THE YALE-HOOVER SERIES ON STALIN, STALINISM, AND THE COLD WAR

PROPAGANDA STATE IN CRISIS

SOVIET IDEOLOGY, INDOCTRINATION, AND

TERROR UNDER STALIN, 1927–1941

DAVID BRANDENBERGER

Hoover Institution
Stanford University
Stanford, California

Yale UNIVERSITY PRESS
New Haven and London

Published with assistance from the foundation established in memory of Philip Hamilton McMillan of the Class of 1894, Yale College.

Yale University Press books may be purchased in quantity for educational, business, or promotional use. For information, please e-mail sales.press@yale.edu (U.S. office) or sales@yaleup.co.uk (U.K. office).

Set in Sabon Roman type by Vonda's Comp Services.
Printed in the United States of America.

Library of Congress Cataloging-in-Publication Data

Brandenberger, David.
  Propaganda state in crisis : Soviet ideology, indoctrination, and terror under Stalin, 1927–1941 / David Brandenberger.
    p. cm. — (The Yale-Hoover series on Stalin, Stalinism, and the Cold War)
  Includes bibliographical references and index.
  ISBN 978-0-300-15537-2 (pbk. : alk. paper)
    1. Propaganda, Soviet—History.   2. Stalin, Joseph, 1879–1953—Influence.   3. Kommunisticheskaia partiia Sovetskogo Soiuza—History.   4. Political culture—Soviet Union—History.   5. Popular culture—Soviet Union—History.   6. Public opinion—Soviet Union—History.   7. Ideology—Soviet Union—History.   8. State-sponsored terrorism—Soviet Union—History.   9. Soviet Union—Politics and government—1917–1936.   10. Soviet Union—Politics and government—1936–1953.   I. Title.
  DK269.5.B73 2011
  947.084'2—dc22

2011014928

A catalogue record for this book is available from the British Library.

This paper meets the requirements of ANSI/NISO Z39.48-1992 (Permanence of Paper).

10 9 8 7 6 5 4 3 2 1

To Sasha, Fedya, and Katia

Contents

List of Illustrations

Acknowledgments

This study has benefited from a number of long- and short-term grants provided by the International Research and Exchanges Board (IREX), with funds supplied by the National Endowment for the Humanities and the United States Department of State under the auspices of the Russian, Eurasian, and East European Research Program (Title VIII); the National Endowment for the Humanities; the Department of State's Fulbright Program; the Davis Center for Russian and Eurasian Studies at Harvard University; and the School of Arts and Sciences at the University of Richmond.

The origins of this study date back to the mid-1990s when I looked into the origins of Stalin's infamous *Short Course* in the former central party archive in Moscow before setting the topic aside as prohibitively difficult. Aspects borrow from chapter two of my book *National Bolshevism: Stalinist Mass Culture and the Formation of Modern Russian National Identity, 1931–1956* (Copyright © 2002 by the President and Fellows of Harvard College) and chapter thirteen of Sarah Davies and James Harris's 2005 edited volume *Stalin: A New History*. I would like to thank Harvard University Press and Cambridge University Press for their permission to reprint portions of these pieces. I would also like to acknowledge my gratitude to friends and colleagues who have read and commented upon aspects of this manuscript—M. V. Zelenov, Serhy Yekelchyk, George Enteen, Erik van Ree, Peter Blitstein, Katia Dianina, Eric Lohr, and David Hoffmann. Discussions with A. M. Dubrovsky,

David Priestland, Polly Jones, and Sandra Dahlke came at important junctures, as did collaborative work on the Harvard Project on the Soviet Social System with Terry Martin and on the *Short Course* with Zelenov. At Yale University Press, Jonathan Brent and Vadim Staklo provided critical support and Margaret Otzel and Kay Scheuer guided the manuscript into print. But I am most grateful to Sasha, Fedya, and Katia for their good humor, and it is to them that this work is dedicated.

A Note on Conventions

The transliteration of terms, titles, surnames, and geographic locations herein adhere to Yale University Press's house style. Exceptions occur in quotations taken from other sources and in the bibliographic citations, which follow the transliteration conventions practiced by the U.S. Library of Congress. Geographic and geopolitical names and spellings used here are those appropriate for a study of the 1930s even if they've changed in recent years (Leningrad, not St. Petersburg; Belorussia, not Belarus; Kiev, not Kyiv). In order to improve readability, frequent terms like "the Party" are not capitalized in the text. For similar reasons, French calques like "etatist" and English constructions like "party hierarchy" are used instead of anglicizing Russian colloquialisms like *gosudarstvennik* and *partiinaia verkhushka*.

Terms and Acronyms

For a complete list of the terms, historical events, and personalities referred to in this volume, see the index.

ACP(b)	All-Union Communist Party (Bolsheviks)
Agitprop	Central Committee Directorate of Agitation and Propaganda
Glavlit	Main Committee on State Censorship
Glavpolitprosvet	Main Political Education Committee
IKP	Institute of the Red Professors
IMEL	Marx-Engels-Lenin Institute
komsomol	communist youth league
Cheka	
NKVD	various incarnations of the secret police
OGPU	
Osoaviakhim	Society for the Support of Aviation and the Chemical Industry
Politburo	Central Committee Political Bureau
RAPP	Russian Association of Proletarian Writers
RSFSR	Russian Soviet Federative Socialist Republic
Sovnarkom	All-Union Council of People's Commissars
SRs	Socialist-Revolutionary Party

Introduction:
Ideology, Propaganda, and
Mass Mobilization

THE USSR UNDER LENIN AND STALIN is often referred to as the world's first propaganda state. That said, if ideology, propaganda, and mass indoctrination are often considered key characteristics of the Soviet "experiment," they've received surprisingly little scholarly attention in recent years. Although many early Sovietologists looked to ideology to explain virtually all the idiosyncrasies of this state and society,[1] more recent generations of scholars have tended to "normalize" Soviet society by focusing on pragmatic political practices (e.g., clientalism, patronage, factionalism, patrimonialism) and normative socio-cultural dynamics (upward mobility, resistance, accommodation, criminality).[2] Under the influence of this work, the Soviet experience has assumed a veneer of "everydayness," transforming Stalinism into the history of "ordinary lives in extraordinary times."[3] This book returns ideology to center stage by revealing the scale and uniqueness of the party hierarchy's engagement with propaganda and indoctrination, as well as the extent to which Stalin and his entourage personally participated in the creation of the official line and party canon.

Authoritarian and ruthless, Stalin and his inner circle were also true believers living in what they believed to be an ideologically charged world.[4] Not only did they see themselves as actors within an epic struggle governed by the Marxist-Leninist historical dialectic, but they believed that an understanding of their historical experience was fundamental to Soviet citizens' formation of a distinctive sense of self. Untold resources were to be devoted to the task of indoctrination, whether through propaganda, education, or mass culture. Still more was to be spent purging the Soviet public sphere of any material that might contradict the official line. Ultimately, the propaganda campaigns of the 1930s that climaxed with the publication of the infamous *Short Course on the History of the All-Union Communist Party (Bolsheviks)* deserve to be considered among the defining projects of the Stalin period, alongside the first Five-Year Plan, the Baltic–White Sea Canal, Magnitogorsk, the defense of Stalingrad, and the storming of Berlin.

But if this book argues that ideology ought to be regarded as one of Stalinism's central characteristics, it does not treat the issue in a monolithic fashion. Instead, it argues that ideology is best addressed from three different perspectives relating to its production, projection, and popular reception. Such three-dimensional analysis reveals that despite the priority that the party hierarchy placed on ideology, it was often treated in a clumsy, haphazard way by members of the ideological establishment, the creative intelligentsia, the press, and party activists. What's more, it was received and internalized by society at the grass-roots in ways that can only be regarded as selective, inconsistent, and superficial. In other words, although ideology meant a lot to Stalin and his entourage, it meant less—sometimes a lot less—to the society over which they ruled.

This failure of the party hierarchy to popularize its ideological worldview and promote a mass sense of revolutionary socialist identity sheds light on many of the distinctive traits that the Soviet experiment assumed during this period. Historically, a number of theories have been advanced to explain the Bolsheviks' hesitancy to pursue more single-minded, radical objectives. Some have argued that the party hierarchs were more interested in political power than they were in revolution and were willing to do virtually anything to retain it.[5] Others have contended that this pragmatism stemmed from the Stalinist elite's revision of Marxist principles, the emergence of domestic etatism, eroding prospects for world revolution, the triumph of administrative power over revolutionary utopianism, and the emergence of nationalist sympathies within the party hierarchy.[6] Still others associate the transformation with increasing threats from the outside world (principally

Hitler's rise to power in 1933) or the exigencies of war after 1941.[7] Some even explain policy moderation by questioning whether the Bolsheviks actually possessed the power to put truly radical ideas into practice.[8] And this position contrasts with those who assert that these programs actually *were* radical in the context of other industrial societies at the time.[9] According to this last interpretation, even though the party hierarchy reversed itself on ethnic, gender, and social equality during the 1930s, such modulations should not be seen as incompatible with the overall Soviet project. Rather, they should be viewed in the context of "a strategic shift from the task of building socialism to that of defending socialism."[10]

This book, by contrast, contends that it was the party hierarchy's failure to popularize a more revolutionary sense of Soviet ideology that necessitated its populist revisionism in the first place. *Propaganda State in Crisis* makes its case by combining an archivally based archeology of the Stalin-era ideological establishment with an interdisciplinary focus on the official line as represented in party study circles, the all-union press, middle-brow literature, theater, film, and museum exhibition. It then complements this examination of the construction and dissemination of ideology with a special investigation into the popular reception of regime rhetoric and imagery. Intent on determining how ordinary Soviet citizens reacted to the wax and wane of the official line, this study focuses on an array of letters, diaries, and memoirs, as well as denunciations, secret police reports, and rare sociological interviews conducted during Stalin's lifetime. Such sources preserve echoes of "authentic" voices from the 1930s that allow for an analysis of the popular resonance of ideologically charged propaganda on the mass level.

Chapter One begins by investigating the approach that Soviet authorities took to mass mobilization during the 1920s, both within traditional contexts (e.g., public rallies, study circles, the press, poster art) and less conventional forums (art, literature, drama, film, museum exhibition, etc.). These venues' embrace of abstract materialism and the avant garde produced an inaccessible mélange of schematicism and anonymous social forces that functioned poorly as mobilizational propaganda—something visible in the collapse of Soviet morale on the eve of the tenth anniversary of the revolution. Focusing on the aftermath of this fiasco, Chapters Two and Three trace how party authorities began to modulate their representation of the official line in order to enhance its accessibility and evocative power. Journalists, for instance, rede-signed their reportage in order to court party activists. Party historians attempted to identify a "usable past" that would make the annals of the Russian revolutionary movement more relevant to Soviet society at large.[11] Propagandists augmented these efforts by launching an ambi-tious Lenin-based personality cult that styled Stalin as the living per-sonification of the Soviet experiment.

None of these approaches proved easy to put into practice, however. Indeed, it appears that veteran party historians and ideologists struggled for years between the late 1920s and mid-1930s to reconcile their long-standing commitment to Marxism-Leninism with the newer, seemingly "bourgeois" approaches to mass mobilization. What's more, Chapters Four and Five reveal that the first to arrive at a truly accessible version of the Soviet usable past were not members of the party's ideological es-tablishment at all, but instead innovators who hailed from the journal-istic and literary ranks of the creative intelligentsia. Their approach, which celebrated contemporary individual heroism and the long-taboo notion of patriotism, met with resistance from party veterans on account of their recourse to conventional, non-Marxist appeals. But as demon-strated in Chapter Six, this new mobilizational strategy elicited a sur-prisingly strong reaction from the society at large, popularizing regime values and priorities on the mass level with remarkable effectiveness.

Chapters Seven and Eight interrupt this success story surrounding the new pantheon of everyday patriots, heroes, and role models with the realization that no sooner had this populist line come into its own than it was blindsided by the most brutal dimensions of the Great Terror. "Unmasked" as enemies of the people between 1936 and 1938, many of the members of the new Soviet Olympus fell into disgrace or disap-peared entirely, taking with them an entire generation of bestsellers, textbooks, and popular dramas for the stage and silver screen. Chapters Nine and Ten demonstrate that public opinion was profoundly shaken by the Terror's slaughter of the society's heroes and role models. Worse, this bloodletting forced the ideological establishment to abandon its hard-won emphasis on heroes and individual heroism and retreat back to sterile schemata and anonymous social forces. A turn of events epit-omized by the notorious 1938 *Short Course on the History of the All-Union Communist Party (Bolsheviks)*, it destroyed years of work on societal mobilization and identity formation.[12]

Chapter Eleven argues that the destruction of the party's usable past between 1936 and 1938 resulted in a broad ossification of the official line in Soviet mass culture. It also clarifies why the party hierarchs rushed to embrace non-Marxist heroes drawn from the annals of the Russian national past even before the release of the *Short Course*. Ultimately, this book concludes that it was the paralysis of the propaganda state during the mid-to-late 1930s that forced the party hierarchs to avail themselves of an array of mobilizational surrogates in order to rally the society. Most controversial among these concessions was their turn to a heavy investment in Russian national imagery, rhetoric, and iconography in a desperate bid for hearts and minds. This sea-change in official propaganda—long assumed by specialists to stem from either cynicism on Stalin's part or exigencies connected with war in 1941—is thus attributed in the present study to a surprisingly contingent, panicky turnabout in official propaganda and ideology. As is clear from early critiques of this transformation—N. S. Timasheff's "Great Retreat" and L. D. Trotsky's "Revolution Betrayed"—the irony of this promotion of nativist, russocentric, and jingoistic emotions was not lost on its contemporaries.

Several terms require clarification before continuing. "Propaganda state" is a turn of phrase that is used in this study to denote political systems that distinguish themselves by their co-option and harnessing of mass culture, educational institutions, and the press for the purpose of popular indoctrination. By nature a top-down governing paradigm, it is promoted by a tight, consensus-driven elite possessing an articulate political ideology and the aspiration to shape public opinion or society itself. A familiar concept in the contemporary world, it was a revolutionary proposal when advanced by the Bolsheviks in the aftermath of 1917. As with other expressions used in this study, the term "propaganda state" is used on the pages that follow in a neutral sense without pejorative inflection or judgment, despite its frequent use in that way during the early years of the Cold War.[13]

"Ideology," according to the official 1940 Soviet definition, is a value-neutral term for a worldview or "a system of opinions, ideas, understandings, and impressions" found in fields such as philosophy, ethics, law, art, science, and religion. Political ideology, therefore, refers to a set of ideas, principles, priorities, and discourses that guide decision-making, legitimate the exercise of power and governance, and aid in the construction of governing culture and practice.[14] According to Terry Eagleton, ideology allows the modern state to reinforce its authority by "*promoting* beliefs and values congenial to it; *naturalizing* and *universalizing* such beliefs so as to render them self-evident and apparently inevitable; *denigrating* ideas which may challenge it; *excluding* rival forms of thought, perhaps by some unspoken but systematic logic; and *obscuring* social reality in ways convenient to itself."[15] Put another way, ideology serves as both ends and means, not only defining political objectives and worldviews, but also acting as a vehicle for the realization of these objectives. Ronald Grigor Suny notes that "ideologies are tools for mobilizing populations, and like political parties they function to coordinate diverse opinions and people." In this vein, according to Suny, modern elites and political entrepreneurs have come to regard ideology—whether defined narrowly as dogma or broadly as political culture—as virtually indispensable.[16] In the context of such modern, social science–informed discussions, ideology in western liberal societies is seen as something almost as ubiquitous and multivalent as discourse and power relations. This is less the case for authoritarian societies and for this reason, the present study treats ideology in the USSR more or less as Stalin-era ideologists did: as both an official political culture and a "top-down" tool for popular indoctrination and mobilization.

"Propaganda," a term closely associated with ideology, describes a deliberate and concerted attempt to use political sloganeering, imagery, and iconography in order to advance a systematic message designed to influence and shape popular beliefs, attitudes, and behavior.[17] Propaganda's persuasive appeal can be direct or oblique and typically assumes one of two modes, emphasizing either rational argumentation or the rallying of sympathy through a variety of emotional registers.[18] Like ideology, the term propaganda is used in here in a sense similar to that current during the Stalin period—as a neutral term without the negative connotations that the word often possesses in modern colloquial English. Officially, the Soviet definition distinguished propaganda from agitation, propaganda denoting a complex, well-rounded set of ideological arguments designed to persuade through educational indoctrination, while agitation described a more simplistic, rabble-rousing sort of sloganeering. A largely heuristic distinction that Lenin originally borrowed from G. V. Plekhanov, this did not prevent Soviet authorities from using the terms interchangeably—a convention that this study likewise adopts.[19]

"Indoctrination," a concept that came into popular currency in the United States during the 1950s, refers to a persuasive process by which ideology is inculcated in the popular mind by means of propaganda and a pervasive political culture. Although it is a neutral term, its semantic reliance on the word "doctrine" suggests that the indoctrinational process is an inherently political one, designed to propagandize a coherent set of ideological principles or ideas at the expense of all other competing worldviews and principles.

"Ideological establishment" is used in this study as an aggregate term for a variety of official circles associated with the production and dissemination of regime propaganda and the official ideological line. Headed by the propaganda and agitational arm of the party's Central Committee, it also included the political directorate of the Red Army, the Commissariat of Education, ranking party historians and Marxist-Leninist philosophers, leading journals and their editorial boards, major newspapers and their editors, and "court" writers and intellectuals. The term distinguishes between these official and semi-official spokespeople and other, lower-ranking non-executive personnel, whether educators, activists, artists, or members of the creative intelligentsia.

"Party hierarchy" is another aggregate turn of phrase that identifies the party and state leaders who devised the official line and supervised its development and maintenance within the ideological establishment. This term improves upon more traditional nomenclature used to describe the decision-making elite in the USSR, inasmuch as while Stalin wielded enormous power during his reign, it would be simplistic and reductionist to attribute to him every decision made during his tenure. Such a puppet-master paradigm not only mythologizes Stalin's leadership capacities (in a perverse inversion of his personality cult), but it also obscures the decisive roles played by ranking party members like A. I. Stetsky, L. M. Kaganovich, and A. A. Zhdanov. Thus "party hierarchy" is used in the pages that follow to signify the small, exclusive group of party members in Stalin's entourage who wielded power in Soviet society during the 1930s.

All of these institutions and practices were designed to influence "social identity," the last of this study's key terms. Identity, as such, refers to the essence of individual or group consciousness—those factors which define the individual's uniqueness and differentiate the "self" or group from others.[20] This, of course, is not to suggest that identity is the sole product of fixed, objective characteristics like ethnicity, gender, or class. Indeed, while this study concentrates on political aspects of the Soviet "self" experienced among Russian speakers in Stalinist society between 1928 and 1941, it readily concedes that identity itself—whether individual or collective—is a much larger, unstable constellation of subjective characteristics that undergoes continuous renegotiation. In other words, this study limits its investigation to political aspects of individual and group identity during the 1930s, rather than attempting to map Soviet identity as a whole. What's more, because this study concerns itself chiefly with *popular* identity and mass consciousness, it focuses on views and attitudes that were broadly held and consistently understood by constituents from all social strata in the interwar USSR. Although elites figure prominently in the pages that follow, this study's scope of inquiry has been designed to focus on opinions and beliefs expressed outside the intelligentsia and party hierarchy.

In its investigation of ideological indoctrination under Stalin, this book exposes a long-overlooked failure that took a massive toll on mobilizational efforts within the world's first propaganda state. Such a fiasco can explain the regime's near-continuous resort to various forms of populist imagery and sloganeering after the start of the 1930s—whether concerning ethnicity, gender, or class. It also provides a new explanation for why propaganda in the USSR paid so little attention to revolutionary values and mores, whether during the Second World War or the postwar's "return to orthodoxy" between 1945 and 1953. Finally, it provides clues to why N. S. Khrushchev and his communist-idealist successors from Yu. N. Andropov to M. S. Gorbachev proved unable to draw upon an enduring sense of mass identity revolving around membership in a common socialist endeavor. Detailing the party hierarchy's failure to promote a sense of revolutionary Soviet identity during the 1930s, this book speaks to one of the core dysfunctions of propaganda and ideology in the USSR over the course of the twentieth century.

1 The Propaganda State's First Decade

ALTHOUGH THE PHRASE "propaganda state" entered academic parlance some fifty years ago as a derogatory epithet for the maintenance of political authority through the manipulation of mass culture, it can also serve as a more analytical label for regimes that demonstrate a preference for aggressive, media-savvy governance. The early Soviet republic, while not a pioneer in the creation of specific genres of propaganda, earned this moniker due to the scale and intensity with which it attempted to disseminate its official line throughout society during its first decade in power. This chapter examines the party hierarchs' construction of a propaganda state over the course of the 1920s, paying particular attention to the obstacles that they encountered during the establishment of a mass indoctrinational system.

The Bolsheviks were of two minds regarding the nature of their society in the years after 1917. For decades, Lenin had argued that the laboring classes were fundamentally ready for radical change—"the majority of the population in Russia, according to its instinct, feeling, and inclination, is sympathetic to a revolution against the capitalists."[1] That said, he also believed that the society lacked the class consciousness and organizational ability to be truly revolutionary on its own—something that doomed it and other like societies to the trials and tribulations of trade-unionism and "constant relapses [. . .] into petty-bour-geois spinelessness, disintegration, individualism, and alternating moods of exaltation and dejection."[2] According to Lenin, the key to overcoming such vacillation and galvanizing a genuinely revolutionary sense of social consciousness was to be found in a vanguard of professional revolutionaries that would supply followers with a sense of ideological vision and discipline. Only consistency, determination, and clarity could convert the emotional spontaneity of "trade-unionism" into a truly resilient and transformative sense of revolutionary consciousness.[3] This class consciousness would not be possible to maintain without a vanguard party; indeed, the broader and more diverse the movement, the more imperative the need was for such an organization.

The emphasis that the Bolsheviks placed on ideological leadership, consistency, and continuity provides one explanation for why the party was so uncompromising about its vanguard position in Soviet society after the conclusion of the revolution and civil war. Social transformation remained incomplete and would require years of concerted action, during which time mere spontaneous emotion—no matter how well intentioned—threatened to derail the entire process. So as before the revolution, the party now attempted to mobilize society by "influencing the mood of the masses."[4] This focus on the need to coax, convince, scold, and chide ordinary workers and peasants into embracing the cause of revolution stands at the foundation of the Bolshevik propaganda state. Put another way, persuasion was seen as key to the realization of the Soviet "experiment." As Lenin wrote in 1917: "the proletariat needs state power, the centralized organization of force, both for the purpose of crushing the resistance of the exploiters and for the purpose of *guiding* the great mass of the population—the peasantry, the petty bourgeois, and the semi-proletarians—in the organization of a socialist economy."[5] As the self-appointed advocates of the proletariat, Lenin and his party repeatedly emphasized the priority that they afforded to public persuasion and indoctrination efforts. This theme runs like a red thread through early Bolshevik writing on how to consolidate the gains of the revolution. Lenin argued in 1917 that "the whole task of the communists is to convince the backward elements" of the legitimacy of their vision. Nine years later, Stalin echoed this basic axiom of revolutionary activity in his definition of good leadership, averring that it consisted of "the ability to convince the masses that party policy is correct and [then] to issue and act upon slogans that will bring the masses closer to the party's point of view."[6] In other words, mere mastery of the laws of Marxism-Leninism or possession of state power was not enough—the Bolsheviks had to "convince the masses that party policy is sound on the basis of their own experience." Only this would "ensure the support of the working class and induce the broad laboring masses to follow its lead." Failure to mobilize the society around the party platform, Stalin added, would inevitably lead to a faltering of popular support for the regime and the defeat of the revolution.[7]

As is well known, the early Bolsheviks expected their liberation of society from capitalist exploitation to result in the emergence first of sympathizers and then of *homo soveticus,* the "New Soviet Person," who would almost automatically demonstrate a sophisticated sense of class consciousness. That said, Lenin and his entourage understood that while this new society was forming, they would need to contend with older "bourgeois remnants" who had been brought up under the old regime. These elements threatened not only to slow the revolutionary transformations underway, but to taint the upbringing of the new generation as well. For this reason, mere sloganeering was not enough; instead, the aggressive reeducation of the whole society was seen as a vital and pressing priority.

While neither Lenin nor Stalin ruled out the use of force to consolidate their ideological gains, coercion was seen as a means of last resort. As Lenin put it, "we must convince first and keep force in reserve."[8] This emphasis on persuasion explains the Bolsheviks' early embrace of the mass media as a means of mobilization and indoctrination. Both Lenin and Stalin frequently referred to the press and various mass cultural venues like literature, theater, and film as "instruments," "tools," and "transmission belts" that would allow the party to disseminate its vision throughout society as a whole. This determination to invest in mass culture was officially endorsed in 1919 by the Eighth Party Congress and routinely reiterated thereafter.[9]

Convinced that the indoctrinational process was fundamentally an educational one, the party hierarchs established the Main Political Education Committee (Glavpolitprosvet) in May 1920 to supervise mobilizational work that until then had been run on a decentralized basis. Lenin endorsed this committee's mandate in November of that year at a major congress of political education workers; shortly thereafter, it was incorporated into the Commissariat of Education in order to improve coordination of indoctrinational efforts.[10] In November 1921, Glavpolitprosvet was complemented by the formation of a department of propaganda and agitation within the Central Committee to supervise mass cultural work. Known as Agitprop, this institution was to work alongside Glavpolitprosvet in order to supervise all official work in the realm of oral and printed propaganda. Glavpolitprosvet was to monitor public educational institutions and libraries, while Agitprop was to oversee ideological work both inside and outside party ranks. Together, they were to prepare the society for conscious participation in the construction of a new socialist order. They retained much of this mandate even after the establishment of an independent press department within the Central Committee in 1924.[11]

Institutions with overlapping jurisdictions, Glavpolitprosvet and Agitprop were charged with interpolating ideology and politics into everyday public life. Glavpolitprosvet looked after the society's schoolhouses, lecture halls, and reading rooms. Agitprop, aside from its engagement with mass culture and the press, oversaw party educational activities throughout the governmental bureaucracy, trade unions, producer and retail cooperatives, and other sorts of organizations. It also aided grassroots party cells in factories, enterprises, and other state institutions in opening or regularizing reading circles for the discussion of basic ideological concepts and texts, party and state policy, and current events. Political literacy courses also proliferated on the mass level, providing neophytes with what was supposed to be a rigorous approach to Marxism-Leninism and the party line on key issues. Staffing such groups with qualified discussion leaders proved to be a constant headache for party cell administrators, frequently forcing the administrators themselves to moonlight as agitators and instructors. Party authorities attempted to compensate for this shortage of grassroots propagandists by forming mobile agitational brigades that would travel to outlying villages in order to popularize the basic tenets of the official line.[12]

Graduates of grassroots courses who aspired to move up in the party would frequently enroll in district or regional party schools, which combined remedial work on grammar school subjects with a more systematic study of party philosophy, history, political economy, and current events.[13] Those who excelled in such programs might ultimately apply for entrance to higher education in one of the USSR's nine communist

universities, where the curriculum likewise alternated between philosophy, party history, and less political subjects.[14] Although graduates of
this system were to emerge well versed in Marxist-Leninist theory, it
would be incorrect to think of party schooling as focusing only on the
production of articulate propagandists. Instead, the system aspired to
produce personnel who would combine a solid background in Marxism-Leninism with the practical training and knowledge necessary to
be effective party officials.[15]

The political curriculum of these early reading circles and more formal courses familiarized activists and students with the writings of
Marx, Engels, and Lenin, supplemented by shorter selections from
major figures in the Russian Social Democratic Labor movement (e.g.,
Plekhanov) and leading Bolshevik ideologues (Trotsky, G. Ye. Zinoviev,
N. I. Bukharin, Stalin, etc.). Terms and concepts—many of them unfamiliar foreign calques—were also rehearsed, ranging all the way from
"capitalism" and "socialism" to "bourgeois" and "proletariat." The
international dimensions of the Soviet experiment were also emphasized
—topics that included the importance of world revolution and the
Comintern, specific working-class movements abroad, and the conceptual distinction between internationalism and nationalism.[16]

This material was taught in tandem with the history of the Bolshevik
movement, from its populist origins during the 1860s through the advent of the New Economic Policy (NEP) in 1921. According to this approach, Marxism-Leninism and its chief precept, dialectical materialism,
provided a set of tools for understanding social relations during the
transition to socialism, while party history supplied empirical proof of
the tools' analytical power. Massive resources were devoted to docu-
menting the revolutionary experience from a historical point of view
during the early years of the Bolshevik regime—prominent party ideologists were drafted to write history textbooks, and entire institutions
were established to collect, organize, analyze, and popularize the memory and legacy of 1917.[17] As noted above, the goal was transformative
rather than merely instructional—something Jochen Hellbeck describes
effectively. "Through a multitude of political-education campaigns," he
writes, "the Soviet regime prodded individuals to consciously identify
with the revolution (as interpreted by the party leadership), and thereby
to comprehend themselves as active participants in the drama of history. They were summoned to internalize the revolution and grant it an

interpretation defined not only by the objective course of history, but also by the spiritual unfolding of their subjective selves."[18] Mere academic study of the annals of the revolution, then, was not enough to guarantee true consciousness on its own, even if Soviet citizens literally immersed themselves in party-sponsored textbooks, memoirs, belletristic literature, and poetry. Visits to exhibits, museums, and the theater were likewise necessary but insufficient. Familiarity with 1917 and mastery of its historical lessons had to be complemented by an internalization of the revolutionary paradigm itself. As the propagandists' journal *Sputnik politrabotnika* argued in 1924, "in order to truly be politically literate, it is not enough to work through theoretical and historical books in the social sciences. One must also be able to independently apply the acquired material to contemporary life. It is necessary to orient oneself in current political life."[19] Revolutionary consciousness, in other words, required the New Soviet Person to identify personally with the history of the party and its struggle. As one member of this new generation, Valentina Kamyshina, put it, history was a defining element of her social identity. "It was through literature and stories told by eyewitnesses that I became acquainted with the events that occurred during my childhood," she wrote. "I accepted the Revolution and with it the Bolshevik regime as part of history—perhaps inevitable. Although my parents often tried to prove to me that life was considerably better under the czarist regime, I argued endlessly that the opposite was true."[20] In pursuit of this goal, students and activists like Kamyshina were encouraged to examine not only the party and society through the lens of 1917, but their own lives as well. This recommendation became a mandatory exercise for anyone within the party, the Komsomol, higher education, and most state and party institutions.[21] Whether they were idealists or pragmatists, careerists or cynics, all upwardly mobile Soviets citizens had to "align themselves with history" in public in order to demonstrate that their individual sense of selfhood and consciousness was firmly grounded in the larger revolutionary narrative of the party and society as a whole.[22] Such individual transformation was seen as the key to larger society-wide progress.

Although one might expect descriptions of these efforts to "align" autobiographical and historical narratives to be expressed in an emotional, romantic, coming-of-age genre—something akin to the German *Bildungsroman*—party officials discouraged this, arguing that true rev-

olutionary consciousness required the disciplining of spontaneous outbursts of passion and excitement.[23] As a result, the dominant mode of
these autobiographical exercises ended up being rather dry and schematic,
due to the need to emplot personal experience according to an impersonal, standardized formula. Marx had proclaimed in the *Communist
Manifesto* that "all the history of the hitherto existing world is the history of class struggle," and this required those engaged in "narrations
of the self" to base their analyses on anonymous social forces, stages of
economic development, and class tensions. Although more traditional
styles of emplotment tended to narrate events according to the reign of
great rulers, the trials and tribulations of famous heroes, and the contours of epic military clashes, the new materialists were taught to dismiss such conventions as superficial and unscientific. Their preferred
mode of expression ultimately produced a generation of history texts,
memoirs, novels, short stories, dramatic works, and political art that
depicted the revolutionary experience in strikingly generic, bloodless
terms.

Of course, the relative heterogeneity of Soviet society during the
1920s prevented any of these historical, artistic, and literary forms from
completely monopolizing public life. This diversity of opinion was aided
and abetted by the relatively modest reach of Glavpolitprosvet, Agitprop, and the ideological establishment, which were themselves divided
over precisely how the ideological tenets of Marxism-Leninism were to
be conveyed to the public. As a sign of the times, dozens of party history textbooks circulated alongside one another, offering contradictory
accounts of the Bolshevik experience.[24] An array of artistic and literary
organizations likewise vied for the right to officially define how the revolution was to be framed in Soviet arts and letters.[25] But as confusing
and conflictual as this state of affairs may sound, it did at least ensure
that discussion of the historical, ideological, ethical, and aesthetic significance of 1917 loomed large in the Soviet press and mass culture
throughout the decade.

Several years before the start of the 1990s' archival revolution, Peter
Kenez published a pioneering account of the USSR's early efforts to
combine ideology, education, and mass culture into a single indoctrinational drive. Although Kenez lacked access to primary sources that
could have documented how ordinary Soviets responded to this initia-

tive, he speculated that many basic objectives were probably realized, especially on a discursive level. Crediting the party's ideological establishment with the broad dissemination of Soviet imagery and iconography—especially in urban areas—Kenez argued that the Bolshevik message assumed hegemonic proportions by the mid-to-late 1920s. Such power, he continued, meant that despite an array of shortcomings, the propaganda state succeeded in inculcating in the society "a political language and a pattern of behavior." "First the people came to speak a strange idiom and adopt the behavior patterns expected of them, and only then did the inherent political message seep in. The process of convincing proceeded not from inside out but outside in. That is, people came to behave properly, from the point of view of the regime, not because they believed its slogans but because by repeating the slogans they gradually acquired a 'proper consciousness.'"[26] An explanation that anticipated aspects of Stephen Kotkin's famous "speaking Bolshevik" paradigm by several years, Kenez's argues that propaganda during the 1920s essentially hybridized persuasion and coercion. Whether or not Soviets sympathized with the central tenets of party ideology and the official historical line, they were forced to accept and internalize these views due to a lack of alternatives. Ultimately, according to Kenez, the hegemony of this new political language and set of practices gave rise to a distinctly Soviet form of social identity.

Research conducted after the opening of the former party and state archives complicates these conclusions by suggesting that official propaganda stressing internationalism, class consciousness, the worker-peasant alliance, and support for Soviet power enjoyed much less social resonance than Kenez supposed.[27] Instead, the populace proved to be fractious enough to resist embracing any semblance of a common sense of community.[28] Particularly striking in the sources is a profound division between city and country, apparently inspired in part by NEP's discriminatory terms of trade. Even before the exacerbation of the so-called scissors crisis in 1926, peasants objected to what they saw as unfair state pricing and taxation. This is visible in sources like the following 1925 resolution from a rural council near Samara that denounced official slogans about the solidarity of the working class with the peasantry:

> We consider the work of the Russian Communist Party [sic, All-Union Communist Party (Bolsheviks)] unsatisfactory, insofar as there is no

equality between the workers and the peasants, the peasants' work is not valued, and little attention is paid to educating the peasants. In good harvest years, the Russian Communist Party [*sic*] does not help improve the peasants' agricultural operations—the peasants aren't given seed for sowing or supplies and the peasants' operations are taxed more heavily than they should be.[29]

Such bitterness led to widespread lobbying for a peasant union and greater local control over government under the slogan "soviets without communists."[30] It also led to isolated outbursts of anti-Semitic, monarchist, and nationalist sentiments in the countryside during the mid-1920s.[31]

Morale among traditional Bolshevik industrial constituencies in urban areas was often not much better than that in the countryside. OGPU reports between 1922 and 1925 indicate that working-class districts and industrial enterprises in Moscow, Leningrad, and other major provincial cities were rife with discontent and irritation over working conditions, unemployment, and party rule.[32] In an industrial suburb of Yaroslavl, for instance, workers were overheard complaining about the party's broken promises, especially its hypocritical celebration of the dictatorship of the proletariat. "Now something bad is taking place—there are no more communists in the party, but only careerists and they joined up just to receive a big salary and live better." Still worse was another overheard conversation, in which one worker announced to a group of comrades:

> All the leaders, like Lenin, Trotsky, and the others, lived and are still living like little princes, just as before; the workers, as under the tsar, are exploited by these comrades and it is hard for a worker to make a living at the present time. If a worker's paycheck under the tsar was enough to buy four pairs of boots, now it is only enough for one pair. Meanwhile, the executives have found themselves soft armchairs, receive big paychecks and don't do anything.

Such observations led still others to hint that it was time "throw off the communists." In Tatarstan, for instance, unemployed workers grumbled that "it's time to tell the communists straight to their faces: 'to hell with you—you can't govern this country.'"[33]

Although OGPU reports contained plenty of this sort of "anti-Soviet agitation" during the early-to-mid-1920s, talk of "throwing off the communists" marked a different kind of inherently political protest that

had been rare since the civil war. Indeed, if discontent had initially focused on the need to reform specific policies (taxation, unemployment,
variable wage rates, the employment of "bourgeois specialists," etc.), in
time this unrest assumed a more politicized tenor and gave voice to
more general complaints about the nature of Soviet power and the need
for regime chance. In Moscow in 1926, for instance, the secret police reported dissatisfied workers' comments to be wide-ranging and bitterly
"anti-Soviet": "the party has turned against the workers," "the workers are being stifled by the party and their demands are not being met,"
etc.[34] Leningrad workers echoed this criticism, denouncing the "fraud-
ulent" nature of the proletarian dictatorship: "they write all the time
and everywhere about our broad democracy at the elections, but all the
while, the All-Russian Communist Party [sic] collective dictatorially ap-
points candidates who are no good for the workers."[35] Life, according
to many such critics, had been better "under the tsar."[36]

Further research is needed to clarify precisely how the party hierarchy responded to reports of such discontent, but it seems likely that the
disappointing information that the OGPU supplied was at least in part
responsible for the leadership's repeated reiteration of the need for aggressive indoctrination efforts during the mid-1920s. What's more, the
perception of mobilizational weakness stimulated by these reports also
likely explains the surge of Agitprop activity surrounding the so-called
War Scare of 1927.[37] The origins of this pivotal crisis date to the second half of 1926, when tension with Great Britain and Poland led to the
release of a series of Comintern communiqués warning of "the danger
of war"—"the international bourgeoisie is organizing a new offensive
against the USSR." Picked up by the Soviet press, this rhetoric was seconded shortly thereafter by speakers like Bukharin at the Fifteenth Party
Conference and the Seventh Plenum of the Comintern Executive Committee at the end of 1926.[38] Bukharin and K. Ye. Voroshilov repeated
these warnings at a Moscow party conference in early 1927, the former
contending that "there is no guarantee that they will not attack us" and
the latter announcing ominously that "we must not forget that we stand
on the brink of war, and that this war will be far from fun and
games."[39] Although intended to be inspiring and mobilizational, such
talk turned out to be so provocative that Stalin was forced to assuage
popular fears of imminent invasion that March.[40] Tensions remained
high, however, spiking later that spring after a series of foreign policy

reversals within which Chinese nationalists attacked the Soviet-aligned Chinese communist party and sacked consulates in Beijing and Shanghai; Great Britain severed diplomatic relations with the USSR; and a "White Guard–counterrevolutionary" assassin killed the Soviet plenipotentiary to Poland. These events, although unrelated, led to the resumption of inflammatory articles in the press about the threat of war with Britain and a vaguely defined coalition of capitalist powers.[41]

At first glance, the war scare came at a terrible time, overshadowing a year that the propaganda state had clearly expected to spend celebrating the tenth anniversary of the revolution.[42] Still, the tensions did offer leaders like Bukharin an unusual mobilizational opportunity, insofar as the war scare provided graphic illustration of Marxism-Leninism's thesis on the inevitability of conflict with the capitalist world. Apparently confident that an actual invasion was not in the offing, the party hierarchy encouraged the ideological establishment to fan the flames of the supposed emergency in order to rally popular support. Local party and Komsomol organizations launched campaigns oriented around the theme of "revolutionary defensism" that summer, and much of this instrumental hype culminated that July with an Osoaviakhim-sponsored Civil Defense Week, which proclaimed that mass participation in military training and industrial production would provide a fitting "answer to Neville Chamberlain."[43]

Scholars have speculated for years that the unforeseen events precipitated by the war scare must have given the party hierarchy considerable pause, whether it be the widespread run on consumer goods and hoarding of staples or rural grain producers' efforts to withdraw from the market.[44] But recently declassified OGPU reports on all-union morale now reveal that concern over these phenomena within the party hierarchy likely paled by comparison with the populace's hysterical reaction to the rumors of war.[45] Instead of rallying the USSR together in the name of industrialization and defense, the war scare precipitated a wave of discord and defeatist rumors that swept the country from Smolensk to Vladivostok. Many peasants, angered by rapidly rising taxes and other sorts of discriminatory measures during the fall of 1926, rebuffed the party's calls for mobilization:

> What sort of defenders are we? They are crushing us with taxes and we are to defend them? [Biisky region]

England is preparing to go to war against the USSR, but the Russian is tired of war and won't go off to fight anyone. Soviet power for us is like a bad dream and a passing phenomenon—sooner or later, it'll disappear and there will have to be a Constituent Assembly. [Krivoy Rog region]

England has told the communists to give up without a fight, and a president will be installed in Russia who England or the peasants want. If the communists do not surrender, England will go to war. We've already spilt enough blood, so it would be good if the communists gave up without a fight. [Amur region]

Soviet power will not get to celebrate its 10th anniversary, inasmuch as no sooner will war begin than the communists will be beaten. [Pskov province]

Soon war will come and they'll give us peasants weapons and we'll turn them against Soviet power and the communists; we don't need a workers' government and must overthrow it and strangle the communists. [Moscow province]

Soviet power will soon meet its end—a single spark would be enough and all the people will rise up and the Red Army will turn Green and head into the woods. [Nizhny Novgorod province][46]

Workers too rejected the regime's call for unity in the face of the external threat, reminding its representatives of their own broken promises.

Soon there will be war and the communists will meet their end. The communists will be beaten at the front and in the rear by the nonparty members, insofar as they've not justified themselves. [Kharkov]

Now no one will go off to fight—you won't find any sheep, as you did in '20. [Kharkov]

We don't have a dictatorship of the proletariat and if war breaks out, we won't fight. [Leningrad]

If we go off to fight, we won't leave those snakes who are drinking our blood here alive. [Irkutsk]

If war is to come, then we'll first beat the local rulers—the ACP members—and then we'll go off to fight England. [Orenburg][47]

Red Army troops, who were often considered a barometer of popular opinion during the 1920s, greeted the war scare with an increased rate of desertion and similarly disloyal talk.[48]

It is unclear, of course, how representative such reports on morale

were as a whole, inasmuch as OGPU, party, and military personnel did
not collect information with the rigor and dispassion of modern social
scientists.[49] Moreover, detailed studies of the war scare within smaller
population groups reveal Soviet citizens on the ground to have reacted
variously to the crisis.[50] That said, the reports that the OGPU submitted to the party hierarchs were overwhelmingly negative, and it was this
material that likely forced Stalin and his entourage to quash the war
scare propaganda that fall.[51] Whether or not the reports offered a truly
accurate picture of popular opinion within the USSR, they did suggest
to the party hierarchy that Soviet society was ill prepared to defend itself.[52]

In the aftermath of the war scare, the party's ideological establishment flailed about wildly as it attempted to explain the fiasco. Its proposals of a wide array of seemingly indiscriminate reforms hint at panic
in the corridors of power. For example, on the eve of the tenth anniversary of the revolution, the Central Committee passed a resolution
criticizing the press for allowing day-to-day coverage of administrative
and economic issues to eclipse ideological ones.[53] Two months later, the
Fifteenth Party Congress decreed that the entire political education and
agitprop system was in need of serious reform, especially in the countryside.[54] Such initiatives indicate not only that the party hierarchy was
concerned about the weakness of its mass indoctrinational program,
but that it had failed to determine precisely what was responsible for
this impotence.

After six months of behind-the-scenes debate, the party authorities
convened a major all-union conference on agitation, propaganda, and
cultural work in Moscow in May and June 1928 in order to discuss further institutional reform. There, the conference participants apparently
issued a scathing evaluation of mobilizational efforts during the first
decade of Soviet power—resources had been wasted, opportunities for
party-state cooperation squandered, and little real indoctrinational
progress achieved. In its proceedings, the conference called for sweeping changes in many areas, from economics, agriculture, and science to
education, nationality policy, popular belief, and the organization of
everyday life—changes that would require unprecedented coordination
between the party, Komsomol, and trade union organizations. Propagandists and agitators in the public schools, the press, the workplace,
and party study circles were to assume a much more concrete, practical

approach to popular indoctrination and focus on issues such as literacy, competency, training, and morale. Moreover, "it is especially important to note that throughout all of this mass agitational work, the task is not merely *to convince* the masses of the correctness of the party line, but also *to organize* them to verify their fulfillment of this line and struggle with any shortcomings encountered along the way."[55] In other words, the party authorities' emphasis on "persuasion" from the early years of the propaganda state was now to acquire a more regimented, comprehensive character.

Unsurprisingly, party, Komsomol, and trade union officials were expected to advance the conference's recommendations in close coordination with state publishing and the press. But as befitted the USSR's status as the prototypical propaganda state, all other institutions within the society's public sphere were also drafted into public service. Accordingly, "literature, theater, film, canvas art, music, radio, and the popular stage—all of these forums must be brought to bear on the widest breadth of society and utilized in the struggle for a new cultural outlook and a new way of life, as well as against bourgeois and petty bourgeois ideology, vodka, philistinism, and narrow-mindedness."[56] As evident from this statement, all the arts and letters were to be organized around a single line—a line that was to be explicitly political and proactive. "No mass cultural work can be apolitical, nor should it be," declared the conference's proceedings. "It must be tightly connected with party agitation, contributing to the masses' acquisition of political experience and facilitating their incorporation into socialist construction in such a way that this participation becomes part of culture, habit, and daily life."[57] This determination to mobilize the entire breadth of mass culture into the service of the state and party was seconded months later at an all-union meeting of editors, where S. B. Ingulov, the head of the Central Committee's press department, was similarly explicit about the need to subordinate newspaper coverage to these mobilizational priorities. "Our fundamental task," he argued, "is to organize the broadest stretches of the toilers around the slogans of the party and the tasks of Soviet construction—those stretches that until the present time have remained inert and backward."[58]

Between the fall of 1928 and the summer of 1929, the Central Committee passed nearly a dozen resolutions that called upon party and Komsomol schools, trade union organizations, and newspapers to begin implementing aspects of these findings.[59] Among the most important of these initiatives was a December 1928 resolution on state publishing, which decreed that all material printed in the USSR was henceforth to be regarded as a tool of mass mobilization. Publishing houses were to produce new literature on all subjects relating to indoctrination that was accessible enough to suit even the least educated members of society. In particular, the industry was instructed to:

> a) pay special attention to the publication of books that popularize Marxism-Leninism and the history of the ACP(b) and its revolutionary movement; b) improve the publication of mass literature on production in order to raise the level of technical knowledge among the workers and peasants; c) develop the publication of popular-scientific literature, connecting it to the socialist reconstruction of the economy and adapting it to promote self-study; d) expand the publication of artistic literature, especially those works that develop relevant political themes and counter the influence of the bourgeoisie, philistinism, defeatism, etc.; and e) provide for mass literature's maximal accessibility (in both form and content) in order to find the broadest swath of readership.[60]

History, then, remained at the core of the party's mobilizational efforts, but now it was—like all other subjects in Soviet mass culture—to be more aggressively popularized in order to make it accessible to a mass audience. Precisely how this popularization was to be accomplished still remained to be decided, however—a question that would haunt the propaganda state and its ideological establishment for years to come.

As is visible from the debacle surrounding the 1927 war scare, a decade of propaganda and agitation revolving around notions of class consciousness, worker-peasant solidarity, and loyalty to the party as the vanguard of the revolution had fallen upon deaf ears. Neither the party, nor the revolution, nor the idea of the dictatorship of the proletariat appears to have enjoyed much sympathy. How should this defeat be understood within the context of the party's relentless indoctrinational efforts?

Although the legacy of the Cold War may sometimes encourage the conclusion that Soviet citizens rejected the ideals of the revolution and socialism from the start, recent scholarship cautions against such an interpretation. Mention of revolutionary themes and values was routine in NEP-era popular discourse, indicating that these ideas enjoyed considerable popular resonance. What's more, a number of studies have demonstrated a well-developed sense of class-conscious identity among certain skilled professions during these years.[61] But if Soviets as indi‑ viduals and small groups embraced aspects of the revolutionary regime's rhetoric and values, they did not as a society respond enthusiastically to the way that these themes and messages were disseminated by ideolog‑ ical authorities through the mass media. Why? In essence, the problem appears to have been one of educational background. Few during NEP had more than one or two years of formal schooling, and much of the society could boast of nothing more than functional literacy. Even among urban residents and party members, educational rates were lit‑ tle better.[62] This meant that Agitprop's aggressive focus on materialism and anonymous social forces was simply too abstract and arcane for much of the society to comprehend, much less embrace.[63]

Perhaps because of its commitment to a Marxist-Leninist worldview, the party's ideological establishment failed to grasp this fundamental miscommunication. Of course, there were other distractions as well dur‑ ing this period, which is often referred to as the "Great Break."[64] The central party hierarchy was in the midst of launching the first Five-Year Plan and agricultural collectivization; it was also attacking its own right wing, having just defeated the political left. Party historians were in sim‑ ilar disarray, paralyzed by internal strife and infighting with their re‑ publican colleagues and "bourgeois" rivals over how to narrate the past.[65] The press and state publishing also zigzagged through these years, uncertain over how to best to adapt to the period's new mobi‑ lizational demands.[66] And if anything, the creative intelligentsia was worst off, divided by literary and artistic factions that were engaged in a self-defeating struggle to regulate how the revolution's ideals were to be depicted on the page, stage, canvas, and silver screen.[67] Occurring against the backdrop of social unrest and continuing rumors of war, this ideological crisis ultimately threatened to undermine the propa‑ ganda state itself.[68]

2 The Search for a Usable Party History

THE MOBILIZATIONAL CRISIS at the end of the 1920s forced Soviet ideological authorities to scramble for a new approach to political propaganda and indoctrination during a period in which they had little time to waste. As much as the October 1917 revolution ought to have been an inspirational event, the party's schematic slogans, caricatured heroes, and arcane philosophical references in the years since had failed to win hearts and minds. The problem, it seems, was twofold. First, the party's agitational efforts were simply too complex for much of its audience to grasp. And second, even among those who were able to follow the propaganda, few found it very compelling, inasmuch as party activists and agitators focused so single-mindedly on promoting the essence of Marxism-Leninism that they failed to connect the subject to more everyday, grassroots concerns.

Such an outcome is not surprising, as the party was in the process of transforming itself from a small, elite organization into a mass political movement. But in the context of these years' cultural revolution, industrialization, collectivization, and dekulakization, the ideological establishment—already wracked by factionalism and social turmoil—could not afford to be paralyzed for long by fundamental questions about how to adapt party propaganda to serve the needs of popular mobilization. This chapter investigates how party historians and activists searched for a usable past with which to galvanize popular support for the Soviet experiment.

Between 1927 and 1931, the party hierarchy issued an array of haphazard decisions that in aggregate belied a major shift in policy regarding agitation, propaganda, mass culture, and the press. If during the 1920s party propaganda and its grassroots activists had generally concentrated on explaining and popularizing the abstract, theoretical dimensions of party ideology for mass consumption, now a more practical, hands-on approach was needed. Propagandists who were accustomed to serving as instructors and consultants were now to become mass organizers and rabble-rousers.[1] Rallies were to combine new industrial production techniques with shock work; sloganeering, study circles, and political education courses were to focus on the application of the tenets of Marxism-Leninism and party history to everyday life.[2] The official line had to resonate more effectively with the practical tasks of industrialization, collectivization, and ideological indoctrination. Political instruction had to become more transparent and propaganda more evocative.[3]

Of course, if such sweeping correctives were difficult to formulate in theoretical terms, they were even harder to realize in practice. Propagandists searched for a way to incorporate the practical realities of everyday life into their formerly arcane discussions. Activists and agitators agonized over how to represent the complexity of Marxism-Leninism within sloganeering appropriate for mass audiences. Party historians struggled over how to restructure their scholarship in order to make it more relevant and accessible to ordinary workers and peasants. And amid this tidal wave of confusion and insecurity, the ideological establishment floundered as it attempted to coordinate such a broad program of reform. Ultimately, little was written, published, or disseminated during these years that would withstand the test of time.

Confusion within the ideological ranks caused by the nearly universal demand for retooling was compounded in late October 1931 by the publication of Stalin's now infamous letter to the journal *Proletarskaia revoliutsia,* which assailed party historians for failing to keep up with changing priorities. Stalin had been concerned about historians' apparent preference for inaccessible scholasticism for years, and now he seized upon one young scholar's willingness to second-guess Lenin as evidence of the continuing hubris of the entire discipline.[4] How could members of the ideological establishment neglect the new mobilizational agenda in favor of continued indulgence in arcane, irrelevant research? How dare they question the party hierarchy in public? Denouncing individual historians and the ideological establishment as a whole, Stalin defamed even fanatic loyalists like Ye. M. Yaroslavsky as "archival rats." Not only was Lenin's legacy to be considered unimpeachable, but ideologists were henceforth to focus on the heroic deeds of party leaders and steer clear of source-study and other "academic" exercises.[5]

While there is some controversy over what precisely precipitated Stalin's intervention—and what his actual intentions were—the ramifications of the letter suggest that mobilization and ideological control were the key issues at stake.[6] Officials like Kaganovich accused ideological cadres of "bureaucratic paper-shuffling" and warned hysterically of "opportunists" within the field who were supposedly using historical scholarship as a Trojan Horse from which to launch attacks on the party's legitimacy.[7] Even those who were not consciously engaged in wrecking were undermining the official line among mass audiences with their indulgence in scholasticism. Oversight was needed in order to guarantee that the ideological establishment would focus on the priorities at hand. As a sign of the times, the fervor with which Kaganovich and other members of the party leadership assailed the field set off a witch hunt within the ranks that not only thoroughly rattled the propaganda state over the next several years, but rendered virtually every book and article on party history and the Soviet leadership obsolete.[8]

The intensity of this scandal illustrates the centrality of the past to the party's construction of a mass sense of Soviet identity. Respect for history within the party hierarchy was hardly new, of course. That said, the publication of Stalin's letter both heightened the subject's priority and effectively nationalized the field, press-ganging even the most cautious party historians into the service of the state.[9] Thus even as the discipline was reeling from an orgy of denunciation, its members were confronted by an array of new demands to be required of all practitioners in the field. Already on December 16, 1931, the Politburo made plans to form a commission to write a new official history of the party. At the same time, Stetsky's Central Committee department of culture and propaganda—Kultprop—was mobilized to identify errors in other canonical books on party history, class struggle, the October revolution, the Comintern, and political literacy in general.[10] A few days later, Stetsky drew up plans for the reorganization and expansion of his whole department to deal with this new set of duties. Ratified in mid-January by the Central Committee, these decisions called for all party history textbooks to be reviewed and, when necessary, to be rewritten entirely for reissue. Party history courses were to be redesigned and party organizations were reminded about appointing qualified people to posts dealing with ideology, agitation, and propaganda.[11]

The priority of such measures was reiterated in 1933 when the results of a routine party purge confirmed the leadership's worst fears regarding its indoctrinational efforts. Ideological ignorance was endemic. "Among a wide swath of party members," *Pravda* noted, "along with a very weak understanding of the party program, its charter, and decisions, even the most basic familiarity with party history is sometimes found to be lacking." The situation in Moscow and Leningrad was shocking, the paper continued, whether in the hallowed halls of the Oriental Institute or on the shop floor at Elektrozavod. In the Ball-Bearing Plant, for instance, a worker named Malkin astonished his examiners by being unable to say when the October 1917 revolution had taken place. But if this was embarrassing, conditions were worse in the provinces, where veteran party members proved unable to identify what Trotskyism was or how democratic centralism differed from democratic socialism. When asked about the party's struggle with the left and the right, a fellow in the Urals named Yakovlev (who claimed to have been a party member since 1905) answered confidently: "The leftists said that we need to give everything to the kulaks and don't need to build collective farms. The rightists said that we need to build collective farms immediately." Such errors warned not only of chronic problems with party indoctrinational efforts, but with the party itself. How could such poorly educated party members rally support among non-party audiences? How could they withstand the challenge of better-versed opponents? How could they identify and root out renegades and wreckers within their own ranks?[12]

Blame for this crisis was initially assigned to grassroots-level agitators, who were failing to raise public consciousness in their study circles and reading groups. This, in turn, led to questions regarding the party's educational system as a whole. Although massive in nominal terms, the system functioned in a strikingly unsystematic way on a day-to-day basis. The competence of instructors varied wildly, as did the quality of teaching supplements. Perhaps for this reason, the party hierarchs' solution to this crisis focused as much on rewriting pedagogical materials as it did on retraining agitational cadres. Stalin and his entourage apparently felt that the creation of a successful standardized curriculum for party schools and study circles would ultimately allow them to worry less about individual grassroots-level agitators. Accordingly, all the information essential for basic political literacy was to be distilled into a handful of almanacs that were to be accessible to even the most poorly educated. And among the most important of these handbooks was to be a series of histories for all levels of the party faithful, as well as more specific works on republican, regional, and local party organizations across the USSR.[13] Reminders not to neglect the "full scale [. . .] of Stalin's executive role" served to ensure that this search for a usable past would contribute to the nascent cult of personality as well.[14] Such calls may at first glance seem odd in light of the party leadership's longstanding obsession with its own history and the dozens of textbooks and readers in circulation during the late 1920s and early 1930s. But the party hierarchy had signaled its dissatisfaction with this literature in 1931 and apparently expected a total transformation on the historical front.

Early in 1932, the Central Committee's call for a new party history led the Marx-Engels-Lenin Institute (IMEL) and the Institute of Red Professors (IKP) to form several editorial brigades in order to write major new multi-volume studies on the subject. Official party patronage was visible in the fact that these brigades brought together leading party historians who did not normally work together—the IMEL team, for instance, included Yaroslavsky, I. P. Tovstukha, N. N. Popov, V. G. Knorin, and V. A. Bystriansky, as well as the Commissars of Education for the Russian and Ukrainian republics, A. S. Bubnov and N. A. Skrypnik. What is more, this brigade was to be supervised by a blue-ribbon commission of party officials that included such luminaries as Stalin, Kaganovich, Stetsky, V. M. Molotov, P. P. Postyshev, O. A. Piatnitsky, and A. A. Adoratsky.[15] Such high-level involvement was completely unprecedented.

As it turned out, this constellation of talent did little to simplify the task at hand. At the first meeting of the IMEL brigade, Popov, a prominent ideologist and an editor at *Pravda,* suggested that the team should quickly write a three-volume history of the party—something that was very much in line with his newspaper's interest in material for mass audiences. Tovstukha, the deputy director of the IMEL and a former secretary of Stalin's, interrupted Popov and argued that they should produce a four-to-five-volume "scholarly" edition instead. This view, in turn, was challenged by Yaroslavsky, Stetsky, and Skrypnik, who believed that the project would require between six and nine volumes to do correctly. Such differences point to a profound disagreement over whether this history was to be encyclopedic or more suitable for broad audiences. Deadlocked, Tovstukha eventually allied with Popov and Knorin against Yaroslavsky, Stetsky, and Skrypnik and appealed to Stalin to resolve the impasse, lobbying for a comparatively simple, four-volume text. Stalin ruled that their instincts were correct and that the work should be "maximally *popularized.*"[16] Stalin's personal involvement notwithstanding, work on the textbook proceeded very slowly.[17] Describing Bolshevik history as monolithic and error-free had always been difficult, and this task was now further complicated by the need to write an account of the party's origins that would be both highly detailed and accessible.

Equally problematic were logistical issues, as Popov, Yaroslavsky, and others proved unwilling to devote much time to the new project.[18] Despite all the calls for change and despite the fact that at least some members of the intelligentsia read Stalin's letter to *Proletarskaia revoliutsia* as a "turning point," these historians underestimated the degree to which the party hierarchy expected their new work to differ from existing literature on the subject.[19] Popov, for instance, had been drafted to participate in the IMEL project and write a separate smaller history for party schools as well.[20] Nevertheless, he focused instead on a new edition of his *Outline of the History of the ACP(b),* a textbook that had gone through fourteen editions by the fall of 1931. Determined now to publish a fifteenth edition, he penned a new foreword in order to distance it from earlier party literature. He also rewrote stretches of the book in order to assume a more critical stance in regard to early members of the revolutionary movement such as Plekhanov and Trotsky and to excise commentary on how Stalin, Molotov, and the *Pravda* editorial board had briefly defied Lenin in March 1917. Although these changes assured Popov's text a new edition, the need for further corrections forced the text into a sixteenth edition in 1935.[21] What's more, this editing and reediting also prevented Popov from focusing on other, potentially more promising projects.

Like Popov, Yaroslavsky had been tapped to participate in the IMEL brigade in early 1932; like Popov, he also appears to have devoted most of his time to saving material he had been working on before the publication of Stalin's letter: a four-volume *History of the ACP(b)* and a beginner's textbook entitled *A Short History of the ACP(b)*.[22] While it was inevitable that both would require revisions after Stalin's letter, the former sustained a particularly brutal mauling during the winter of 1931–1932 after Kaganovich denounced it as "history tinged with the hue of Trotskyism."[23] Such harsh treatment stunned Yaroslavsky, as he was not only a prominent party historian and a member of the party's Central Control Commission, but a member of the editorial boards of *Pravda, Bolshevik,* and *Bezbozhnik*.[24] Unwilling to accept defeat, he immediately attempted to blunt these attacks before they ruined his career. Perhaps taking a cue from those on the party's left whom he had hounded in years past, Yaroslavsky recanted his sins in public even as he lobbied behind the scenes for a thoroughgoing political rehabilitation.[25] He even wrote directly to Stalin to assure the general secretary that his errors were correctable and that his books still showed "the most initiative in the field."[26]

A veteran of disciplinary infighting already in the late 1920s, Yaroslavsky probably realized that such gestures were not enough to guarantee his future. For that reason, he matched his acts of public and private repentance with a complete and total rewriting of the fourth volume of his *History of the ACP(b)*. Errors in the first edition had included mention of Stalin's wavering support for Lenin in the spring of 1917, and this forced Yaroslavsky to scour the sources in search of an authoritative document that would refute charges that Stalin had defied Lenin's direct orders. Eventually, he concluded, "it's best to say what Stalin himself said in the introduction to *Lessons of October*."[27] A risky gamble that Yaroslavsky had successfully wagered in 1927, it now failed to win approval from party authorities, and both the fourth volume and a projected fifth foundered shortly thereafter.[28]

In the wake of this defeat, Yaroslavsky returned, on Stetsky's advice, to the shorter (and thus less problematic) *Short History of the ACP(b)*. Redrafting and expanding the textbook to foreground Stalin's role in

Fig. 1: Ye. M. Yaroslavsky, early 1930s. VTsIK photo—collection of the author.

party history, he corrected its approach to Stalin's hesitation in 1917 by citing a new memoir exonerating the general secretary that had just appeared in *Pravda*. As several commentators have noted, the appearance of this exculpatory account in a paper that Yaroslavsky himself edited seems a little too convenient to be coincidental.[29] In any case, its publication resolved Yaroslavsky's crisis and allowed him to move forward with the revisions. It was in this edition that Yaroslavsky also began to address another major problem in party history. How could Stalin be styled as one of the founding fathers of Bolshevism if he hadn't held a major position in the central party organization until 1912? Yaroslavsky's solution was to treat the first nine years following the party's 1903 break with the Mensheviks in the Russian Social Democratic Labor Party (RSDLP) as a time of division and discord. Only in 1912, at a conference in Prague, he claimed, were the Bolsheviks able to straighten out their platform enough to form a separate, full-fledged party. Prague was already an important conference, insofar as it was after this meeting that Stalin was first appointed to the party's Central Committee, so Yaroslavsky now moved to describe the consolidation of the party and the cooption of Stalin into its leadership as if they were related. Although he admitted parenthetically that Stalin did not actually attend the conference and was promoted in absentia, he had nevertheless managed to link Stalin to the origins of the Bolsheviks' mature party organization. A cynical rearrangement of the party's first decade, it was greeted as a stroke of genius by many within the ideological establishment.[30]

Yaroslavsky completed his revisions to this textbook in early 1933 and sent the new manuscript directly to Stalin, aware of the fact that only the latter's intervention could get his book through the brutal review stage. In an accompanying letter, he wrote: "I am sending you the draft of my textbook on the history of the ACP(b), which I have completely reworked. I corrected it in the most meticulous way, keeping in mind all of your and Com[rade] Stetsky's directives [. . .]. No single critic could be more strict and demanding of my work than I have been myself. In this sense, the work has turned out thrice corrected [*trizhdy ispravlennaia*]." Nervous about the fate of his manuscript, Yaroslavsky sent another copy to Kaganovich, assuring him that he had revised over a third of the book and written several new chapters on Stalin from scratch. Equally important, he had designed the book with a mass audience in mind, aiming "to provide something which ordinary party and Komsomol members need right now as they *begin* to study party history."[31] Convinced or simply frustrated by the available alternatives, Stalin and Kaganovich conceded that the new manuscript had potential. Yaroslavsky was summoned to a private audience for further consultations and was forced to endure at least one more round of meddling by Stalin, Kaganovich, Stetsky, and Postyshev before the textbook was allowed to go to press.[32] Published in two volumes in late 1933 and early 1934 under the title *History of the ACP(b),* it enjoyed only modest print runs, suggesting that the hierarchs regarded the text as only a temporary solution.[33]

As marginal as Popov's and Yaroslavsky's new editions were, the fact that they made it back into print after 1931 distinguished them from the books of many other party historians and commentators, like Zinoviev, V. G. Yudovsky, V. O. Volosevich, and V. I. Nevsky.[34] Indeed, very little else was republished in 1932 and 1933. Aside from a difficult new book on dialectical materialism, the only other new texts to be published during this chaotic period were written by Ingulov and B. M. Volin, two party functionaries who were now working as high-ranking censors at Glavlit.[35] Their "political grammars" combined party history with social studies and civics—a successful formula that allowed them to get away with only limited detail on the party's historical experience. Demand was high for such texts, and both went into second editions in 1933 and third editions a year later.

It would be wrong, however, to assume it was merely the meddling of the party hierarchy that forced Yaroslavsky, Popov, Ingulov, and Volin to repeatedly revise their textbooks after 1931. Publishing in general fell under unprecedented scrutiny during these years, being blamed ex post facto for insufficient ideological vigilance in print during the late 1920s. Accusations in the press of complicity in anti-Soviet conspiracies were compounded by a 1933 Central Executive Committee resolution that threatened to hold state institutions responsible for loosely defined "wrecking" activities occurring within their jurisdictions. As a result, OGIZ, the official state publishing house, declined to release eighty-eight books in 1933 alone.[36] Such alarmism quickly became a union-wide phenomenon—in the Transcaucasus, the local party bureau not only backed away from publishing the memoirs of prominent Old Bolsheviks such as S. Karakash, but subsequently denounced these "politically dangerous" works for "perverting and falsifying party history and discrediting the [prerevolutionary] Bolshevik underground in the Transcaucasus."[37] A. S. Yenukidze's fall from grace between late 1934 and mid-1935 likewise began with the publication of memoirs concerning the Transcaucasian revolutionary underground that were judged to be insufficiently Stalin-centric.[38] Such events reveal the subject of party history to have become hyper-politicized in comparison to the relatively liberal and heterodox conditions of the 1920s. Moreover, this new orthodoxy was complicated by the fact that the doctrinal interpretation of party history was not completely worked out in the early 1930s—if the party hierarchs had a fairly clear idea of how their experience was to be viewed, the ideological establishment had yet to figure out how to convert the bosses' banal platitudes and simplistic explanations into an articulate, convincing, and inspirational narrative. The result was false start after false start.

Perhaps the only truly new party history text to be published during these years was written by another veteran member of the ideological establishment—Knorin—who, like Popov and Yaroslavsky, had also been drafted into contributing to the IMEL brigade. Like his colleagues, Knorin had better things to do: not only was he a ranking official in the Comintern, but he had been appointed to head a parallel textbook project at the IKP, where he led a new department devoted to political literacy and curricular materials. Knorin's IKP brigade of veteran party historians and instructors appears to have settled relatively quickly in 1932 on the goal of writing a modest single-volume party history, perhaps due to Stalin's advocacy of a "maximally popularized" text.[39] That said, this brigade soon experienced enough problems to require changes in staffing in 1933; even after this restructuring, leadership of the group oscillated back and forth between Knorin and B. N. Ponomarev several times.[40] Ultimately, however, Knorin's efforts were vindicated in early 1934, when his brigade succeeded in releasing a textbook under the title *A Short History of the ACP(b)*.[41]

Although heralded as a new leader in the field, Knorin's text troubled its editor after its release in light of questions regarding the degree to which it actually broke with the past. These misgivings were likely catalyzed by the publication of party and state resolutions during the spring of 1934 that criticized "sociological" approaches to history for their tendency to eclipse both chronology and the historical events them-

Fig. 2: V. G. Knorin, 1933. RGASPI, f. 495, op. 65a, d. 9797, l. 6.

selves.[42] In the end, these concerns led Knorin to publish an article in *Propagandist* in which he defended his text's ideological correctness and highlighted its "innovative" dimensions. In this piece, he placed particular emphasis on the priorities that had ostensibly structured the *Short History*'s approach:

> *first,* [we were] to lay-out the history of the party against the backdrop of elementary references to the civic history of the USSR; *second,* [we were] to present facts, events in party history, and party decisions in chronological order, with specific mention of the dates of events and party decisions; *third,* [we were] to present this in a popularized, short textbook on party history [. . .]; *fourth,* [we were] to supply textual material that is written on an acceptably high theoretical level.[43]

Echoing the party and state decrees mentioned above, this account allowed Knorin to cast his textbook as anticipating all the new priorities in the field. As everyone now knew, history was to be lively, animated, engaging, and relevant to people's everyday lives. Schematicism and attention to anonymous social forces was no longer to structure the way historical materialism was taught. "Sociological" analysis was to give way to historical cause-and-effect.

Truth be told, many of Knorin's claims in this article were rather forced, insofar as his *Short History* had been sent to press months before the new decrees were promulgated. Still, his book did satisfy a few of the new demands. For example, it boasted a narrative that was heavily grounded in names and dates and unfolded according to a rigorously chronological sequencing of events. Moreover, although it was first and foremost a history of the party, it did contextualize this experience within that of the history of the USSR and the Moscow-centered international communist movement. Abstract theoretical issues and other esoteric subjects too were toned down, in part to afford Stalin a central role in the *Short History*'s account. As Knorin himself put it, one of his brigade's most important tasks had been "to sketch and demonstrate the *great historical figure of Stalin* in its full greatness."[44]

Unsurprisingly, party members and the Soviet elite looked forward to the appearance of such new textbooks with great anticipation, as they had been searching for a reliable party history since 1931. *Proletarskaia revoliutsia* spoke for its readership when it reiterated the need in 1934 for a text that could serve as a "'finely honed party weapon' for the training of hundreds of thousands of party members and candidates, as well as non-party activists." That said, the journal was not willing to endorse either Knorin's text or the new editions of older textbooks as *the* solution to the crisis in the indoctrination system. The new and revised texts were apparently far from perfect and required "detailed discussion [. . .] and serious Bolshevik criticism of their shortcomings." Moreover, "it also should be mentioned that there is still no popular textbook that is small in scale and designed for the broad masses, party members, and non-party activists."[45] Like Popov's and Yaroslavsky's texts, then, Knorin's *Short History* represented no more than a temporary respite in the ongoing crisis of the propaganda state.

But although *Proletarskaia revoliutsia* was uncongratulatory about the situation at hand, weren't party historians at least finally recovering from the debacle of 1931? Weren't Knorin's book and the IMEL brigade's continuing work on its four-volume party history—as slow and plodding as it was—evidence of marginal progress?[46] Perhaps. But if a few historians and a single brigade were making slow headway, party history as a field was marked by endemic confusion within the ideological establishment and mounting discontent within the party hierarchy. Stalin recalled the situation in harshly critical terms several years later:

> the Central Committee knew that there was a mass of short and not-so-short courses [*nekratkie kursy*], guides, and political grammars of every Popovist, Bubnovite, Knorinist, and Ingulovite stripe. The Central Committee knew that there was a heap of guides, textbooks, political grammars, and readers and that the people found this confusing. Party members didn't know which one to rely on. None of the textbooks, courses, readers, or political grammars had the Central Committee's endorsement and sanction and this confused people further. People didn't know which was the best to follow—Yaroslavsky, [P. N.] Pospelov, Knorin, Bubnov, Popov or something else. With such a plethora of textbooks, there was no unified view, nor was there one that had the endorsement of the Central Committee. All of this created confusion in the popular mind and our party cadres did not know what to follow, which compass to latch on to. They quietly supposed that if Yaroslavsky's textbook or Pospelov's was being given out, that meant that it had the sanction of the Central Committee, but at the same time they had their doubts about whether there really was such sanction. And in fact, there was no such Central Committee sanction.[47]

According to Stalin, the inability of party historians to devise a canonical textbook spoke of a systemic failure on the part of the ideological establishment to synthesize the previous decade's diverse literature on party history—pamphlets, brochures, speeches, anthologies, readers, and memoirs—into a single, animated, evocative narrative.[48] A difficult task under any circumstances, it was further complicated by the hierarchs' apparent inability to articulate their vision of the official line and by the instability of the official line itself. In the case of the Knorin text, for instance, the book had failed to anticipate the full extent of the emergent break with schematic "sociological" analysis, despite its author's connections within the party hierarchy. True, the text invoked an impressive array of names and dates in the proper chronological order, but, all too often, it still allowed anonymous social forces and collective agents like "the party" and "the working class" to dominate the narrative. Worse, despite the *Short History*'s focus on Lenin and Stalin, its frequent commentary on Kaganovich, Molotov, and Voroshilov, and its passing mention of a handful of other Old Bolsheviks (Ya. M. Sverd-lov, F. E. Dzerzhinsky, V. P. Miliutin, I. I. Skvortsev-Stepanov, and Bub-nov), it neglected to animate its account with everyday heroes and accessible role models. Indeed, of the roughly three dozen historical per-sonalities to figure in the text, the vast majority were either enemies or repentant oppositionists, whether on the left (Trotsky, Zinoviev, L. B. Kamenev, Ye. A. Preobrazhensky, G. L. Piatakov, A. G. Shliapnikov, T. V. Sapronov, G. Ye. Yevdokimov, V. M. Smirnov) or on the right (Bukharin, M. P. Tomsky, A. I. Rykov, M. I. Frumkin, M. N. Riutin, N. A. Uglanov). Finally, the textbook utterly failed to incorporate into its narrative any discussion of "Soviet patriotism"—a key ideological concept that was introduced just months after the text's release. Such a remarkable lack of coordination and foresight within the ideological establishment serves today as a reminder of the degree to which party policy was evolving on an ad hoc basis. Ultimately, this trial-and-error approach to mass mobilization must share part of the blame for the stunning series of ideological missteps and false starts that repeatedly set back the party's search for a usable past during the early-to-mid-1930s.

Although many commentators justifiably regard the years between 1933 and 1936 to have been a respite from the radicalism of the Cul-tural Revolution, few within the ideological establishment would have agreed. Of particular concern during these years were indoctrinational efforts among the party rank-and-file and these cadres' low level of po-litical sophistication.[49] Kaganovich gave voice to these misgivings in early 1934 at the Seventeenth Party Congress, noting that indiscriminate admissions into the party between 1929 and 1932 had extended mem-bership to people who were ill educated and utterly unaware of many of the basic tenets of the official line. "It is necessary to admit," he as-serted, that the ideological establishment had failed to "test, train, and assimilate" these green recruits. The 1933 party purge had likewise failed to expel all of those unqualified to enjoy party membership. Ac-cording to Kaganovich, the party needed to redouble its efforts to bring the rank-and-file into line, both by increasing investment in political ed-ucation and by expelling those who failed to master its lessons.[50]

Amid this concern over the purity of the party faithful, S. M. Kirov was assassinated inside Leningrad party headquarters on December 1, 1934. Never satisfactorily explained, the murder of this major party boss touched off a firestorm of political hysteria within the upper reaches of the party, where even the most powerful seem to have feared that a plot was underway within the ranks to undermine the Soviet political system.[51] Leningrad party headquarters, after all, was located in the Smolny complex, the birthplace of the October 1917 revolution. How could a criminal act of this magnitude have transpired on such sacred ground? A secret circular issued in mid-January 1935 to all party organizations quickly announced in shrill terms that Kirov's murderers— a conspiracy ostensibly headed by Zinoviev—represented something "utterly new and without precedent in the history of our party." Struggling to explain Kirov's death in Marxist-Leninist terms, the communiqué blamed factionalism, ideological complacency, and lack of vigilance among party members on the mass level. The historical dialectic had apparently warned of the inevitability of such treachery, but insufficient awareness of the party's past experience with deviation and factional infighting and an obsession with purely technical expertise had allowed for the infiltration of subversive elements. "Knowledge and understanding of our party history," the circular concluded, "is the most important means by which to guarantee party members' total revolutionary vigilance." Henceforth, it was decreed that: "party members' instruction in party history must be elevated to a level worthy of the party. This includes study of each and every antiparty group in our party's history, their methods of struggle against the party line and their tactics. This also includes our party's tactics and methods of struggle against the antiparty groups—the tactics that have made it possible for our party to overcome and crush these groups." According to this circular, party history was now to be defined largely by the Bolshevik leadership's longtime struggle with internal dissent. "Party members ought to become familiar with not only how the party fought and defeated the Kadets, Socialist-Revolutionaries, Mensheviks, and anarchists, but also how the party fought and defeated the Trotskyites, Democratic-Centrists, Workers' Opposition, Zinovievites, right deviationists, rightist-leftist freaks, and so on." Although the text of this circular was classified and read aloud only within closed party assemblies, similar rhetoric surfaced in public newspaper coverage of the January 1935 show trial that convicted Zinoviev and Kamenev of complicity in the plot.[52]

With its stern warnings about the connection between political literacy and vigilance, the January 1935 circular drove many local, regional, and republican party organizations to review their rolls in a search for potential conspirators.[53] Little of the enormous amount of paperwork that this investigation generated during the late winter and spring of 1935 has been made available to researchers, but the material that does exist at the former central party archive in Moscow is very useful for assessing the state of grassroots-level party organizations on the eve of the Great Terror.[54] It is clear, for instance, that any hint of organized opposition within the local party organizations was almost completely overshadowed by more fundamental problems of political illiteracy. Many local officials and propagandists even turned out to be unable to explain what the so-called Zinovievite opposition was. Compounding this widespread incompetence was the fact that the investigations quickly revealed many of the party's lauded study circles and courses to exist only on paper. And even when such classes actually met, attendance was poor. Serko, for instance, a ranking Komsomol member on the "Belarus" kolkhoz near Dzerzhinsk, explained his refusal to attend such classes by saying that he "didn't need political literacy" and that most of his rural cohort felt the same way. Another Komsomol, Korba, the editor of a local newspaper, declared defiantly: "I don't need to know the history of the party for my work. I can get by without it and therefore skip going to class."[55] *Pravda* repeatedly assailed such apolitical attitudes during the spring of 1935, attributing widespread apathy in the ranks to a poor grasp of the party's history and heroes.[56]

Even those who regularly attended reading circles or party courses probably learned relatively little, due to ineffective instruction. Uninterested or overburdened with other responsibilities, many party activists and agitators read neither newspapers nor fictional literature; few others went to the theater or movie house.[57] Often, they didn't even read their own textbooks. When officials in Ivanovo checked up on an agitator named Belov before a study session on "The Party in the Struggle for October," they discovered that he was too ill prepared to answer even elementary questions.[58] Poor organization compounded such incompetence. And even when instructors were ready to teach, their pedagogical techniques only increased the confusion over the party line on the mass level. Typically, instructors led their groups through prescribed lessons in the curriculum by insisting that assigned texts be learned by rote—an approach that was not only unevocative, but ignored the question of whether the material was ever really understood, much less mastered. A shortage of up-to-date textbooks, supplementary materials, and visual aids further aggravated the situation.[59] Even when texts by Popov, Yaroslavsky, and Knorin were available, they often proved to be too complex and confusing to be used successfully at the grassroots level.[60]

The result was a reliance on uneven lectures and formulaic classroom dialogues that at times produced incredibly confused exchanges. In Moscow's Doromilovsky Factory, for instance, a *Pravda* correspondent was horrified to witness one such study circle session on the "liquidators," a faction within the prerevolutionary social democratic movement that sought reform within the system rather than through illegal means. According to the correspondent, he witnessed the following question-and-answer drill:

INSTRUCTOR: Who were the liquidators?
STUDENT: The liquidators were a tendency within the Bolshevik party.
INSTRUCTOR: No, the liquidators were agents of the counter-revolutionary bourgeoisie.
STUDENT: Okay, the liquidators were Mensheviks, and the Mensheviks supported the tsar.

According to the *Pravda* correspondent, not only was the instructor's correction of the first student's answer too vague, but he compounded this error by allowing the second student's conflation of liquidatorism, Menshevism, and monarchism to go unchallenged.[61] Other classroom scenes were too sensitive to be reported in such public forums. For example, when a certain N. I. Vitushchenko in an Azov basin study circle was asked to identify all the members of the Politburo, he named everyone except for A. A. Andreev. When his instructor pressed him for the final name, he innocently guessed "Trotsky," revealing how little he knew not only about recent party history, but about current events as well![62]

While teaching information as basic as key names, dates, and events ought to have been fairly routine, many instructors proved reluctant to entertain even elementary questions, lest queries from the floor expose how little they themselves actually knew. One Yakovenko, for instance, an agitator in the Black Sea port of Kerchensk, bluffed in early 1935 when asked what the difference was between the Bolsheviks and other social democrats in the years before the revolution. His answer—"that the Bolshevik party distinguished itself by following the Marxist-Leninist line"—was at best simplistic and at worst little more than a tautology. When a Tambov activist named Mikheev was asked why the Provisional Government had wanted to arrest Lenin in 1917, he indiscreetly revealed that the founder of the future USSR had been accused of "high treason" and then failed to point out the irony of the charge.[63]

Misconceptions abounded as a result of such pedagogical weakness. Some students, like a worker named Krylov in Moscow, would write down incorrect information presented in class and then commit it to memory. In Krylov's case, he had memorized an explanation for the rise of the Russian revolutionary movement—"the torture of political prisoners"—that elided not only the laws of historical materialism, but the role of party leaders such as Lenin and Stalin. Other students were led to question fundamental principles of Soviet rule. In one case, archival documents describe a study circle debate over whether or not it was truly possible to build socialism in one country. Some expressed doubts, while others expressed complete confidence in its realization. After all, "in Germany, the fascists are also building socialism!"[64] Although an innocent mistake, this relativism was viewed as heresy and even agitation of a deliberately "anti-Soviet" nature by party authorities.

If many grassroots party officials were apparently unaware of the implications of their own ignorance, others apparently were. One party report from early 1935 passed on the admission of a woman named Vladimirova:

> I am politically illiterate and know how difficult this makes things for me. Non-party people ask me questions about rationing and I am able to provide answers, but if they were to ask me about the former Zinovievite opposition, I would not be able to answer and would begin to hem and haw [*plavat'*]. This is why we must increase our political literacy along with our class vigilance.[65]

Mikhin, another party member, was even more blunt, confessing to being completely unaware of the degree to which the party was defined by its struggle with internal opposition. "I am ashamed to admit," he said, "that although I've been a party member since 1924, I didn't know about this whole struggle that Zinoviev and Kamenev were waging against the party."[66] Still others vowed to correct their erroneous ways. A Komsomol member in Minsk named Baranovsky, for instance, announced that he was now determined to invest more seriously in his political education: "I've never spoken at meetings because I did not study well and didn't know what to say. But after reading the circular and working through it, I've realized that it's not enough to work well in production—you also need to know the party's history."[67] Widespread reports of such passivity, timeserving, and incompetence within local party organizations during the late winter and spring of 1935 provoked a revival of discussions in the press of the importance of party history to the training of the rank-and-file.[68]

While party officials likely found the sentiments of Baranovsky and the others laudable amid the deluge of bad news during the first half of 1935, such statements only further embarrassed the ideological establishment, which had been trying to field a truly authoritative history textbook since 1931. *Pravda* criticized state publishing houses' attempts to address this need with new editions of obsolete texts by the likes of Popov, Yaroslavsky, and Knorin already in March 1935, dismissing these books as ill suited for the present situation. "Party history textbooks suffer from major problems," the paper claimed. "They're laid out too schematically. Propagandists complain that the textbooks are entirely inadequate when it comes to their discussions of antiparty groups' tactics, as well as the methods with which our party is struggling with them." Not only did the texts fail to supply information now judged to be critical to promoting vigilance within the party ranks, but they were still dogged by persistent problems of accessibility. Quoting Postyshev, *Pravda* demanded that these materials be rewritten to avoid the "dry, bookish language" of the present editions. Justifying its demands, the newspaper again connected the question of the usable past to current priorities:

> The study of party history must be engrossing and full of the revolutionary satisfaction that comes from work on mastering the combat tasks of the Bolshevik party. Only this sort of study will be able to train communists and Komsomol members to rally more and more new strata of laborers to the task of active socialist construction and the struggle with the enemies of the party and the persistence of attitudes that stem from already-defeated antiparty groups.

Party activists and agitators, according to Postyshev, had to be better trained. They had to have better textbooks to rely on—detailed, thorough texts rather than the stopgap political grammars and other handbooks presently in use. And they had to be better read and informed in order to connect key lessons on party history to literature, art, cinema, and current events both in the USSR and in the world at large.[69]

In the midst of this discussion in the press, Stetsky summoned a number of leading members of the ideological establishment to his Central Committee department of culture and propaganda on March 10 for a wide-ranging discussion of the crisis.[70] The next day, Yaroslavsky wrote a letter to Stalin in which he conceded that much of the miserable state of party education was attributable to the inaccessibility of its textual materials. He proposed to rectify the situation by reorganizing party education into a centralized, three-tiered system. On the most basic level, political neophytes would study a curriculum structured around a short, animated, still-to-be-written textbook that would flank vital information about party history with illustrated material on the party's "heroism and people." Students would then move on to material organized around a textbook like Knorin's recent *Short History,* "although here it would be necessary to avoid schematicism" and "liven up the examples." Finally, the most politically mature party members would study their history according to a detailed, two-volume text that would devote two-thirds of its narrative to the post-1917 period. Yaroslavsky offered his *History of the ACP(b)* as an example of such an advanced reader. Key to the success of this proposal, Yaroslavsky averred, would be active input from the party hierarchy about the priorities around which this new generation of texts should be constructed.[71]

Internal party reports, combined with Yaroslavsky's lobbying and the criticism in the press, pushed Stalin and his entourage to correct the situation not only on the textbook front, but throughout party education as a whole. In late March 1935, the general secretary gave an extended speech to the Orgburo in which he assailed the quality of party educational programs and adopted Yaroslavsky's call for a three-tiered indoctrinational system.[72] At that same meeting, the party leadership passed a Central Committee resolution calling for new infrastructure, greater discipline, and more accountability in party education—an initiative quickly seconded by the Leningrad party organization, which was still reeling from the Kirov murder.[73] Evidently unsatisfied with these measures, the hierarchs took further action between that April and June. First, directives were issued instructing all local party organizations to update and verify their membership rolls in order to purge slackers, criminals, deviationists, and "dead souls" from their ranks.[74]

Second, Stetsky's massive department of culture and propaganda was broken up into five smaller departments dedicated to more focused work on agitation and propaganda, state publishing and the press, cultural enlightenment, school policy, and science.[75] Third, Stalin and the other Central Committee secretaries met to draw up a new, more detailed agenda for party history textbooks. Fourth, the hierarchs passed yet another Central Committee resolution that reiterated the need for improvements in history instruction among party members. Courses, classes, and circles had to be rethought; new curricular materials had to be made available.[76] The repeated issuance of such decrees testifies both to the continuing priority of such efforts and a growing sense of impatience over their fulfillment.

Most important among these various measures was probably Stalin's meeting with the Central Committee secretaries during the spring of 1935—a little-understood event that is described only obliquely in correspondence between Stetsky, Yaroslavsky, and Stalin. Apparently, it was at this meeting that a whole array of textbook projects were either commissioned or re-endorsed. Ingulov and Volin were to combine forces on a new, co-authored political grammar. Knorin, Yaroslavsky, and Pospelov were to produce a new, collectively written popular history text for mass audiences. And the IMEL brigade working on the four-volume academic history (now under the leadership of M. D. Orakhelashvili) was to continue to soldier forward, flanked by another new brigade at the same institute now instructed to quickly produce a shorter two-volume history text for grassroots propagandists and party activists.[77] Reactions to this agenda indicate that even experts in the field felt totally overwhelmed.[78]

Help in alleviating the tension between supply and demand appeared only a month later, from entirely unexpected quarters. L. P. Beria, a rising Georgian party boss, had been attempting to curry favor with Stalin since early in the decade and one of his initiatives—a Tbilisi research institute devoted to the study of the prerevolutionary Transcaucasian underground—now bore fruit. Although only marginally literate, Beria had made a name for himself in 1934 by publishing a ghostwritten article in *Bolshevik,* the party's main theoretical journal, on Stalin's role in his region's revolutionary movement. Now, he followed this successful trial balloon with an ambitious, two-day presentation to the Tbilisi party organization in July 1935 in which he outlined a new interpretation of Stalin's rise to prominence within the Bolshevik party. Aside from exaggerating Stalin's role as a militant within the Transcaucasian underground, Beria established two other interrelated myths that would come to define party propaganda for over two decades. First, he argued that from the earliest years of the twentieth century, Lenin had always considered Stalin one of his closest, most able lieutenants— a contention that the party boss supported with a grossly simplified rendering of early party history. Second, Beria seized upon Yaroslavsky's treatment of the Prague conference in order to postdate the actual founding of the Bolshevik party to 1912. This depreciation of the Bolshevik movement between 1903 and 1912 to little more than factionalism within the RSDLP won Stalin a place at the table at what would now be referred to as the Bolshevik party's founding conference—an impression Beria reinforced by obscuring the fact that Stalin never actually made it to Prague. A brilliant exercise in smoke and mirrors, this narrative received quick endorsement from ideological authorities in Moscow and would script the contours of early party history until the mid-1950s.[79]

A potential answer to calls for a new approach to party history, this speech was promptly serialized in *Pravda* for an all-union audience under the title "On the Question of the History of the Bolshevik Organizations in the Transcaucasus." Although there is some doubt over the degree to which Beria's ghostwriters coordinated their work with ideological authorities in Moscow, the party hierarchy does not appear to have hesitated before authorizing the publication of the address as a book slated for mass consumption.[80] Stetsky, for instance, issued a directive commanding all party organizations to have their "activists, propagandists, and party members study C[omrade] Beria's presentation [. . . ,] which has provided new material of the richest kind on the role of C[omrade] Stalin as our party's leader and theoretician. Special seminars are to be organized to help activists and propagandists work through C[omrade] Beria's presentation."[81]

But if Beria's text satisfied some of the hunger for new material, it was at best an incomplete solution. Although it addressed critical questions about periodization and Stalin's role in party history, it confined its commentary to the general secretary's tenure within the prerevolutionary Transcaucasian underground, supplying little new about his service to the party and state after 1917. Worse, the book's lesser pro-

tagonists—a little-known cast of Georgian, Armenian, and Azeri Bolsheviks—were too obscure to serve as popular heroes or role models. In
some circumstances, this volume might have satisfied a portion of the
demand for instructional literature; in mid-1935, however, it did little
to make sense of Kirov's murder or the new revelations about treachery within Old Bolshevik ranks. To make matters worse, Zinoviev's and
Kamenev's public admissions of guilt, compounded by closed-door proceedings that spring and summer against Yenukidze, Shliapnikov, and
others, not only led to more arrests, but to more problems with indoctrinational efforts as well. Fanatic ideological vigilance provoked a
wide-ranging purge of public libraries in mid-1935 that targeted party
histories and memoiristic writing judged to deviate from the poorly defined general line.[82] This, in turn, led to the closure of major organizations blamed for disseminating politically suspect material, such as the
Society of Old Bolsheviks, the Society for Former Political Prisoners,
and their publications, *Stary Bolshevik* and *Katorga i ssylka*.[83] This
propaganda pogrom threw party study circles into chaos, as activists
panicked over what must have seemed like the impending collapse of the
entire party canon. Their fears were confirmed when the results of the
party's verification campaign came in somewhat later on. According to
the survey, the rank-and-file had a stunningly poor grasp of the party's
past and its relevancy to the present and future.[84]

With no solution to the crisis at hand, the authorities gambled on a
number of temporary, stopgap measures to shore up the situation. The
IMEL and IKP reassigned almost all their qualified personnel in order
to staff pressing textbook projects.[85] Ingulov and Volin rushed their new
co-authored political grammar into production, while Ingulov hurriedly
updated another introductory reader of his own for rerelease.[86] The
press published articles on how instructors could make the most of
flawed textbooks and provided party ideologists with a forum within
which to publicize the new priorities for party education.[87] Major meetings of pedagogues and propagandists were likewise convened to discuss
these issues in greater depth.[88] And more unorthodox initiatives can be
linked to this new set of priorities as well. For instance, a revolutionary
new narrative of party history was unveiled in 1936 within the context
of a massive new museum devoted to Lenin's memory. Situated around
the corner from Red Square in the former seat of the Moscow City
Duma, the Central Lenin Museum offered 21 rooms of exhibits, 15 of

which were arranged in chronological order. Referred to by *Komso-molskaia pravda* as a "school of Bolshevik history," its exhibits mapped the rise of the communist party according to Lenin's career as visionary, revolutionary, and statesman.[89] Like Beria's history of the Transcaucasus revolutionary movement, these texts and installations attempted to fill some of the vacuum and at least temporarily satisfy demand for new historical materials. In the end, however, each of these measures exacerbated the crisis instead of ameliorating it. Beria's book was too obscure and foreign. Volin and Ingulov's political grammars were too superficial. The advice in the press was too complicated for all but the best-trained grassroots instructors, while the descriptions of the party's agenda and its conferences were too brief to offer real practical help. Even the Lenin Museum missed its target, lionizing its namesake and his disciple instead of providing a sweeping narrative on party history. Potentially useful as curricular supplements, these texts—whether printed on the page or displayed under glass—were powerless to rectify Soviet indoctrinational problems on their own.

In late 1935, as the fourth anniversary of Stalin's letter to *Proletarskaia revoliutsia* neared, Knorin, Yaroslavsky, and Pospelov submitted their new two-volume text for approval to the Central Committee under the title *History of the ACP(b): A Popular Textbook*. Based on Knorin's *Short History of the ACP(b)*, the book—now nearly 900 pages in length and graced with over 200 illustrations—was heralded by Stetsky and others as the panacea that the party's educational system had been waiting for. So lavish was the book's projected layout and formatting that it was expected to completely monopolize Moscow's printing presses and paper stockpile once it was approved for publication.[90]

But despite Stetsky's excitement over the text, it failed to win Stalin's approval. As is evident from the one surviving copy of the book's page proofs, Stalin gave it a quick read in late 1935 or early 1936 and made a handful of factual corrections and comments in the margins before putting it aside.[91] Although it is unclear precisely why Stalin rejected the text, it is likely that at least two things aroused his displeasure. First, although the *Popular Textbook* was considerably more dynamic and evocative than its predecessors, it was very long and—despite its title—not really suitable for mass audiences. Second, it was dominated by a verbose play-by-play narrative that offered little in the way of larger observations, generalizations, or lessons associated with the party's historical experience. In other words, the book did not satisfy the party's need for a didactic work that would rally opinion at the grassroots. Stalin's dismissal of the text left its authors little choice but to return to the drawing board in search of a truly popular approach to party history.[92]

When Stalin and his inner circle paused to take stock of the situation on the historical front in early 1936, they could not have been very pleased. Years of effort had produced little more than a bibliography of obsolete, unusable readers at a time when instructional leadership was absolutely necessary. Why, with seemingly unlimited resources at their disposal, hadn't the various Knorins, Yaroslavskys, Popovs, and Ingulovs been able to get it right? Part of the problem lay in the historians' unwillingness or inability to embrace a truly populist mode of writing suitable for mass audiences. Accessibility demanded dramatic storylines, animated prose, dynamic description, and a cast of engaging heroes and villains—characteristics that appear to have been antithetical to how these devout Marxist-Leninists believed history ought to be written.

But although the ideological establishment bore considerable responsibility for aspects of the crisis, blame must also be assigned to Stalin and his entourage. It was, after all, the hierarchs' fault that their political careers were proving to be impossible to describe in positive, ideologically consistent terms. It was their fault that their clumsy, ad hoc approach to governance bore little resemblance to the building of socialism according to the scientific laws of Marxism-Leninism. And it was their fault that they had delegated the ungrateful task of reconciling these inconsistencies to historians without first providing them with a clear understanding of what was expected. Such obstacles would have to be resolved if the party hierarchy was ever to identify a version of the usable past that could contribute to popular mobilization.

3 Personifying the Soviet "Experiment"

AS SOVIET IDEOLOGISTS struggled during the early 1930s to develop a canonical textbook on party history for use with mass audiences, many also became involved in propagandizing Stalin's personal role in the history of the Bolshevik movement. This was to some extent unavoidable, of course, as ideological cadres strained in the wake of Stalin's letter to *Proletarskaia revoliutsia* to demonstrate their loyalty to the party leadership in general and the general secretary in particular. But it also suggests that many of these specialists did not consider the party catechism and Stalin's cult of personality to be mutually exclusive and instead believed that all such priorities contributed to official indoctrinational efforts and, by extension, Soviet identity formation. This chapter therefore examines the development of Stalin's personality cult as a form of mass mobilizational propaganda.

The notion that the cult of personality played an integral role in Soviet ideological affairs contradicts much of the existing literature on the subject, which since 1956 has echoed Khrushchev's denunciation of the cult as a function of Stalin's personal psychosis.[1] That said, it corresponds closely to modern social scientists' observations that charismatic leadership and personality cults tend to emerge in developing societies where ruling cliques aspire to cultivate a sense of popular legitimacy.[2]

Scholars since Max Weber have posited that if coordinated effectively, charismatic leadership can promote consensus even in societies that are poorly integrated or lack a greater sense of patriotism, community, and rule of law.[3] Such observations explain much about Soviet ideologists' recourse first to the Lenin cult after 1924 and then to Stalin's cult of personality after 1929. Despite massive investment in reconstruction and industrialization, the USSR lagged woefully behind its neighbors in both socio-economic and institutional terms during the 1920s and early 1930s. It was a place where, in the words of one commentator, "most of the components of civil society or of the modern state were missing: a reliable bureaucracy, a unitary consistent notion of citizenship or polity, [. . .] or even a sense of psychological inclusion."[4] These conditions, combined with the increasing threat of war after 1933, virtually drove Soviet ideologists to mobilizational exigencies like the personality cult.

Of course, such an interpretation of the Stalin cult is a distinctly modern one, grounded in social anthropology and cross-cultural analysis. Yet it is interesting to note that Stalin's intuitive understanding of the cult's role in Soviet society conformed quite closely to this point of view. In the mid-1930s, for example, he commented to M. A. Svanidze that "'the people need a tsar,' i.e., someone to revere and in whose name to live and labor."[5] Shortly thereafter, he elaborated on this point with Leon Feuchtwanger, contending that the cult did not focus on his personality so much as on his role as the personification of socialist state building in the USSR.[6] Over time, this conflation of the cult with broader propaganda efforts became so routine that Stalin eventually even assigned his official biography a central role in the party catechism.[7] Such gestures, despite their obvious immodesty, confirm that that the cult was designed to serve first and foremost as a mechanism for political mobilization, advancing a larger-than-life hero capable of embodying the power, legitimacy, and appeal of the Soviet experiment.[8]

This chapter investigates the cult's performance as a vehicle for mass mobilization by examining the production history of Stalin's official biography. The construction of this text provides an ideal case study for appreciating the charismatic dimensions of the cult of personality: not only was Stalin's *Short Biography* one of the most seminal propaganda texts of its day, but Stalin's biographers left behind a remarkably detailed paper trail despite Soviet publishing houses' routine destruction of manuscripts and correspondence.[9] In genre terms, biography is also well suited to such an investigation, having at least as much relevancy to the cult as the portraiture, sculpture, verse, and poster art that is so well remembered today. One of the most ancient forms of writing, biography dates back to early religious hagiography; in modern times, the genre enjoys unparalleled popularity within the reading public due to its compelling subject matter, its emphasis on temperament, character, and accomplishment, and its tight narrative focus on a single protagonist. Few other forms of communication, it would seem, are so suited to the promotion of charismatic authority.[10]

Stalin's official biography has surprisingly humble origins. Although commentary on Stalin was not uncommon in the USSR in the years following the October 1917 revolution, early party propaganda did not generally dwell on individual personalities aside from Lenin and a handful of other senior party members.[11] Indeed, it wasn't until the mid-1920s that the compilation of several hundred descriptive profiles of leading Bolsheviks for the *Granat Encyclopedic Dictionary* necessitated the production of a serious biographical statement on Stalin. Tovstukha, the general secretary's former assistant, drafted the manuscript. The final result, describing Stalin's career through 1924, boasted a narrative which—if largely fictional—was at least quite accessible.[12] It appeared in 1927 both in the encyclopedia and as a separate fourteen-page brochure, complete with frontispiece, entitled *Joseph Vissarionovich Stalin: A Short Biography*. Published in large, bold type in a modest print run of 50,000, it was a relatively unassuming production.[13] Slightly enlarged, this biography resurfaced in 1929 during the commemoration of the general secretary's fiftieth birthday, when it ran in *Pravda* on December 21 as an unsigned "official" complement to articles by Kaganovich, Voroshilov, and others in the paper's jubilee double edition. On the back page, OGIZ advertised the original 1927 pamphlet and heralded the imminent publication of a new, more elaborate biography. Aimed at a wide audience, it had been "designed for every literate worker and peasant" and was to be printed in massive numbers.[14]

This new focus on the celebration of an individual like Stalin was indicative of the broader reorientation of ideological efforts underway during these years detailed above. Difficulties with social mobilization within this poorly educated society during the late 1920s had compelled party ideologists to search for alternatives to Soviet propaganda's long-standing focus on materialism and anonymous social forces. OGIZ likely decided to commission its book on Stalin after realizing that propaganda oriented around the general secretary both complemented the longstanding Lenin cult and answered calls for more animated, accessible, and less impersonal propaganda.

Despite assurances to the contrary, however, the OGIZ biography never saw the light of day. This is rather curious, insofar as Stalin's 1929 jubilee is generally considered to mark the launching of the Stalin cult and Tovstukha's thin brochure was clearly insufficient to play a central role in the new campaign. But aside from the publication of a small article in the *Minor Soviet Encyclopedia* and a number of chapters or sub-chapters in party history textbooks and political grammars, nothing even vaguely reminiscent of a Stalin biography rolled off the presses during these years.[15] How is one to explain this peculiar lacuna? Although some have attributed the lack of an official biography during the early 1930s to modesty on Stalin's part, this conclusion seems rather unsatisfactory.[16] By 1934, sixteen and a half million copies of Stalin's various works were in circulation, complemented by increasingly large amounts of hagiography in the party press.[17] Modesty, then, did not prevent the production of a new biographical statement.

Instead, Stalin's biographers likely struggled with the contradictions involved in constructing a cult of personality within a society that was at least ostensibly committed to a materialist view of history. As noted above, this materialism had focused on class analysis and discouraged interest in individual actors for much of the 1920s; now, although most agreed that the approach had not worked, few had any idea how to improve upon it. The party's deification of Lenin offered little guidance, in part because he had not been venerated during his lifetime and in part because Stalin's claim to his mantle remained contested. Somewhat more helpful was Plekhanov's work on the role of individual actors in the Marxist dialectic. Plekhanov, who was far from uncontroversial within the Bolshevik ranks, had argued that historic individuals should not be dismissed by materialists, as they were representatives of greater social forces. Political and military leaders, as well as famous reputations in science and the arts, were propelled forward in history by pre-existing socio-political movements; they could even accelerate or retard this historical process, although this ability was more a function of their understanding of the laws of history than their personal charisma or talent. This accommodation was important for members of the Soviet ideological establishment, as it allowed historic individuals to be used to personalize and animate historical narratives without contradicting the Marxist maxim that "the history of all hitherto existing society is the history of class struggle."[18] Such ideas had circulated at the margins of the Lenin cult for nearly half a decade by 1929; still, it was only after considerable hesitation that the ideological establishment decided to invest in Stalin-centered propaganda in order to augment the inscrutable nature of Marxism-Leninism with a tangible, living hero familiar to one and all.

But if Stalin's OGIZ biographers found their assignment challenging from an ideological standpoint, the situation was further complicated in October 1931 by the publication of Stalin's letter to *Proletarskaia revoliutsia*. As detailed in the preceding chapter, Stalin's letter called into question virtually all existing party propaganda and swept away much of the nascent hagiography of the Stalin cult that had emerged. Propagandists and party historians were now under direct orders to write for a mass audience and to focus on the heroic deeds of party leaders rather than the more subtle analysis of theory and practice.

Some of the confusion surrounding the fluctuating official line on heroes was resolved in the spring of 1932, when *Bolshevik* published an unusually wide-ranging interview with Stalin conducted by the popular German biographer Emil Ludwig. Aware of the general secretary's respect for a broad array of historic individuals from Lenin to Peter the Great, Ludwig pointed to the difficulties that such famous personalities created for historical materialists. Stalin parried, arguing that the two were not as incompatible as Ludwig alleged. Their subsequent conversation laid down a reliable set of rules to guide the gradual evolution of Bolshevik attention to the "great men of history" over the course of the next few years:

LUDWIG: Marxism denies the leading role of personality in history. Don't you see a contradiction between a materialist understanding of history and the fact that you nevertheless recognize a leading role for historic personalities?
STALIN: No, there is no contradiction [. . .]. Every generation is met with certain conditions that already exist in their present form as that generation comes into the world. Great people are worth something only

insofar as they are able to understand correctly these conditions and what is necessary to alter them [. . .].

LUDWIG: Some thirty years ago when I was studying at university, a large number of German professors who considered themselves to be adherents of the materialist understanding of history assured us that Marxism denies the role of heroes and the role of heroic personalities in history.

STALIN: They were vulgarizers of Marxism. Marxism has never denied the role of heroes. To the contrary, it gives them a significant role, albeit in line with the conditions that I have just described.[19]

Thus as Stalin had argued in *Proletarskaia revoliutsia* just months earlier, it was not only acceptable, but imperative that party propagandists focus on the heroic public service of individuals at the fore of major social movements. Put another way, he was essentially endorsing Plekhanov's position, although without mentioning the controversial theorist by name.

Although the nuances of this subject seem to have stymied OGIZ's biographers, they did not discourage the growth of the cult as a whole, which expanded exponentially during these years as members of the establishment attempted to prove their loyalty in a frenzy of deferential writing.[20] Such tendencies were reinforced by the party hierarchs' call for a broad reconceptualization of party and civic history, as well as their official endorsement of Socialist Realism in literature and the arts (which is detailed in the following chapter). These latter initiatives stemmed from the party hierarchy's loss of confidence in the previous decade's focus on abstract schematicism and anonymous social forces and its new call for animated narratives, populated by a pantheon of identifiable heroes and villains. Indeed, the general secretary and his entourage were to play a key role in this new Soviet Olympus—something made more explicit in an appeal by P. F. Yudin in early 1934: "The greatest people of the epoch stand alongside us—we had Lenin and we now have Stalin, Molotov, Kaganovich, and Voroshilov. But people with such intelligence or revolutionary sweep-of-the-hand as our leaders don't yet figure into our artistic literature. It is imperative to represent such people in our literature."[21] If Yudin's announcement could be mistaken as referring exclusively to the *belles lettres*, a similarly timed statement by Kaganovich was more programmatic. Conceding that the general secretary's reputation was well known, he claimed that this was not enough. "The role of Comrade Stalin," the party boss averred, "still awaits its comprehensive and profound evaluation."[22] *Proletarskaia revoliutsia* made this biographical agenda completely transparent later that year:

> The biographies of Lenin, Stalin, and an array of exceptional figures within our party—[Ya. M.] Sverdlov, Dzerzhinsky, [M. V.] Frunze, etc. —have an enormous significance in the popularization of our party's history. To the present day, there are no biographies of Lenin or Stalin written for the broad masses; there are no dynamically written biographies of Sverdlov, Frunze, Dzerzhinsky, and others.
>
> The biographies of Lenin published by the IMEL to commemorate the tenth anniversary of his death (by [P. M.] Kerzhentsev, Yaroslavsky, and others) suffer from major shortcomings. They do not provide a living portrait of the ingenious leader. They are more like party histories than they are biographies of the party's founder. The careful preparation of biographies of the founder of our party, its leaders, and its exceptional figures is a major task for our party historians—biographies, written for the broad masses of workers and collective farmers. These biographies should not be dry lists of facts and dates from their lives, activities, and struggles; they should instead illuminate in an appealing way the living portrait of a Bolshevik—illuminate the lives and activities of the founders and leading figures of our party, which are so rich and worthy of emulation.[23]

Despite this agenda's clear priority, however, efforts during the mid-1930s to develop more animated, evocative propaganda oriented around the party leadership did not immediately produce results. Although ideologists and party historians slowly began to reframe their Marxist-Leninist analysis in more populist terms, political literature remained dominated by arcane theoretical tracts, poorly annotated speeches, and crude sloganeering. Chronic indoctrinational problems persisted as a result: when a certain Petrushenko in the provinces was asked who Stalin was in a study circle in 1935, his answer—"someone like the tsar used to be"—got him reported all the way to Moscow.[24] Petrushenko's example illustrates why the absence of a Stalin biography was so keenly felt, inasmuch as such a narrative offered an excellent opportunity for synthesizing the party's corpus of abstract theory and abstruse rhetoric into a coherent, compelling statement on what it meant to be Soviet.

Part of the delay in developing such texts seems to have stemmed from the fact that Stalin lacked confidence in many of his potential biographers. The *Proletarskaia revoliutsia* scandal had proven that even the most loyal were sometimes a bit too critical in their approach to such tasks—how could the party guarantee that they would not unintentionally undermine the overall objectives of the propaganda campaign? And if such a possibility existed, would it not be exploited by the regime's opponents? Such fears explain why Stalin's chancellery quickly asserted a monopoly over how the general secretary's biography, likeness, and writings were disseminated for public consumption. They also explain why Stalin not only vetted biographers himself, but discouraged groups as venerable as the Society of Old Bolsheviks from mounting even temporary exhibitions about him.[25]

Thus if Stalin's hesitancy to appoint an official biographer is sometimes seen as evidence of his discomfort with the nature of the personality cult during the 1930s, his refusal to authorize certain projects is better read as a sign of extreme caution over who would be tapped to carry out this all-important task.[26] Kirov appears to have been selected to author such a text in the early 1930s before L. V. Nikolaev's bullet cut short his nascent literary career. M. Gorky, the most revered of the court *litterateurs,* also considered an invitation to develop a manuscript before diplomatically sidestepping the offer.[27] In the end, biographical projects enjoying real potential emerged from within the Stalinist establishment. Beria, as noted in the preceding chapter, engineered the establishment of a Stalin Institute in Tbilisi in February 1932 while still a rising party boss. A development inextricably linked to the emergence of the personality cult, this institute proposed to gather and systematize the local historical record as it pertained to the general secretary's career in the Transcaucasian underground. As its charter noted: "along with the collection of all materials pertaining to the revolutionary activity of Com[rade] Stalin, the institute is also assigned the task of organizing scholarly research to work out issues concerned with Stalin's biography and his role as theoretician and organizer of the party, particularly including the study of Stalin's role as organizer of the revolutionary workers' movement in the Transcaucasus."[28]

Tbilisi did not monopolize the research for long, however. That same year, IMEL deputy director Tovstukha resumed his interest in chronicling Stalin's career. One of his first moves was to begin shifting relevant documents from Georgia to Moscow in order to prepare for the publication of Stalin's collected works.[29] Territoriality quickly became an issue, however, as Tbilisi's prerogative was asserted first by M. G. Toroshelidze and then by Beria and his client, E. A. Bedia. Beria's rising prestige in the party gave him a tremendous advantage, allowing him to sideline local rivals like Toroshelidze and publish an article of his own in *Bolshevik* in mid-1934 on Stalin's service in the prerevolutionary Transcaucasus underground. In the wake of this coup, he had Bedia use the resources of the Tbilisi institute—now known as the Tbilisi division of the IMEL—to expand his Stalin-centered history of the Transcaucasus Bolsheviks into a book-length study.[30]

Infighting soon divided the field. In Moscow, Yaroslavsky joined the fray and began gathering material for a book about Stalin through official and unofficial channels in late 1934, perhaps believing that such a project would restore his reputation within the ideological establishment. "I am working on a book that I am certain will be useful to the entire party as well as to the Transcaucasian comrades," he wrote to a Georgian party official in early 1935. Writing to Tovstukha, Yaroslavsky asked for help and advice, speaking of the need to publish "a fairly detailed, popularized biography." Tovstukha responded rudely that while there was no doubt about the pressing need for such a book, Yaroslavsky was the wrong man for the job. "It will not turn out as a *biography* of Stalin—it will just be another history of the party and Stalin's role therein." "A detailed biography of Stalin," averred Tovstukha, "one exceptionally vivid and rich in facts," would take years to complete. Denying that he was writing a Stalin biography of his own, Tovstukha flatly refused Yaroslavsky's request for assistance.[31]

Insulted by Tovstukha's tone, Yaroslavsky refused to be discouraged. Instead, he wrote back that he had allies in the Politburo and would proceed with his planned biography with or without Tovstukha's assistance.[32] Unbeknownst to Yaroslavsky, however, it was actually Tovstukha who enjoyed the party hierarchy's favor, and he found Yaroslavsky's demands presumptuous and threatening. Tovstukha, it turns out, had been in ongoing discussions with Stetsky at Agitprop for some time about the idea of such a book and believed himself to have been appointed Stalin's official biographer.[33] Determined to checkmate his rival, Tovstukha wrote to Adoratsky, the then-director of the IMEL, that "if Yaroslavsky moves toward what I am working on [. . . ,] please steer him away decisively."[34]

Stymied by this stonewalling, Yaroslavsky wrote first to Stetsky and then directly to Stalin, explaining that he hoped to write a biography of the general secretary for young audiences. "I could write a good, useful, and needed Bolshevik book, for which there's enormous demand," he noted to Stalin. When these missives went unanswered, he attempted to convince his patrons in the Politburo—particularly G. K. Ordzhonikidze—to overrule Tovstukha and Adoratsky. In August 1935, he again appealed directly to Stalin:

> C[omrade] Stalin! Sergo [Ordzhonikidze] called me today [. . .] and said that he had talked to you about my planned book *Stalin*. Only you can remove the exceptional obstacles that he told you about—it is imperative that either you or Comrade Poskrebyshev order the IMEL or the Archive of the October Revolution to allow me to use *all* the available materials and documents. Otherwise, they will not permit me to make use of them.[35]

Stalin's response, scrawled across Yaroslavsky's letter, was dismissive. "I am against the idea of a biography about me," he averred. "Maksim Gorky had a plan like yours, and he also asked me, but I have backed away from this issue. I don't think the time has come for a Stalin biography." Although some commentators have viewed this response to be a sign of Stalin's hesitancy regarding the cult, it's probably better read as hesitancy regarding Yaroslavsky himself.[36] After all, the personality cult had been going through a period of rapid expansion during the early 1930s, and this only increased after the assassination of Kirov in December 1934. Yaroslavsky's problem was that he had yet to fully overcome the reputation for political unreliability that he had acquired in 1931.

Political reliability, of course, was a major concern throughout the society in the wake of the Kirov murder. As noted in Chapter Two, when local officials responded in early 1935 to the Central Committee's call to root out the supposed Zinovievite conspiracy, they instead found their fiefdoms rife with more mundane problems related to political indoctrination and mass mobilization.[37] Particularly embarrassing was the discovery of an entire subculture of dissembling and political joke telling, a good portion of which assaulted party leaders in highly biographical terms. In 1935, for instance, Kirov and his untimely demise stood at the center of this unofficial culture of political humor. Mean-spirited gossips such as a bookkeeper on the Moscow-Donbass railroad named Savitsky referred to the fallen party boss as a lecherous Casanova who had finally been done in by a jealous husband. Reports sent to central authorities during that spring list scores of Soviet citizens— including party members—who had been caught trafficking in such disrespectful talk.[38] Others got away with it, like the vandal in a Moscow suburb who scrawled "he got what he deserved" under a portrait of the martyred boss in early 1935.[39]

Such talk alarmed party and secret police officials because of its propensity to precipitate even more explosive discussions within society at large. Attacking Kirov was bad enough, but officials feared that those willing to defame the martyred boss might attack the general secretary as well. And NKVD reports demonstrate this fear to have been well founded. Some, for instance, accepted the official story that Kirov had been the victim of a Zinovievite assassination plot, but added snidely that "it's too bad that they got only one."[40] Others did not bother to be so oblique about the object of their discontent, stating bluntly that in order for things to improve, Stalin would have to die. Folk couplets, or *chastushki,* were even composed to this effect.[41] One of those denounced for making such statements, a party member and railway employee named Mankov, was surprisingly forthright in his speculation: "Killing Kirov is nothing—Soviet power won't perish on account of that. It'd be different if they were to kill Stalin, but that won't be easy, as he's guarded like the tsars used to be."[42]

As is evident from Mankov's provocative comparison, such commentary assailed the party leadership in both personal and symbolic terms. Stalin's position as Lenin's heir also was a matter of frequent contention. Two Komsomol members, for instance, were overheard in February 1935 arguing over whether Stalin was qualified to lead:

KUZNETSOV: We had a genius in Lenin but now we don't have anyone.
SMYSLOV: What about Comrade Stalin?
KUZNETSOV: You think this is a genius that you've found? Anyone can be that sort of genius as long as the newspapers write about him.[43]

Kuznetsov's sarcastic connection of flattering newspaper coverage on Stalin with the party's efforts to style him as Lenin's successor suggests that the ubiquity of the cult at least at times hamstrung its ability to persuade within society at large. Of course, less articulate forms of protest were more common. A student named Potseluenko, for instance, was caught in February 1935 defacing a portrait of Stalin in his party history textbook.[44] Elsewhere, people deciphered the acronym SSSR as "Shoot Stalin, Save Russia," poked the eyes out of portraits of Politburo members, and labeled images of Kaganovich "kike" (*zhid*).[45]

Party officials were so threatened by this proliferation of gossip, dissembling, and political joking that they did not attempt to determine which of these actions were conscious expressions of political dissent and which were more spontaneous outbursts of disrespect. Weak indoctrination efforts were blamed for this heretical behavior, and arrests quickly followed under Article 58/10 of the Soviet criminal code (the statute outlawing "anti-Soviet agitation").[46] Pyrkov, a second-year student in a technical school in Balakovsky, was turned over to the police for telling the "most outrageously counterrevolutionary jokes." Far away in Tadzhikistan, a certain Trofimov's sardonic connection of Kirov's murder with the end of bread rationing—"Kirov was killed and bread became cheaper; if Stalin is killed, things will get even better"— earned him a ten-year prison sentence.[47] Ultimately, the NKVD arrested some 43,686 people on charges of anti-Soviet agitation during 1935 alone, over half of whom were accused of swapping jokes and couplets, vandalizing portraits of party leaders, and speculating about the fate of Kirov, V. V. Kuibyshev, and other Bolshevik bosses.[48]

The party's aggressive response to this sort of behavior ultimately testifies to more than just intolerance within Stalin's entourage. Apparently, the party leadership was concerned about the fragility of Soviet society's foundational myths—particularly the cult of personality. As noted at the head of this chapter, the Stalin cult performed an important political function in the USSR during these years by casting the general secretary as a symbol of unity and the charismatic embodiment of the Soviet experiment. Political humor and joke telling posed a direct threat to this sacralization of Stalin as a central icon of Soviet ideology and explains why such practices were met with charges of "anti-Soviet agitation."[49]

Gossip and dissembling, of course, were treated as evidence of more than just sedition. The existence of such provocative talk in society also demonstrated to party officials in the most graphic of terms the extent to which indoctrinational efforts were failing to inculcate a proper attitude toward authority within the population at large. Such a shortcoming again reiterated the need for a central, biographical narrative to organize and systematize indoctrinational efforts predicated on the cult.

Many, from Tovshukha to Toroshelidze and Yaroslavsky, aspired to supply the missing text, but it was actually the party boss Beria who succeeded in publishing the first major biographical statement on Stalin, thanks to a combination of personal ambition and administrative resources at his disposal.[50] As noted above, Beria followed his 1934 *Bolshevik* article with an address to the Tbilisi party organization in the summer of 1935 in which he proposed a new, highly detailed account of Bolshevik revolutionary activity in the Transcaucasus. A largely biographical narrative, this speech used Transcaucasian party history as a convenient vehicle with which to explore Stalin's past and establish a firm chronology of his professional activities in the underground. Interestingly, the speech's focus on Transcaucasia, as well as its reliance on the Tbilisi IMEL archive and the testimony of hand-picked local party veterans, also allowed Beria and his ghostwriters to skirt later, more controversial episodes in the general secretary's career that were confounding his other potential biographers. Stetsky and the ideological establishment in Moscow endorsed this vision and first serialized Beria's speech in *Pravda* before publishing it in a massive hardcover edition.[51]

But as adept as Beria's book was at describing Stalin's days in the Transcaucasian underground, its detailed focus on obscure, prerevolutionary events, and little-known non-Slavic surnames made it a challenging text for the mass readership. As one propagandist named Roitberg would complain later at a conference,

> I believe that the biography of our leaders and heroes should occupy a large place in our political training work. What can I say about Comrade Stalin's biography? Our people know Pushkin's biography quite well, but know Stalin's biography poorly, and we are not teaching it in the right way for this to improve. The following fact I can relate to you from school: one day, I came upon the fourth pioneer squad and these 11–12 year-old kids were sitting there and reading [Beria's] biography of Comrade Stalin. I asked: "Who gave you this book?" The teacher had. And there were such words as *dashniak*s and RSDLP and they didn't know what a *dashniak* was [. . .]. I had a story about Stalin that had been printed in *Pravda* [. . .] and I took it to them. "Give me that book because I really need it and read this for the time being." The kids read it and got interested.[52]

Inaccessible and over-encumbered with detail, Beria's book was at best only a partial solution to the Central Committee's call for new materials, doing little to galvanize the restive party ranks or reinforce the cult of personality.[53] Worse, the rumor mongering and joke telling uncovered during the Kirov investigation heightened the need for a more comprehensive, popularized biography at a time when other projects were faltering. Tovstukha succumbed to illness and died without completing so much as a working draft of his project. Toroshelidze's grumbling about Beria's book (or rumors to that effect) precipitated his arrest.[54] Yaroslavsky lacked the support of the party hierarchy. And none of Stalin's other sometime-biographers—M. V. Volfson, Volin, etc.—stepped forward to fill the void. For all its resources, the cult of personality had failed to secure for the general secretary a court biographer, whether from the ranks of the party nomenclatura or the creative intelligentsia.

As this comedy of errors dragged on into 1936, a full biography did finally appear, emanating from the French left, of all places. Frustration with Stalin's potential biographers at home had led Agitprop into talks in the mid-1930s with a series of distinguished Western authors such as Feuchtwanger, André Gide, and Henri Barbusse.[55] Barbusse readily agreed to the proposal, as the French communist was already at work on an IMEL-sponsored book about Stalin for western audiences (and an accompanying film) that would complement his pro-Soviet books on Georgia and the USSR. Contractual arrangements were made, therefore, to publish the book not only in the western capitals, but in Moscow as well.[56]

During the summer of 1934, Barbusse submitted a flattering literary treatment of Stalin's political career to Stetsky for vetting as he turned to his screenplay. His manuscript quickly presented Stetsky with a major headache, however. True, the French communist was a loyal friend of the USSR and, as a foreigner, was generally allowed to stray a bit from the party line in the press.[57] But his manuscript was full of factual and conceptual errors. Barbusse had linked Stalin's greatness to his personality rather than his mastery of the broader Marxist-Leninist laws of history and development. Similarly, the general secretary's struggle with the opposition was described as a clash of personalities rather than ideologies. Worse, while the manuscript went to great lengths to characterize Stalin as a brilliant tactician with a flair for political infighting, it neglected to balance this description with a discussion of him as a philosophical visionary.[58] On the whole, Stetsky had to doubt whether Barbusse was really much of a Marxist at all.

But as problematic as the text was, it was also highly readable and offered a dynamic portrait of Stalin as well as a scathing indictment of
Trotsky, Zinoviev and Kamenev. Moreover, it was the only biographical project of its scope underway. Stetsky therefore appears to have offered Barbusse a domestic contract for the book at the same time that
he attempted to impress upon the writer the need for major alterations
to the manuscript. Barbusse, pleased with what he understood to be an
endorsement of his vision, informed *Literaturnaia gazeta* of his plans to
publish the book simultaneously in France, Great Britain, Holland, and
the USSR during the coming year.[59]

Although the biography was indeed published abroad during 1935,
work on its Russian translation slowed due to Barbusse's failure to recast the biography in more materialist terms.[60] Even in revised form,
Barbusse's celebration of Stalin's greatness continued to marginalize
both the role that ideology played in Soviet society and the threat that
enemies still posed to the accomplishments of the revolution. Further revisions proved impossible, however, as Barbusse fell ill and then died
that August. Stetsky, caught between the proverbial rock and a hard
place, ultimately opted to publish the book, but only with a disclaimer
that noted that although the volume had considerable merit, it was unsuitable for use as a party history textbook. It was published in early
1936, first in serial form in *Roman Gazeta* and then, shortly thereafter,
as an attractive hardcover book.[61]

Despite the eventual release of Barbusse's volume, then, the situation
with Stalin's official biography remained eerily similar to that surrounding party history. Circa 1935, Soviet society was at least nominally awash in literature and art related to the personality cult. As with
the party history canon, however, if this material was more or less ubiquitous, it was too disorganized and inconsistent to function effectively
as an ideological tribune. Worse, both party historians and participants
in the personality cult found themselves at an impasse over how to
adapt their fields to the evolving demands of the propaganda state.

But if these projects ground to a halt almost simultaneously, it would
be a mistake to assume that they stalled for the same reasons. One of the
most remarkable aspects of this story is the amount of infighting that
appears to have gone on behind the scenes within the ideological establishment, dividing Stalin's potential hagiographers against one another.

At first glance, this seems rather peculiar in light of the Stalinist intelligentsia's collective participation in rituals associated with the cult—by the mid-1930s, celebration of Stalin's reputation had become a customary way for public figures to pledge allegiance not only to the general secretary, but to the Soviet experiment as a whole.[62] Evidence of this can be found in the panegyrics to Stalin that punctuated public addresses by card-carrying Stalinists like V. P. Stavsky and A. A. Fadeev, as well as by other, more independent figures such as B. L. Pasternak, I. G. Ehrenburg, and V. S. Grossman. But it is important to remember that other impulses also played a role in the involvement of artists like I. I. Brodsky and A. M. Gerasimov in the cult. After all, successful portraits, sketches, literary works, and biographies promised lucrative rewards in the form of official commissions and royalties, as well as less tangible perks associated with political patronage and protection.[63] High stakes, then, fueled the expansion of the personality cult during the early-to-mid-1930s and help explain some of the bitterness and rancor that characterized the competition between Stalin's prospective biographers.

Of course, other factors contributed to the failure to produce a usable biography as well. As noted previously, party historians agonized over the emplotment of Bolshevik history, straining to frame pragmatic, ad hoc decision-making within a systematic Marxist-Leninist narrative governed by the historical dialectic. Stalin's official biographers faced a different set of challenges associated with reconciling the emergent personality cult with the genre of modern biography. According to Stalin's letter to *Proletarskaia revoliutsia* and his interview with Ludwig, party leaders were to be valorized for both their heroic deeds and their prescient grasp of the historical dialectic. But how could the official record of an iconic symbol like Stalin accommodate the rites of passage, angst, and self-doubt that distinguish the modern biographical genre from other, more impersonal sorts of narration? How could Stalin both personify the monolithic nature of the party and experience personal trials and tribulations along the way? Tovstukha demonstrated an acute awareness of this narrative tension when he predicted that Yaroslavsky's biography would turn out to be just another party history textbook rather than a truly compelling account of Stalin's life and times. Ultimately, these genre problems, combined with the inelegancies of Stalin's own career, conspired to hamstring the personality cult during the mid-1930s.

4 The Cult of Heroes and Heroism

WHAT IS REMARKABLE about the array of false starts and misfires surrounding the development of party history textbooks and the personality cult during the early-to-mid-1930s is the degree to which these projects failed to take advantage of new developments in Soviet art and letters during these years. First, the various Yaroslavskys, Knorins, Volins, and Ingulovs were slow to shift from the abstract schematicism of the 1920s to the concrete, animated narrative structure of the early 1930s. Second, aside from their enthusiasm for Stalin's cult of personality, they were reluctant to embrace the new emphasis on individual heroism that appeared at about the same time.

At first glance, this hesitation is especially puzzling, as the celebration of historic individuals and famous reputations has traditionally played a key role in modern mobilizational propaganda.[1] Not only do famous personalities tend to be broadly accessible, but they provide mass audiences with role models to identify with and emulate. In the USSR, however, this sort of rallying call was largely rejected during the 1920s by the ideological establishment as a "bourgeois" convention incompatible with the tenets of historical materialism. Instead, official emphasis was placed on class-based imagery with such a fervor that it came to govern the idiom within which Soviet propagandists worked, despite the fact that these themes never enjoyed much societal resonance. Perhaps for this reason, even after the party hierarchy called for a new stress on heroic words and deeds during the early-to-mid-1930s, members of the ideological establishment hesitated over the role that historic individuals were to be afforded within the official line.

In spite of this institutional paralysis, the celebration of heroes and heroism came to dominate the wider vistas of Soviet mass culture during the early-to-mid-1930s. Names like N. A. Izotov, A. G. Stakhanov, V. K. Bliukher, and M. I. Tukhachevsky became ubiquitous, personifying the elusive nature of the party line and Soviet identity that Stalin and his entourage had been trying to define since the late 1920s. This chapter traces this movement of heroes to center stage in the propaganda state, attributing the about-face in the official line to an unexpectedly diverse group of cultural agents outside of the traditional ideological establishment.

Despite the emergence of the Lenin cult and the creation of a number of iconic protagonists in Soviet fiction during the 1920s, debate raged within the new creative and literary intelligentsia over how heroes were to be treated in a socialist society. For radicals, class analysis and dialectical materialism called into question not only the centrality of the canonical classics, but the literary norms and conventions governing basic issues of emplotment, characterization, and the role of the protagonist in narrative prose. Many felt that it was time for the complex, internally conflicted characters of nineteenth- and early twentieth-century fiction to give way to more didactic, publicly minded protagonists. Some, like A. S. Serafimovich, even attempted to write novels within which the working class was cast as a single collective hero and individual characters were reduced to two-dimensional sociological archetypes.[2] Such literature coexisted in an uneasy truce alongside works produced by more moderate communists, fellow travelers, and the remains of the prerevolutionary publishing industry, which continued to print nineteenth-century classics and foreign literature in translation well into the 1920s.[3]

Toward the end of the decade, many literary radicals gradually found ways to reconcile with their more mainstream colleagues and the canon itself, heeding calls to "study the classics" even as they attempted to create a new literary tradition. Class consciousness remained the order of the day, of course, but now controversy concerned how best to deploy individual protagonists in socialist literature. Should these publicly minded characters give voice to internal doubts and confusion in their revolutionary struggle, or should they personify the party line's unwavering confidence, consistency, and vision? RAPP, the biggest and most powerful of the period's literary organizations, played a major role in this debate. Intriguingly, although RAPP is best remembered for its fierce criticism of non-communist writers and its tendency to evaluate authorial talent on the basis of social origin, it was also known between 1927 and 1932 for its championing of a surprisingly conventional mode of literary realism, populated by ideologically doctrinaire but otherwise complex protagonists. According to Katerina Clark's memorable formulation, Soviet literature shifted during these years first to "little heroes" and then to increasingly bigger ones.[4]

But how are these changes in literature and the arts relevant to a better understanding of Soviet ideological efforts? It turns out that at about the same time that the ideological establishment was beginning to search for new, more populist mobilizational techniques in the aftermath of the 1927 war scare, a motley group of writers, journalists, artists, and publishers were attempting to steer the propaganda state away from its abstract focus on materialism and class.[5] Pointing to the marginal results of recent mobilizational drives, they talked—hesitantly at first—about the need to popularize the official line by directing greater attention toward the human experience of socialist construction. Even the most orthodox reading of Marxism-Leninism, they argued, could accommodate discussion of emblematic individuals who embodied the ideological values and priorities held by society as a whole. These heroes, in turn, could convey a sense of Soviet identity and class consciousness to the reading public at large, personifying the revolution and socialist construction with badly needed role models.

Perhaps the most famous of these partisans was Gorky, who even before his permanent return to the USSR from abroad in 1932 expressed concern over the ideological establishment's failure to promote a popular sense of Soviet identity.[6] Mulling over an appropriate vehicle for his propaganda initiative, Gorky won official permission to launch the monthly *Our Achievements* in 1928. He followed this up between 1929 and 1931 by reviving *The Lives of Remarkable People,* a popular prerevolutionary biography series, and by launching two new documentary book series, *The History of Plants and Factories* and *The History of the Civil War in the USSR,* as well as another monthly, *USSR in Construction.*[7]

Gorky's initiatives proved to be compatible with similar sentiments among a number of leading journalists and much of the mainstream RAPP movement, all of whom were responding in one way or another to the party's 1928 directive to mobilize print culture in the name of socialist construction.[8] *Komsomolskaia pravda* was perhaps the most innovative of the major newspapers, but other dailies followed in time, showing unprecedented interest in individual workers involved in the realization of the first Five-Year Plan.[9] Journalists' focus on socialist accomplishments and the valor of ordinary workers won acclaim at the Sixteenth Party Congress in 1930, resulting in calls for still more attention to be devoted to the productive dimensions of shop floor culture.[10] *Pravda* scolded the press in May 1931 for its incomplete implementation of these demands, noting that little had been done to identify and publicize these new paragons of proletarian virtue. According to a lead editorial, propaganda surrounding socialist construction still required thoroughgoing reform:

> the release of the journal *Our Achievements* under M. Gorky's editorship is only a first step toward depicting the heroism of everyday life on the new sites of socialist construction, where the problems of Bolshevik tempos are being worked out and where the task of "catching up and overtaking" [the capitalist powers] in a maximum of 10 years is being decided.
>
> [. . .] We are not bad at excoriating the remnants of bureaucratism, indolence, and Oblomovism, but we've not yet succeeded in depicting the degree of heroism with which the proletariat is building the socialist economy. Similarly, our press hasn't raised the question of how to reward our heroes of labor properly. The press has not taken advantage of concrete state and party resolutions recognizing the best inventors, shock workers, technicians, etc. in order to lead the millions to new, even greater victories. This is because the press has yet to depict as it should the heroes in the forefront of the struggle for the plan.[11]

Responding to its own call to arms, *Pravda* then moved to rectify this shortcoming by establishing a stable feature entitled "The Country Must Know Its Heroes," which would henceforth splash biographies and photos of prominent Soviets across a two-page spread with some regularity.[12] Perhaps the most famous of these early heroes was Izotov, a champion coal miner and shock worker in the Donbass, who was introduced to the paper's readership in May 1932 by a journalist looking for a role model with whom to make headlines.[13] Political poster art too shifted from a reliance on idealized representations of workers, peasants, and soldiers to photographs of actual, identifiable personalities.[14] Even pioneering organizations like RAPP redoubled their support for this new focus on heroes and heroism.[15] And although RAPP was shuttered along with other independent literary groups in 1932 to make way for a single Writers' Union, much of the organization's basic agenda was canonized within Socialist Realism, the new union's officially recognized method of artistic expression.[16]

But if Gorky was connected to much of the early literary activity surrounding this new interest in socialist heroes and protagonists, he at least initially felt that his *History of the Plants and Factories* series was key to the popularization of an "authentically" Soviet usable past.[17] Only fragments of the series' main editorial archive survive, but what remains suggests that from the start, Gorky connected the project to the cause of Soviet identity formation.[18] As N. G. Shushkanov, the series' managing editor, noted, *The History of Plants and Factories* was to be "a tool for mobilizing the workers to create socialism."[19] Official endorsement of the project's goals in the fall of 1931 is visible in both official decrees and the list of party luminaries appointed to supervise the project: Kaganovich, Postyshev, Bukharin, Yenukidze, Stetsky, Andreev, L. Z. Mekhlis, and A. V. Kosarev.[20]

Part of this endorsement was a matter of timing, of course, as Stalin had just issued his broadside against party historians in *Proletarskaia revoliutsia* and effective mobilizational literature was in short supply.[21] Conveniently, Gorky had little respect for professional historians.[22] But more fundamentally, he agreed with people like RAPP leader L. L. Averbakh that the working class ought to be writing its own history. According to both Gorky and Averbakh, working-class historians now ought to begin supplying Soviet society with their own inspirational tales of yore, much like the RAPP-inspired workers who were attempting to reinvent literature, music, and the arts during these years.[23]

In some ways, of course, Gorky's doubts concerning professional party historians were justified. They struggled in vain to produce accessible work during these years, despite being rebuked in *Proletarskaia revoliutsia* for their reluctance to write for a mass audience. Gorky's working-class chroniclers, however, were no more successful than their academic rivals, even under the tutelage of professional writers and journalists.[24] Although the various *History of Plants and Factories* projects collected enormous amounts of material from the grassroots level —sketches, diaries, interviews, reminiscences, etc.—these sources tended to overwhelm their amateur historians and frustrate all attempts to make sense of the bigger picture. Worse, the worker-generated accounts suffered from an excessive focus on the technological dimensions of factory life—a shortcoming that this writing shared with the turgid journalism and "production novels" of the First Five-Year Plan.[25] Page after page of these accounts indulged in the seemingly endless description of shift work, production schedules, productivity targets, and socialist competition in an apparent attempt to hybridize narrative storytelling with orthodox materialism. Gorky and Shushkanov's repeated entreaties to their authors to break with such tendencies reveal that the celebration of iconic individual workers and role models was more important to *The History of Plants and Factories* project than the detailed description of socialist construction itself.[26] Ultimately, these shortcomings led the series to be virtually co-opted by professional ghostwriters and journalists, even as its patrons continued to describe the project as "a new form of heroic epic."[27] A paraliterary genre somewhere between fiction and journalism, it had a celebratory focus on individual heroism during socialist construction (as well as the revolution and civil war) that anticipated by several years Zhdanov's famous definition of Socialist Realism at the first Congress of the Soviet Writers' Union—"a combination of the most sober, matter-of-fact realities and the most heroic and grandiose prospects."[28]

All this initial work on animating official propaganda between the late 1920s and the early 1930s took on a decisive role in Soviet mass culture in the spring of 1934. The catalyst for this discursive ascendency was the developing drama surrounding the stricken arctic research vessel Cheliuskin, which had become trapped in the ice of the Chukchi Sea in October 1933. Captain V. I. Voronin and expedition leader O. Yu. Shmidt coordinated the crew's efforts to ride out the winter, but by early 1934, it became clear that the Cheliuskin was unlikely to survive the crushing pressure of the surrounding ice. This grim prognosis came true on February 13, when hull ruptures forced the ship to be hurriedly evacuated before it sank. Shortly thereafter, seven air force pilots—A. V. Liapidevsky, M. V. Vodopianov, I. V. Doronin, N. P. Kamanin, M. T.

Ванкарем. Уэллен.

Ляпидевскому, Леваневскому, Молокову, Каманину, Слепневу, Водопьянову, Доронину.

Восхищены Вашей героической работой по спасению челюскинцев. Гордимся Вашей победой над силами стихии. Рады, что Вы оправдали лучшие надежды страны и оказались достойными сынами нашей великой родины.

Входим с ходатайством в Центральный Исполнительный Комитет СССР:

1) об установлении высшей степени отличия, связанного с проявлением геройского подвига, — звания «Героя Советского Союза»,

2) о присвоении летчикам: Ляпидевскому, Леваневскому, Молокову, Каманину, Слепневу, Водопьянову, Доронину, непосредственно участвовавшим в спасении челюскинцев, звания «Героев Советского Союза»,

3) о награждении орденом Ленина поименованных летчиков и обслуживающих их бортмехаников и о выдаче им единовременной денежной награды в размере годового жалования.

И. СТАЛИН. В. МОЛОТОВ. К. ВОРОШИЛОВ.
В. КУЙБЫШЕВ. А. ЖДАНОВ.

Fig. 3: "Heroes of the Soviet Union." Top: textbook illustration of Shmidt and the Cheliuskin's rescuers (from upper left: Shmidt, Liapidevsky, Molokov, Kamanin, Vodopianov, Doronin, Slepnev, Levanevsky). Bottom: Stalin's congratulatory telegram to the rescuers, hailing them as "worthy sons of our great motherland." From B. Volin, *Politgramota* (Moscow: Partizdat, 1934), 221; *Pravda,* April 14, 1934, 1.

Slepnev, S. A. Levanevsky, and V. S. Molokov—were dispatched to search for and then rescue the Cheliuskin's 104 surviving crew members, now stranded on an ice floe. Upon their completion of this harrowing feat two months later, the pilots were honored with a new class of award, the Order of the Hero of the Soviet Union. In early June, they were reunited with the crew of the Cheliuskin in Moscow for a ticker-tape parade and reception attended by Stalin and ranking party and state officials.[29]

Although the Cheliuskin saga received a huge amount of media coverage throughout the rescue operation, the announcement of the awards produced an unprecedented wave of discussion in the press over what constituted Soviet heroism. A prominent editorial in *Pravda* connected the Cheliuskinites' valor to the new celebration of labor heroism and contrasted the new Soviet Olympus against the heroes of the capitalist West:

> The bourgeois world is searching in vain for heroes but isn't finding them. The ruling capitalist class needs heroes, as its leaders are frightened by their own flabbiness and insignificance. Shameful theories are being advanced about the imperative of war as a means of teaching bourgeois youth to be brave and reviving the ancient spirit of chivalry. Lacking contemporary role models, the bourgeoisie instead is summoning the shadows of the past, falsifying and updating even the most decrepit of legends. In a number of capitalist countries, daring bandits and smugglers are held to embody the bourgeoisie's romantic ideal. The children of the rich dream of becoming people as fearless as Al Capone and [John] Dillinger, or as resourceful as the detective Sherlock Holmes. The Plutarchs of the contemporary bourgeoisie look to find their role models for the next generation in the police station or thieves' den.
>
> In the Soviet world there is no need for such heroic mythmaking. Our heroism is reality. Our children's groups play "Cheliuskin" while our adolescents dream of feats of labor and science. Our role models—the heroes of the proletariat's struggle and the heroes of socialist construction—are full of revolutionary passion, and they are now joined by a brilliant new gallery of heroes from the Cheliuskin. They learned to triumph on the ice at the same time that we have been learning how to triumph over setbacks in the struggle for socialism.[30]

Coming at a critical time, this editorial is very revealing. Despite its emphasis on reality, the editorial's conflation of fictional and nonfictional heroes from the capitalist world hints at Soviet officialdom's enthusiasm

Fig. 4: Advertisement for *Cheliuskin: Heroes of the Arctic,* dir. Ya. M. Poselsky (Soiuzkino-khronika, 1934). From *Vecherniaia Moskva,* July 5, 1934, 4.

for the period's hybridizing of literature, journalism, and propaganda. Assuming an unabashedly mobilizational posture, *Pravda* declared that contemporary heroes and those from the recent past were to fulfill two basic roles. Not only were they collectively to embody the goals and priorities of the revolution and socialist construction in accessible, populist terms, but they were to provide Soviets from all walks of life with concrete, individualized examples of how to be model citizens. These directives promptly received official endorsement at the Writers' Union conference that August, where delegates repeatedly referred to the Cheliuskinites as templates for the heroes of the future.[31] Shmidt was even summoned to address the forum and share his insights on what distinguished his comrades from ordinary men and women.[32] Songs and a major newsreel documentary were released at about the same time, keeping the Cheliuskinites in the limelight for much of that fall.[33]

To be sure, early books in *The History of the Plants and Factories* series reveal that such priorities defined Gorky's project even before the Cheliuskin rescue. For example, *The People of the Stalingrad Tractor Factory,* a 1933 prosepography on the massive industrial site, was almost entirely concerned with the heroism of ordinary people in extraordinary circumstances. Sneering contemptuously that "there is no place in bourgeois literature for these things," Ya. Ilin, the volume's editor and a former executive at *Komsomolskaia pravda,* announced that the "new masters" of the USSR were a major new priority for Soviet letters.[34] And while Ilin and his contributors stressed the importance of avoiding sensationalism in their accounts, many of the biographies in *The People of the Stalingrad Tractor Factory* ended up revolving around individuals whose stories were exceptional, if not utterly implausible.[35] Accounts about skilled workers alternated with Red Army veterans, women, ethnic minorities, reformed criminals, and youthful idealists. In one way or another, however, all bore some resemblance to that of G. Remizov, an earthy diamond-in-the-rough who described his journey of self-realization in highly personal but didactic terms. Born into the anonymous ranks of the illiterate peasantry, Remizov journeyed to Stalingrad in 1931 to take a job at the new factory. There, he quickly developed a keen interest in self-improvement, education, and upward mobility, remembering:

> I loved to study. I would regularly buy more and more books with each paycheck I received. I bought a two-volume set of Lenin, paying two-twenty. Then I bought Bubnov, which I used to get through party history —I paid a ruble sixty-five for it and another two rubles to have it hardbound. Most people here get their party history from Popov's big book. Then I bought a book on Russian grammar and some math books; I studied fractions and then bought some belletristic works, sometimes for twenty kopeks, sometimes for thirty.

On-the-job training, in other words, apparently led to political consciousness and cultural refinement. According to *The People of the Stalingrad Tractor Factory,* Remizov's taste in reading informed other aspects of his personal life as well, underscoring the role that ideological literacy played in everyday life. Narrating his move from the factory barracks to a private room, Remizov noted that among his first purchases, he acquired "portraits of Lenin, Stalin, and M. M. Litvinov, a poster of the Battleship Potemkin, and another depicting the 1918 execution of the Baku commissars" in order to decorate the walls of his new accommodations.[36] Such naïve idealism, expressed in a chatty, folksy idiom, permeated *The People of the Stalingrad Tractor Factory.* Averbakh had sought precisely this style of narration from his writers and linked its effectiveness to its personal focus in his conclusion to the book. "It seems at first that this book is about individual people. But it actually turns out to be a celebration of the victorious advance of the collective wisdom of millions." Taken as a whole, the book provided a rich illustration of how "backward peasant lads are transformed into shock workers, inventors, and specialists in labor rationalization—all of them supporters of socialist construction."[37] Consciously emplotted as a pageantry of heroes, *The People of the Stalingrad Tractor Factory* was lauded in the press for its engaging, vivid style.[38]

Similar objectives defined other early volumes in *The History of Plants and Factories* series like *Stories of the Moscow Metro-Builders* and a book on the G. G. Yagoda Children's Labor Colony, as well as related volumes such as *Motherland of Factories.*[39] Several other works —on the Moscow–St. Petersburg highway, Moscow's Trekhgorny Plant, and the Zlatoust and Verkhisetsky Plants in the Urals—also embraced these principles, although their exclusive focus on the prerevolutionary period probably limited their propaganda value somewhat.[40] Perhaps the most infamous of the Gorky volumes was *The Stalin Belomor–White Sea Canal,* a work that focused on the Soviet-era rehabilitation of political prisoners under the ostensibly paternalistic supervision of the NKVD. Written by a team of professional authors including Vs. V. Ivanov and M. M. Zoshchenko, the book exemplified the degree to which this series was prepared to invent Soviet heroism from whole cloth when needed.[41]

Building on the case studies supplied by *The History of Plants and Factories* series, Gorky proposed in early 1934 to shift some of the series' resources to an even more personality-driven project entitled *The People of the Second Five-Year Plan.*[42] But his last great love was really another series entirely—his famous *History of the Civil War in the USSR.* As with *The History of Plants and Factories,* Gorky's interest in this project dated back to the late 1920s, when he first brought the idea to Stalin's attention:

> For two years, I've been talking [to people] about the need to publish a history of the civil war for the peasantry.
>
> The peasants don't understand this history because they can't appreciate it as a whole. It's important that they know why the working class began the war, that they know that the working class saved the country from foreign capital and slavery, that they know—in figures and tables—what sort of losses the various Denikins, Kolchaks, Wrangels and Yudenichs inflicted in terms of blood, lives, and economic destruction, and that they know what role [N. V.] Chaikovsky's beloved SRs and other "minor gods" played under them.
>
> Such a book must be very accessible. It seems to me that we should have the military's high command and political directorate appoint a commission to gather all the needed material and arrange it in chronological order. Popular writers [belletristy] should then turn this raw material into something literary. I would eagerly suggest Aleksei Tolstoy—he'd be very useful for this sort of work—and [M. A.] Sholokhov, the author of Quiet Flows the Don, and Yu. [N.] Libedinsky. Of course, their work will need to be looked over. The book should be published in a massive print run so that there will be a copy in every village and so that it'll be read as if it were a novel.[43]

Although Gorky soon broadened his project's intended audience beyond the peasantry as he expanded his plans from a single book to an entire series, he retained the idea of relying on professional authors to transform "raw material" from the civil war into a usable past. Ideally, he wrote to Stalin, each volume would consist of "reminiscences and memoirs of the participants, which have been organized and verified by military historians and Marxist historians, and then polished by creative literary talents in order to maximize their clarity and accessibility." Sholokhov was recruited to this task, as were Ivanov and N. I. Kochkurov (who wrote under the nom de plume A. Vesely); after the series won Central Committee endorsement in July 1931, some fifty professional writers joined the endeavor in one capacity or another. Gorky even put together an artistic editorial board staffed by writers—F. V. Panferov, Ivanov, D. Bedny, L. M. Leonov, K. A. Fedin, M. Ye. Koltsov, R. P. Eideman, and I. K. Mikitenko—to ensure literary control over the legion of historians recruited to work on the project. Although the series was to be monitored by a main editorial board comprised of party functionaries, the artists were granted day-to-day control.[44]

In spite of the talent available to him, Gorky took special pains to style his project as more than just a literary treatment of the civil war. It was also to be more than a military history—Gorky wrote to the chair of the Leningrad party committee in 1931 that although the *History of the Civil War in the USSR* would not neglect war-related concerns, its narrative was most concerned with "the party's role in organizing the masses." Moreover, it would complement Gorky's other mass mobilizational work as well:

> *The History of the Civil War* must depict the working class in its struggle with the class enemy. *The History of Plants and Factories* will depict the working class first—before October—as the unskilled labor that created bourgeois culture and then depict it in the same way as the energy that is now creating socialist culture. These books, I hope, will serve as a good means of developing the masses' class and revolutionary identity, while at the same time helping lead the world proletariat.[45]

Put another way, despite their disparate themes, the two series were expected to closely complement one another.

Ironically, party patronage and the participation of the creative intelligentsia did not exempt *The History of the Civil War in the USSR* from many of the dilemmas that party historians were confronting during the early 1930s. The series was also forced to contend with stylistic controversies that plagued *The History of Plants and Factories*—balance, tone, and rhetoric were often as difficult to resolve as questions of historical fact, agency, and interpretation.[46] This is clear from a harsh letter that Gorky wrote in mid-1933 to the civil war series' managing editor, I. I. Mints, in order to complain about the quality of drafts chapters from the project's first volume. Excessively journalistic and wordy, they apparently alternated between shrill sloganeering and discussions that could only be described as "limp" and "boring."[47] According to Mints, Gorky repeated over and over again during these years that the professional writers on staff were to serve as literary commissars rather than mere consultants, actively policing the historians' work.[48]

Perhaps as a result of such reminders, Mints's brigade turned in a surprisingly colorful draft of the series' first volume in late 1934.[49] Gorky declared the work acceptable from a literary point of view and passed it on to the party hierarchy for political vetting.[50] Stalin was not so easily satisfied, however, and subjected the manuscript to a meticulous reading between late 1934 and mid-1935. Later that August, he sat down with the main editorial board at Gorky's dacha to explain his corrections in a running monologue that lasted over three hours. Hailing the book's overall focus and emplotment, he criticized a number of sections that focused on minutia at the expense of the big picture. In particular, he wanted the text to more clearly distinguish the Bolsheviks from their socialist rivals in mid-1917 and cast more attention on the threat of factional activity within the party.[51] Stalin was also critical of what he felt was the draft's excessively florid, metaphorical language. Mints's brigade had apparently overshot the mark in stylistic terms, producing a manuscript that was so "literary" that it appeared flamboyant and whimsical in places; much of Stalin's commentary attempted to distinguish good paraliterary historical writing from rhetorical excess.[52] Mints described the essence of the general secretary's objections years later:

> Stalin was pedantically interested in formal exactitude. He replaced "Piter" in one place with "Petrograd," "February in the Countryside" as a chapter title (he thought that suggested a landscape) with "The February Bourgeois-Democratic Revolution," [and] "Land" as a chapter title (a "modernism," he called it) with "The Mounting Agrarian Movement." Grandiloquence was mandatory too. "October Revolution" had to be replaced by "The Great Proletarian Revolution." There were dozens of such corrections.[53]

Although pedantic, such corrections did not indicate that Stalin wanted the text rewritten in a strictly academic manner. Despite his objections, the general secretary remained committed to having the revolution portrayed in dramatic terms, complete with a cast of clearly defined heroes and villains. After these revisions were complete, Mints quoted Stalin as saying that "the book has turned out well—it's written simply and has a lot of interesting material." Perhaps even more telling was Stalin's congratulations to the editorial brigade itself: "You've done your work well—the book reads like a novel."[54]

Published in late 1935, *The History of the Civil War in the USSR* rolled off the presses as a beautiful, large-format edition boasting a dramatic storyline embedded with mention of dozens of revolutionary heroes and illustrated with numerous reproductions, engravings, inserts, and maps.[55] The volume, according to Elaine MacKinnon, was explicitly "popular in form, with colorful illustrations, photographs, and a prose style that is more characteristic of fictional narratives than scien-

tific treatises." Elaborating on its populist, literary character, MacKinnon adds that the book's contents alternated between "clear images of
good and evil, positive and negative. The narratives read like fiction,
with many short sentences and continual effort to build a sense of tension and drama in the unfolding of events. Enemies are clearly defined.
The role of workers, soldiers, and peasants is highlighted, despite in-
numerable references to Stalin and other Bolshevik leaders, thereby
providing at least token recognition of the project's primary goals."[56]
Reviews advertised the volume's accessibility and dynamism as the
dawn of a new era in popular historical propaganda. They also looked
forward to the second volume in the series, insofar as the first one ended
rather abruptly on the eve of the Bolshevik seizure of power in October
1917.[57]

The fanfare surrounding this series—along with that of *The History
of Plants and Factories*—indicates that journalists and critics in the
press were aware of the significance of this watershed in Soviet mobilizational propaganda. Gorky and his brigades had provided Stalin and
the Soviet leadership with a glimpse of a truly usable past, populated by
readily identifiable heroes and villains—something that they had been
searching for since the late 1920s. And although these works were far
from all-encompassing in scope, they provided reliable templates for
other members of the creative intelligentsia to follow as they began to
embrace this new mandate.[58]

Of course, the official stress placed on accessible, didactic literature
during the early 1930s was reflected not only in Gorky's various projects. Soviet mass culture as a whole also focused on party history, the
revolution, civil war, and industrialization in fiction, poetry, art, photography, and film, and this only became more pronounced as time went
by. But as noted at the start of this chapter, although the celebration of
popular heroism was the order of the day, and although authors frequently focused their work on fictional protagonists instead of actual
shock workers and army commanders, they still wrestled with the concept of heroism in the same way that their journalist and historian contemporaries did. For instance, one of the most famous early Socialist
Realist novels, N. A. Ostrovsky's *How the Steel Was Forged* (1932–
1934), is a fragmentary, episodic work revolving around the civil war
exploits of Pavel Korchagin, a fictional character based on Ostrovsky

himself. Korchagin, a natural rebel, instinctively understands right from wrong but only slowly develops a truly Marxist understanding of class conflict under the tutelage of his brother, a Bolshevik sailor, and a female Komsomol activist. Over the course of the novel, Ostrovsky uses Korchagin to demonstrate that the ultimate meaning of life can be found only in revolutionary struggle. Early reviews of the first parts of this novel expressed concern that Korchagin was insufficiently heroic and excessively insecure; in response to this criticism, Ostrovsky and his editors not only altered the depiction of Korchagin in later installments, but revised and rereleased the first editions as well. They also strengthened the contemporary relevance of Ostrovsky's tale by interweaving the narrative into the context of the prerevolutionary and revolutionary years and by including Lenin, Stalin, Kosarev, I. E. Yakir, D. P. Zhloba, and N. P. Chaplin as peripheral characters.[59] By the time of Ostrovsky's death in 1936, *How the Steel Was Forged* had become one of the most canonical works of Socialist Realism.

Other older novels went through a similar process of revision in order to better conform to the new emphasis on didactic heroism. A major prototype of the Socialist Realist novel, F. V. Gladkov's 1925 *Cement*, focuses its *Bildungsroman* narrative on Gleb Chumalov, his estranged wife Dasha, and their efforts to restart a cement factory after the conclusion of the civil war. Gladkov's tale concerns competing visions of economic recovery during NEP—communist idealists' call for a continuation of class war and radical collectivism versus pragmatists' advocacy of a *modus vivendi* with petty bourgeois elements. His protagonists personify these conflicts in private as well as in public: Chumalov is a rough, rash dynamo with progressive dreams for the factory who grows impatient with the party bureaucracy and his independently minded wife. Dasha expresses this emancipation through leadership of the local women's section of the party and sexual liaisons with Red partisans and the party executive Badin. As Soviet literature's tolerance for such contradictions waned in the 1930s, Gladkov rewrote key sections of this narrative to make Chumalov and his wife better role models. Chumalov becomes less vulgar and explosive; Dasha comes to regret her infidelities and refuses Badin's advances. The end result is a more harmonious storyline that focuses less on the protagonists' conflicted interiority and interpersonal relations and more on their struggle in the workplace.[60] Like Korchagin, Chumalov exchanges his rebelliousness for the discipline of a party activist.

Another novel by Gladkov, *Energy,* evolved according to a similar pattern. Begun between 1926 and 1927 and published in 1932, *Energy* casts an entire brigade of workers at the Dniepr Hydroelectric Plant as its collective hero and protagonist. Initially, the schoolgirl Katia Bychkova, party activist Miron Vatagin, director Baleev, and engineer Kriazhich display little character or personality aside from what was necessary to depict their relationship to their work. Over time, however, Gladkov revised the novel in order to strengthen its engagement with its individual protagonists and flesh out their maturation from sincere but shortsighted workers into fully conscious labor heroes and role models.[61]

Panferov's *Bruski* likewise increased the stress that it placed on the heroic over time in its treatment of the postrevolutionary peasantry. Begun in 1927, *Bruski* initially casts its protagonist, Kirill Zdarkin, as a conflicted character who experiences doubt over the party's agricultural program and his own commitment to the cause. Some of this wavering is expressed in dialogue, both with others and with himself; other dimensions are reflected in bouts of sexual impotence. When not afflicted with this metaphorical weakness of character, Zdarkin tends to be manic—something epitomized by his wild behavior with an array of secondary characters and his impulsive decision to draw a gun on local peasants during grain collection in 1930. Much of this was rewritten between 1933 and 1935 to make Zdarkin a more calm, unambiguously positive hero without such tortured interiority.[62]

Libedinsky's *Commissars* also concerns the fate of civil war heroes after the start of NEP. In this 1926 novel, a number of political officers gather together for retraining—an ideal context for a series of character studies through which to investigate the connection between social origin, class, and consciousness. Libedinsky was a leading member of RAPP and a close associate of Averbakh, and his *Commissars* originally revealed a strong interest in the flawed nature of its everyday protagonists. Some of *Commissars'* political officers are frustrated or confused by NEP's concessions to the market; others adapt a bit too easily to the resumption of capitalist economic relations. Quite successful as a novel, *Commissars* nevertheless went through a number of editions in the late 1920s and early 1930s as changes in literary politics required its protagonists to become less complex and more didactic.[63] While minor when compared with the more sweeping revisions to the other "classics," the changes to *Commissars* indicate how attentive state publishers were to the party's changing demands.

Poetry followed prose in its celebration of the heroic. A. A. Surkov was one of the early pioneers of this theme, focusing in the mid-1930s on lyric discussions of valor and self-sacrifice during the civil war. Particularly notable is a poetic tribute to the Red Army officer corps, entitled "Commanders." In this piece, Surkov hails an array of heroes for their service in defense of the republic between 1917 and 1921 and their contribution to security and rearmament in the years since:

> Our units were all there, in the fight,
> The Bolsheviks are men of steel, all right.
> Breaking the grip of this hydra's claw,
> And leaving the world in awe.
> Voroshilov, Budenny, and Bliukher came to the fore,
> With Chapaev, Yakir, Shchors, and Parkhomenko.
> We followed them through fire and ocean swell,
> Through a flood of lead and shrapnel hell.[64]

As in the fiction of Ostrovsky, Gladkov, and others, Surkov used specific heroes to personify the valor of the society as a whole.

Similar objectives are visible in the period's pictorial art, portraiture, and sculpture. A good case in point concerns a major exhibition mounted in 1933 to celebrate the fifteenth anniversary of the founding of the Red Army. The exhibit's mission statement boasted that the art for the exhibition had been explicitly designed to "rally the people to new victories and summon the masses to strengthen the defense of the socialist fatherland," in part through the realistic depiction of actual Red Army soldiers and officers in their everyday service to the state. This new emphasis on realism and accessibility was deliberately contrasted with earlier exhibits of military art and propaganda, including the anniversary shows mounted in 1923 and 1928. Although these shows had been judged to be successes at the time, in retrospect they looked both immature and overly dependent on the avant garde. As the official introduction to the 1933 exhibition put it, one of the "fundamental creative conclusions" drawn from past experience was the need to develop "Soviet thematics" and "depart from illustration toward a deeper, more realistic and representational language." The end result, as the exhibition catalog makes clear, was a massive collection of canvas, sculpture, and poster art devoted to concrete, heroic subject matter. Of 628 pieces on display, most depicted Red Army troops in battle or engaged in training exercises. One hundred dealt with prominent political and military leaders in various contexts and detailed some 60 different famous personalities, ranging from Lenin, Stalin, and Voroshilov to Tukhachevsky, Bliukher, Yakir, Eideman, S. M. Budenny, Ya. B. Gamarnik, A. I. Kork, A. I. Alksnis, I. P. Uborevich, A. A. Khalepsky, and I. P. Belov.[65] A similar focus on famous personalities in the armed forces is evident in El Lisitsky's famous *Workers and Peasants' Red Army,* a large-format photography album published in 1934.[66]

Heroism likewise came to dominate the silver screen during these years. Defense- and party-oriented themes were, of course, no strangers to the Soviet cinema before the mid-1930s, but many of the most famous features—A. P. Dovzhenko's *Arsenal,* D. Vertov's *Three Songs of Lenin,* etc.—were criticized for their avant garde "formalism" and inattention to accessibility.[67] Better received were newsreels that regularly provided coverage of major parades, military exercises, and everyday life within the ranks; indeed, this journalistic medium probably provided nearly as many images for discussion and emulation during the early 1930s as Ostrovsky and Gladkov.[68] But perhaps the most famous mass culture coup linked to the new heroic thematics was the cinematic blockbuster *Chapaev,* shot by the Vasiliev "brothers" in 1934.[69] Hurriedly readied to mark both the seventeenth anniversary of the revolution and the fifteenth anniversary of the Soviet film industry, *Chapaev* was ostensibly based on D. A. Furmanov's 1923 novel of the same name. That said, the Vasilievs' idiosyncratic acknowledgment of this debt in their film's opening credits—"based on the materials of D. A. Furmanov and A. N. Furmanova"—hints at a more complex story. It turns out that Furmanov himself had written a screenplay based on his semi-autobiographical novel in 1924, only to have it rejected by the NEP-era Leningrad Film Studios, perhaps due to its unfashionable focus on a single, iconic individual. Eight years later (and well after Furmanov's death in 1926), his widow attempted to revive the idea with a screenplay of her own, apparently sensing the change in the way mass culture was beginning to treat individual heroes. This time, Lenfilm offered the script to G. N. and S. D. Vasiliev, who recognized its potential and sat down immediately with Furmanova to develop a more simple, cinematic screenplay. Discarding many of the original novel's secondary characters, the Vasilievs also eliminated much of the nuance and complexity of both the story's eponymous hero and its first-person narrator, Klychkov. In the novel, Klychkov is depicted as a politically conscious but insecure military commissar who initially assumes a patronizing attitude toward V. I. Chapaev on account of his illiteracy, political ignorance, and penchant for arbitrariness and brutality. Furmanov, in other words, characterized Chapaev as the embodiment of peasant anarchy and used Klychkov to personify the party's struggle to harness and discipline this elemental rage. The Vasilievs realized that they could not emplot a screenplay in 1934 around such an extreme standoff and recast Klychkov (now renamed Furmanov) as a patient, capable, and self-confident mentor. Chapaev, too, is reworked in order to offset his lack of book learning with a strong sense of raw political intuition that he expresses in colorful, folksy idiom.[70] As the Vasilievs put it shortly thereafter,

> It was necessary to combine Chapaev's legendary, epic nature with a realistic depiction of him [. . .]. It was necessary to create a Soviet hero, not according to the traditional way that it's done in films, but in such a way that the audience would believe in him and believe that such a hero could actually have existed. If you offer up a hero with superhuman characteristics, with all the expected heroic contours, you hear from the audience, "Yes, he's certainly a hero, but I could never be like him." The whole point was to induce the audience into believing in the hero's basic realism and believe his image on the screen, and to fall in love with him, and want to be like him [. . .].[71]

Such statements reveal how seriously Soviet artists took the period's call for dynamic role models and iconic individuals during the early-to-mid-1930s.

Chapaev ended up foregrounding the issue of personality at the expense of class—something that until then was virtually unheard of in Soviet cinema. Such disregard for ideological orthodoxy unnerved the head of the state film directorate, B. Z. Shumiatsky, when he was asked to show a rough cut of *Chapaev* to Stalin a few days before its November 7, 1934 release. This concern turned out to be well founded, as the general secretary initially responded with suspicion and displeasure to *Chapaev*'s opening scenes. Indeed, it was only at the film's twenty-minute mark that he finally began to grasp the appeal of the story's unconventional heroism. According to Shumiatsky, Stalin experienced something of an epiphany during this screening and would request repeated showings nearly a dozen times that November as he shared the film with members of his inner circle. Saluting the film's charismatic

Fig. 5: Newspaper advertisement for *Chapaev*, dir. Vasiliev brothers (Lenfilm, 1934); iconic still featuring Chapaev and his lieutenant, Petka. Advertisement from *Vecherniaia Moskva*, November 15, 1934, 4.

populism and broad accessibility, Stalin declared *Chapaev* to be "good, clever, and tactful" and predicted that it would "mean a lot in educational terms."[72] He repeated this statement in his jubilee message to the film industry in January 1935, announcing with satisfaction that films like *Chapaev* "mobilize us to perform new tasks and remind us both of the achievements and of the difficulties of socialist construction." Unwilling to leave his endorsement of the film at that, Stalin then took Dovzhenko aside and suggested that he ought to shoot a film about "the Ukrainian Chapaev," N. A. Shchors.[73]

It should be noted, of course, that *Chapaev* was not the first mass-audience film on Soviet themes to foreground heroism. Agitprop had been demanding accessible films since the late 1920s and had taken delivery of its first heroic dramas, *Counterplan* and *Maksim's Youth*, in 1932 and 1934, respectively.[74] *Counterplan* begins with what was a fairly predictable factory-floor standoff between Pasha, an idealistic but naive apprentice; Babichenko, a drunken and politically backward old-timer; Skvortsov, an engineer who secretly mourns for the *ancien régime;* and Vasia, a savvy and charismatic leader of the local party cell. Importantly, *Counterplan* endows these characters with a sense of humor and humanity, producing a film that is both ideologically didactic and accessible. This combination, according to authorities like V. B. Shklovsky and G. M. Kozintsev, amounted to a major breakthrough.[75] *Maksim's Youth,* released alongside *Chapaev* two years later, focuses on the early career of a Bolshevik revolutionary, foregrounding a similar pattern of political maturation from spontaneity to consciousness. No less schematic than *Chapaev, Maksim's Youth* was aided by talented acting and a clever screenplay, which gave the young Maksim an exciting, almost scandalously non-Bolshevik start in the revolutionary movement.[76]

Together, these three films signaled the beginning of a new era in Soviet cinema. Two other features—*Peasants* and *Aerograd*—picked up on these aesthetics of popular heroism in 1935 in order to depict rural communities divided along class lines. In each case, ordinary individuals step forward to expose enemies hidden within the local population, revealing heroism and class consciousness to be as important in the early 1930s as they had been between 1917 and 1921.[77] Even more inventive was another film from 1935 about a provincial flight school directed by Yu. Ya. Raizman. *Flyers* begins with a dashing, risk-taking pilot

Fig. 6: Advertisement for *Peasants,* dir. F. M. Ermler (Lenfilm, 1935). From *Vecherniaia Moskva,* March 29, 1935, 4.

Fig. 7: Advertisement for *Flyers,* dir. Yu. Ya. Raizman (Mosfilm, 1935). From *Vecherniaia Moskva,* April 16, 1935, 4.

named Sergei Beliaev being disciplined for his gratuitous antics in the air. One of his former students, Galia Bystrova, learns from his errors and rises to a position of responsibility in the flight school, eventually serving as the test pilot for a new airplane design. Bystrova's combination of youth, talent, bravery, and self-control proved both inspiring and politically laudable, as is visible from *Izvestia*'s review: "There are new people in *Flyers*. And they are cast in such a way that we have the right to demand that all our master artists go to Raizman to study how to depict the modesty, depth, and genuineness of these new people, the people of our country."[78]

This discussion of the heroic in Soviet cinema would not be complete without a few words about one final film: 1935's *Dzhulbars*. This film narrates the story of an aging Central Asian patriarch, Sho-Murad, his granddaughter Peri, their German Shepherd, and the commander of a nearby border guard detachment, Tkachenko. At the start of the tale, Sho-Murad is saved by Tkachenko and gives the rescuer his dog, Dzhulbars, in gratitude. In the meantime, a number of embittered locals including several former notables plot to attack a state caravan. When they follow through with their plan, kidnapping Sho-Murad and Peri in the process, Tkachenko and his men come to the rescue, assisted by Dzhulbars. Predictably, the film casts Central Asian society as divided between tradition and prospects for change; it adds a heavy dose of Orientalism as well by indicating that the only route to Soviet industrial modernity was through outsiders, as symbolized by the coveted caravan and the garrison of Slavic-looking border guards. Although the caravan turns out to be transporting a consignment of textbooks and other ideological literature, the chief source of enlightenment in the film is Tkachenko, who is as brave and compassionate as he is respectful of local culture. In contrast to Chapaev, Tkachenko is politically literate, a party loyalist (as is clear from the portrait of Yagoda hanging in his quarters), and unfazed by his unfamiliar surroundings. Capable of maintaining order without offending native sensibilities, Tkachenko is both a commissar and a gentleman. As a reviewer in *Izvestia* was quick to point out, Tkachenko's character is also informed by the service he and his unit perform in defense of the USSR:

> The audience watches the lives of those who guard our borders—the Soviet border guards—with great interest. Calm and brave, they bear their difficult guard duty at the furthest reaches of the Soviet state. Their dif-

ficult and dangerous work inspires admiration. Looking at them, one becomes very confident that the enemy will not find a single crawl-space, nor a single loophole, through which to enter our territory. This confidence is reinforced even more when we see that all the residents of the local villages rise up as one to defend the Soviet land at the first signal from the border guard command.[79]

In other words, *Dzhulbars* not only offered audiences a host of unambiguously heroic soldiers, but it provided an example of how their honorable conduct could inspire similar values within the population at large.

During the second half of the 1930s, at about the same time that *Dzhulbars* was being readied for release, the campaign surrounding Soviet heroism expanded to encompass a new group of populist heroes. As before with the Cheliuskinites, the catalyst was an eye-catching event on the grassroots level: A. G. Stakhanov, a miner at the Central Irmino Mine in the Donets Basin, had set a major record for coal extraction during a single six-hour shift. Initially an event connected with the local shock worker movement, it quickly caught the attention of the party hierarchy and then of the entire society once it was publicized in the all-union press.[80] Journalists and party bosses sensed that Stakhanov's feat could be used to stimulate productivity on the shop floor and elsewhere in the economy and began popularizing accounts of average workers and peasants who set production records or demonstrated unusual mastery in their fields of expertise. Within months, the Stakhanovite movement eclipsed shock work as a mobilizing principle as ordinary Soviets in industry and agriculture responded to the newspaper coverage with widespread participation in a wave of what was called "record-mania." As Lewis Siegelbaum summarizes,

> On September 19, Aleksandr Busygin was credited with forging a record number of crankshafts at the Molotov Automobile Works in Gor'kii. Given a shift norm of 675, Busygin had managed to turn out 966. Two days later, Nikolai Smetanin lasted 1,400 pairs of shoes at the Skorokhod Shoe Factory in Leningrad. Then, from the Donbass, it was reported that Petr Krivonos, an engine driver on the Slaviansk-Lozovaia line, raised his average speed to more than forty kilometers an hour; from the Nogin Mill in Vychuga, word went out that Mariia and Evdokiia Vinogradova, working in two different shifts, had managed to supervise the operation of 94 and a few days later 100 Northrup automatic weaving machines;

Mariia Demchenko brought in 523 centners of sugar beet per hectare; Ivan Gudov set a record for machine milling; [Vasilii] Musinskii sawed 221 cubic meters of wood, far above his norm of 95; and so forth.[81]

The results of this activity were hailed in mid-November in the Kremlin at an all-union conference of Stakhanovites in industry and transportation, where outstanding representatives of the movement spoke about how they had defied expectations and set new production records. They also used the conference hall podium to call for their new ideas and techniques to be applied throughout the remaining sectors of the economy.[82] In his speech, Stakhanov credited Stalin with the creation of a society that made such accomplishments possible and thanked him for "the happy life of our country" and "the happiness and glory of our magnificent motherland." Stalin agreed that such labor heroism was possible only within a socialist economic system and lauded workers like Stakhanov for the productivity increases that were apparently revolutionizing Soviet society. "Life has become better," he famously announced, "and happier too." This quotation became a slogan for the entire period overnight.[83]

Five additional meetings were subsequently held between December 1935 and March 1936 in order to foreground champion combine and tractor drivers, Machine-Tractor Station executives, and specialists in animal husbandry, linen, and hemp.[84] These meetings dominated the central press, which featured page after page of delegate speeches and pictures of the ongoing proceedings. State publishing also printed lasting tributes to these sessions—both bound stenographic transcripts and celebratory albums—in order to extend their mobilizational and inspirational impact.[85] Bukharin hailed this new cohort of heroes, noting that although the old regime had also had its celebrities, they were usually either criminals, parasites, or idle members of the nobility and clergy—"it didn't matter who they were, as long as they weren't working people." But now, he continued,

our heroes and heroines are people of labor. They're not nuns, nor are they Simon Stylites. They don't wear chains of penance, nor do they spend their whole lives fasting. Instead, they eliminate poverty, destroying its stinking roots and rolling back its lack of culture. They want to enjoy all the joys and pleasures of life. But they aren't heroes of pillows, slippers, and robes—they're heroes of labor, struggle, creativity, genuine feats, strong characters, and mighty passions.[86]

Fig. 8: New Marshals: Voroshilov, Yegorov, Tukhachevsky, Bliukher, and Budenny. From *Pravda,* November 21, 1935, 1.

Bukharin then pointed to the key role that labor played in the reputation of people like Stakhanov, Busygin, and Demchenko, emphasizing the degree to which their accomplishments were the result of nothing more unusual than hard work and political consciousness.

Just after the start of the first Stakhanovite conference, central newspapers broke another major story—the elevation of Voroshilov, Tukhachevsky, Budenny, Bliukher, and A. I. Yegorov to the rank of Red Army Marshal. Yakir, Gamarnik, Uborevich, Belov, B. M. Shaposhnikov, B. M. Orlov, and S. S. Kamenev followed, becoming first-rank commanders in the military hierarchy. M. Ye. Koltsov framed the promotions in *Pravda* in heroic terms, referring to the new marshals as "Suvorovs" and contrasting their accomplishments to the impotence of the imperial Russian general staff during the First World War.[87] Several weeks later, promotions were extended to the secret police establishment, when Yagoda was elevated to the post of General Commissar and Ya. S. Agranov, G. Ye. Prokofiev, V. A. Balitsky, S. F. Redens, L. M. Zakovsky, and T. D. Deribas became first-rank commissars. *Pravda* published pictures and biographies of each of these chekists, stressing their vigilance and service in the name of the revolution. Most interesting, however, was the degree to which the press stressed these heroes' relentless devotion to the society's well-being:

> Who among them has not frequently looked death in the eye? Who among them has not become acquainted with the strength and treachery of the enemy, which will don any mask in the struggle with socialism? But this has strengthened rather than weakened the majestic sense of proletarian humanity that one finds in the heart of every one of these honorable chekists—the commissars as well as the majors, lieutenants, and sergeants that they've trained. The entire world is impressed by the bright examples of this humanity in action, by the examples of reeducation and reforging of new people—in labor colonies, on the Belomor and Moscow-Volga Canals—the thieves and bandits, both major and minor predators, and all the dregs of humanity that the capitalist world spat out and left the proletarian state to inherit.[88]

As disingenuous as this commentary may seem in retrospect, it confirms the inspiring, unifying role that Soviet heroism was supposed to play in the USSR.

Finally, between December 1935 and March 1936, a series of conferences was held in Moscow with representative of a number of non-Russian republics and autonomous regions. Patterned after the Stakhanovite conferences, these meetings brought together leading party executives and workers from Tadzhikistan, Turkmenistan, Armenia, Azerbaidzhan, Buriatia, and Georgia for highly publicized meetings with party and state leaders.[89] Much like the other celebratory conferences, these receptions did not so much focus on well-known republican leaders as demonstrate that there were people on the periphery engaged in work which was every bit as heroic and impressive as that found in more central regions of the USSR. Non-Russian collective farmers, workers, and activists dominated the headlines for weeks on end. It was at this series of meetings that Stalin posed for his famous photos with the Tadzhik schoolgirl Mamlakat Nakhangova, a champion cotton picker, and Gelia Markizova, the daughter of a Buriat party boss.

In the wake of these events, it will come as no surprise that the celebration of heroism rose to such a crescendo in mass culture as to enjoy absolute ubiquity throughout Soviet society. Within this atmosphere, several blockbuster films were released that focused on subjects related to the Cheliuskin expedition and the recent celebration of the NKVD. *The Courageous Seven* narrates the struggle of six young prospectors and a stowaway who venture to the frozen wastes of the arctic in order to search for natural resources. *Inmates,* based on a play by N. F. Pogodin, depicts NKVD labor camp guards' efforts to rehabilitate wreckers, career criminals, and prostitutes. Another major film, *The Party Card,* concerns Anna, a model worker, and the loss of her identity papers (which turn out to have been stolen by her erstwhile husband, the concealed wrecker Pavel). Anna is expelled from the party for her carelessness but remains determined to explain the mishap and eventually uncovers her husband's role in the crime. The final scene depicts Anna holding her husband at gunpoint as she tries to turn him over to the NKVD. A storyline oriented around anti-heroes rather than heroes, it was described in *Pravda* as an instructional tale about the perils of insufficient vigilance. Press coverage described the film as offering the possibility of redemption to people who make mistakes but then correct their errors instead of covering them up.[90]

More conventional were several other films offering differing emplotments of Socialist Realism's spontaneity-into-consciousness paradigm. In *The Baltic Deputy,* an initially resistant elderly scientist (patterned after K. A. Timiriazev) gradually transforms into a staunch ally of the Bolshevik cause. *We Are from Kronshtadt* begins by celebrating the civil war heroism of an Old Bolshevik martyr, Vasily Martynov, but then shifts to focus on the personal and political maturation of the sole survivor of Martynov's lost unit, Artyom Balashov. This theme of personal struggle also included physical handicaps, as is evident from the plotline of *The Motherland Is Calling.* In this film, an injured test pilot named Igor Novikov successfully overcomes the limitations of an old war wound in order to return to the skies after a German surprise attack. Although fundamentally a defense-themed film, *The Motherland*

Is Calling was also a study in heroism and determination; its original title, *The Face of a Hero,* testifies to the stubborn bravery and grim charisma that Novikov embodies throughout.[91]

Less ideological depictions of heroism also emerged at this time—something epitomized by the film *Girlfriends,* which revolves around three childhood friends who enlist as nurses during the defense of Petrograd in 1919. Each of the three distinguishes herself under fire at the front and demonstrates willpower and bravery every bit equal to her male counterparts. A feature perhaps aimed at teenage girls, it depicts one of the nurses pleading with her comrades on her deathbed to "recruit more girls to the cause—there are too few of us in the Komsomol." Stalin seized upon this line as he watched the film during a prerelease screening in the Kremlin, commenting that *Girlfriends* would be "enormous in its mobilizational meaning."[92] Shumiatsky waxed confident over the USSR's diverse cinematic repertoire between 1935 and 1936, revealing in passing that each new film was evaluated according to a set of standards set by *Chapaev*'s success two years earlier.[93]

Of course, the developing cult of popular heroism in industry and the Red Army was not universally embraced throughout Soviet mass culture between 1932 and 1936. As noted above, the ideological establishment hesitated to embrace the new thematics; theater, too, appears to have been slow to develop a new repertoire revolving around such themes. Beginning in the wake of the Cheliuskinites' rescue, prominent directors and playwrights called for the theater to stage similar stories of drama and valor.[94] A year later, however, authorities like A. N. Afinogenov and V. M. Kirshon acknowledged with disappointment that only half of what was playing in theaters was thematically "Soviet," and much of that repertoire consisted only of comedies. Serious political theater, such as it was, focused exclusively on fallen members of the old regime and reformed criminals. More resources were needed in order to break away from the classics and develop compelling storylines oriented around Soviet heroes. Only this would allow the theater to become a veritable "school of socialist conduct, mores, and aesthetics." Although some plays were eventually mounted around these guidelines—*Chapaev, Never Surrender,* etc.—they too were judged to be excessively complex, inaccessible, and insufficiently didactic.[95]

But with the exception of the theater, Stalin-era mass culture between the late 1920s and the mid-1930s was utterly transformed by its new focus on popular heroes, role models, and iconic personalities. In marked contrast to the previous decade's preference for schematic emplotment and a sterile focus on materialism and anonymous social forces, the new line was accessible, appealing, and even populist in its conventional focus on ordinary heroes drawn from the ranks of Soviet society. Stalin provided consistent support for this shift in propaganda, commenting somewhat laconically during these years that the orthodoxy of the 1920s had won the party few converts because "the people do not like Marxist analysis, big phrases, and generalized statements."[96] Something properly credited to writers, journalists, and other members of the creative intelligentsia, this triumph reveals in passing the degree to which party historians and ideologists had ceased to play a key role in the propaganda state during the early-to-mid-1930s.

5 The Pageantry of Soviet Patriotism

THE OFFICIAL CELEBRATION of famous reputations and personalities in Gorky's series, *Chapaev,* and elsewhere in mass culture in the USSR dovetailed with the emergence of another new rallying call during the early-to-mid-1930s: "Soviet patriotism."[1] Promotion of this ethic, especially alongside the simultaneous stress placed on heroes and the multiethnic "Friendship of the Peoples," marks the high point of party populism during the mid-1930s. That said, leading ideologists and party historians initially failed to embrace this imagery and rhetoric, apparently as uncomfortable with the idea of a socialist motherland as they were with the other mobilizational innovations of this period. This chapter examines the hesitancy with which the ideological establishment approached the issue as well as the way in which Soviet patriotism nevertheless ended up transforming the public face of the propaganda state during the mid-1930s.

For seasoned members of the Stalin-era ideological establishment, the use of patriotic appeals was at least initially as counterintuitive as the veneration of "the great men of history." Patriotism—a form of loyalty defined by community rather than class consciousness—has traditionally been condemned by Marxists as having more in common with nationalism than internationalism. Hardly an exception to this rule, early

Soviet ideologists dismissed the sentiment, invoking Marx and Engels' famous statement that "the workers do not have a fatherland." And while Bolshevik propaganda made some use of patriotic-sounding imagery during the revolution and civil war, these appeals are best seen as instrumentalist in nature. Close examination reveals references to the defense of Soviet Russia between 1918 and 1921 to have stemmed from revolutionary rallying calls rather than calls for the protection and advancement of more conventional national traditions or cultural values. Even on a rhetorical level, the Bolsheviks made this distinction, consistently using the term "defensism" (*oboronnichestvo*) in the place of the more colloquial Latin cognate "patriotism."[2]

Years later, after the start of NEP-era pragmatism, the inauguration of Stalin's "Socialism in One Country" thesis, and the launch of non-Russian nativization (*korenizatsiia*) programs, patriotism remained the antithesis of class consciousness, standing for the defense of parochial self-interest, ethnic particularism, and bourgeois chauvinism. As the *New Encyclopedic Dictionary* put it in 1927, "the love of the motherland that is cultivated by bourgeois governments is a wellspring of nationalism. Patriotism is a foreign concept to the proletariat, who rise above narrow, national boundaries [. . .]. Patriotic sentiments stand in opposition to the brotherhood and peaceful cooperation of all peoples." The *Encyclopedia of Government and Law* went even further, dismissing patriotism as a reactionary notion designed "to justify imperialist bestiality and deaden the proletariat's class consciousness."[3] Samuel Harper, a left-leaning American tourist, concluded from such talk that the emerging society was "not handicapped by patriotism." Comparing patriotic beliefs to religiosity, he observed that they were "sentimental idealisms to the materialist Bolsheviks," who had better ways of rallying social support to the Soviet cause.[4]

But just as Harper's travelogue started to appear in U.S. bookshops a few years later, Soviet leaders began to call this militancy into question. During a major speech in February 1931, for instance, Stalin noted that although Marx and Engels had been right that "in the past we didn't have and could not have had a fatherland," it was important to be careful about applying this maxim to the present. After all, "now, since we've overthrown capitalism and power belongs to the working class, we have a fatherland and will defend its independence."[5] Stalin's statement was a major extension of his "Socialism in One Country" thesis, insofar as he now proposed to stress the importance of state sovereignty as much as the viability of an autarchic socialist economy. Months later, it fell to the editors of the *Minor Soviet Encyclopedia* to harmonize Stalin's new definition of Soviet patriotism with the previous decade's strident sense of proletarian internationalism. Reiterating the view that patriotism had long served as "a flag behind which to conceal the expansionist and reactionary tendencies" of the bourgeoisie, the encyclopedia conceded for the first time that revolutionary movements had the capacity to engender a patriotic emotion of their own. "During the transitional period [and] the period of proletarian construction" that follow a successful revolution, "the working class may establish a state of its own, which becomes a socialist fatherland (and ceases to be a fatherland of the exploitative classes). The Paris Commune was the first to declare itself the fatherland of the toilers. Now, the USSR is the fatherland of the international proletariat and toilers of the world." Internationalist rather than nationalist, Soviet patriotism promised support for worldwide revolutionary movements at the same time that it advanced claims to more conventional statehood. Indeed, all revolutionary movements abroad were now to look to Moscow with the same sense of loyalty that the Russian, Uzbek, and Tatar proletariat did, inasmuch as one day, under Soviet guidance, "all borders between countries will disappear and the entire world will become the workers' fatherland."[6]

Although significant, Stalin's 1931 statement was not a total watershed, inasmuch as the Comintern had been publicizing such a line abroad since the late 1920s.[7] What's more, this new rhetoric was slow to catch on, circulating rather quietly alongside more traditionally revolutionary, internationalist sloganeering throughout the early 1930s, indicating that Stalin's initiative was more of a trial balloon than a policy reversal.[8] Perhaps the most tangible effect of this shift in semantics occurred in military study circles, where a series of new textbooks first introduced the concept of the fatherland (based on the 1928 Comintern program and Stalin's recent speech).[9] Instruction in the public schools and party study circles also reflected this change after official decrees called for teachers and agitators to begin balancing their esoteric talk of world revolution with increasingly concrete, factual lessons about the USSR and its history, geography, and culture.[10] An inconsistent and halting shift that was very much at odds with the radicalism of the ongoing Cultural Revolution, this ideological turnabout ran parallel to the wide-ranging sea changes that would swamp the literary and artistic world in the next few years.

Amid all this turmoil, compounded as it was in late 1931 by Stalin's letter to *Proletarskaia revoliutsia,* one would think that party historians and ideologists would have literally fallen over each other in their efforts to sift through Stalin's recent speeches and identify overlooked priorities like this new-found love of country. Curiously, though, it was the political directorate of the Red Army, rather than the ideological establishment or even the press, that first responded to Stalin's call, flirting with the concept for the next few years. In the end, it took Stalin to return the concept to the fore—something he did in the spring of 1934. On April 14, he published a congratulatory telegram to the pilot-rescuers of the Cheliuskin in which he hailed their service to the "motherland."[11] Four days later, he placed the word squarely in the center of Soviet political discourse as he edited several dozen slogans for publication in the press in preparation for May Day:

> The imperialists are preparing for new wars and an attack against the USSR. Workers of the world! Down with those who'd provoke war! ~~Like a granite wall,~~ Defend the USSR, the ~~bulwark~~ *motherland* of all workers.

> Greetings to the young fighters of the Red Army, who will take their oath on the 1st of May in the name of the power of the workers and peasants, in the name of ~~the working class of the whole world~~ *our motherland.*

> Long live the second Five-Year Plan—the Five-Year Plan which has marked the ~~completion of the technical reconstruction of the people's economy~~ *strengthening of the might of our motherland* and the construction of a classless socialist society. Onwards to new victories!

> Long live the scientific and technical workers who are working hand in hand with the working class in the great task of building socialism and strengthening the defens~~ive capabiliti~~es of ~~the USSR~~ *our motherland.*[12]

Using the word "motherland" in public for the first time in years, the general secretary's editing of these slogans transformed them from by-now routine internationalist expressions of worker solidarity into much more etatist, state-centric statements of political pride and loyalty.[13] When *Pravda* published the slogans as its lead editorial a day later, it added one more slogan for good measure that must have been approved by Stalin's secretariat only hours before it appeared in print: "Workers, collective farmers, and shock workers of this socialist construction site! Join your organizations, join Osoaviakhim, and in doing so provide for the steadfast defense of our socialist motherland."[14] Within weeks, the term had been subsumed into the center of the regime's official lexicon, stimulated by the celebration of the Cheliuskinites' rescuers as Heroes of the Soviet Union.[15]

It is hard to say precisely what determined the timing of this intervention in the press, in part due to the loss of critical holdings from the former party archives.[16] Germany and Poland had just signed a non-aggression pact in January 1934. Hitler had also just completed his savage rout of the German communist party, giving the Austrian government the confidence to crush its own small rebellion of radical workers in mid-March 1934.[17] At about the same time, several Soviet air force pilots defected to Poland, Turkey, and other neighboring countries.[18] Circumstantial evidence suggests that all of these events combined to put Stalin on the defensive. As is well known, Stalin talked extensively about the German-Polish treaty and security issues at the Seventeenth Party Congress.[19] Later that spring, he and his entourage moved to reorganize the instruction of civic history in the public schools around more statist goals.[20] Finally, it was at this time that the party hierarchy proposed a new legal statute on treason—expressed in Russian as "betrayal of the motherland"—which criminalized an act that had not received much attention since 1917.[21]

This new interest in patriotism was also stimulated by more systemic efforts to enhance the mobilizational effectiveness of party propaganda during the spring of 1934. Many of these long-term priorities are visible in the new decrees on the instruction of civic history and geography in the public schools, which the party hierarchy promulgated right after the May Day holidays.[22] As outlined above, these decrees' scope was massive, affecting far more than just the schoolhouse curriculum. Aside from restoring the importance of chronology and cause-and-effect within historical narratives, they required that abstract "sociological" theory be deemphasized in favor of a more conventional reading of Russo-Soviet and world history. Heroes and villains, among other tropes, now received unambiguous official endorsement.[23]

These announcements in the press set the stage for the appearance of a series of new articles revolving around love of the motherland and commitment to one's society. Most important was an article by G. Vasilkovsky, entitled "The Highest Law of the Land," which appeared in *Pravda* on May 28 alongside coverage of the Cheliuskin rescue. Echoing Stalin's 1931 commentary, Vasilkovsky declared that although Marx and Engels had been correct in 1848 that "the workers do not have a fatherland," the October 1917 revolution had changed everything by giving rise to the world's first genuine workers and peasants' state. What's more, not only had the revolution succeeded in abolishing capitalist exploitation and private property, but it had eliminated ethnic inequality as well. These changes, according to Vasilkovsky, combined to create all the conditions necessary for the whole society to unite together for the first time and provide a groundswell of patriotic support for the party and state. Crediting the Bolshevik leaders and the Russian people with transforming their "backward, Asiatic, and forever spat-upon country of the rod into an advanced industrial and collective-farming superpower," Vasilkovsky traced their special revolutionary love of country to the martyred radicals of the past, from the Decembrists of 1825 and regicides of 1881 to those who manned the barricades in 1905 and stormed the Winter Palace in 1917. A surprisingly russocentric statement for these years, it was derived from Lenin's and Stalin's beliefs regarding the leadership role of ethnic Russians in imperial Russia and the USSR and was apparently regarded as compatible with the party's otherwise stridently internationalist brand of patriotism.[24] Indeed, Vasilkovsky was quick to affirm that the USSR was the motherland of the international proletariat rather than the private preserve of a more conventionally constructed ethnic or civic nation. Workers and peasants from around the world were said to be looking to the Soviet Union for help in their own revolutionary struggles; Western intellectuals, too, were apparently drawing inspiration from Moscow as their forefathers had from Paris after 1789. Ensuring the survival of this bastion of socialism, according to Vasilkovsky, was a profoundly patriotic endeavor.[25]

Vasilkovsky's dramatic broadside was seconded by an editorial in *Pravda* two weeks later that shared the paper's front page with coverage of the Cheliuskin crew's return to Moscow. Referring to the explorers and their airborne rescuers as the epitome of Soviet patriotism, the piece waxed rhapsodic about their valor, their "limitless love and devotion to their motherland" and their willingness to "defend the inviolability of Soviet borders." Reiterating Stalin's statement about how the advent of the Soviet motherland had become possible only through the revolution's abolition of capitalist exploitation, *Pravda* added that the Cheliuskinites were precisely the sort of heroic role models that the society needed in order to help even the least educated "express their own willingness to defend their motherland and the honor and glory of the USSR."[26]

Such essays and editorials prioritizing national defense were hardly new, of course—literary journals had been publishing "defensist literature" (*oboronnaia literatura*) for years, especially since the late 1920s.[27] Now however, defensism was to be subsumed into the campaign surrounding Soviet patriotism, obliging ordinary citizens to literally stand guard over the USSR's geographic borders, territorial integrity, and internal security.[28] On a more metaphorical level, defensism also referred to support for the construction of socialism and other domestic party and state priorities. Ultimately, such semantics converged to conflate popular loyalty with patriotism, national defense, and shock industrialization. *Pravda* reinforced the significance of this new sense of allegiance in June 1934 by publishing the Politburo's new statute on treason that condemned those guilty of the crime to death by firing squad.[29] Henceforth patriotism became the highest law of the land, serving as a litmus test of loyalty to the party, state, society, and economic system. Defense of the motherland was now to be treated as a greater priority than the advancement of the worldwide socialist cause.

Exiled Mensheviks read this announcement in Paris with a mixture of disbelief and horror, alleging in their paper *Sotsialistichesky vestnik* that the party hierarchy's embrace of patriotism was a sign of ideological deviation, if not outright heresy.[30] Bukharin responded to their allegations in print only a few days later, contending that concepts like patriotism, motherland, and fatherland were actually fully compatible with the expectations and norms of contemporary Soviet society. Conceding that these terms had figured prominently in the most hated, chauvinistic dimensions of old regime propaganda, Bukharin again took the opportunity to drive home how 1917's elimination of the capitalist system had allowed Soviet workers and peasants to recast such terms for use within the context of their new socialist world. Patriotism, according to Bukharin, was not only an honor, but a duty for loyal Soviet citizens in all walks of life.[31]

Koltsov, a regular *Pravda* correspondent and essayist, also contributed to this ongoing discussion that summer. Perhaps uncomfortable with the russocentric undertones of Vasilkovsky's article, Koltsov focused on the importance of internationalism to popular loyalty among the peoples of the USSR. Virtually ignoring internationalism's connection to the outside world, however, he focused on the term's secondary meaning in Russian parlance: the interethnic relations between the various peoples of the USSR. Koltsov began by referring to the paradox that Bukharin had just identified—that the pseudo-patriotism of the tsarist period had been noxious and chauvinistic enough to offend Russian and non-Russian alike. According to Koltsov, the only people to espouse patriotic feelings before 1917 had been dyed-in-the-wool monarchists and reactionaries; everyone else, from ordinary peasants to A. S. Pushkin and T. G. Shevchenko, had found it impossible to think about the Romanov regime in patriotic terms. Only in the wake of the revolution, after the landowners and capitalists had been swept away and exploitation abolished, had the people apparently begun to experience a true sense of patriotic loyalty and affection for their society. Russian and non-Russian, no longer divided by class or ethnicity, could now finally work alongside one another in harmony in order to realize the promise of socialism.[32] *Krasnaia zvezda* reiterated this line shortly thereafter to mark Constitution Day, attempting to succinctly define the concept of "motherland":

The Soviet Union has always been the motherland of our country's millions of toilers, but today that word sounds especially joyful, especially proud, and especially persuasive.
—*My motherland* is these wondrous people, the enthusiasts of socialist construction on the kolkhoz fields and in the plants and factories.
—*My motherland* is the magnificent wealth of our country: oil, coal, and metal.
—*My motherland* is the thousands of socialist plants and factories, lush collective farm fields, blooming gardens, and orchards.
—*My motherland* is the schools, technical institutes, theaters, clubs, radio, and other powerful components of our socialist culture.
—*My motherland* is *the great Bolshevik party and its brilliant and wise helmsman, C[omrade] Stalin, under whose direction our country has become a mighty socialist redoubt, a country of the great brotherhood of all nationalities, an indomitable defensive fortress.*
   This is what every proletarian, every collective farmer, and every honest worker says.

[. . .] *The USSR is my motherland, my fatherland, and my country—* this is what the workers of the world say.[33]

On the same day that *Krasnaia gazeta* made its case, K. B. Radek published an article in *Izvestia* that argued for a more classically internationalist meaning of patriotism. He began by referring to his own background as a Polish Jew and German revolutionary who nevertheless had looked to the USSR as his fatherland since 1917. According to Radek, the fact that people like him had been welcomed to the Soviet cause distinguished patriotism in the USSR from the chauvinistic nativism found in ostensibly "patriotic" bourgeois societies. Breaking away from his own biography, Radek then went even further in characterizing the implications of this internationalist rallying cry. "Our motherland is not just the motherland of those who are laboring and struggling under the capitalist yoke at the present time," he wrote. "It's built on the ashes and bones of all those who've fought for the emancipation of the toilers, in all times and all places. After all, it is their trials and tribulations, which Lenin studied and thought through, that lie at the foundation of our victories." Although Radek did not explicitly criticize Vasilkovsky or Koltsov for their narrower views of Soviet patriotism, he was uncompromising about the principled direction in which he thought the campaign ought to go.[34]

Whether because of the preparations for the upcoming Writers' Conference or the continuing celebration of Soviet arctic exploration, Radek's challenge went unanswered for an entire month. In early August, however, *Pravda* issued an unsigned article entitled "On the Motherland" as part of its regular "Propagandists' Corner" rubric that provided an official definition of the relationship between patriotism, nationalism, and internationalism. Rehearsing the now familiar history of patriotism's bourgeois origins, the piece then identified its Soviet incarnation as something entirely new, demonstrating a higher set of values stemming from the October revolution and the cause of socialist construction. Although some lip service was given to the revolution's internationalist appeal among working-class movements abroad, the core of the article concerned Soviet unity on the domestic front.[35] In November, *Bolshevik* offered a large article entitled "On the Socialist Motherland" that reemphasized the difference between bourgeois and socialist loyalty to one's society. Soviet citizens of all walks of life were assumed to be eager to support their society, insofar as it was organized along Marxist-Leninist lines. Only late in the piece did *Bolshevik* also reiterate calls for members of the working class abroad to regard the USSR as their motherland.[36] Molotov confirmed the direction of this line while speaking at the Seventh Congress of Soviets in early 1935. Although he echoed Radek's favorable contrast of Soviet patriotism against European nationalism, he focused the bulk of his commentary on the symbiotic relationship between industrial development and domestic loyalty to the party and state.[37] Overall, the message was clear to all those following the debate: although it was correct to interpret internationalism as referring to both multiethnic harmony on the domestic front and cooperation with revolutionary movements abroad, the former was to always take precedence. Soviet patriotism, in other words, began at home.

This is not to say, of course, that slogans referring to the USSR as the motherland of the world proletariat subsequently fell into disuse; instead, a routine developed within which such sloganeering assumed an auxiliary relationship to the increasingly central emphasis placed on domestic development and national defense. *Izvestia* ran an editorial in February 1935 detailing the USSR's political, economic, and military achievements before concluding that "we've built a socialist fatherland and [now] we'll be able to defend it."[38] According to an editorial in *Pravda* the following month, it was the USSR's state-led industrialization drive, education, and culture that inspired in Soviet citizens a "burning feeling of boundless love, their selfless devotion to their motherland and their profound responsibility for her fate and defense." Internationalism, to the extent to which it continued to play a real role in such discussions, served merely to remind people of the distinctiveness of their system against the darkening backdrop of European fascism. *Pravda* concluded its editorial by reminding its readership that genuine patriotism was possible only under socialism, insofar as the concept presupposed that people's class interests would align closely to those of their state and society at large. This coincidence of individual and societal priorities was impossible in the capitalist world, where economic elites' selfish pursuit of wealth inevitably drew them into conflict with other elites, state institutions, and the laboring masses. Such had been the case in Russia before 1917 and was still the case elsewhere in the world. Only the USSR, declared *Pravda,* could claim to be the object of genuinely popular affection. Authoritative commentators such as D. A.

Zaslavsky and Stetsky reaffirmed this line during key holiday celebrations on November 7, 1935 and January 21, 1936.[39]

Shortly thereafter, *Komsomolskaia pravda* summarized these new testaments to the uniqueness of Soviet patriotism while presenting a vision of the motherland that was surprisingly conventional. Russian in historical terms, the contemporary USSR was a multiethnic state dominated by workers and peasants engaged in the grand project of socialist construction. Great emphasis was placed on the borders of the USSR, which marked the physical extent of the motherland, as well as Soviet geopolitical, ideological, and economic interests. Insofar as the USSR was surrounded by hostile powers intent on its overthrow, defense of the Soviet borders was described as the sacred obligation of all those loyal to the revolution, whether at home or abroad.[40] *Pravda* reiterated the case for Soviet uniqueness at about the same time, highlighting the multiethnic nature of the society during a reception for dignitaries from the Buriat-Mongol ASSR.[41] The Friendship of the Peoples had played a key role in domestic propaganda since late 1935, when a series of receptions in Moscow celebrated Tadzhik, Turkmen, Armenian, and Azeri contributions to the USSR, and this would continue into March 1936 when a Georgian delegation was fêted in the Kremlin.[42] This "internationlist" patriotic rhetoric climaxed in the rehabilitation of the Cossacks as a social institution shortly thereafter. A Russo-Ukrainian population that had served as a military caste under the old regime, the Cossacks had been persecuted under the Bolsheviks for their loyalty to the tsar and participation in the White movement during the Civil War. Now, however, even the Cossacks were to be embraced by the Friendship of the Peoples, *Pravda* proclaiming that today's Cossacks were no longer divided in their loyalties and in fact longed for an opportunity to serve in defense of the Soviet motherland.[43]

Nearly two years after his first stridently internationalist article on Soviet patriotism, Radek returned to the subject in an article published on May Day, 1936. The most thorough-going discussion of the subject to appear in print since the inception of the campaign, Radek's article proposed to resolve how Soviet patriotism could be both internationalist and statist at the same time. Putting this sense of loyalty into historical perspective, he noted that patriotism in the European context dated back to 1789, when it had originally been deployed by the bourgeoisie against the vestiges of the feudal system. If this had been a progressive historical development at the time, the bourgeoisie's subsequent use of patriotic sloganeering to distract the working class and peasantry from their legitimate class interests was not. Nineteenth-century Marxists, according to Radek, had attempted to counter patriotism's influence by exposing it as a "masking ideology" that interfered with the expression of workers' innate class identity. The controversy that this caused was only truly resolved by the Bolsheviks' seizure of power in 1917, when they succeeded in reconciling proletarian internationalism with a revolutionary sense of patriotism in order to harmonize class interests with love of country. According to Radek, the uniqueness of this accomplishment, possible only in the USSR, justified Soviet patriotism's heavy focus on domestic unity in the postrevolutionary period.[44]

Radek's fall from grace later that year limited the influence that his exegesis had on the ongoing celebration of Soviet patriotism. It was not, for instance, reprinted in a handbook entitled *Our Socialist Motherland* that was published in late 1936 in order to make important articles on patriotism more easily accessible to grassroots agitators.[45] Nevertheless, increasingly routine use of the term in Soviet mass culture harnessed it as an accessible way to promote socialist construction, nationality policy, and defense of the USSR. It was now common for commentary in the press to connect the sentiment to concrete accomplishments and dozens of contemporary heroes from the multiethnic ranks of industry, agriculture, the armed forces, and the security services—Stakhanov, Izotov, Busygin, the Vinogradova sisters, Smetanin, Gudov, Musinsky, Demchenko, Shmidt, Liapidevsky, Vodopianov, Voroshilov, Budenny, Tukhachevsky, Bliukher, and Yagoda—all of whom demonstrated by example how patriots were able to contribute to the Soviet experiment.[46]

Official encouragement for Soviets of all ages, creeds, and social origins to love their motherland had a major impact on discussion circles and party education courses during the mid-1930s. Komsomol instructors, for instance, were told to complement theoretical work with material drawn from current events and the usable past. As one directive explained, "facts and examples from contemporary life give students a complete impression of historical events" as well as provide a powerful context within which to "train students in the spirit of Soviet patriotism."[47] Without such a focus, even the most enthusiastic Komsomol members might lose focus and lapse into complacency. Now, *Pravda* urged, was no time for modesty. "It's not so rare for certain young men and women to grow up on their own, somehow unaware of their fathers' and mothers' torturous and heroic past in the struggle with tsarism and in the battles of the Civil War for Soviet power [. . .]. Wherever the school and Komsomol sideline such an upbringing, you find the beginnings of hostile class influences."[48] The key to continued vigilance and struggle, according to party officials, was the sense of patriotism that the study of history and emulation of heroes provided.

Pravda returned again and again to the subject of enlivening class presentations by connecting the past to the present and regularly referring to the bigger picture. One commentator criticized several propagandists' discussion of the Mensheviks' support for the Provisional Government in 1917, noting that while this sort of material was factually correct, it failed to identify the large issues at stake. "Working through the Mensheviks' position on the defense of the 'motherland,'" the correspondent wrote, the propagandists neglected to contrast this treachery against more genuinely patriotic impulses. Specifically, the propagandists failed "to say a single word about the victorious proletariat's great sense of motherland, nor did they say anything about how we must defend our fatherland from the enemy." Such a oversight meant that the instructors had forfeited a valuable opportunity to connect their discussion to ongoing mobilizational priorities. "The history of the party is not just historical material," the correspondent reminded his readers. "It's through history that we are training today's builders of socialism."[49]

Part of the problem with party education, as alluded to above, was its reliance on texts that did not talk explicitly about Soviet patriotism. Neither elementary readers by Ingulov and Volin, nor party history textbooks by Yaroslavsky, Popov, and Knorin even mention love of country. Most of the books that augmented these curricular mainstays were no better, whether *USSR—the Country of Socialism*, Beria's *On the Question of the History of Bolshevik Organizations in the Transcaucasus*, or Voroshilov's *Stalin and the Red Army*.[50] Because these books were so colorless and unevocative, both the mass press and specialized pedagogical journals encouraged instructors to bolster their oral presentations and classroom discussions with more populist material from mainstream mass culture.[51]

Pravda's efforts to supply such mobilizational material ranged from accessible accounts of revolutionary events to articles on civics and geography. An editorial in the summer of 1935 even encouraged its readers to tour the far-flung regions of the USSR in order to become personally acquainted with the diversity of the society. Explicitly contrasting this exploration and sincere curiosity with the capitalist world's imperialism and colonial exploitation, the editorial denounced the notion that local culture was a low priority within the modern industrial state. Such an attitude, according to *Pravda,* was an example of leftist foolishness: construction of a socialist society would be impossible without a thorough understanding of local customs, needs, and expectations. The editorial then called upon members of the artistic and scholarly elite to produce materials to aid the society in its understanding and appreciation of this ethnographic diversity through literature, theater, cinema, and popular science. Evidence of the seriousness of this proposal is visible in the editorial's demand that such work be thoroughgoing and not amount to "cheap exotica."[52]

This call to artists to devise ways of publicizing the Friendship of the Peoples was complemented less than six months later by *Pravda*'s announcement of preparations underway for an upcoming exhibition devoted to the twentieth anniversary of the Red Army. Among the various thematic categories of art to be displayed was canvas and sculpture grouped under the slogan "Defense of the Socialist Motherland: An Endeavor for the Entire Society." This exhibition's precursor, mounted in 1933 to celebrate the Red Army's fifteenth anniversary, had gone to great lengths to break away from earlier styles of abstract, avant garde art. The twentieth anniversary, according to *Pravda*, would complete this shift by displaying art that saluted both heroism and patriotic service to the motherland.[53]

Aside from such agenda setting, the press was also eager to display successful examples of patriotism in the arts for appreciation and emulation. Among the first members of the creative intelligentsia to step forward to supply this sort of celebratory material were the Ukrainian poets L. S. Pervomaisky and M. F. Rylsky. They offered pieces in *Izvestia* in mid-1935 that defined the Soviet motherland somewhat generically as a bountiful expanse dotted by factories, chimneys, and canals.[54] Surkov published a poem entitled "Fatherland" in *Pravda* in mid-1935 that borrowed from the developing official line in order to celebrate the

1917 revolution as the founding act of a multiethnic society oriented around the needs of the common people. He followed this poem with "The Song of Youth" in the fall of that year, which combined the emerging patriotic rhetoric of the period with the ongoing celebration of Soviet heroism. Both these pieces developed themes that the lyricist had already explored in a collection of patriotic poetry entitled *Motherland of the Brave,* which had rolled off the presses earlier that year.[55] N. Sidorenko echoed Surkov's revolutionary thematics in his "Motherland of October" in November 1935, while the Tatar poet M. Sadri picked up on Surkov's mention of national liberation in early 1936.[56] Sadri's piece, along with those by Surkov and Rylsky, was republished later that year in a brochure for use in structuring radio broadcasts, indicating their importance within the campaign.[57]

But if some members of the creative intelligentsia were quick to grasp the emerging direction of the official line, others, like most party historians and members of the ideological establishment, were far more hesitant.[58] *Pravda* appears to have tried to accelerate this transition by giving visibility to patriotic pioneers like Surkov and by spending hundreds of column inches promoting others. Indeed, even when members of the creative intelligentsia did not fully embrace the new priorities, *Pravda*'s critics wrote about them anyway. A good example of this is I. I. Kataev's short story "The Meeting," published in his collection *Fatherland* in 1935. A tale about the postcollectivization Russian countryside, it concerns I. A. Kalmazov, a Jewish party propagandist from Odessa who is dispatched to a distant village to help a local activist bring in a potato crop. At the climax of the story, Kalmazov realizes that rains threaten the village's harvest on the eve of Pokrov, a three-day religious feast celebrating the intercession of the Virgin Mary. Kalmazov convinces the peasants to skip their holiday and secure the harvest, delaying his own return to the city in order to help. The potatoes are brought in, the peasants drink in celebration, and Kalmazov realizes that he's learned more than he expected from his experience in the countryside. If this reading of "The Meeting" indicates that the short story's basic themes revolve around a reconciliation of urban modernity and rural tradition, *Pravda* claimed that the text was a metaphor for the mobilization of all of society around a patriotic sense of duty and responsibility.[59] A forced reframing of the story, it is reminiscent of radical nineteenth-century literary critics' use of the popular press to advance their own ideological agendas (although in this case done at the behest of the state).

Another example of a critic's injection of patriotic values into a story primarily concerned with class consciousness is *Izvestia*'s November 1935 review of Afinogenov's play *Far Away*. In the play, an ailing brigade commander, M. I. Malko, is stranded in an isolated village by a train accident. Over the course of a single day, he turns the entire community on its head, helping a former Red Army soldier overcome his malaise and two women combat their superstition and passivity. He also starts up a mentoring relationship with a female Komsomol activist half his age. *Izvestia* acknowledged the presence of traditional Soviet tropes in Afinogenov's play—old vs. new, faith vs. rationality, spontaneity vs. consciousness, naïveté vs. experience—and agreed that the play's characters personified these political tensions. But it also claimed that the characters, when taken together, made up a group portrait of the Soviet motherland as well.[60] Such a conclusion seems strange, not only because it is unfounded, but because it was utterly unnecessary, given the other strengths of the piece. Only the new-found priority of all-inclusive patriotism can explain the odd spin that *Izvestia* put on the play.

Less forced was the press's treatment of *Motherland*, another piece for the stage by B. M. Levin. A narrative that explores the intertwined fates of four childhood friends, it begins in 1914 and then segues through 1917 and 1920 into the 1930s. Petr Tuganov is introduced as a privileged young noble who delights in bossing around one of the local peasant youths, Nikolai. Petr barely notices Sonia, a Jewish playmate, who worships the ground he walks on. He does acknowledge Liuda, his social equal, who secretly has feelings for Nikolai while realizing the hopelessness of this love. In the second act, the four are briefly reunited at a variety show in Moscow in 1917 where Liuda and Sonia are to sing in front of an audience that includes Petr, now an officer in the army of the Provisional Government. Backstage, Sonia confesses to Liuda that she is still in love with Petr, while Liuda confides that she's stayed in touch with Nikolai, who's been imprisoned for denouncing the war. Just as Sonia takes to the stage, however, a group of Red guards burst into the theater to announce the Bolsheviks' seizure of power. Nikolai, within their ranks, greets Liuda and disarms Petr, who rudely brushes Sonia aside and rushes off to alert his superiors to the unrest. During the play's third act, set in 1920, the audience learns that Nikolai has joined the Red Army. Liuda too has joined the revolution and married a communist, while Sonia has gotten involved with a disreputable entrepreneur and Petr has joined the White army and its Japanese allies. The play's longest act is its fourth, which begins in Harbin, a White Russian community in Manchuria, in the mid-1930s. There, Petr visits Sonia, who lives in lonely bourgeois luxury, longing to return to her motherland. Petr speaks openly about being a spy who feigns poverty during his missions into the USSR in order to avoid drawing attention to himself. The scene then shifts to Moscow, where Liuda now lives. Petr, having committed some dastardly act of sabotage in Kiev, flees to Moscow, where he makes contact with Liuda. Liuda suspects nothing and offers her old friend shelter. She also invites him to a collective farm in the USSR's western borderlands where their old friend Nikolai, a political agitator, is hosting a reunion for his peasants' upwardly mobile sons and daughters. Petr accepts the invitation, hoping to escape across the frontier. Once at the collective farm, Petr attempts to enlist the help of a grumbling old peasant to get closer to the border. Instead, the peasant turns Petr over to the authorities, protecting his motherland and countrymen from the spy. Aside from stressing the theme of vigilance, Levin's *Motherland* offered his audiences four different forms of patriotism: Petr's elite revanchism, Sonia's nostalgia, Nikolai and Liuda's enthusiasm for the new society, and the old peasant's love for his family, neighbors, and region. *Komsomolskaia pravda* hailed the intentions behind the play, noting that it "exposes the hostile, counterrevolutionary essence of these Tuganovite notions of motherland and demonstrates the Soviet people's historically new sense of fatherland. This makes B. Levin's *Motherland* deeply relevant and moving, as well as idealistically oriented."[61]

A similar borderland theme is explored in Dovzhenko's film *Aerograd*, which was released in November 1935. A story initially conceived with Fadeev, *Aerograd* deals with the struggle of a peasant community against local anti-Soviet elements and Japanese infiltrators in a heavily forested border region of the Soviet Far East. Dovzhenko's protagonist, Stepan Glushak, a hunter and former Red partisan from the Civil War years, takes the lead in this effort, ultimately killing his friend of fifty years, Vasily Khudiakov, for taking part in the conspiracy. *Aerograd*'s message was a simple one: the times dictated that Glushak exchange his

Civil War–era class-consciousness for patriotism. Appearing in the wake of the Kirov murder, the film emphasized this point by stressing the connection between domestic discontent and hostile powers abroad; it also forced Glushak to choose between friend and country. Ultimately, Glushak's choice is rewarded not only by the defeat of the insurrection, but by the construction of a new socialist city, Aerograd, as an outpost of Soviet power in the region. Songs composed for the film popularized this message—to take just one example, D. B. Kabalevsky and V. M. Gusev's "Rise Up, Partisans!" proclaimed: "Long live our motherland! / We'll lift the red banner up high, / Over our Red Far East / No foreign banners will ever fly!"[62] *Pravda* concluded with satisfaction that the film was "about a close, unbreakable bond with the people, about hatred for the enemy, and about limitless love for the motherland." *Trud's* evaluation was similarly lyrical: "*Aerograd* is a heroic poem about love for the motherland. Its heroism is not pompous, nor is it shrill, but calm, stern, inwardly focused, and justified. [. . .] This film makes us love our motherland even more and nurtures within us feelings of Soviet patriotism. It's a victorious song about our motherland."[63]

A third film about the borderlands, *The Thirteen,* was released by M. Romm less than six months after *Aerograd* in March 1936. It focuses on a unit of border guards and a handful of civilians as they make their way across a windswept Central Asian desert toward a base where they will be relieved of duty and sent home. Stumbling across an oasis in the middle of a sandstorm, they discover a cache of weapons belonging to a *basmachi* commander named Sheremet-khan and realize that this notoriously elusive rebel and his fighters are headed their way. One guard is sent for reinforcements while the remaining twelve vow to tie down the *basmachi* until aid can arrive; ultimately, only one survives. Such self-sacrifice is depicted in patriotic terms, most evidently in the eulogy pronounced to commemorate the martyrs' feat at the end of the film: "They died a brave death as honorable sons of the socialist motherland. We shall remember their names!" Prompt invocation of these surnames—a combination of Slavic-, Tatar-, and Turkic-derivatives—demonstrates another facet of the film's thematic message: the evocative power of the Friendship of the Peoples. Finally, *The Thirteen* subtly connected domestic opponents of the Soviet regime to adversaries abroad by outfitting Sheremet-khan as an officer in the British expeditionary forces.[64] Genuinely suspenseful, Romm's film drew a patriotic line in the Central Asian sand.

Another film released alongside *The Thirteen,* entitled *We Are from Kronshtadt,* projected a similarly sober and grim sense of patriotic loyalty based on the recent past. In this epic about the 1919 defense of Petrograd, an Old Bolshevik named Vasily Martynov is appointed commissar over a rag-tag group of Baltic fleet sailors at Kronshtadt and is then dispatched with them to the nearby coast to slow the advance of White forces under N. N. Yudenich. Although initially successful, Martynov's unit is overrun and only the most questionable member of the group, Artyom Balashov, escapes with his life. Initially unsure about what to do, Balashov rises to the challenge of his circumstances and returns to Kronshtadt to report the defeat. Once there, he also wins permission to lead reinforcements back to relieve another unit facing the same bloody fate. Throughout the film, slogans of loyalty to the revolution among party members alternate with expressions of concern for the population of Petrograd among the more rough-and-tumble members of the Kronshtadt garrison. In this sense, Ye. L. Dzigan's film marched in step with Surkov's lyric poetry about the manifold meanings of 1917. *Pravda*'s review of *We Are from Kronshtadt* seized on Balashov's taunting challenge to the White forces at the end of the film— "So, who else wants a try at Petrograd?"—in order to report that "this rejoinder resonates with the sound of the Red Army and Red Fleet's heroic past. It also resonates with a warning to today's enemies that they will be beaten and defeated even more mercilessly than 16 years ago, in October 1919. They will be beaten and destroyed everywhere where they dare to tread on Soviet soil." *Pravda,* in other words, saw a direct connection between the crucible of world revolution years earlier and the contemporary priority of defending the USSR. *Izvestia* agreed, proclaiming that the film expressed "the big truth of our history."[65]

Defense also played a major role in *The Motherland Is Calling,* a film released in April 1936 by A. V. Macheret. A story that revolves around a test pilot named Sergei Novikov and the outbreak of war with Nazi Germany, it opens with Novikov taking a new plane through trials so rigorous that he reopens wounds acquired during the civil war. Celebration follows his return to base, followed by hospitalization. While recuperating, he learns that Germany has launched a surprise attack on the USSR and that his son has been killed in an air raid. Hearing the

Fig. 9: Advertisement for *We Are from Kronshtadt,* dir. Ye. L. Dzigan (Mosfilm, 1936). From *Vecherniaia Moskva,* January 8, 1937, 4.

proverbial call of the motherland, Novikov manages to return to his unit, engage an enemy bomber squadron, and shoot down the aircraft responsible for killing his son. Unsurprisingly, *Pravda*'s review of *The Motherland Is Calling* focused on the relationship between Novikov's personal valor and his love of country: "It's possible to say without any doubt that the film finds its mark. The theme—the defense of the motherland and Soviet patriotism—is exceptionally timely during these dark days [. . .]. And Sergei Novikov and his family are just a general depiction of the millions of Soviet patriots, who anywhere, anytime, will answer the call of the motherland: exterminate and annihilate the enemy!" Macheret must have been pleased by such reviews, as they resonated closely with his ambitions for the film. As he noted to *Kino,* from the start, he and his team "wanted most of all to mobilize audience members on an emotional level, and not through historical material, but through [contemporary] material on the possibility of the threatening storm of war."[66] Within a few years, *The Motherland Is Calling* would be criticized for its naïve "hurrah patriotism" about the USSR's undefeatable esprit de corps and technical know-how. But from the perspective of the interwar years, Macheret's film was also unusually prescient in its anticipation of the coming armageddon.

Fictional subjects like the idealized showdown with Nazi Germany in *The Motherland Is Calling* were complemented by dozens of documentary newsreels during these years that also waxed patriotic about the primacy of the Soviet armed forces. One of the first of this genre was *The Battle for Kiev,* which paired documentary coverage of maneuvers in the Kiev military district with historical and contemporary commentary on the city and its civilian population. Presiding over the event were a number of celebrities from the Red Army general staff such as Voroshilov, Budenny, Yegorov, and Yakir; also captured on screen were members of the Ukrainian party elite, such as Postyshev, Popov, S. V. Kosior, and G. I. Petrovsky.[67] *Belorussian Maneuvers,* which followed about a year later, turned audiences' attention to the Polish border and focused more narrowly on tank and cavalry exercises. Like *The Battle for Kiev,* it also spent considerable time on Voroshilov and Budenny, shown inspecting the troops and conversing with everyone from local commanders to Tukhachevsky, Yegorov, and Uborevich.[68] *Troop Maneuvers of the Moscow Military District* similarly spoke of the air and land forces of the Red Army in breathless terms. Hailing the capabilities of the average Red Army soldier, the film also tipped its hat to celebrities within the command staff, lavishing attention on Yegorov, Tukhachevsky, Uborevich, Kork, Yakir, Alksnis, Belov, and others.[69] These three films were complemented by the release of *Tactical Exercises of the Far Eastern Red Banner Army,* which focused on infantry maneuvers and artillery exercises under Bliukher's command.[70] In each case, a flurry of images of troops, equipment, and armor, presided over by famous members of the general staff, was framed by either evocative intertitles, an inspirational male narrator, or a rousingly patriotic musical score about the Red Army's readiness for war.

Ultimately, defense-oriented Soviet patriotism became a staple of regime propaganda alongside other campaigns focusing on popular heroism and the Friendship of the Peoples. A marked departure from the previous decade's emphasis on materialism, class, and anonymous social forces, this valorization of famous patriots ultimately precipitated the formation of a new pantheon of Soviet heroes, socialist myths, and modern-day fables that would inculcate regime values in the society "by example." Alongside heroic Bolsheviks from the revolution and civil war, this populist propaganda celebrated exemplary party leaders, Komsomol activists, non-Russians from the republican party organizations, Red Army commanders, secret police officials, and shock workers in industry and agriculture. People like Tukhachevsky, Bliukher, Yegorov, Uborevich, and many others quickly became household names.

At the same time that this new patriotic ethic in Soviet society was promoting specific champions to replace the impersonal materialism of the 1920s, it was also subtly reinterpreting the meaning of internationalism. If internationalism had initially described Soviet workers' cooperation and solidarity with the workers of the world against the forces of capitalism and counterrevolution, now the term increasingly pointed to the cooperation and solidarity of the peoples of the USSR against hostile foreign forces. In this sense, internationalism came to be almost synonymous with the Friendship of the Peoples and tended to downplay the USSR's common cause with working-class movements abroad. Of course, some of the term's original semantic associations with international revolution did survive into the mid-1930s—particularly in regard to foreign affairs (e.g., Austria in 1934, Abyssinia in 1935, and Spain between 1936 and 1939). They also appeared from time to time in Soviet mass culture (e.g., the 1936 blockbuster *Circus*).[71] That said, on the whole, these elements played a distinctly secondary role to the increasingly popular theme of domestic unity and the shared duty of national defense.

Circa 1935–1936, then, Soviet propaganda cast the USSR as a colorful and dynamic pageantry revolving around patriotism and the building of socialism. Populist heroic tales from the recent past served to provide a common narrative that the entire society could relate to—a patriotic rallying call with greater social application than the previous decade's narrow and impersonal focus on materialism and class. Facilitated by Soviet journalists, *litterateurs,* authors, poets, and cinematographers, this accessible, evocative line came closer to articulating a truly Soviet sense of a usable past than party historians or ideologists ever would.

6 The Popularity of the Official Line

INASMUCH AS IT WAS THE DUTY of Soviet mass culture and the press to mobilize public opinion, it should come as no surprise that *Pravda, Izvestia,* and other leading newspapers during the mid-1930s accompanied their new focus on patriotism and heroes with the testimonials of common citizens who responded with delight to the turnabout in official propaganda. In June 1934, for instance, A. P. Mukhin and several fellow airplane mechanics announced that they, like the heroic rescuers of the Cheliuskin, were prepared to fulfill any mission that the party or state demanded of them. In another letter, N. Rakitin and R. Blumental vowed on behalf of the members of their tank unit to emulate the patriotism of the Cheliuskin crew and its rescuers in their defense of the motherland. In a third piece, the playwright Levin reproduced a conversation that he had purportedly overheard between three schoolboys on a street in central Moscow:

FIRST BOY: So who would you like to be? Shmidt or one of the flyers?
SECOND: I'd like to be one of the flyers.
FIRST: But why not Shmidt?
SECOND: Because it's hard to imagine being him.
THIRD: I— . . . I— . . . I— . . .
OTHERS: Well, what about you?
THIRD: I'd like to be a Cheliuskinite, Shmidt, and one of the flyers.

OTHERS: Well, aren't you clever. That's too easy—you have to choose.
THIRD: Uh . . . um . . . well, I'd just like to be a Hero of the USSR—it
  doesn't matter what kind.[1]

Such accounts suggest the new propaganda line to have enjoyed considerable popular resonance.[2]

Of course, using official sources to document such support presents a host of methodological problems. For that reason, this chapter triangulates such testimony against that found in private letters, diaries, memoirs, and secret police reports in order to better establish how Soviet society reacted to the new discussion of heroes and patriotism that became so ubiquitous in the press and mass culture during these years. Even such an approach, however, is complicated by the pervasive violence, coercion, and chaos that were so characteristic of Stalinist governance during the mid-1930s. Ultimately, it is important to concede, therefore, that discussion of public opinion in the USSR is difficult enough to preclude anything more than a glimpse of interwar popular *mentalité*.[3] That said, the fact that party authorities clearly attempted to rule with the carrot as well as with the proverbial stick during these years justifies even a tentative investigation of how Soviet citizens responded to the propaganda state's newly populist initiatives.

Personal diaries, archival records, and memoiristic accounts from the mid-1930s suggest that Mukhin, Rakitin, and Blumental were far from alone in their response to the discussion of heroism and patriotic sentiments in the press. Isaev, for instance, a soldier stationed in the Far East, announced to his study circle in the spring of 1936 that he found the celebratory coverage of leading members of his generation at the Tenth Komsomol Conference inspiring as he thought about his place within Soviet society.[4] Press coverage of this congress had a similar effect on a school-aged Komsomol aspirant in a small Belorussian town at the opposite end of the USSR. Referring to Kosarev's famous speech on Soviet patriotism, M. Molochko wrote of his enthusiasm for the way in which the Komsomol chair framed the question of popular loyalty to the USSR: "The 10th Congress of the All-Union Leninist Communist Youth League has opened. Kosarev's report was most of all a speech about how people ought to be brought up. It has a remarkable effect. Strong, passionate, and profound words."[5] Nor were Isaev and Molochko alone in how they regarded such ideological statements.[6] L. A. Potemkin, a

Komsomol activist in Sverdlovsk, wrote in his diary in early February 1935 about his reaction to Molotov's speech about Soviet patriotism at the Seventh Congress of Soviets. According to Potemkin, Molotov's speech demonstrated:

> how clear, just, reasonable, and noble are the policies of the dictatorship of the proletariat. How majestic and grand are the successes of the policies of the wisest party of all mankind as it creates a joyful, bright, beautiful life for all men. And the overwhelming majority of the population (millions) of our country [who are] attempting to build a socialist society consciously and actively are New Men in the prehistory of mankind. Men [of the future,] of the true history of mankind.[7]

From such examples, it is clear that people like Isaev, Molochko, and Potemkin tended to accept the epic terms in which the authorities framed the new concepts. Indeed, even when Soviet citizens either did not entirely understand what they were reading in the press or flatly disagreed with party policy, they still often expressed themselves in ways that reveal an elemental sense of patriotism.[8]

Perhaps unsurprisingly, popular interest in Soviet heroism and a patriotic sense of common cause appears to have matured for many in much the same way as it did for Mukhin, Rakitin, and Blumental. For Molochko, for instance, such feelings date to his concern over the fate of the Cheliuskin expedition in 1934—a preoccupation that led him to write in his diary about the eventual rescue in euphoric terms: "April 24, 1934—The Cheliuskinites, who lived on the ice for two months under the daily threat of death, have been saved by the hero-flyers. This is genuine heroism in the name of common interests [. . .]. I can't convey the feelings that I experienced from this news."[9] Molochko, of course, was only one of many to react breathlessly to these events. A. Likhachev, the director of Moscow's School No. 7, noted to *Pravda* that from the very start of the crisis, his students had followed daily news updates in the press and on the radio with great concern. Aside from encouraging teenagers to take an interest in current events, Likhachev continued, the drama on the ice also could be credited with inspiring Soviet youth to take a new interest in science, positive role models, and far-flung regions of the country. Perhaps most important, the Soviet pilots' eventual rescue of the Cheliuskin crew apparently had given his students a valuable lesson about "their debt to the motherland."[10] *Pravda* columnist Zaslavsky went even further in an accompanying piece, asserting that the Cheliuskin crew's teamwork in the arctic had served to popularize abstract Marxist-Leninist concepts like collectivism.[11] Although both Likhachev and Zaslavsky clearly exaggerated the ethical and philosophical impact of the events on Soviet society, it is true that the celebrity of the protagonists involved proved inspiring even to those who ordinarily had little affection for such spectacles.[12]

The reason for this broad surge of interest in patriotic heroism stems from several factors. First, whether covering the drama of the Cheliuskin rescue or the subsequent struggle of Stakhanovites to set new production records, the Soviet press tended to emphasize the suspense, risk, and stakes involved in these endeavors. This was not only a natural way to emplot such narratives, but it also invited readers to make a connection between contemporary Soviet heroism and that of yesteryear. According to such commentary, a metal worker's valor or a tractor driver's perseverance was just as heroic as the revolutionary derring-do of the Bolshevik old guard in 1917. As one Komsomol member recalled years later: "We read articles in *Komsomolskaya pravda* about the heroism of Komsomol members in winter work or in the construction of the new town of Komsomolsk-on-Amur, and believed that the activities of some Komsomol organizations could, indeed, bear some comparison with the romantic exploits of Komsomol members during the Civil War."[13] Commentators like Anna Krylova point out that members of the post-1917 generation felt insecure about their lack of revolutionary credentials and sought out the opportunity to distinguish themselves under fire.[14] Such emotions, stimulated by the press and mass culture, explain a lot about Soviet youth's enthusiasm for the drama surrounding heroism and patriotic valor in industry, agriculture, and civil defense.

Of course, it was not only the press that encouraged ordinary Soviet citizens to believe in the importance of the new line. Publications, including those within Gorky's *History of Plants and Factories* series, also served as sources of inspiration and models of personal conduct. In September 1935, *Pravda* reported that an early book in the series on the Highmountain Iron Mine was one of the most sought-after titles within the ranks of the Red Army.[15] A year later, it reported that public libraries were finding it impossible to satisfy demand for the first volume of Gorky's series on the civil war.[16] Interviews with readers revealed a host of explanations for this latter book's popularity:

I am 42 years old. I have never read a more understandable or interesting book in my life than the first volume of the *History of the Civil War in the USSR*. Most important is that the language is simple. I study in party school from textbooks and I must say that [that material] comes with difficulty. The language in which these textbooks are written is difficult, but in the *History of the Civil War*, everything is understandable. [Collective farm chairwoman S. K. Nagornaia, Kharkov province.]

The contents of the book genuinely express the struggle and heroism of the working class of our country in its preparations for the Great Proletarian Revolution. The role of the communist party and its leader is clearly shown. [Komsomol member Zhiliaev, Kursk province.]

Although I've studied the history of the party and civil war in institute, study circles, and the army, I never learned many of the facts that are illuminated in this book. The relationship between the various parties, their differences, and the commonality that all bourgeois parties shared in the face of the proletarian revolution; the struggle and difficulties of the Bolshevik party's work; the devotion of the popular masses to the great Lenin's cause—all of this is presented in this book in a bright, lively, and engaging way. [Architect B. A. Melnikov, Baku.][17]

Over and over, readers credited the text's populist dimensions—its animation and focus on clearly identifiable heroes and villains—with making the *History of the Civil War in the USSR* accessible to the broadest possible audiences. Stalin had noted to Mints that the book read like a novel, and his opinion was clearly shared by the public at large.

Fictional literature, of course, also served as a conduit for mobilizational propaganda during the mid-1930s. Although often criticized today for its artistic shortcomings, Socialist Realism enjoyed a wide readership during these years, insofar as it packaged ideologically correct thematic material within a conventional narrative genre.[18] A series of interviews conducted with former Soviet citizens after the Second World War revealed that most still recalled the titles and authors of the most memorable books that they had read during the 1930s.[19] Sholokhov was almost unanimously admired for the perceived realism and honesty of his depiction of the civil war and collectivization. His *Quiet Flows the Don* was perhaps the most frequently mentioned; *Virgin Soil Upturned* also appears to have been a favorite.[20] Panferov, too, was remembered with affection for his *Bruski*.[21] Predictably, Gorky enjoyed prominence in the popular mind, in large part due to the readability of his early novels and plays and his later stature within the Soviet artistic establishment.[22] A. Avdeenko and Fadeev were associated with memorable works, as were humorists like I. A. Ilf and Ye. P. Petrov (the latter apparently more for their *One-Story America* than for *The Golden Calf* and the trickster Ostap Bender).[23] And despite changes in the literary canon after 1932, other prominent writers of the 1920s like Gladkov, Serafimovich, and Zoshchenko also managed to retain a measure of their early popularity, as did poets like V. V. Mayakovsky.[24] Millions of copies of these works of fiction were sold during these years, complementing long lines at public libraries.[25]

Perhaps the most emblematic of the writers was Ostrovsky, whose semi-autobiographical *How the Steel Was Forged* was revered both by Soviet youth and by the author's own revolutionary generation. One worker named Kogan from Moscow's Paris Commune Factory waxed rhapsodic about how realistic she found Ostrovsky's writing: "You forget that you're reading a book and feel as if you are a participant in the events as they are described and as if you are hearing Pavel Korchagin's voice." Mogilevsky, a worker at the Kaganovich Ball Bearing Factory, went even further, noting how tempting it was to identify directly with Ostrovsky's protagonist. "Pavel Korchagin is not simply a self-portrait. He is a wonderful, generalized portrait [for all of us]. In the hero of his novel, Ostrovsky has shown us a genuine Bolshevik, a person of the new epoch." A model activist, Korchagin also served as a useful exemplar of Bolshevik self-criticism. Pagubina, a colleague of Kogan's at the Paris Commune Factory, found this particularly helpful, contending that "through Pavel, the author depicts the new [Soviet] man [. . .]. You can't help analyzing your own life and attempting to take the same path. This book ought to be treated like a textbook, an example, a model of a heroic life." Others reported similar feelings of humility and gratitude, one woman even deciding to return to school after reading the book. A construction worker at the Red Army Theater named Yefremkin reported that the novel had such a strong effect on him that he immediately signed up to join the Komsomol.[26] Diaries and postwar interviews with Soviet refugees confirm the affection that people from all walks of life felt for the book, describing it not as a piece of didactic literature, but as a realistic model for proper Soviet conduct.[27]

Gladkov's *Energy* evoked almost as much excitement. Bryskin, a worker at the Stalin plant in Moscow, announced at a public discussion of the work that he had read it with "great intensity, eagerness, and enthusiasm. I read it in a few evenings, never putting it down. I skipped all my classes at technical school—I skipped everything so that I could finish the book more quickly." Bryskin's explanation for what he found so compelling in the book echoed that of another worker, Rozhnova. "When I read Gladkov's novel," she claimed, "its heroes reminded me of the people whom I meet all the time at the plant. I've had the opportunity to meet guys who absolutely don't take anything into account—not their time, not their health—they just work, organize, and lead their brigades, relieving others at work in order to help. And when you read Gladkov's novel, you are simply stunned by how much Gladkov was able to get into the consciousness of this sort of person." A third worker, Gurevich, added that although Gladkov's novel was at least nominally oriented around a single, far-off construction site, its appeal was much more broad, whether at the Stalin plant or others like it. According to him, the novel boasted "a broad, generalized character, insofar as Dnieperstroy is a typical example of socialist construction during the first Five-Year Plan. And the types of characters who are highlighted in the work are characteristic of all those involved in socialist construction."[28] Put another way, Gladkov had endowed his protagonists with a distillation of all the qualities that distinguished the Soviet working class, producing an array of quintessential role models and labor heroes.

Audiences not only read such works of fiction attentively, but tended to express their reactions to the books in the political terms in which they were written or reviewed. Bryskin, for instance, virtually quoted Ilin, the editor of *People of the Stalingrad Tractor Factory*, as he described his enthusiasm for *Energy*. "This book didn't grip me because of some daring subject or a plot twist, nor because I wanted to know what would happen to the wreckers." It was, instead, the protagonists' "character-types" that had attracted and held his interest.[29] In Molochko's case, he reported enjoying A. Kron's play *Rifle* because of the proactive way in which it dealt with the issue of reforming criminals and street children. He found S. Basko's *Amelka* to be much less satisfying as an artistic work due to its inability to satisfy the same criteria. "The book has a lot of political mistakes," Molochko wrote. "Basko doesn't depict anything from socialist construction—only the personal life of a 'very poor' young railway watchman. The ending is extremely unsuccessful. These days, we would have been a lot more interested to learn about how the boy was rehabilitated."[30] Evgeny Dobrenko contends that this sort of such political engagement with fiction was one of the hallmarks of Socialist Realism's "ideal" reader.[31]

As successful as works by Ostrovsky, Sholokhov, and Gladkov were, another, older example of the genre—Furmanov's *Chapaev*—rivaled their popularity, especially after the Vasiliev brothers released their cinematic adaptation of the book.[32] Shortly after the film's première, Stalin asked Shumiatsky how *Chapaev* was being reviewed in the press, apparently concerned that it should reach the broadest possible audience. When Shumiatsky replied that several newspapers had responded to the film in either lukewarm or critical terms, Stalin personally called Mekhlis at *Pravda* in order to have his paper print an immediate corrective. "Critics," the general secretary chided, "need to learn how to review correctly and not write incorrect things, especially about such an enormously talented and sensible film."[33] A truly mass-appeal feature, *Chapaev* quickly set records for ticket sales and sold-out movie houses —upwards of 50 million tickets were purchased for the film during the mid-1930s alone. A. T. Marian, a rural activist, wrote in his diary in euphoric terms about the film's effect on his comrades in early 1935:

> February 23. I took a hundred members of the [village] youth to Tiraspol. There they saw the film *Chapaev*. The impression was indescribable. Our audience saw in Chapaev their own peasant fellow, who conquers everyone with his fearlessness, bravery, ability to fight, and his ability to organize Red Army troops and lead them into battle. In so doing, he becomes a threat to the White Guard generals. Vasily Ivanovich, Commissar Furmanov, Petka, and Annushka have become heroes for our youth, who greeted an array of moments in the film with loud, approving applause.[34]

Shumiatsky spoke of this enthusiasm in society-wide terms, claiming that *Chapaev* was so popular that almost as many adults were quoting lines from the film as schoolchildren were playing "Reds vs. Whites" on playgrounds, courtyards, and side streets all across the country.[35] And if some of these adolescent "Chapaev Assaults" are known to have occasionally spiraled out of control, more innocent versions of the game would be enacted and reenacted deep into the decade.[36]

Other films, such as F. M. Ermler's *Peasants,* also proved to be popular—and often in ways that dovetailed with Soviet newspaper headlines.[37] A drama about political vigilance, *Peasants* followed the swine

Fig. 10: Newspaper sketch of crowds in front of a movie house for a showing of *Chapaev*. From *Vecherniaia Moskva*, September 23, 1934, 1.

breeder Gerasim Platonovich from his work on a collective farm and his marriage to a local activist to his eventual exposure as an undercover kulak saboteur and murderer. According to *Pravda*'s coverage of one post-screening discussion on the Black Sea coast, audience members correctly gauged *Peasants* to be a cautionary tale not only about the latent kulak threat in the countryside, but about the capacity of such concealed class enemies to manipulate local officials and other representatives of the Soviet order.[38] As one peasant named Privalov noted, "the struggle for a better life and collective farm prosperity demands caution. The enemy is tricky about masking himself. He is quiet and mild-mannered. Haven't there been instances, after all, when the enemy was even able to use certain former Red Partisans for his own devices?" Privalov and his comrades were quick to speculate about how they might detect even the most cleverly hidden wreckers in the future. They also proved to be harsh and unforgiving in relation to Varvara, the activist who allowed herself to be deceived by the enemy. In the end, they concluded, the only real hero in the film was Nikolai Mironovich, the head of a local machine-tractor station's political department. Particularly admirable was his ability to relate to his peasant neighbors in unassuming, earthy terms while not compromising his ideologically informed sense of vigilance or his willingness to subordinate self-interest for the good of the collective.[39] Summarizing their general impressions, another audience of collective farmers near Moscow wrote a group letter to Ermler commending him for his film: "Your picture will summon collective farmers to a new struggle for Bolshevik collective farms, for collective farmers' prosperity, and for culture, cleanliness, steam baths, and barbershops—for the bright new life that we owe to the communist party and our beloved leader, C[omrade] Stalin!"[40] Soviet audiences, in other words, proved willing to allow the popular press to connect even the most specific films to the broader cause of societal mobilization.

Dzigan's *We Are from Kronshtadt* benefited from a massive publicity campaign surrounding its spring 1936 release. Tickets sold so fast in urban areas that it was reportedly necessary to buy them days in advance. In its first week, the film drew 307,000 people from the Soviet capital alone; literally all of Moscow was said to be repeating its famous line: "So, who else wants a try at Petrograd?" In the same period, 120,000 people saw the film in Kiev, even though copies dubbed into Ukrainian were not yet available. In Minsk, where the film was showing only on a single screen, 5,000 people saw it on the first day of its release. Even in the small city of Stalino, it was seen by 20,000 people in 3 days, including some 3,500 from a local metallurgical plant. By 1939, the film had sold 30 million tickets.[41] Such numbers indicate enduring support, on both an official and an unofficial level. As the head of the political directorate of the Black Sea Fleet commented to *Pravda*: "The film demonstrates how poorly equipped and hungry fighters fought for their socialist motherland. The film instructs us on how we ought to love our motherland, which had given us such a joyous life. The film arms us and summons us to perform great feats." Some found it realistic enough to wonder whether it was really just a work of fiction. Students from the far north, for instance, wrote to a central newspaper asking for more information about Dzigan's transformative protagonist. "Could *Pionerskaia pravda* tell us whether C[omrade] Balashov is still alive and where he works at the present time? Does he know about our heroes' conquests and our joyous times?"[42] In other words, was the fictional Balashov aware of how his feat had contributed to the material and emotional well-being of Soviet society?

The fact that correspondence of this kind survives to the present day in Dzigan's personal archive suggests that the director took great interest in the mobilizational impact of his film. This impression is strengthened by the fact that he wrote a book about *We Are from Kronshtadt* after its release in order to share what he believed to be the secret of its popularity. Arguing that other recent films by directors such as Eisenstein and Dovzhenko—*Strike, Arsenal, Earth,* and *Aerograd*—had been too artistic to be accessible to broad audiences, he theorized that truly mass films had to balance four factors. "In a complete work," wrote Dzigan, a film's "ideological content, the grammar of its construction, its style, and its subject matter must always be maintained in a state of dialectical harmony." Excessive investment in a film's aesthetics, he implied, not only alienated audiences, but detracted from the feature's political meaning, emplotment, and *dramatis persona*.[43]

The Thirteen, which appeared right on the heels of *We Are from Kronshtadt,* suggests that Romm too found a formula that provided for accessibility without pandering. Audience surveys conducted in Leningrad reveal that people related to the contemporary subject of the film just as emotionally as they did to Dzigan's historical epic, even though the drama was set in the faraway wastes of Central Asia rather than the northern capital. Indeed, in some senses, audience members may have experienced an even more intimate connection to *The Thirteen*. Beker, a survey participant, referred to Romm's film as a powerful propaganda vehicle, inasmuch as "the film, with its harsh simplicity, produces an inexpressible impression. The fact that everyone turned out to be in the right place at the right time is far from coincidental. They are people of our era, [a time] that advances such brave and simple people [. . .]. This is a film that will mobilize the masses." Arstakhov, another member of the Leningrad audience, surpassed Beker in his judgment of *The Thirteen*'s pertinence to the interwar period. Stressing the effectiveness of the film's dramatic emplotment, he argued that its contemporary subject matter tended to blur the line between fiction and reality. "When only one was left of the initial thirteen," Arstakov reported, "and when the *basmachi* began their advance, the picture got so alarming that I am sure that if the action had taken place on the stage instead of on the screen, someone from the audience would certainly have jumped up and leapt behind the machine gun."[44] The idea of returning such a weapon to service probably occurred to Arstakhov after seeing Chapaev do something similar at the end of the 1934 blockbuster. But even if that is not the case, Arstakhov's statement demonstrates the degree to which *The Thirteen* caught and held his attention.

Documentary newsreels, although frequently neglected in studies of mass culture, also held considerable sway over their audiences.[45] This is demonstrated most visibly in the diary of the Komsomol activist Potemkin quoted above. Potemkin devoted considerable space in his daily entries during the mid-1930s to films he had seen, commenting excitedly about G. V. Aleksandrov's *Happy-Go-Lucky Fellows,* Raizman's *Fliers,* S. A. Gerasimov's *The Courageous Seven,* and Aleksandrov's *Circus.*[46] But perhaps his longest set of entries was reserved for a documentary film about Kirov that was hurriedly compiled for mass audiences after the party boss's assassination in late 1934. Beginning with general impressions, Potemkin noted that he and his fellow movie house audience members watched the documentary with rapt attention. "The film *Kirov* makes an extraordinarily valuable and strong impression. The enormous thirst of our leaders to study, live, and work is reflected in the enormous interest with which everyone in the auditorium holds their breath as they follow every action and movement of their beloved leaders." Such a reaction is not surprising, insofar as less than two months had passed since Kirov's dramatic martyrdom and the inquisition that followed. Potemkin then proceeded to detail his own reaction to the film, indicating the degree to which he regarded Kirov as a personal hero:

> I want to study as comprehensively as possible the turbulent, multi-faceted life of S. M. Kirov, who was so selflessly dedicated to the cause of world communist revolution. The documentary did not encompass all of his colossal activity in its entirety, but in each individual incident, insignificant though it may be in size, the seething energy of Mironych blazes forth. It is a graphic, living example of the Bolsheviks' work, leadership, and managerial concern.

Particularly memorable for the activist was the documentary's extended coverage of one of the party leader's speeches at a teachers' conference in Azerbaidzhan. According to Potemkin, Kirov's "genuinely revolutionary, emotionally enrapturing speech captivates the listener with its profound sincerity and precision, which enrich the meaning of words and reveal the enormous significance of the sentences. It convinces you that the oratorical art of the school of Lenin and Stalin is the most paramount, mighty, and delightful of the arts." Thrilled by the animated image of his idol, Potemkin was also struck again by the tragedy of his death. "In this film," he continues, "you reexperience the enormous loss that inflames the columns of intrepid workers, millions strong, and their unquenchable hatred toward our class enemies." Attempting to redeem the loss, he noted at the end of the diary entry that "you leave the auditorium rapt in an irrepressible, impetuous, headlong drive to work with Kirov's magical solicitude, initiative, and energy." Evidently, Potemkin returned again and again to his memories of Kirov, even showing his rhapsodic diary entry on the film to his sister. Her reaction —that he submit the review for publication in the local newspaper—indicates that his evaluation was very much in step with what others were saying about the film.[47]

Museums complemented the mobilizational power of the page, stage, and screen by providing another way for Soviet citizens to personally connect with objects and scenes from the recent past. The year 1935, for instance, saw 200,313 people tour Moscow's Museum of the Workers and Peasants' Red Army.[48] Some were drawn to the museum out of a sense of curiosity stimulated by other aspects of Soviet mass culture. An engineer named Maliuchikov, for instance, was quoted as saying that among the books that he had recently picked up, "I read *Chapaev* with avid interest. After that, I went to the Red Army museum several times and studied Chapaev and his comrades-in-arms—this book and its hero created an unforgettable impression for me."[49] Others came to the museum for help with the study of party history, inasmuch as textbooks— especially on the civil war—were virtually unavailable until the emergence of Gorky's *History of the Civil War in the USSR* late in 1935. A female student from the Timiriazev Academy testified to this function of the museum, noting on the pages of its guest book that "having visited the museum [. . .], we leave with a profound and deep feeling that will help us a lot in our further studies of the civil war and the history of the ACP(b)." Another visitor, a worker from the Yaroslavl station train yard in Moscow, placed a stronger emphasis on the personal dimensions of party history in his comment. "For us, the Museum of the

Workers and Peasants' Red Army is the best sort of political school imaginable, as it tells of the civil war and the heroic feats of our beloved leaders C[omrade] Stalin, C[omrade] Voroshilov, and C[omrade] Budenny."[50] A group of collective farmers from the Crimea summarized such sentiments in verse in the same guest book:

> Sing of our great motherland, heart of mine,
> Protect every border, valley, and mountain.
> There's never been greater news until this time—
> Than to be a patriot of the great Stalin![51]

Despite the emphasis that museum exhibits would seem to have placed on material culture, these inscriptions suggest that the overall message that the institution conveyed to its visitors concerned personal heroism and patriotic loyalty.

As impressive as the record of the Red Army museum was, it was surpassed during the following year by the Central Lenin Museum after its opening in May in central Moscow. A museum founded to aid in the study of party history as well as Marxism-Leninism, it hosted 2,000 visitors a day during its first month, overwhelming even this institution's generously outfitted resources. *Komsomolskaia pravda* quoted one of those exiting the museum—a librarian named N. S. Kolosova— as waxing rhapsodic about the degree to which the exhibits had helped her to grasp the party's purge of factionalists and opportunists from its ranks. "Visiting the museum," she said, "gave me much more than our numerous textbooks do. Here I was able to see with extraordinary clarity how the life of the proletarian revolution's leader flowed in the struggle for the party and for the purity of its line. The museum showed me how V. I. Lenin and I. V. Stalin's friendship stretches like a red thread through the entire history of the party." Visibly frustrated with the complexity of the party history curriculum, Kolosova found clarity and simplicity within the museum's exhibition halls. Perhaps this was due to its mapping of party history through the intertwining careers of just a handful of people. Perhaps it owed its accessibility to the fact that its reading of the Bolshevik experience was sequenced in a linear narrative and studded with an array of engaging visual aids and a minimum of text. Indeed, even when aspects of the presentation required the digestion of printed material, this often took the form of poster montages and leaflet displays, or party decrees and telegrams under glass bearing Lenin's and Stalin's signatures. As one visiting party history instructor confirmed, "in the museum I saw a mass of wonderful, extremely rare documents which will help me talk in new ways about the many interesting stages in our party's struggle."[52] Ultimately, the impact of the museum was apparently persuasive enough to convince many of its visitors of Lenin's and Stalin's inseparability during their struggle for the Bolshevik cause.[53] Only one other institution in Moscow—Lenin's mausoleum—could depict the leader in more graphic terms.[54]

Other sorts of mass mobilizational forums seem to have served as broad symbols of loyalty to the Soviet cause, even if nominally organized around narrow, specific issues. Parades, state funerals, and elections were the most curious in this regard, inasmuch as their topical specificity often appears to have been lost amid the loud celebration of patriotism during the 1930s.[55] May Day, for instance, originally commemorated the victims of Chicago's 1886 Haymarket massacre before becoming an occasion for socialists and anarchists worldwide to celebrate the cause of organized labor in the late nineteenth century. In Stalin's USSR, however, this holiday was gradually stripped of its spontaneity and class consciousness and transformed into a state celebration of Soviet power and military might. This is clear from Molochko's account of the annual celebration in his provincial town:

> we were standing on the street, watching the Red Army demonstration. The infantry marches by at attention, legs and arms moving in unison; the heavy weapons rumble across the bridge—here comes the artillery; the flyers march by; and then the cavalry with their sabers drawn. The sun reflects off these sabers, kissing them. Then some light tanks drive by [. . .]. Here is our strength. Here is our defense.[56]

The impression created by Molochko's diary entry is confirmed by a similar entry from the notebook of a Leningrad student, A. A. Aleksin, within which he describes an exchange he overheard between two members of the proletariat right after May Day. According to Aleksin, the conversation started with one complaining to the other about his fellow workers on the shop floor:

FIRST WORKER: If everyone is going to work like this . . . that'll be the end of Soviet power . . . Bandits will come and steal everything [. . .] That'll be the end of Soviet power.

SECOND WORKER: Grisha—Grisha, that's . . . you stop that talk. Don't you know what Soviet power is? It's a marble wall 350 feet high. It's not only smooth but lathered in soap as well . . . Go ahead, just try to climb to the top—there's no way to get even a foothold. Bandits? They'll gnash their teeth and give up.[57]

Intriguing here is how the second worker transformed the first worker's connection of Soviet power and labor productivity into a question of national defense. Other symbols associated with labor activism and world revolution were similarly skewed during this time. As Molochko noted in his diary after attending a pioneer ceremony, "at the gathering, [...] there was an orchestra from the musical studio. It was very joyous, and when they began playing a march—the 'Internationale'—your heart became really light and happy because you're living in the USSR."[58] This anthem, in other words, had ceased to bear any connection to the French Revolution or the world socialist movement and now evoked only patriotic, Soviet associations.

More conventional public events and celebrations likewise appear to have forfeited the opportunity to stress all but the most basic of political values. Military parades on February 23—Red Armyman's Day—and other occasions, provided an opportunity for the expression of patriotic sentiment, both within the ranks and throughout society at large.[59] Diaries of the period indicate that parades in Moscow, Leningrad, and the republican capitals on May Day, November 7, and other holidays also served to offer commoners a chance to see the country's civilian, party, and military leadership in person. For those on Red Square, the climax of any parade was catching sight of Stalin.[60] *Izvestia* confirmed that major crowds assembled in Kiev for a parade in the fall of 1935 following local military maneuvers in hope of a glimpse of notables from Voroshilov and Budenny to Postyshev and Kosior.[61] Close contact with such famous personalities in the provinces was at least as powerful, as Molochko describes in an account of Budenny's impromptu visit to Mogilev:

> More and more people gathered. I was pressed from all sides but didn't waver in the crush of people. Finally, the doors flew open and Semyon Mikhailovich [Budenny] came out of the buffet. The working people greeted him with thunderous applause and cries of "Hurrah!" He went to his car and then began to clap with everyone else [...]. It was a long time before the people were able to calm down, as the great joy of being able to gaze upon this legendary civil war hero literally blinded and deafened everyone.[62]

Both parades and these more intimate events were filmed, of course, in order to promote via newsreel the impression that party, state, and military leaders were not only popular, but accessible within society at large.

Molochko's reaction to seeing Budenny indicates that he and many of his contemporaries idolized members of the Soviet elite. Stalin, of course, was virtually deified by the mid-1930s, complicating public emulation of the role he played in Soviet public life. Others like Budenny, however, cultivated a more approachable image that appears to have to have enjoyed broad resonance on the mass level. M. I. Kalinin, too, enjoyed quite a following, largely due to his reputation as the USSR's "all-union peasant elder" (*vsesoiuznyi starosta*).[63] Dozens of other celebrated names from the ranks of the party and military, as well as industry, agriculture, science, and the arts, were also treated as heroes for veneration and emulation. Some ordinary Soviets appear to have regarded anyone with a civil war pedigree as a member of the Soviet Olympus.[64] Others idealized specific individuals on account of character traits that distinguished them from other members of the patriotic pantheon. Kirov, Voroshilov, Tukhachevsky, Yakir, and others all had their private followings.[65] Still others were lionized at the grassroots by professional constituencies, Red Army soldiers in the Far East saluting Bliukher, border guards hailing Yagoda, and so on. Fragmentary evidence suggests that party and military figures were embraced with greater frequency than labor heroes and other civilians, perhaps because their deeds were seen as more daring and patriotic, their speeches more dynamic, or their reputations more historic. In many cases, their steadfast service to the party and state was celebrated in greater detail than that of the rather one-dimensional miners, metal workers, and tractor drivers who tended to pass fleetingly across newspaper headlines during these years. Ultimately, these figures' conduct may simply have been considered more heroic than the frequently scorned Stakhanovites.[66] No matter what the precise reason, however, in the end, the propaganda state's emphasis on heroism and patriotic conduct resulted in the creation of several dozen genuinely popular personality cults in Soviet society during the mid-1930s.

Amid discussion of this propaganda coup, it would seem appropriate to question for a moment why this material on the page, stage, and silver screen appealed to audiences who had just witnessed firsthand the excesses of shock industrialization, agricultural collectivization, and dekulakization. Part of the likely answer stems from the compelling nature of positive heroes, the promise of the future, and the contemporary threat posed by enemies both at home and abroad. But another part of the answer has to do with the ubiquity of the party hierarchy's message within Soviet society during these years. As Jeffrey Brooks has noted in regard to Soviet journalism, a conspicuous lack of alternatives during the 1930s allowed official mass culture to dominate popular impressions of the Soviet experiment, not only among "friendly readers who had a stake in the system," but among great swaths of the apolitical and disengaged as well. Indeed, the official line "increasingly resembled what M. M. Bakhtin [. . .] called an 'authoritative discourse'" —"a 'monologic' discourse like religious dogma or accepted scientific truth" that assumes enough of a hegemonic role in society to define everyday reality and stifle disbelief among even the most critical thinkers.[67] Diaries of the period reflect this dynamic in their repetition of official mass culture's choice of lexicon and imagery, as do the amateur testimonials that ordinary Soviet citizens wrote for their local newspapers with titles like "Heroes of Our Time."[68] This also can explain why literally everyone knew who Korchagin was and why so many could reproduce Balashov's quip from the end of *We Are from Kronshtadt* word-for-word.

This hegemonic effect of Soviet mass culture was heightened by the way that Agitprop ran study circles and party education courses. According to official instructions, grassroots-level agitators were not only to read lectures and lead discussions, but they were also to collect scrapbooks of newspaper cuttings and decorate bulletin boards with articles and pictures of leading members of the Soviet Olympus.[69] They were to chaperone their tutees on field trips to museums, parades, local landmarks, and the theater.[70] Advice columns in the press instructed them not only to keep up with contemporary literature, drama, and cinema, but also to pay close attention to what their students were reading. They were to know which authors were to be included on recommended reading lists (Gorky, Sholokhov, Ostrovsky, Tolstoy, Furmanov, Serafimovich, Fadeev, and Avdeenko, as well as Pushkin, A. S. Griboedov, N. V. Gogol, N. A. Nekrasov, and L. N. Tolstoy); equally important, they needed to know which names were not to be included on such lists (S. A. Yesenin, A. Bely, F. M. Dostoevsky, etc.).[71] In other words, when properly set up, these groups excelled at inculcating specific values in their participants.

Of course, as noted above, these groups were were not generally run well enough to fully satisfy all the party's expectations. Still, many did manage to focus on the virtues of heroism and patriotic service to the motherland—concepts that were accessible and engaging. That said, these themes tended to overshadow less appealing and more arcane aspects of the curriculum rather than provide an entry-point into more difficult subject matter. In a 1934–1935 annual report from the Leningrad Military District, for instance, officials confessed that political education was producing mixed results. Almost all units reported that within the general curriculum, the theme "Our Motherland —the USSR" tended to be the most readily mastered. Much weaker were topics related to the civil war, Soviet nationality policy, and the international workers' movement.[72] Officials in the North Caucasus Military District reported much the same thing, noting that the majority of Red Army soldiers and officers performed well in classes focusing on the Soviet motherland, the USSR's geopolitical position on the world scene, and major issues concerning party policy. Less satisfactory was work related to the civil war, foreign revolutionary movements, and the nuances of party history, especially its struggle with internal enemies.[73] These results also were mirrored in a major report from the Belorussian Military District. There, a commander named Rutkovsky turned out to be so ignorant when it came to party history that he was incapable of answering a single question correctly. For example, when asked what the relationship of the Bolshevik party had been toward the Provisional Government after the February 1917 revolution, he asserted that the party had conducted itself "loyally." Only the traitor Zinoviev, averred Rutkovsky, had come out against the government. Mikhnitsky, Rutkovsky's colleague, proved to be slightly better prepared, but still stumbled over how to explain the concept of dual power and the essence of Lenin's April Theses. Worse, he apparently believed that the party had focused its efforts between the two revolutions of 1917 on convening a constituent assembly, somehow forgetting about the struggle with other socialist parties and the Provisional Government that culminated with its seizure of power. Performance within the district's ranks was little better; troops floundered when quizzed on issues regarding the civil war, the party's struggle with counterrevolution, nationality policy, and the origins of the Comintern.[74]

In sum, then, this report concluded that the only areas of satisfactory work concerned topics such as "Our Motherland—the USSR." The reasons for such selective success are fairly predictable. First, an increasingly conventional interpretation of Soviet patriotism in mass culture and education had prioritized domestic issues over internationalist ideals. Second, this theme was reinforced by newfound attention to Soviet heroes who distinguished themselves in defense of the USSR. Third, grassroots-level activists and agitators found it impossible to complement material on these subjects with equally compelling propaganda on party history. The end result was that if aspects of official indoctrination efforts had improved dramatically since the late 1920s, key dimensions related to party ideology and history remained weak and ineffective.

What, then, was the overall effect of this inspirational but unbalanced official line? Between 1950 and 1951, scores of Soviet refugees, former POWs and ex-*Ostarbeiter* laborers were interviewed about the persuasive appeal of the Soviet propaganda state. One former Komsomol member testified that the mobilizational campaigns of the early 1930s had had an important effect on his sense of self and membership in Soviet society:

> In spite of material difficulties, such as the constant food shortage which was particularly acute at this time, neither I nor the other young people around me had any anti-Soviet feelings. We simply found in the heroic tension involved in the building of a new world an excuse for all the difficulties [. . .]. The atmosphere of undaunted struggle in a common cause —the completion of the factory, engaged our imagination, roused our enthusiasm, and drew us into a sort of front-line world where difficulties were overlooked or forgotten.[75]

Many things can explain this fearless sense of enthusiasm amid the storm of industrialization and collectivization: youthful energy, ideological passion, a non-materialist sense of ethics, and so on. But Soviet mass culture also played a major role with its celebration of patriotism and its official pantheon of heroes, providing a higher goal, an ideological code of honor, and a sense of belonging to offset the hardships and discontent of the period. As another former Komsomol member noted, "everything around me helped to foster this feeling: the bright and lively movies shown at the time, the gay songs that were popular, and the feats of Soviet airmen, scientists, and Arctic explorers, which captured the imagination of the young." Continuing, he added:

> I had faith in the Party and government leadership which had abolished food rationing, had begun to build large numbers of schools, "palaces of culture," youth clubs, and children's technical exhibitions, and had given the traditional Christmas tree back to the young ones. I believed in the leaders who had made it possible for the best men of the country—men such as [V. P.] Chkalov, [V. K.] Kokkinaki, [M. M.] Gromov, Shmidt, and others—to display their talents and bring glory to our homeland. In other words, I had faith in Stalin and his comrades-in-arms.[76]

Famous memoirists of this generation like K. M. Simonov and G. K. Zhukov concur about the role that Soviet patriotism and heroes played in galvanizing their belief in the Soviet experiment.[77] In many senses, it is impossible to overstate the contribution that this propaganda made to mobilizational efforts in the USSR during these years.

By 1935–1936 then, the ideological establishment's exchange of abstract, schematic, and obscure sloganeering for a new sort of propaganda had begun to have a transformative affect on Soviet society. The party hierarchy was clearly aware of the success of the new line, insofar as it invested more and more in these new agitational genres with each year that passed. Parallel campaigns against vestiges of the 1920s' line—the "Pokrovsky school" in history, "vulgar sociology" in literary criticism, and "formalism" in the arts—reinforced the accomplishments and accessibility of the new line.[78] Ultimately, even ordinary Soviet citizens appear to have sensed the sea change in propaganda and public opinion itself—something visible in a letter that an anonymous correspondent wrote to the Menshevik editors of *Sotsialistichesky vestnik* in Paris in 1935:

> They talk about it in Soviet institutions, factory smoking rooms, student dormitories, and commuter trains. . . . it's a sense of *national pride. Russia* has again become a Great Power and even such powerful states as France desire her friendship [. . .]. Narrow-minded bureaucrats in Soviet institutions who have long been quiet now confidently talk of national patriotism, of Russia's historic mission, and of the reviving of the old Franco-Russian alliance, [notions which] are greeted approvingly by their Communist directors [. . .]. There is clear panic among Communist idealists.[79]

Six months later, another correspondent provided an even more nuanced analysis of the mood within Soviet society. "It is entirely too early, if you please, to talk about genuine patriotism among the peasants," the pseudonymous "X" wrote. "It's another thing completely in the city, however, among the intelligentsia and bureaucratic groups. Here, the patriotism is genuine, having matured especially fast after the victory of fascism in Germany. All here have become patriots of the Soviet way of life."[80]

7   The Murder of the Usable Past

BY ALL RIGHTS, propaganda concerning party history and Stalin's personality cult should have played a prominent role in the celebration of heroism and patriotic valor that emerged during the early-to-mid-1930s. Dozens of books patterned after *The History of Plants and Factories* series appeared during these years, after all, flanked by novels like *How the Steel Was Forged* and films like *Chapaev*. But while much of this torrential wave of literary and celluloid agitation can be said to have popularized party leaders and advanced the personality cult, the fact remains that these themes lacked a central narrative that could have provided focus and context for the official line. A central dysfunction of the party's ideological establishment, this failure to advance a single, systematic message designed to shape popular beliefs, attitudes and behavior ultimately blunted some of the potential of Soviet propaganda during the mid-1930s.[1]

Blame for this shortcoming, ironically, lies with the party ideologists themselves, who spent much of the early-to-mid-1930s engaged in foot-dragging and resistance. And no sooner had these party historians and propagandists finally begun to consider retooling than much of the usable past was suddenly swept away during the years of the Great Terror. This chapter investigates these ideologists' slow acceptance of the newly populist nature of Soviet propaganda—a dynamic field of persuasive expression that by the mid-1930s had enlisted virtually the whole creative intelligentsia. It also examines the devastating toll that the purges exacted not only on the cultural, artistic, and ideological elites, but on their new modes of mobilizational propaganda as well.

As counterintuitive as it seems, party historians and ideologists repeatedly fell out of step with party propaganda during the early-to-mid-1930s, failing to adopt and embrace new paraliterary techniques that would have allowed them to popularize their work on Bolshevik history and the Stalin cult in officially prescribed terms. In hindsight it is not entirely clear whether this failure was a sin of omission or commission. Some probably never quite grasped what they were supposed to be doing, while others may have considered the celebration of heroes and patriotism to be sensationalistic pandering best left to the mass press. In any case, it was only in 1935 that the party hierarchy decided to take a more direct role in its search for a usable past, meeting several times to discuss the problem, issue advice, appoint new editorial brigades, and pass resolutions calling for improved pedagogical strategies. Leading ideologists then publicized this agenda in the press[2] and convened a series of conferences to address the problem, first with consultants from the Institute of the Red Professors and the academic subcommittee of the Central Executive Committee, and then with provincial propagandists and agitators.[3]

At first, it must have seemed as if this heightened engagement would produce results. Knorin, Yaroslavsky, and Pospelov compiled a major new manuscript—their *Popular Textbook*—and the IMEL appeared ready to deliver a similarly promising two-volume instructional aid for propagandists and party activists. Neither production managed to live up to expectations, however. The IMEL brigade stalled during the fall of 1935, while Knorin, Yaroslavsky, and Pospelov's mistitled 900-page volume failed to win Stalin's endorsement later that winter. These setbacks, if in some ways quite unexpected, were in other respects quite predictable. Almost five years after Stalin's letter to *Proletarskaia revoliutsia*, the party hierarchy had placed responsibility for its new initiative in the hands of three people who had repeatedly failed to deliver results in the past. True, all were quintessential insiders: Knorin had just been appointed deputy chief at Agitprop; Yaroslavsky sat on several prominent editorial boards and the Party Control Commission; and Pospelov edited *Bolshevik* alongside the other two. But despite such proximity to power, none of them had ever shown any enthusiasm in their historical work for the heroes, patriotism, or the dramatic style of storytelling that now offered hope for a real mobilizational breakthrough.

Of course, the troika was hardly alone in its recalcitrance—many party historians refused to recognize the advantages of this approach to party propaganda during these years.[4] Other members of the field, however, proved more willing to consider the innovation. In January 1936, for instance, the historians B. A. Romanov and S. N. Valk wrestled with the issue of accessibility as they discussed plans for a new textbook on the history of the USSR. Sensing their lack of experience in the area, they even entertained the notion of recruiting the novelist Tolstoy and children's author K. I. Chukovsky to aid in the construction of an appropriate narrative.[5] Later that March, as *Pravda* announced an open competition for this textbook contract, it issued an explicit call for professional writers to apply their talents to the project:

> [this] competition, with its demand for an artistic narrative, is addressed in part to our masters of the creative word. Could there possibly be a more worthwhile or honorable task for a Soviet writer or artist than participating in the creation of a text that will become the standard reference book for our young Soviet generation? The great English writer Dickens wrote his *A Child's History of England* with love and enthusiasm. H. G. Wells wrote a book on world history. The historical value of these works has never been highly rated by bourgeois historiography, but the language in which they are written is unparalleled. Pushkin never considered his work *The History of Pugachev* [sic] to be irrelevant; Tolstoy himself wrote the textbooks for his school at Yasnaia Poliana.[6]

M. A. Bulgakov, among others, expressed interest in writing such a textbook before returning to his more famous exegesis on the Soviet experiment, *The Master and Margarita*.[7]

Party historians, unlike their state historian colleagues, were never subjected to such a humiliating competition, largely due to the sensitive nature of the subject that they were expected to discuss.[8] That said, the party hierarchy clearly expected them to take advantage of the new trends in mass culture and produce work that was both accessible and populist.[9] After the twin textbook fiascos of late 1935, however, confusion again reigned within the ideological establishment. Knorin, Yaroslavsky, and Pospelov mothballed their *Popular Textbook* rather than attempt to rework it into something more satisfactory. Knorin and Pospelov returned to their duties at Agitprop; Yaroslavsky likewise resumed his various responsibilities, devoting all the spare time he could find to updating his older textbooks—chiefly *The History of the ACP(b)* (last published in early 1935) and *A Short History of the ACP(b)* (last published in 1931)—to reflect the new stress on accessible, populist storytelling.[10] Similarly exhausted, the leadership of the IMEL also paused to reevaluate its projects. The brigade working on the two-volume text for propagandists and party activists—now under Popov's de facto leadership—pushed back its deadline by a year to December 1936.[11] More dramatically, the books were literally closed on the brigade that had been working on the institute's four-volume scholarly history since 1932.[12]

Of course, this attrition did not make party history any easier to write. Tracing the Bolsheviks' trajectory from the prerevolutionary underground through 1917 and into the mid-1930s, the remaining authors struggled not only with issues of style, tone, and language, but with how to combine abstract theory with a concrete chronological progression of events. Balance too was important, for if the prerevolutionary period was easier to write about, the postrevolutionary experience was increasingly prioritized by the party hierarchy. Of equal concern was the construction of a narrative which was not only animated, but which would connect the more arcane, esoteric, and abstruse dimensions of the party's past to the broader contours of Russo-Soviet history on either side of the revolutionary divide. Also difficult must have been the challenges associated with the continual renegotiation of Stalin's role that the evolving personality cult required—something which not only complicated depictions of the general secretary, but which hampered efforts to publicize a diverse variety of other Bolshevik heroes as well.

Such concerns, however, must have seemed almost academic after the onset of the Great Terror in the late summer of 1936. Although the first stage of the purges chiefly concerned long-time pariahs like the left "Trotskyite" oppositionists Zinoviev and Kamenev, their kangaroo-court ordeal at the First Moscow Show Trial produced coerced testimony alleging that party and state institutions were also rife with traitors. Suspicion focused in particular on apparently loyal ex-Trotskyites like Piatakov and Radek, who had held prominent positions in Soviet state and society after recanting their association with the left opposition years earlier. Rumors and forced confessions quickly ensnared scores of other former leftists within this second make-believe Trotskyite conspiracy, leading to new waves of repression. Rightist leaders like Bukharin, Rykov, and Tomsky were also implicated by these developments—something exacerbated by Tomsky's decision to commit suicide upon hearing the news. In early January 1937, Piatakov, Radek, and an array of other high-ranking former leftists were induced to confess to outrageous crimes during the Second Moscow Trial. Bukharin, Rykov, and the former right opposition were again mentioned as conspirators in this trial—accusations that received further development in the tense environment of the party's February-March Central Committee Plenum that followed. Here, Stalin also fed the flames by calling upon ordinary citizens to aid the "responsible organs" in uncovering treachery within the ranks of the party, Komsomol, Comintern, Red Army, secret police, and state bureaucracy.[13] By the spring of 1937, denunciation from below and accelerated repression from above had begun to tear gaping rents in the fabric of the Soviet elite, on both the left and the right.

Arrest of the best and brightest within party and state institutions—people like Miliutin, Chaplin, Ya. E. Rudzutak, N. K. Antipov, F. G. Khodzhaev, and A. I. Ikramov—not only dealt a punishing blow to the establishment, but cut deeply into the new Soviet Olympus as well. Heroes turned into villains overnight, causing propagandists to scramble to pull down portraits in public places and strike the names of the fallen from the historical record. In a pattern that was to repeat over and over after each wave of the purge, books were removed from circulation and entire volumes rewritten due to their now unacceptable celebration of recently exposed "enemies of the people." A good example concerns a manuscript that was being developed around the Moscow metro's construction agency, Metrostroy, as a part of *The History of Plants and Factories* series. S. V. Zhuravlev notes that although this volume was slated to be a centerpiece of Gorky's series, "work on the book was undermined in 1936. Mass repressions, beginning in Metrostroy, affected the members of the editorial board under Kosarev and likewise the best and most active of the workers, specialists, and construction leadership —that is, precisely those people who were supposed to 'populate' this fundamental book on the history of the metro."[14] This same phenomenon would repeat itself over and over with propaganda projects ranging from industrial zones like Magnitogorsk to Moscow's Stalin Auto Plant.[15] Mature projects revolving around the histories of Moscow's Bolshevik Factory and Leningrad's Kirov Works proved impossible to complete. Completed volumes like *The History of the Karl Marx Factory* and the history of October railroad turned out to be unsuitable for release. And already-released titles had to be recalled—1936's volume on the Yagoda Children's Labor Commune, for instance, was removed from circulation after its namesake's arrest in early March 1937.[16] Averbakh's fall doomed the popular *People of the Stalingrad Tractor Factory* and contributed to the fate of the infamous 1934 volume on the Belomor Canal, already crippled by the disappearance of other brigade members and many of the book's NKVD "heroes."[17] Similar problems stalled four of the five projected volumes of the *People of the Second Five-Year Plan* series and several parallel projects on subjects such as the history of the Petrograd Soviet.[18] On January 31, 1938, the entire Plants and Factories publishing house was shut down and its archive seized, terminating work on over a hundred projects in various stages of completion.[19] Fortunately for Gorky, his death in 1936 spared him from having to witness this ignominious end to his revolutionary dream.

Other projects outside *The History of Plants and Factories'* rubric also collapsed as arrests consumed their *dramatis personae*. Long-planned histories of famous local party organizations were abandoned, to be revived as sterile institutional histories only in the 1960s. Histories of the Komsomol, too, became impossible to write.[20] A. V. Shestakov's important 1937 USSR history textbook for the public schools required revisions only months after its publication when Bubnov, the Commissar of Education, was arrested.[21] Volin and Ingulov's 1935 *Political Grammar,* rereleased in 1937 to account for the purge of former rightists, was similarly jeopardized by Ingulov's own arrest that December. The number of books affected by this mayhem is legion.

But if the outset of total chaos in party propaganda can be dated to the February-March 1937 plenum, the celebration of Red Army heroes was curtailed later that May by the bloody purge of the officer corps that began with the so-called Tukhachevsky Affair. Prominent titles such as the second edition of S. Ye. Rabinovich's Red Army textbook on the civil war and L. A. Kassil's *Parade on Red Square* were among 1937's many victims.[22] El Lisitsky's famous *Workers and Peasants' Red*

Army disappeared from use at the same time, due to its full-page portraits of Tukhachevsky, Gamarnik, Yakir, Alksnis, Eideman, Uborevich, and Khalepsky, as did the glossy exhibition catalogue from the 15th anniversary of the Red Army.[23] Further waves of terror within the ranks —particularly the arrests of Yegorov and Bliukher—sealed the fate of Ingulov and Volin's *Political Grammar* and just about brought down Shestakov's textbook as well.[24]

Of course, while the sagas involving these texts and albums are instructive, all pale in comparison to the fiasco surrounding the monumental first volume of *The History of the Civil War in the USSR*, published in 1935. Authorities were forced to pull this famous tome from circulation and off library shelves in early 1937 after it was found to be littered with the names of Old Bolsheviks who had vanished during the ongoing purges.[25] When a second edition of the book finally appeared in 1938, the original text had been stripped of numerous photographs, illustrations, and some twenty-seven pages of text, not to mention all passing references to fallen luminaries like Piatakov and Rykov. Indeed, nearly half of the fifty-odd heroes in the first edition either were now classified as "enemies of the people" or had been stricken entirely from the narrative.[26] Beria's book on the history of Bolshevism in the Transcaucasus ran into similar problems, requiring rerelease in late 1936, and then again in 1937 and 1938.[27]

Responsibility for keeping track of such problems lay with Glavlit, the Main Directorate for Artistic and Literary Affairs, which since 1922 had supervised not only prepublication editing, but post-hoc censorship as well.[28] This latter duty, which consisted of recalling books and blacking-out text and pictures from still-circulating volumes, was governed by an ever-expanding list of banned titles and authors that Glavlit distributed every ten days to its subordinates at provincial printing presses, bookstores, and libraries. These bulletins were typically accompanied by boilerplate declaring that "any portrait, statement or mention of any of the above-listed individuals is subject to seizure, whether photographic, lithographic, done in oil on wood, canvas or fabric; embossed on medals or tokens; or contained in photomontages or negatives on glass or celluloid." Some such formulas included other sorts of artistic representation like statuary as well, making Glavlit the USSR's chief watchdog throughout the realm of mass culture.[29]

Armed with such lists (unofficially known as the Talmud), even the most humble Glavlit staffers on the ground enjoyed sweeping powers to interdict the circulation of material judged to be compromised. Hardest hit were the libraries. One former Soviet citizen remembered years later that "the books were constantly checked" at such institutions during the purges.

> Suppose a Party man was arrested. The catalog cards of his books would immediately be taken out [of all public card catalogs]. That this was being done would be checked by secret investigators. In the library there was a secret room in the cellar where the banned books were placed. A Party worker worked there. Some of the books were banned because they showed Stalin and Trotsky together. Others were banned because in a photograph Stalin's sleeve had a fold in it that could be interpreted as a swastika, etc. Some books were banned because they had a preface, say, by Zinoviev. Since all the Republics had to publish political literature in their respective languages, this meant a multitude of books.[30]

Control of old material, in other words, was as axiomatic to the propaganda state as the coordinated release of new material.

Highly bureaucratic, Glavlit claimed to systematize and rationalize the activities of its subordinate censors on a union-wide scale, enforcing tight, consistent control over the USSR's 70,000 libraries and reading rooms while precluding the debilitating effects of arbitrariness and human error. At least theoretically, the system was designed to guarantee control over what little remained of the Soviet public sphere. But as efficient as the Glavlit system was, it lost its grasp of the situation in the spring and summer of 1937 after the mass purge of the party and military got underway. Wave after wave of repression stretched Glavlit's analytical abilities to the breaking point; its lists first fell days and then weeks behind in their identification of material to sequester or destroy. Many local activists, agitators, librarians, and even censors, anxious to avoid accusations of complacency or trafficking in "counterrevolutionary contraband," responded to this crisis by preemptively purging their collections of everything mentioning fallen heroes even before Glavlit itself issued the order.[31] Enormous amounts of material, including books and periodicals containing only passing mention of enemies of the people, were consumed during the chaos: everything from flimsy propaganda pamphlets and framed classroom portraits to textbooks, encyclopedias, party congress stenograms, and the collected works of people as prominent as Lenin, Voroshilov, and Frunze.[32] An internal investigation at Glavlit in October 1937 under Mekhlis confirmed that the institution had lost control over censorship activities on the mass level. According to Mekhlis, although the Glavlit administration was trying to regain the initiative, its choice of tactics was only making matters worse. Apparently, the agency was now instructing its personnel on the ground to remove material from libraries, bookstores, and reading rooms on the basis of a crudely compiled list of arrested authors rather than a more careful analysis of the questionable volumes' content. Not only did this approach to censorship accelerate the removal of still-valuable literature from circulation, but it also unintentionally disseminated damning information on the scale of the purges.[33]

Grasping the dimensions of this crisis only in December 1937, the party hierarchy attempted to limit the Terror's destruction of its indoctrinational infrastructure by purging the Glavlit administration at the same time that it reinforced the central censorial administration's authority over its personnel in the field. Now, local staffers were forbidden to sequester print, celluloid, or representational propaganda without explicit authorization from the party hierarchy. The arbitrary withdrawal of books, periodicals, film, and artwork not listed in Glavlit's bulletins was also no longer to be allowed, even when material in circulation seemed compromised by the presence of names or likenesses of known enemies of the people. Even books making prominent mention of disgraced heroes were to remain in circulation until they could be replaced by newly sanitized editions.[34] These orders, while understandable from the point of view of central officials aghast at the destruction of entire libraries, offered little or no advice about how to retain such materials for popular use without violating standards of political vigilance and orthodoxy. Were offending pictures and text to be blackened out? Excised? Pasted over by newsprint or pictures cut from magazines? The dangerous ambiguity surrounding these orders explains why it should come as no surprise to learn that they were routinely ignored in the field, allowing the nearly wholesale destruction of compromised propaganda materials to continue unabated until the end of the Terror.[35]

Even before chaos engulfed Glavlit, people like Yaroslavsky who were involved in the development of new textbooks must have looked on helplessly at the censors' ruthless destruction of historical literature. How could anyone compile a grand narrative on party history under such conditions? At first, it's likely that they attempted to confront the challenge that the Terror posed to their work by carefully removing mention of individual party members as they fell.[36] In time, however, the randomness of the purge revealed this to be an exercise in futility— there was no way to anticipate who would be the next to be arrested, and this transformed the editorial process into a nightmare of never-ending proportions. Aware of the penalty for allowing enemies of the people into print and unwilling to gamble on their ability to predict who within the party would survive the Terror, party historians changed tactics and simply deleted from their narratives mention of all individuals who were not either fixtures of Stalin's inner-most circle (e.g., Molotov, Kaganovich, Voroshilov, Yezhov), long-dead martyrs (Frunze, Dzerzhinsky, Kirov), members of the Soviet Olympus (Stakhanov, Bliukher, Molokov, Chkalov, I. D. Papanin), or known enemies of the people (Trotsky, Zinoviev, Kamenev).[37]

At first glance, this grim methodology appears to have supplied party historians with an effective way of coping with the chaos of the purges. Further examination, however, indicates that the superficiality of this approach probably only heightened its adherents' peril. First, it forced party historians to abandon all pretense of creating an animated story-line populated by a diverse variety of inspirational heroes—precisely the sort of usable past that the party hierarchy was demanding. Second, it did nothing to resolve their confusion over the nature of the official line. Stymied once again, Yaroslavsky and his colleagues looked in vain to the party press and officials like Stetsky for any hint of where the leadership was headed. Archival documents, however, testify only to ideological confusion and paralysis.

Predictably, as the Terror mounted, so too did calls from all levels of the party organization for a canonical text that could serve as an almanac or reference book in troubled times.[38] Stalin stoked this sense of ideological panic in his speech at the February-March plenum, where he blamed the rank-and-file's lack of vigilance on their poor understanding of the official line. "Master Bolshevism," he commanded. Prioritize "cadres' political education."[39] These demands contributed not only to the tension in the air, but to a formal resolution calling for further educational reforms. Stalin capitalized on this mandate shortly after the plenum's conclusion, forwarding to the Politburo a proposal for a new two-tier system of "Party" and "Leninist" courses for discussion in early April.[40]

Amid the frenzy of denunciation and arrest that followed the plenum, Yaroslavsky hurriedly submitted to Stalin a new draft of his *Short History* that he had spent the past year revising. Stalin asked Stetsky to take a look at it, and the latter promptly submitted the manuscript to a blistering critique.[41] Stalin took a close look at Stetsky's review and then rescheduled the Politburo's discussion of educational reforms in order to first sketch out his own broad critique of recent work on party history. A terse memorandum that showed no awareness of the effect that the purges were having on the field, it did outline what the general secretary considered to be the literature's overall defects. "Our textbooks on party history are unsatisfactory for three main reasons," Stalin wrote. "They are unsatisfactory because they present party history without connection to the country's history; because a simple discussion of events and facts in the struggle with tendencies [in the party] is given without the necessary Marxist explanations; and because [the texts] suffer from an incorrect formulation and an incorrect periodization of events." Continuing, Stalin noted that particularly the history of factionalism required more treatment: already a major theme of the Bolshevik experience, this was now to become its defining feature. The purpose of this focus was obviously twofold, providing a historically informed explanation for the ongoing purge of concealed enemies within the party while at the same time justifying Stalin's demands for heightened political vigilance. Much more attention was also to be given to prerevolutionary Russian political and economic history, which would inform the context and imperative of otherwise obscure interparty debates. Accounts of the postrevolutionary period were to be similarly bolstered. According to Stalin, every chapter and major division of these texts was to be prefaced with pertinent information on Russo-Soviet state history in order to ensure that the books would not read like some "light and unintelligible story about bygone affairs." He then concluded his memorandum with a table that laid out in unambiguous terms what he considered to be the correct periodization of the party's history.[42]

Stalin circulated this memorandum among his colleagues in the Politburo and then assembled the group for a meeting in mid-April, with Knorin, Popov, Mekhlis, B. M. Tal, and A. I. Ugarov. Two resolutions emerged from their discussion. The first established a commission to organize the general secretary's new two-tiered training courses and supply them with curricular materials.[43] The second, on party history itself, ordered Knorin, Yaroslavsky, and Pospelov to again join forces in order to write the flagship text for the upper tier of the new educational system. Knorin and Yaroslavsky were also to update and streamline their older textbooks for use in the lower tier and elsewhere in society. Officially freed of all other commitments, the troika was given four months to produce a breakthrough.[44]

Few traces of Knorin, Yaroslavsky, and Pospelov's collaboration survive from early that summer—something that indicates that an array of factors may have interfered with their work. Yaroslavsky had been upset by Stetsky's review of his *Short History* and focused closely on the Politburo-commissioned revisions to another of his older mainstays, *Sketches of the History of the ACP(b)*.[45] Knorin wrote an explanatory article about Stalin's memorandum for several leading party journals and then also probably began revising his obsolete 1934 text.[46] Pospelov spent this time revising a piece that he perhaps intended for the IMEL's again-delayed two-volume textbook for propagandists and activists.[47] Such behavior is odd enough to beg the question about what prevented the troika from focusing exclusively on its central mandate. Were the historians intimidated by the nature of the assignment? Did personal rivalries complicate their collaborative work? Did they somehow believe that they could satisfy the party hierarchy with a revised version of their 1935 *Popular Textbook*?

Perhaps the best explanation for the troika's peculiar behavior stems from the Terror's savage assault on the Soviet elite, which during the spring and early summer of 1937 was consuming not only historic individuals, but historians themselves. Colleagues like Orakhelashvili, L. M. Lukin, S. M. Dubrovsky, V. I. Zeimal, A. G. Slutsky, A. I. Urazov, D. Ya. Kin, and Ye. P. Krovisheina all "disappeared" as arrests swept through the profession.[48] Popov's exposure as an "enemy of the people" on June 17 brought his IMEL brigade's work on the two-volume text for propagandists and agitators to an abrupt end.[49] And the arrest of Knorin himself a week later—"a Polish and German spy," according to Stalin[50]—likely drove Yaroslavsky and Pospelov to despair as it threatened their project with total collapse. This probably indicates why so little archival material survives from the troika's work in during these months, inasmuch as Knorin's arrest likely forced Yaroslavsky and Pospelov to either turn hundreds of pages of notes and drafts over to the NKVD or destroy this paper trail themselves.[51] Internal IMEL reports indicate that this wave of repression within the ideological establishment left the institute almost totally paralyzed.[52]

Days after Knorin's arrest, Yaroslavsky submitted to Stalin a new draft of his *Sketches of the History of the APC(b)*, accompanying it with a note claiming that he had recently been focusing all of his energies on the manuscript. While it is certainly possible to regard this as a sign of Yaroslavsky's respect for deadlines, the phrasing of his note probably ought to be read as the historian's desperate attempt to distance himself from Knorin. Stalin took a look at the 800-page typescript, ordered it laid out in publisher's galleys, and then lightly edited it before passing it on to Stetsky.[53] The general secretary must have given it a relatively positive appraisal, because while Stetsky's eventual review was critical, it focused on narrow questions of fact and interpretation rather than more fundamental flaws. Stalin accepted the constructive tone of the report and forwarded it to the rest of the Politburo members for their sanction.[54]

Perhaps as important as the fact that Yaroslavsky's manuscript was more or less acceptable was the fact that it was now really the only option left to the party hierarchy. The IMEL's four-volume academic history had collapsed in 1936, its two-volume text had been compromised by Popov's arrest, and the Politburo's newly commissioned collective textbook had just been crippled by Knorin's unmasking.[55] This ultimately meant that when Stetsky reported back to Yaroslavsky regarding the fate of his revisions, he came bearing both good and bad news. Specifically, if the text had considerable potential, it was also excessively long and choked with factual material.[56] As Yaroslavsky recalled later, "after that project was presented [to Stalin] and after it was looked over by members of the Politburo, we were told: 'Make it twice as short, so that it will run no more than 240 pages in length.' [This was] a very difficult task—you can't just scrunch such a thing down [*srazu ne sozhmesh'sia*]—and this took an awful lot of work."[57] To help with this time-consuming editing, Stetsky commandeered a brigade of specialists from the IMEL—Pospelov, V. G. Sorin, M. S. Volin, and others —to help with the redrafting. Yaroslavsky, for his part, appears to have returned to work with little protest, understandably uneager to lose the favor of the party hierarchy and risk sharing the fate of Knorin, Popov, and others.[58]

Fig. 11: Ye. M. Yaroslavsky and P. N. Pospelov at work, late 1930s.
RGASPI, f. 629, op. 1, d. 141, l. 22.

Of course, this party history text was hardly the only project to be
stymied by the Terror. Propaganda surrounding Soviet arctic exploration that had enjoyed such a high profile between 1934 and 1936
waned as the purges threatened the institutions that had sponsored the
Cheliuskin expedition.[59] Aviation, too, came under fire from a variety
of different angles. The purge of the Red Army in the summer of 1937
resulted in the arrest of air force commander Alksnis, two of his successors, and about two-thirds of the air force's officer corps by 1939. At
roughly the same time, a series of spectacular accidents embarrassed Soviet civil aviation and called into question the reliability of its technical
specialists. The arrest of prominent designers and executives followed
soon thereafter.[60]

But perhaps the most acutely felt propaganda fiasco stemmed from
the purges' ruinous effect on the 20th anniversary of the October revolution in 1937. Evidence of the importance of this event can be seen in
the Central Committee's decision in March 1936 to invite nine play-

wrights and ten screenwriters to compete against one another for the right to create a major public spectacle to commemorate 1917 as the "turning point in the history of humanity." Told to focus on Lenin and his role in the revolution, these authors were also implicitly expected to adhere to the party hierarchy's rulings on historical work since Stalin's letter to *Proletarskaia revoliutsia*.[61] Invitation to compete in such a contest was an honor and promised a major reward to its victor; the party hierarchy anticipated a large windfall as well, as the competition was expected to generate a host of new works for the stage and screen during the jubilee year. Predictably, questions about the emplotment and casting of 1917 inhibited the authors' work almost immediately, as did somewhat less-expected disagreement over how Lenin was to be depicted. In regard to the latter debate, the chair of the competition jury and head of the Lenin Museum, N. N. Rabichev, demanded restraint and historical exactitude; Shumiatsky offered contradictory advice, recommending that the leader be interpreted artistically. In the end, only one screenplay and four plays turned out to be even remotely acceptable, with two of the latter number requiring major rewrites before final acceptance.[62]

The single clear triumph of the competition was A. Ya. Kapler's *Lenin in October* screenplay, which Romm hurriedly shot and edited for the screen during the summer of 1937.[63] Kapler and Romm's film proposed to weather the purges by focusing its attention on a narrow, somewhat dull narrative chronicling Lenin's conspiratorial preparations for revolution during the month of October 1917. Like Yaroslavsky and Pospelov, Kapler and Romm limited their cast of characters to Lenin and a handful of revolutionary martyrs (Dzerzhinsky, Sverdlov, M. S. Uritsky), excluding all but one current party boss—Stalin—from the screenplay. What's more, even though Lenin took center stage in the film (sharing it with a fictional foil, Comrade Vasily), his casting took few risks. As Karen Petrone writes,

> Kapler and Romm did not portray Lenin as a brilliant theoretician, a keen politician, or a tactical genius, but rather as a source of moral authority. The film created a likeable, modest, genial, and grandfatherly Lenin who inspired the revolution but relied on Stalin to help organize it. This folksy and spiritual depiction of Lenin downplayed his intellect so that the film did not undermine Stalin's image as a wise and all-

knowing leader. By depicting Stalin as Lenin's faithful and active young deputy, Kapler and Romm employed the sacred image of Lenin as a revolutionary leader to identify him as Lenin's only legitimate successor.[64]

On the whole, Kapler and Romm's strategy paid off, as the film both opened more or less on schedule and remained in circulation throughout the period. *Pravda* hailed the production as "a film created for the masses. It will be equally understandable for people of the most varied cultural and educational levels in light of its accessibility, its vividness, and the concreteness of its historical material." *Izvestia* predicted that the film would play a key role in how the society thought about the revolution, insofar as an ever-increasing percentage of the country's youth had not personally witnessed the October events.[65]

But if *Lenin in October* was a success within the context of the Terror, it was only a marginal instrument of propaganda or the personality cult. The film was slow and uneventful and the actors playing Lenin and Stalin supplied exacting but otherwise unremarkable performances, offering little suspense or insight into their characters' personality or vision.[66] Similar problems of scale and perspective paralyzed other aspects of the personality cult during these years. As noted above, perhaps the greatest problem was the absence of a biographical text that could supply a central narrative for the cult. The only available book of any merit was Barbusse's biography, which not only was questionably Marxist, but diverged from the party line on important questions like the nature of the left and right deviations. Authorizing this biography's publication despite their better judgment, the party hierarchs signaled their hesitancy by including in an August 1935 Politburo resolution on the IMEL an order to produce an ideologically correct biography as soon as possible. Internal IMEL planning documents subsequently noted that the task was assigned to a loose group of insiders including Mekhlis, Pospelov, and Tal; Adoratsky and Stetsky were to edit the text and hand it in by November 1, 1936.[67]

In the meantime, Barbusse's biography initially proved skeptics like Stetsky wrong. Released in early 1936, it was not only popular, but its unrelenting attacks on Trotsky even appeared to anticipate the party's renewed assault on the former left opposition during the first stages of the Great Terror.[68] Unfortunately, as the purges widened in early 1937, these arrests undermined the continued use of the book in a chain of

Fig. 12: Advertisement for *Lenin in October,* dir. M. Romm (Mosfilm, 1937). From *Vecherniaia Moskva,* December 10, 1937, 4.

events that illustrates how the unpredictable nature of the Great Terror came to cast a shadow over the personality cult itself. Early objections to Barbusse's references to the fallen Yenukidze were now quickly compounded by mention of other new-found "enemies of the people" like Radek; by the fall of 1937, this list had expanded to include Bukharin, Rykov, Knorin, Bubnov, Popov, Orakhelashvili, Piatnitsky, and S. F. Grinko. The fate of the biography was sealed in 1938 following the arrest of Yegorov, V. I. Shorin, N. V. Krylenko, and Stetsky himself.[69]

To a certain extent, the Barbusse debacle was eclipsed by new editions of Beria's book and a document collection on Stalin and the Red Army by Voroshilov.[70] The viability of these books and a handful of other document collections and institutional histories amid the carnage should not be particularly surprising. After all, unlike traditional historical and biographical narratives, these texts did not have to detail Stalin's personal relationship with the party and military elite. Beria's book was a opportunistic history of the prerevolutionary Transcaucasus region. The document collections offered little narrative aside from brief introductions to letters, telegrams, and reports that had been hand-picked for publication. And the institutional histories focused on anony-mous organizations, production units, and historical agents like "the party" and "the working class" that allowed them to avoid mention of specific members of the nomenclatura whenever possible. Thanks to this brevity and selectivity, successful examples of these genres typically risked removal from circulation only when their authors or editors fell victim to the purges.

Of course, such volumes offered at best only a temporary solution to the problem at hand. Not only did they make for difficult reading, but they were too narrow to provide an overall sense of the era. Indeed, this literature actually had the effect of stimulating new calls for a major Stalin biography. G. M. Dimitrov, for instance, called in late 1936 for a book on the leader to serve as the centerpiece of a new series on "The Remarkable People of the Working Class."[71] Internal IMEL documents also persistently listed the biography as a major priority. That said, the Mekhlis-Pospelov-Tal team failed to deliver its manuscript in Novem-ber 1936, whereupon the task was reassigned to the IMEL's deputy di-rector, Ye. I. Korotky. Korotky, too, missed his August 1937 deadline, despite that fact that all he was expected to do was revise and update the text that the late Tovstukha had been developing between 1927 and 1935. The task was then passed along to another IMEL insider, M. A. Saveliev; he, like his predecessors, allowed his deadline in 1938 to come and go without producing any tangible results.[72]

Such a record indicates that although the idea of a comprehensive bi-ography retained its importance, the task of actually writing it had be-come something akin to Russian roulette. When called to account for its failures, the IMEL demurred, averring that its authors had failed to gen-erate the needed text "for a whole array of reasons."[73] Clearly, part of the problem stemmed from the Terror, as each wave of arrests trans-formed everything even mentioning its victims from prescribed literature into proscribed contraband. But excessive veneration could also create problems for prospective biographers. In 1938, for instance, Stalin sharply rebuked Detizdat, the Children's Publishing House, for a bio-graphical project demonstrating what was alleged to be a "Socialist-Revolutionary tone":

I am decisively opposed to the publication of *Stories of Stalin's Childhood*.

The little book is filled with a mass of factual errors, distortions, exaggerations, and undeserved praise. The author has been misled by fairytale enthusiasts, liars (perhaps "honest" liars) and sycophants. A pity for the author, but facts are facts.

But that is not most important. Most important is that the book has a tendency to inculcate in the consciousness of Soviet children (and people in general) a cult of personalities, great leaders [*vozhdei*] and infallible heroes. That is dangerous and harmful. The theory of the "heroes" and the "mob" is not a Bolshevik theory but an SR one. *The SRs say:* "Heroes make a people, transform a mob into a people." "The people make their heroes," *say the Bolsheviks.* This little book will assist the SRs. Every such book will contribute to the SRs and *will harm* our general Bolshevik cause.

I advise you to burn the book.

I. Stalin.

February 16, 1938.[74]

Stalin's rejection of this emplotment paradigm must have caused his potential biographers to despair. He was technically correct, of course: theoretically, the party line on historic personalities had stated quite clearly since 1932 that leaders emerge from among the people at specific historic junctures governed by the Marxist dialectic. In practice, however, Soviet mass culture routinely characterized Stalin as playing a broader, more paternalistic role in the society—something to which the general secretary almost never objected. In the end, such an erratic, unpredictable attitude toward the literary dimensions of the cult virtually stymied the production of biographical material on the general secretary.[75]

It's long been known that the Soviet party and state nearly collapsed under the onslaught of the Great Terror. The Central Committee was paralyzed by the loss of 99 of its 139 members. Regional party organizations ceased to function after having been stripped of their leaders and most able personnel. Engineers and industrial planners disappeared, leaving economic targets unmet. Arrests among teachers and administrators hamstrung public schooling on all levels. Repression also crippled the Red Army, which was forced to surrender 3 of its 5 marshals, 13 of its 15 commanders, 8 of its 9 admirals, 50 of its 57 corps com-

manders, 154 of its 186 divisional commanders, all 16 of its army commissars, and 25 of its 28 army corps commissars. Until now, however,
relatively little has been known about the effect that the Terror had on
the propaganda state itself. As hard as the purges hit the party, military, and civilian elite, nowhere were its effects as total and all-encompassing as in the ideological sphere. Aside from hobbling the ranks of
the ideologues themselves, the Terror undermined the celebration of history, contemporary heroes, Soviet patriotism, and even the personality
cult, neutralizing the beneficial effects that these campaigns were having on popular mobilizational efforts.

Assessments of the wider context surrounding the Terror differ on its
lasting effects. A recent study of the Red Army argues, for instance, that
most accounts exaggerate the role that the purges played in subsequent
military dysfunction and failure. Destruction of the command staff did
not, it seems, lead inevitably to the disastrous Winter War with Finland
or the Nazi surprise attack of June 22, 1941.[76] Similar criticism could
probably be leveled at the literature on Sovet weakness in economics,
science, and diplomacy between 1938 and 1941 as well.[77] But while
such revisionist caution may have considerable merit in some fields, it
would not seem to apply to assessments of the ideological establishment
during these years. Not only did the Terror consume an entire generation
of able party historians and ideologists—Bukharin, Bubnov, Popov,
Knorin, Ingulov, etc.—but it tore gaping wounds in the emerging body
of military, party, and production heroes who had succeeded where
others had failed in advertising the promise of the Soviet experiment.
The effect of this slaughter is difficult to exaggerate, as demonstrated in
the concluding chapters of this book.

8 Mass Culture in a Time of Terror

FOR MEMBERS OF THE CREATIVE INTELLIGENTSIA involved in the campaigns revolving around Soviet heroism and patriotism, the 20th anniversary of the October revolution in 1937 offered a major opportunity to publish new works, stage new plays, screen new films, and display new art dedicated to the Bolshevik cause. A number of major socialist realist novels had already begun to appear during this period, of course—Tolstoy's *Road to Calvary*, Sholokhov's *Virgin Soil Upturned*, etc.—but literary journals and the press called between 1935 and 1937 for still more new work about the revolution that could be published specifically to commemorate the anniversary.[1] Though this was in many senses a logical and even predictable demand, its realization was inhibited first by the reigning confusion over the official historical line and then by the bloody mayhem of the purges. These circumstances drove N. N. Nakoriakov, the head of the State Literary Publishing House, to complain bitterly in September 1937 that he would have little to contribute to the jubilee. "We had the intention of publishing a series of works on civil war themes, but plans are one thing and the reality of our program is another." Regrettably, he continued, "we have no [new] works on the theme of 'Heroics of the Civil War,' due to the fact most of our authors are late in handing in their works."[2] Although Nakoriakov did not specify precisely what was responsible for these nearly universal delays, it is reasonable to assume that the purges' destruction of Old Bolshevik and Red Army ranks had necessitated the total revision or abandonment of many of the projects underway.

This chapter examines how the Terror affected Soviet mass culture and the arts, focusing on the printed page, the theatrical stage, the movie house screen, and the exhibition hall. It also devotes considerable attention to party education efforts, both on the shop floor and at the tribune. Ultimately, it argues that the Great Terror brought key aspects of Soviet mass culture to a virtual standstill between 1936 and 1938.

Socialist realism enjoyed wide popularity within the reading public of the 1930s—particularly authors such as Sholokhov, Ostrovsky, Gorky, Tolstoy, Panferov, Gladkov, Serafimovich, Ilf and Petrov, and Zoshchenko. Among those writing for the stage, N. F. Pogodin, Afinogenov, and A. Ye. Korneichuk were best remembered.[3] That said, the declining fortunes of the avant garde and formalist movement hobbled Soviet theater and opera during the mid-1930s, conspiring with ill-fated repertoire choices to ruin V. E . Meyerhold's theatrical school as well as Bulgakov's *Molière*, D. D. Shostakovich's *Lady Macbeth of Mtsensk District,* and Bedny and A. Ya. Tairov's *Epic Heroes,* among many others. Perhaps more than even the belles lettres, then, the theatrical world looked to the 20th anniversary of the October revolution as an opportunity for redemption. But although the Writers' Union had 28 plays in preparation for the anniversary in January 1936 (including the nine involved in the Central Committee's jubilee competition), much of this work ground to a halt even before the start of the purges, despite the enormous support that the party and state afforded revolutionary thematics.[4] As in other artistic genres, many of these complications stemmed from the chaos surrounding party history. Speaking at a May 1936 meeting of theatrical personnel from the Soviet Writers' Union, a playwright and lyricist named V. P. Volzhenin revealed that he hoped to create something for the stage about "our reality, where heroism has become a part of everyday life." The trouble, as he confessed to the audience, was how to depict the context within which his drama was to unfold: "The demands of creating an October repertoire are so serious that, to be honest, I dread the thought of even picking up my pen." His colleague A. M. Goldenberg (who wrote under the nom de plume Argo) seconded Volzhenin's nervousness, alluding to the instability of the party line on history in his speech:

> If my comrades ask me what I am writing now for the 20th anniversary, I'd have to answer with shame and dismay that I cannot imagine how I'd sit down with a blank piece of paper in front of me and describe what I am thinking and writing. The situation is changing so much that it is difficult to speak of the 20th anniversary. If even encyclopedias are being released these days with corrections, how is it possible to imagine the atmosphere that will exist a year from now? I won't be able to begin writing at least until the 19th anniversary passes.

Volzhenin's and Goldenberg's forthrightness about their misgivings apparently caused considerable unease in the hall. Yu. P. German, another playwright, attempted to put a positive spin on their doubts, but ended up sounding only menacing. "This uncertainty in some people's comments and the frustration that we see is actually a welcoming sign," he bluffed. "It means that everyone understands the responsibility that is presently before them."[5]

Some pressed on, of course. Ya. O. Boiarsky presented a fairly optimistic picture of the situation a year later, noting to *Literaturnaia gazeta* in May 1937 that the jubilee committee expected submissions on Lenin for the competition from at least seven prominent authors and playwrights including Tolstoy, Korneichuk, Ivanov, Mikitenko, S. N. Dadiani, and K. A. Trenev. Other plays slated for performance during the anniversary included N. Ye. Virta's *Land,* S. I. Amaglobeli's *Master of Happiness,* V. N. Bill-Belotserkovsky's *The Border,* S. I. Vashentsev's *Our Days,* V. A. Kaverin's *The Sole Gleaming Sail,* N. N. Nikitin's *Baku,* V. P. Kataev's *Actors,* L. V. Nikulin's *Port Arthur,* Yu. I. Yanovsky's *Thinking of Britanka,* and three versions of Ostrovsky's *How the Steel Was Forged.*[6] Mikitenko, a Ukrainian playwright, was the first to complete his submission for the competition—*When the Sun Rises,* a historical drama about the revolution in Kiev—and proceeded to stage it late that spring. Unfortunately, his flattering depiction of Gamarnik as one of the heroes of the period resulted in the play's closure in early June after the commander's suicide. Mikitenko himself was arrested and shot later that October, at least in part due to mistakes with his ill-fated drama.[7] Amaglobeli's arrest likewise derailed his play's staging.[8] Other projects stalled or stumbled for more artistic reasons. In the end, only two of the competition's Lenin-centered plays—Korneichuk's *Pravda* and Trenev's *On the Banks of the Neva*—were judged to be fit for the stage. Equally embarrassing, only a third of Boiarsky's longer list of prospective plays, by Virta, Nikitin, Kataev, and Yanovsky, were actually performed during the jubilee celebration.[9] Pogodin's play *The Man with a Gun,* which premiered a week after the festivities, was immediately subjected to a scathing critique by ideological authorities on account of its depiction of Lenin and Stalin and pulled from the repertoire for revisions.[10] The end result, in other words, was a near-total fiasco.

The experience of one of the most prominent playwrights to be invited to participate in the Central Committee's competition—Afinogenov—provides useful insight into the challenges that members of the creative intelligentsia faced during these years. A leading member of RAPP in the late 1920s, Afinogenov became one of USSR's best-known dramatists after Stalin's endorsement of his *The Eccentric* in 1929.[11] He survived the reorganization of the arts in 1932 as a tireless advocate of socialist thematics on the Soviet stage, only to run into problems himself, first with *The Lie* (1933) and then with *Hail, Spain!* (1936), both of which advanced characters who were apparently excessively complex and insufficiently heroic.[12] Such problems were serious, but not fatal—although Afinogenov was criticized for his incomplete conversion from RAPP's preference for "ordinary" protagonists to Socialist Realism's stress on triumphalism, he did not face the devastating charges of formalism that many of his contemporaries did. And not only did Afinogenov preserve his reputation as one of the theatrical world's agenda-setters, but he retained his place in the Central Committee's competition as well.

But if issues of focus and characterization did not end Afinogenov's career, the arrests of Yagoda, Averbakh, and Kirshon, his former patron and associates, nearly did. Attacked for these ties at a meeting of the Moscow Association of Playwrights in late April 1937, he was expelled in quick succession from the governing board of the Writers' Union, the party, and the commemorative competition.[13] In the aftermath of this crisis, Afinogenov retreated to the isolation of his country dacha to await arrest, oscillating for the better part of a year between emotions of anger, despair, and the determination to remake himself into an orthodox soldier of the party. Afinogenov's jubilee play, *The Great Choice,* was one of the experience's chief casualties and was left to languish even after the playwright's halting rehabilitation in 1938.[14]

Although Afinogenov miraculously escaped the Terror, none of his popular plays—*The Eccentric, Fear, The Lie, A Distant Point, Hail, Spain!* etc.—returned to the stage until after Stalin's death. A similar dynamic poisoned the *oeuvres* of dozens of other writers and playwrights as well. I. I. Kataev's arrest in 1937 doomed his *Fatherland.* The disappearance of other prominent authors and poets—Averbakh, Babel, Koltsov, Vesely, A. K. Gastev, M. P. Gerasimov, V. P. Kin, V. T. Kirillov, V. V. Kniazev, B. P. Kornilov, G. K. Nikiforov, N. M. Oleinikov, L. S. Ovalov, B. A. Pilniak, A. I. Piotrovsky, V. P. Pravdukhin, F. F. Raskolnikov, S. M. Tretiakov, A. K. Voronsky, etc.—had a correspondingly deadly effect on their creative work as well.

Equally destructive was the banning of works by otherwise reputable writers that mentioned recently exposed enemies of the people in positive terms—a tactic that a variety of authors had used to ground their fictional storylines within the glory days of the revolution and civil war. Ostrovsky's *How the Steel Was Forged,* for instance, was forced into a new edition in 1937 after the censor noticed passing mention of prominent civil war Red Army commanders like Yakir and Zhloba, as well as the Komsomol boss Chaplin. Sholokhov's *Quiet Flows the Don* was repeatedly reissued during the 1930s to remove mention of Zhloba, Krylenko, S. I. Syrtsov, and V. A. Antonov-Ovseenko.[15] Virta's novel *Loneliness* was seized for its approving mention of Tukhachevsky.[16] Serafimovich's *Iron Flood* came under fire for the resemblance of its character Kozhuk to the purged Ye. I. Kovtiukh.[17] Even Furmanov's *Chapaev,* as well as his related short story, *Red Landing,* had to be withdrawn and reissued on account of their mention of Kovtiukh and I. S. Kutiakov.[18] A complete accounting of such censorial interventions likely would require a whole monographic study, as even an incomplete list is very long. If Ye. G. Bagritsky ran afoul of the authorities for his mention of V. M. Primakov, Ye. D. Zozulia got into trouble for his sketch on Bliukher, Zoshchenko for his hailing of the NKVD boss S. G. Firin, and Kassil for his association of Budenny with Bliukher in one book and his inclusion of a picture of Bliukher, Yegorov, and Tukhachevsky in another.[19] Panferov erred in dedicating several volumes of *Bruski* to Ya. A. Yakovlev and I. M. Vareikis; K. G. Paustovsky in writing an entire book about Bliukher; M. A. Svetlov in his mention of P. Ye. Dybenko; and Chukovsky in his quotation of the critic Kornilov and the Ukrainian Commissar of Education V. P. Zatonsky.[20] In each case, the offending piece was sequestered and then either permanently removed from circulation or defaced with India ink to obscure the offending passages until it could be reissued.

Aside from such cases, a number of otherwise orthodox editions fell under scrutiny during these years for their inclusion of commentary or prefaces by contributors whose names could no longer appear in print. Gladkov's *Energy* was seized in 1938 due to a foreword written by Stetsky.[21] Literally dozens of books published by the Academia Publishing House shared the fate of an edition of Gorky's early poetry, which was condemned for a foreword written by Kamenev while he was still director of the press.[22] The collected works of party hierarchs such as Lenin, Voroshilov, and Sverdlov also suffered from this sort of scrutiny after enemies were unmasked in the publishing wing of the IMEL.[23] In some cases, the offending chapter could be torn free of the binding or cut out of the book with a sharp knife; in others, the entire book had to be removed from circulation. Few were republished before the 1950s.[24]

As noted previously, the only truly successful new work released for the twentieth anniversary of the revolution was the film *Lenin in October*.[25] But aside from this masterwork of political correctness, there were a number of other features between 1937 and 1938 that managed to advance versions of the usable past without falling victim to the censor. *For the Soviet Motherland*, released at the same time as Kapler and Romm's film, followed a group of cadets stationed on the Finnish frontier in Karelia during the last stages of the civil war. Much of the storyline, which was based on a novel by G. S. Fish, concerns this detachment's daring winter raid into the nearby Lake Kimas region and evokes themes relating to their love of the motherland, their hatred of the enemy, and their willingness to die in the name of national defense.[26] Quite similar in scale, timing, and genre was *The Baltic Sailors*, which dealt with Stalin's suppression of two White Guard mutinies near Kronshtadt in 1919. *Uchitelskaia gazeta* waxed rhapsodic about the film, proclaiming it to have "great educational significance." According to the newspaper, "it enflames Soviet audiences with a profound hatred of the interventionists and White traitors, who attempted to defeat our young Soviet republic; it nurtures in its audiences bravery, determination, and a burning love for and dedication to our wonderful motherland and a readiness to defend her from all enemies to the last drop of

Fig. 13: Advertisement for *For the Soviet Motherland,* dir. R. Muzykant and Yu. Muzykant (Lenfilm 1937). From *Pravda,* October 16, 1937, 6.

blood."[27] *Volochaevka Days,* a third film about foreign incursions during the early years of the Soviet republic, looked east instead of west to celebrate the defeat of Japanese occupiers in the Khabarovsk region at the hands of local partisans and units of the Red Army.[28] All of these films focused on group heroism rather than than a single famous protagonist, an approach defended by directors like the Vasilievs on account of its ideological merits. "We want our audiences," they wrote, "to see in this film the united image of a great people who has risen to defend its Soviet land and whose heart is full of love for its country and hatred for the enemy. It is in fact this people who is the positive hero of the film. Each member of this people, in his own way, shares the same goal; each member of this people, while preserving his individuality, acts as a part of this united, comprehensive image."[29] Although not as dynamic as *Chapaev,* this focus on a collective hero made up of generic, nearly anonymous protagonists was acceptable from the perspective of the official line. Moreover, it produced features capable of weathering the purges.

Fig. 14: Advertisement for *The Baltic Sailors*, dir. A. M. Faintsimmer (Belgoskino, 1937). From *Vecherniaia Moskva*, December 19, 1937, 4.

Other revolutionary-era films celebrated fictional individuals instead of group heroism. *The Return of Maksim,* the second part of a cinematic trilogy about its eponymous hero, focused on Maksim's maturation from labor organizer to Bolshevik activist during the leadup to the events of 1917.[30] It was followed quickly by the cinematic version of Pogodin's *The Man with a Gun,* which tracked the trials and tribulations of Ivan Shadrin, a peasant draftee during the First World War who eventually finds his way to Lenin's side at Smolny in October 1917.[31] Both of these films, like *We Are from Kronshtadt,* used the society-wide convulsions of the revolution as a backdrop for character studies of "ordinary" individuals' political maturation from emotional spontaneity to artic-ulate class-consciousness.

In addition to his own trilogy, Maksim also enjoyed a bit part in yet another of the period's epic films: Ermler's *The Great Citizen.* A bio-graphical narrative, it traced the rise of P. M. Shakhov from factory manager to regional Bolshevik party boss during the NEP years and climaxed with Shakhov's death at the hands of a Trotskyite assassin in 1934.[32] Drafted and redrafted between 1935 and 1937, *The Great Citizen* pitted the progressive, patriotic Shakhov and his dream of building socialism in one country against concealed enemies within the party who conspire to undermine the USSR and turn the revolutionary society over to foreign capitalists abroad.[33] Ermler's depiction of Shakhov made *The Great Citizen* an important film for several reasons. First, unlike Chapaev, Maksim, and other protagonists of mid-1930s Soviet cinema, Shakhov was cast as a static figure, fully developed and conscious of his revolutionary duty from the first minutes of the four-hour film.[34] Second, Ermler's Shakhov was designed to be only a semi-fictional character, both physically and professionally reminiscent of Kirov and standing at the helm of an unnamed city resembling Leningrad. Shakhov struggles in the film with renegades within the party (A. D. Kartashov and S. V. Borovsky) who evoke associations with Trotsky and Bukharin—an impression that is strengthened late in the film when it becomes clear that they are both acting on the orders of not only Trotsky and his foreign handlers, but Piatakov as well. This fusing of fiction and reality allowed the film to depict the struggle between its protagonists and malefactors with a maximum of realism, while at the same time not complicating the broader tale of Shakhov's martyrdom with mention of his prototype's close relationships with fallen party members like Yenukidze and Orakhelashvili. Although Ermler was far from the first to practice this sort of blurring of fiction and reality, his particular approach was extremely successful. The film was hailed as a great success and an important instructional aid. Not only was Shakhov described as a role model for the new generations, but his life experience captured a key moment in recent party history. *Sputnik agitatora* concluded authoritatively that *The Great Citizen* "teaches us to recognize the methods and tactics of the Trotskyite-Zinovievite-Bukharinite scum and provokes in us a feeling of anger and hatred for this human waste. The film teaches us the necessity of keeping vigilant and being steadfast, firm, and observant. Every agitator should watch this film, organize a collective viewing of it, and tell his audience about this motion picture's profound meaning." Another critic agreed, writing: "this picture will be quite a useful aid for studying party history. *The Great Citizen* teaches vigilance and the ability to differentiate enemy from friend and friend from enemy."[35]

But to what extent should Ermler's unusual narrative strategy be understood as a conscious attempt to weather the purges? At first glance, such an idea seems unlikely. Ermler began work on *The Great Citizen* in 1935, well before the start of the Terror. What's more, after the success of *Peasants,* he enjoyed enough latitude with the film authorities to experiment with cinematic genre for purely artistic reasons —an opportunity he would later explain allowed him to create this explicitly parahistorical, "conversational" film.[36] That said, if Ermler's work on the film predates the purge of the former left and right opposition between 1936 and 1938, it took shape during the NKVD's bloody investigation of the Leningrad party organization in the wake of Kirov's murder—circumstances that would have immediately brought a genuinely biographical screenplay to a halt. Seen in this light, Ermler's decision to cast his protagonist as Kirov-like rather than Kirov himself appears too convenient to be coincidental.[37] Some audience members questioned the motives behind this finesse, but—judging by the mountain of fan mail in Ermler's personal archive—they loved the film anyway.[38]

The prescient nature of Ermler's decision to fictionalize his protagonist is particularly visible when contrasted against Dovzhenko's experience with Shchors, "the Ukrainian Chapaev." Like Ermler, Dovzhenko endured a grueling ordeal of revision after revision between 1935 and 1937 as he brought his cinematic vision of the Ukrainian martyr into accord with that of the party hierarchy and its historians. And like Ermler, Dovzhenko probably felt some relief as *Shchors* neared completion in 1937. But as he was shooting the last segments of the film that fall, the NKVD arrested I. N. Dubovoy, Shchors's former aide-de-camp, whom Dovzhenko had cast as a hero and who was supposed to comfort the mortally wounded commander at the end of the film. Needless to say, this turn of events forced Dovzhenko to rewrite the screenplay and reshoot much of the film, delaying its release by over a year and calling into question the director's political reliability.[39]

But *Shchors* was hardly the only film whose release was stymied by the Terror.[40] *First Cavalry Army,* for instance, was another major civil war epic that dated to 1935 and modeled itself on *Chapaev.* Developed by A. G. Ivanov, Ya. M. Bliokh, and B. A. Lavrenev under the Vasilievs' mentorship, the project quickly won the support of Lenfilm and the Red Army's political directorate. The latter organization arranged for the brigade to consult repeatedly with leading commanders, from Voro-shilov and Budenny to A. Ye. Shchadenko and O. I. Gorodnikov, indi-cating the importance of the film. Nonetheless, Voroshilov, Shchadenko, and Gorodnikov hesitated to share their reminiscences with the authors, aware of the sensitivity of the historical events they had witnessed. Shortly thereafter, Voroshilov and Budenny asked to be written out of the screenplay entirely. Even so, the brigade managed to produce a script in early 1937 that won the approval of the general staff; it was ready to go into production that summer when purges within the ranks consumed key characters including Tukhachevsky and I. T. Smigla. The fall of Yegorov and Shorin a year later sealed the screenplay's fate.[41] Amazingly, Dzigan took up the subject with Vs. V. Vishnevsky shortly thereafter, apparently believing that they could tell the story of the First Cavalry Army without its key figures. Again and again, Dzigan had to confront problems with emplotment and Vishnevsky had to endure re-peated interventions from Voroshilov and Budenny before they would sign off on their screenplay. In the end, Dzigan and Vishnevsky would spend three years negotiating how to tell the story before their version of the film was permanently shelved at the start of the Second World War.[42] Ivanov had only slightly better luck with his *Parkhomenko*. Ac-cording to the author, he and his editors were forced to rewrite the screenplay some 15 times during the Terror years, delaying the film's release until 1942.[43] Petrov-Bytov's panoramic *Defense of Leningrad* stalled for similar reasons during these years; it wasn't until 1941 that a heavily edited version finally appeared as *The Defeat of Yudenich*.[44]

While new films on sensitive historical subjects were worrisome for the authorities, equally troubling was the removal of already released films from circulation when they were rendered politically obsolete by the purges. As noted above, even the slightest glimpse of an enemy of the people was enough to bring about the wrath of the authorities. For example, a commemorative documentary film about Lenin that Stalin had authorized in 1935 had to be seized and reedited in 1937 in order to remove images of "the Trotskyite Radek" before it could be distrib-uted during the annual commemoration of Lenin's death.[45] The fall of Yagoda temporarily suspended showings of feature films like *Inmates* and *Dzhulbars* during the spring of 1937; it appears that *Miners* and *The Courageous Seven* were briefly removed from circulation at about the same time.[46] Vertov's *Three Songs of Lenin* was pulled from distribution that June on account of its shots of Bukharin, Radek, Kamenev, Tomsky, Tukhachevsky, Yagoda, and Rudzutak.[47] The same director's *Lullaby* could be shown only later that year after stock footage of a state reception was distorted in order to obscure glimpses of Gamarnik.[48] Many other long-forgotten documentary films likewise fell victim to the Terror, including *I. V. Stalin's Report on the Draft Constitution, I. V. Stalin's Campaign Speech to Voters from the Stalin District, On the Arctic Circle, The Papaninites, The Stalinist Tribe, The Country of Soviets,* and *The Moscow-Volga Canal.*[49] Apparently also on this list was Stalin's favorite documentary from 1934, *Heroes of the Arctic (The Cheliuskin).*[50] Dozens of newsreels also were also withdrawn and shelved, whether individual installments of established series like *Soviet Cinema Journal, The Socialist Village, USSR on the Silver Screen, The Victorious March of Socialism,* and *Guarding the USSR,* or stand-alone shorts such as *The First of May in Moscow, The Struggle for Kiev, Red Cavalrymen, The Wondrous Year, Beloved Sergo Ordzhonikidze, Epic Heroes of the Motherland,* and *The Festival of Stalinist Eagles.*[51] Few of these latter documentary films and newsreels appear to have undergone the editing necessary to allow their rerelease.[52]

The purges complicated other aspects of Soviet mass culture as well, from museum and gallery exhibits to the painting of mobilizational art.[53] Two shows were particularly affected: 1938's commemoration of the 20th anniversary of the Red Army and 1939's famous Industry of Socialism exhibition.[54] Some artists of the period were arrested in connection with their celebration of the heroes of yesteryear; others like Gerasimov struggled to avoid career-ending mistakes.[55] Jan Plamper, who interviewed Gerasimov's son-in-law V. Shabelnikov in the late 1990s, tells the story of being invited to visit the late painter's studio in northern Moscow. There,

> one large painting, where some of the paint had begun to peel off, caught my attention: a still life with lilacs, obviously painted from the lilac trees in the garden outside the studio. Shabelnikov explained that this had originally been a group of political leaders. While Gerasimov was painting it at the height of the Great Terror he kept receiving calls from the Party's Central Committee, announcing that "unfortunately, comrade X has also turned out to be an enemy of the people." At first, Gerasimov painted over individual figures, adding a palm leaf or a column here and there. When the number of "enemies of the people" became unmanageable Gerasimov simply covered the entire group portrait with lilacs, lest

he be accused of providing an arena to the condemned enemies of the Soviet Union.[56]

Another monumental picture dedicated to the First Cavalry Army is mentioned in the memoirs of A. G. Ivanov, who visited Gerasimov's studio in 1937. According to Ivanov, the canvas in question displayed several blotted-out faces and other tell-tale traces of self-censorship. Still another work of Gerasimov's that the artist intended for the Industry of Socialism show—"A Session of the Council of the People's Commissariat of Heavy Industry"—had to be abandoned after the arrest of Piatakov and others.[57] Brodsky, one of Gerasimov's rivals within the artistic establishment, was similarly confounded by the attrition of Soviet heroes in 1936–1938. "Brodsky burned many canvases," a colleague of his concluded tersely after the war.[58]

Predictably, such difficulties drove artists to narrow the scope of their subject matter and either focus tightly on Stalin and his immediate entourage or return to the stock images of anonymous workers, Red Army soldiers, and peasants that had dominated propaganda art at the end of the 1920s. One author attempted to defend this new depersonalized focus, claiming that art had been selected for the 1938 Red Army exhibit that was "artistically expressive and accurate in its depiction of the honorable path toward the construction, struggle, and victory of the Red Army and Fleet" while avoiding "faux-heroism" and "special effects."[59] Of course, such generic imagery had not been popular during the years of the first Five-Year Plan and was no more readily sought after now. Visitors looked in vain for exceptions to this rule at exhibitions and left disappointed inscriptions in comment books about their inability to find the heroes who had been virtually ubiquitous only a few years earlier.[60] It wasn't until 1939, after the end of the purges, that a few Soviet artists began to return to the idea of celebrating contemporary celebrities.[61]

If the Terror hobbled successful aspects of Soviet mass culture like literature and the arts, it had an even more devastating effect on vulnerable areas such as the party educational system. Most immediately affected was the curriculum, which had been a source of frustration and anxiety even before the purges. Here, as bad as the situation had been since 1931, it now only got worse. In mid-1937, for instance, orders were sent to all provincial, regional, and republican party organizations to blacklist texts by Popov and Knorin, as well as any edition of Yaro-slavsky's *History of the ACP(b)* issued before 1936. Material written by the Volin-Ingulov team and by Ingulov and V. A. Karpinsky was like-wise slated for sequestering as soon as revised editions could be issued. Official communiqués reassured anxious agitators on the local level that new political grammars and party history textbooks would be released as soon as possible. That said, the arrest of key figures including In-gulov himself in December 1937 extended this wait by nearly a year.[62]

Because of the dearth of officially endorsed textbooks, organizations like the Red Army's political directorate recommended that introduc-tory courses and study circles focus their efforts on auxiliary materials such as Kalinin's *What Has Soviet Power Done for the Toilers?* and other basic titles. Stetsky, Ingulov, and N. Baransky's *Our Motherland* was also recommended before Ingulov's arrest in December 1937 and after the start of 1938 once a new edition has stripped the volume of his name. Stetsky's arrest that spring again suspended its use, however, forcing Baransky to reissue the book with Pospelov as his coauthor in order to get it back into circulation.[63] Similar problems plagued more advanced courses as well, forcing better-prepared students to make due with Molotov's *Toward the Twentieth Anniversary of the October Rev-olution,* the *Twenty Years of Soviet Power* anthology, and *USSR—the Country of Socialism.*[64] In the absence of an acceptable party history, all such makeshift materials were taught within a historical narrative sup-plied by the concluding chapters of Shestakov's *Short Course on the History of the USSR,* which was hurriedly excerpted and rebound in pamphlet form.[65] This latter text was apparently so important to the curriculum that it was not removed from circulation after the purge of Yegorov and Bliukher in 1938—instead, orders were telegraphed to all regional Red Army political departments to paste newsprint over the portraits of the marshals and blacken out their names with India ink.[66]

The Shestakov text was not the only thing that the party educational administration borrowed from the public schools, however. Even be-fore they co-opted this text, party officials were planning to dramatically increase the proportion of state history within their party history courses.[67] A Komsomol Central Committee plenum resolution from mid-1936 and a circular from February 1937 attempted to spell out this new agenda for all courses and study circles meeting under the organi-zation's auspices. Reflecting the priority of balancing instruction of

Marxist-Leninist theory with everyday practice, grassroots-level agitators were told that they must

> accompany their presentations with facts and examples from modern life and give their audiences a complete impression of the historical events indicated in the curriculum and of all the major periods of the struggle of the Bolshevik party and Soviet power for the victory of socialism in the USSR. Explaining the achievements of socialist construction and the USSR's constitution, the propagandist must inculcate in his audience the spirit of Soviet patriotism [. . .]. Studying the basics of political literacy, the circles' participants must receive a complete impression of the activities of the founders and leaders of the communist party—Comrades Stalin and Lenin, as well as their brothers-in-arms: Sverdlov, Dzerzhinsky, Kirov, Kuibyshev, Molotov, Ordzhonikidze, Kaganovich, Kalinin, Voroshilov, and others.[68]

Such directives ultimately made their way into print, both in the all-union press and in more specialized journals devoted to agitational work among civilian and military personnel.[69]

Increased centralization was also discussed as a response to party education's mixed record, for although the system was recognized for its enormous array of grassroots-level study circles, lectures, and courses, many of these offerings were simply too homegrown and uneven to meet the party hierarchy's increasingly orthodox demands.[70] Criticism in internal party and Komsomol reports from 1936 to 1937 focused in particular on local agitators' leadership. One interregional survey of personnel revealed most instructors to possess "an exceptionally low level of political and educational preparation." In the Voronezh region, for example, half the local propagandists had only an elementary school diploma and had attended no more than basic political training courses. In the Sverdlov region, 41 percent of local personnel had not even managed that much. Even near the Soviet capital, in the Volokolamsk district, only eight of 63 propagandists could boast of any specialized training at all.[71] A Komsomol study from Kharkov revealed similar results.[72]

Just as in the early 1930s, unqualified instructors between 1936 and 1938 struggled more with their basic responsibilities than those possessing adequate background. But in the nervous climate of the purges, party officials took particular interest in the political implications of incompetent grassroots agitation. In the above-mentioned report on Komsomol education in Kharkov, for instance, an inspector reported that local Komsomol members had only a halting understanding of the context surrounding the October 1917 revolution. In the Tiniakov Factory, students were under the impression that "dual power" meant when "the Mensheviks and SRs styled themselves as Bolsheviks." Across town in the Kharkov Tractor Factory, a study circle on party history was run so poorly that students were unable to summarize even the basic tenets of a socialist economy. Worse, when several of those present questioned the feasibility of the party's plans for "socialism in one country," no one including the instructors proved able to assuage their doubts.[73]

Such awkward situations must have been terrifying for study circle leaders during the Terror—in the Kharkov Tractor Factory case, questioning "socialism in one country" not only challenged one of Stalin's most famous contributions to Marxism-Leninism, but it echoed objections to the party program voiced by renegades like Trotsky. Some group leaders panicked at such suggestions, fearful of where they might lead. One teacher in Kiev went so far as to rebuke such a questioner and hold him after class to inquire what had led him to take such an "anti-Soviet" position. This interrogation also attempted to establish who the questioner's parents and close friends were.[74] Other discussion leaders devised more "pedagogical" solutions to such problems by staging debates in class in order to induce students to correct one another. Such tactics tended to be only marginally more successful, however, and occasionally ended in absolute disaster. As one former Soviet citizen explained to an interviewer after the war:

> the debates on Marxism and Soviet history [were] usually prearranged and lack[ed] spontaneity. Cliche metaphors, such as the one that "it is easier to break one match than a dozen," [were] repeated "ad nauseum" [sic] to demonstrate the superiority of Communism. Student[s] [. . . did] not express their opinions, in order not to draw suspicion on themselves. I remember some debates we had in our schools. One of them, curiously enough, ended in the victory of a student who had to defend the views of Trotsky. Following this incident, all further debates for the year were cancelled.[75]

Over time, such reactions on the part of teaching personnel discouraged all but the most perfunctory of class participation, as did ominous calls from above for students' questions to be written down.[76] Subsequently, formalism, particularly didactic lectures, rote memorization, and question-and-answer drills, came to dominate party education. Participants later recalled avoiding meetings, leaving early, or dozing off whenever possible. Truancy became enough of an issue in some enterprises that cloakrooms had to be locked to ensure that participants would stay until the end of their sessions.[77]

Of course, not all students were content with being merely time-servers. Inadequate instruction, an absence of texts and study aids, and a broadly felt sense of anxiety about the ongoing purges often drove the idealistic and curious to seek out answers for themselves. One Komsomol member in Kharkov named Tarnopolsky was caught in late 1937 professing heretical views to other members of his local organization. An investigation eventually revealed that when the inquisitive teenager had been unable to find answers to his ideological questions either on his own or within his local party committee, he turned for help to one V. Bliumental, a local engineer who had been excluded from the party in 1928 for Trotskyism.[78] Others were reported to party authorities or the secret police for discussing taboo subject matter like Lenin's testament or circulating banned literature such as Trotsky's My Life and Zinoviev's 1924 textbook on party history.[79]

As noted above, reports of chaos and confusion throughout the system, combined with the exposure of concealed enemies in central party and state institutions, led Stalin to lash out at party educational and indoctrinational efforts at the February-March Central Committee plenum. Denouncing members of the nomenclatura who continued to emphasize technical expertise rather than a thorough mastery of party history and ideology, Stalin demanded reforms that would centralize the party education system into a two-tiered set of "Party" and "Leninist" courses.[80] An idea that Stalin had been toying with since at least 1935, it appears to have been designed in part to differentiate between mass indoctrinational activities and higher party education. Party propaganda, agitation, and indoctrination on the mass level under this proposal were to remain populist, retaining an emphasis on heroes, the personality cult, patriotism, and the Russo-Soviet usable past. These priorities also would continue to govern mass culture and the press, as they had since the early-to-mid-1930s. Higher levels of the system, however, were to stress a more rigorous and orthodox approach to party ideology and deemphasize populist aspects of official propaganda. The Politburo ratified Stalin's proposal in April 1937 and set up two commissions to design the new courses and educational materials. As noted above, Yaroslavsky and Knorin were drafted to rewrite their older textbooks for the lower tier of the new system and to develop a more advanced history with Pospelov for the upper tier.[81]

Chapter Seven casts Knorin's subsequent arrest later that June as crippling this new initiative to finally develop an authoritative narrative on party history. Here, it becomes clear that Knorin's fall was even more significant than that, inasmuch as his arrest paralyzed textbook projects for both tiers of the new educational system and thus effectively scuttled Stalin's entire plan for systemic reform. Yaroslavsky's subsequent failure to produce satisfactory revisions to his older text that July delivered the coup de grâce to any remaining hopes for the launch of a new party educational system during the fall of 1937.[82]

Faced with ideological panic at the grassroots and few remaining alternatives, the party hierarchy sent Yaroslavsky back to work, this time assisted by Pospelov, Stetsky, and a group of IMEL researchers. Such measures, however, did little to ameliorate the increasingly desperate situation on the ground. *Pravda* warned that Soviet social stability and security would be impossible to guarantee without improvements in the political educational system and noted that the near-collapse of indoctrinational efforts was already leading to an increase in discipline problems and the circulation of "criminal verses and counterrevolutionary songs" among the country's youth.[83] Internal party reports painted an even grimmer picture, blaming the absence of effective agitation for widespread hooliganism and the trafficking in anti-Soviet jokes and illegal nationalist literature.[84] The propaganda state was in the throes of total crisis.

In aggregate, it is difficult to exaggerate the destructive effect that the Terror had on mass culture and party educational efforts during the mid-to-late 1930s. Canonical novels, plays, motion pictures, and textbooks were consumed in the bloodletting between 1936 and 1938. What's more, the purges effectively compromised a whole array of more general propaganda tropes that had been key to improvements in mass mobilization since the early 1930s. In particular, the purge of the Soviet Olympus hampered the ability of activists to illustrate Soviet values like heroism, valor, and patriotism through the invocation of famous names from the party, military, and civilian elite. Unable to even publish a tenable Stalin biography for much of the 1930s, the regime found that the Terror's destruction of its heroic pantheon stymied its efforts to instill a positive sense of Soviet identity in the restive society.

Although revealing, the collapse of the party educational system during the Terror should probably come as no surprise, as it had been in turmoil for years by the time the First Moscow Trial opened in the fall of 1936. The crippling of Soviet mass culture is more eye-opening, insofar as it has long been assumed that this was the propaganda state's greatest strength. But by the end of the purges, what had been a dynamic mobilizational machine lay in ruins, undermined by social paranoia and a predatorial censor. This pathetic state of affairs is perhaps best epitomized by the arrest of a minor party official in Kursk in early 1939 for anti-Soviet agitation. According to official reports, his crime consisted of using old newspapers as a makeshift tablecloth and, in so doing, draping a large, handsome portrait of Tukhachevsky over the front of his desk for all to see.[85] Such hysteria stopped Soviet mass culture in its tracks between 1936 and 1938.

9   Public Opinion Imperiled

IN HIS MEMOIRS, K. M. Simonov remembered back to 1937, when he was just 22 years old:

> probably like the majority of people—at least the majority of the young people of my generation—I thought that the criminal case against Tukhachevsky and other military officers was probably correct. Who would have benefited from sentencing and executing such people as Marshal Yegorov and Tukhachevsky, the Deputy People's Commissar and the head of the general staff, if they weren't guilty? I had less of an opinion of the others than I did of these two, but they were all in my youthful consciousness the pride of the Red Army and its command staff. Who would have arrested and then sentenced them to be shot if they were innocent? There was no reason to doubt, of course, that there had been some sort of frightening conspiracy against Soviet power. Doubts simply never came to mind because there was no alternative: either they were guilty or what was happening was utterly incomprehensible.[1]

As influential as Simonov's memoirs have been, his recollection of how "the majority" of his generation felt about the purge of the Red Army high command is rather misleading. This chapter demonstrates that the society's reaction to the fall of the Soviet Olympus was not only highly varied but clouded by misgivings and doubt. Doubt over the veracity of the accusations; doubt over the motives of those responsible for the charges; and doubt about the nature of the Soviet experiment that for many years had been personified by the valor and devotion of these heroes. Such glimpses of how society reacted to the fall of these heroes are drawn from letters, diaries, and secret police reports; further illustration is provided by interviews conducted with Soviet refugees in West Germany between 1950 and 1951 and memoirs written either during Stalin's lifetime or just after his death. In aggregate, these accounts paint a devastating picture of what the purges did to popular morale between 1936 and 1938.

The USSR's embrace of the usable past during the early-to-mid-1930s gave the party hierarchy tremendous mobilizational power over Soviet society, but only as long as Stalin and his comrades-in-arms kept their story straight. Indeed, the renewal of interparty tensions, mass arrests, and executions in the wake of the December 1934 Kirov murder had a palpable effect on the growing social consensus.[2] The fall of the party veteran Yenukidze in mid-1935 only added to the popular anxiety and confusion, especially within the left-leaning intelligentsia. A. G. Solovyov, for instance, a professor at Sverdlov University in Moscow, devoted an entire day's entry in his diary to the event:

> June 10. Unpleasant news. Yenukidze, one of the oldest Bolsheviks and one of the founders of the Baku social democratic party at the end of the previous century, has been expelled from the party on charges of personal impropriety and removed from his post as secretary of the USSR's Central Executive Committee. Another Old Bolshevik, [A. E.] Badaev, received a reprimand and was removed from his post as chair of the All-Union Central Electoral Committee for the same thing. [G. N.] Voitinsky says that when they went on a business trip to the Far East to present some medals, some people denounced them for their licentious behavior in the train car. For some reason, this is hard to believe. Both these fellows are almost 60 years old, senior citizens, and veteran party members in high positions. They're not total fools.[3]

Sarah Davies reports that the news of Yenukidze's disgrace was read as a sign of something considerably more serious than personal misconduct, even outside the intelligentsia. The scandal "led to demands that all the higher ups [verkhi] be checked, including those in the Central Committee, since the real root of the country's problems lay with them and not with the grassroots [nizy]. These sentiments grew more pronounced as the regime itself encouraged vigilance toward those in positions of power."[4]

The situation escalated in 1936–1937 with the first major show trials. Former Soviet citizens described the fall of prominent heroes and party veterans as "impressive" and "astounding."[5] Rumors circulating on a collective farm near Voronezh during discussions of the soon-to-be ratified USSR constitution in October 1936, for instance, mourned that "Zinoviev and Kamenev were prominent figures and popular among the people. They would have been voted into the government in a secret vote, and to prevent this, those in power had them shot."[6] Such sympathies among the peasantry are peculiar, as both Zinoviev and Kamenev had been in detention since early 1935 and had never been associated with rural policy. As with support for Trotsky voiced in the countryside during these years, this sort of commentary should be considered less a sign of articulate oppositionist sympathies than a clumsy defense of the status quo against the return of the political turbulence of the early 1930s.[7]

Although such rumors alarmed the secret police during late 1936, they were apparently not very widespread. This probably stems from the fact that the defendants at the First Moscow Show Trial were, for the most part, members of the former left opposition who had not played any real role in public life since they had last been lionized in the press a decade earlier. That changed, however, as the focus of the purge expanded. As one former Komsomol member later put it, "then came the year 1937":

> A number of officers and political functionaries began to be arrested. The newspapers were increasingly filled with the fateful words "enemy of the people." "Enemies of the people" had penetrated [in]to the Komsomol leadership, there were "enemies of the people" among writers, "enemies of the people" everywhere [. . .].
>
> I was accustomed to trusting the Party leaders and to believing every word which was printed in *Pravda,* and I did not doubt at this time that my relatives and friends who had been arrested by the organs of the NKVD had really been secretly plotting against the Soviet regime. However, I could not understand one thing: why had they begun to plot against the regime? Who were they working for and what advantage did it bring them?
>
> In the course of all these years this was the first question to which I could not find an answer, and like a worm it bored deeper and deeper into my mind.[8]

This testimony is noteworthy as it indicates that while ordinary citizens were willing to believe that there was a domestic fifth column in need of exposure, they were less willing to accept that the traitors had been uncovered within the ranks of the Soviet Olympus. Similar sentiments are visible in the statement of a former Soviet citizen who recalled later the confusion caused by the arrest of Yagoda, whose service to the state had been celebrated for years—particularly during elections to the Seventh Congress of Soviets' Central Executive Committee in February 1935 and then during his elevation to General Commissar later that year. "We elected Iagoda," complained the informant, and "then they declared him the enemy of the people [and] took down his portraits, one after another. People didn't know for whom it was safe to vote."[9] Similar reactions of confusion and loss of faith were reported from as far away as Kirgizia and Azerbaidzhan.[10]

Of course, while some individuals arrived at such conclusions on their own, others were forced to confront the confusing situation in conversations with friends and colleagues. Reflecting upon the series of events that brought about his eventual crisis of faith, Petr Kruzhin wrote after the war: "the first jolt to this contented mood came from my friend, Igor Snezhinsky. He took me aside during recess [in high school] and said: 'Don't you think that all these trials are fabrications of Stalin's? After all, he's destroying the old Communists, the 'Leninist Guard,' those who in their day established Soviet rule and who now, apparently, are preventing Stalin from seizing power and becoming a dictator." Such sentiments caught Kruzhin off guard:

> I did not want to think that the Party of Bolsheviks was ceasing to be a party and becoming an instrument of dictatorship. Snezhinsky was determined to convince me. He showed me his father's files, containing newspapers and periodicals with the reports of Party congresses and conferences. I had not seen these documents before. Once I had read them, however, and studied Stalin's own logic with which he had demolished every attempt by the opposition to defeat the party's "general line," I became more convinced than ever of the validity of the "scientific foundation" of Stalin's whole policy. I was particularly impressed by the comparison between an article in *Bolshevik* by Karl Radek concerning the trial of Kamenev and Zinoviev in August 1936, where Radek had covered the defendants with abuse, and his own confessions from the dock during the Pyatakov case. Radek's hypocrisy and duplicity, so clearly revealed in this comparison, robbed me of all sympthy for him.

Kruzhin summarized the experience in the following way: "I rejected my friend's suggestion that Stalin was exterminating those who stood in his way. At the same time, I became aware that the 'Trotskyite' and 'Zinovievite' trials were arousing among my classmates doubts which were undesirable from a Party point of view."[11] As will become clear below, Kruzhin proved able to resist such misgivings for less than half a year.

Although Stalin was generally quite savvy about mobilizational propaganda, his public statements during the Great Terror tended to exacerbate the emergence of such doubts. For instance, in an effort to elicit social support for the purges in early 1937, he called for party bosses to listen to the voices of the "little people" in his infamous speech to the February-March party plenum.[12] A populist bid for increased vigilance, Stalin's invitation instead triggered a deluge of denunciations that blackened even the most pristine reputations within the Soviet elite. Now, no one was above suspicion. The resulting chaos in the party hierarchy, propaganda, state publishing, and mass culture brought even the most basic political education and indoctrinational efforts to a standstill. Worse, it began to undermine the heroic stature and reassuring image of the party's most sacred leaders.

But if the arrest of party bosses was disconcerting, it was the fall of the military high command that really shattered public confidence in the Soviet system. Public concern over problems in the Red Army can be dated to late May 1937, when the party press reported that Gamarnik, head of the political directorate, had shot himself rather than submit to questioning by the NKVD. The fact that such a figure could be suspected of wrongdoing (and be troubled enough to commit suicide rather than uphold his innocence) was something than many found disconcerting. Was anyone beyond suspicion? As a person in Leningrad put it shortly thereafter, "now I don't trust any member of the Central Committee. Today, Gamarnik shot himself and tomorrow they'll arrest Kalinin."[13]

Gamarnik's suicide produced enough murmuring and outcry in Soviet society for the NKVD to attempt to categorize the various types of discontent. According to a June 6, 1937 report, there were nearly a dozen different kinds of reactions: 1) panic; 2) defeatism; 3) loss of confidence state and party leaders; 4) loss of confidence in the military and political leadership of the army; 5) loss of confidence in the press; 6) sympa-

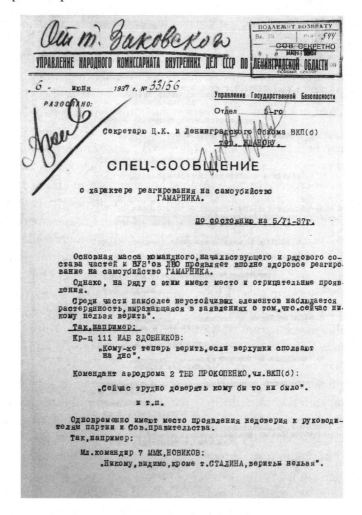

Fig. 15: Special Report on reactions to Ya. B. Gamarnik's suicide from
the Leningrad NKVD. TsGAIPD SPb., f. 24, op. 2v, d. 2498, l. 1.

thy for Gamarnik's plight; 7) doubt over the truthfulness of Gamarnik's
connections with anti-Soviet elements; 8) connection of Gamarnik's suicide with the transfer of Tukhachevsky to the Volga military district; 9)
loss of confidence in orders given by the army command; and 10) counterrevolutionary outbursts aimed at discrediting party and Soviet state
leaders.[14] A damning assessment, it suggested that popular morale and

the credibility of the press, army, and Soviet leadership depended in large part on the reputations of the heroes who were now falling victim to the purges. Of particular concern within the ranks were widespread discussions about the reliability of both senior officers and the military's political directorate. A lieutenant in the Caspian fleet, Sosulin, claimed, for instance, that "insofar as Gamarnik had authority over everything in the army, we should have doubts about all the political directorate's directives." A lieutenant named Kopyov seconded this opinion, noting bluntly: "we should put less faith in the political officers and listen more to the military commanders." Enlisted men expressed the same doubts, one soldier named Beliaev in the 9th artillery regiment announcing that "I'm not going to go to any more political classes—everything said there is a lie."[15]

Tukhachevsky's arrest—announced in *Pravda* on June 11—was especially traumatic, as he was almost as recognizable as Voroshilov and Budenny during the mid-1930s. Even the nonpolitical bibliophile A. A. Krolenko labeled this event "a sensation" in his diary.[16] A. V. Gorbatov, a Red Army general, recalled the confusion that this arrest caused him and his comrades-in-arms in vivid terms:

> This news really stunned me. "How can it be," I thought, "that men who took such a part in routing the foreign interventionists and internal reactionaries, who have done so much for the maturation of the army, and who as communists have experienced such hardship, have suddenly become enemies of the people?" In the end, after mulling over a host of possible explanations, I accepted the answer that was most common in those days: "you can take the wolf out of the forest, but you cannot take the forest out of the wolf" [*Ved' kak volka ne kormi, on vse v les smotrit*]. Such a conclusion was circumstantially based on the fact that M. N. Tukhachevsky and several other people arrested with him hailed from rich families and had been officers in the tsarist army. "Obviously," many people mused at the time, "they fell into the nets of foreign intelligence organizations while abroad."[17]

A former sailor in the merchant marine remembered the announcement of Tukhachevsky's unmasking vividly: "I remember coming to school and someone was taking off his portrait [from the wall]. Then all of the boys would scratch out his picture in the textbooks [and] scribble derogatory phrases about him. Now that made me think how could that happen, how could that be?"[18] Another former Soviet citizen seconded this impression, noting that "no one could possibly believe" that Tukhachevsky was a traitor.[19] Similar misgivings appear in party and secret police reports on the popular mood in Leningrad. According to Davies, "everywhere people asked, 'Whom do we trust now?'"[20] A teacher from Belorussia vividly remembered this aspect of the Terror from the days of his youth:

> We students were very concerned [about the arrests]. When Tukha-chevski's case appeared in *Pravda* (1937), everybody knew that something was wrong in the Kremlin. The first article in *Pravda* did not say that Tukhachevski was under arrest. It only said that he was transmitted [*sic*, transferred] to some other region. But everybody knew that it was a big lie. One week later, Tukhachevski was tried and sentenced to death. After Tukhachevski's execution, one could see in men's washrooms such inscriptions as: "Tukhachevski is our leader," "Down with Stalin," etc.[21]

Although such views seem to express general support for Tukhachevsky, others seem to have believed in the Marshal so unconditionally that they accepted the official story that he had been plotting to depose Stalin, transforming the nature of the act from a treacherous crime to a patriotic deed. According to one contemporary, Tukhachevsky was "the head of the national military opposition. He had my sympathy. He was a man of high culture and great military talent."[22] Others reported not knowing precisely what to think and concluded only that the role model's arrest had had a very negative effect on public morale.[23]

The situation eroded still further as news circulated during the summer of 1937 of the arrest of dozens of other famous names from the leading ranks of the Red Army, navy, and air force—Yakir, Uborevich, Kork, Eideman, B. M. Feldman, and others. Gorbatov, who knew Yakir personally, described the news as a "terrible blow" that he initially found as hard to rationalize as he did the arrest of Tukhachevsky. "Deep down, I nursed the hope that it was only a mistake—'it will be sorted out and he will be released.' But this was the sort of thing that only the closest friends risked saying to one another."[24] Afinogenov too, even amid all his problems following his own expulsion from the party, expressed shock and disorientation at the arrest of the officers.[25] Kruzhin, who had been a stubborn party loyalist in the Komsomol, also recorded similar doubts in his diary. As he remembered later,

> In May 1937, the head of the Political Administration of the Red Army, Jan Borisovich Gamarnki [*sic*], shot himself. The papers reported that he had become entangled in counterrevolutionary connections. Soon after-

ward, they told of the execution of Tukhachevsky, Uborevich, Yakir, and other worthy heroes of the Civil War and leaders of the Red Army. These were not just Party bosses whose number was up. They were the pride of the land as far back as I could remember, and the foundation of our hopes, if we should clash with the capitalist West or with Nazi Germany. The reports that they had sold themselves to foreign espionage made no sense to me. When I pasted the articles about the execution of the military leaders into my diary I added the note: "What can all of this mean?"[26]

Another former Soviet citizen claimed that the arrests that followed the fall of Tukhachevsky marked a turning point in his impressions of the regime as well:

INFORMANT: Until 1937 I thought that [party propaganda was true and that if the papers said something,] it must be like that. I was 16 years old at that time. In 1937 in connection with the execution of Tukhashevsky [sic] and the military conspiracy, I stopped believing in the Soviet Power.
INTERVIEWER: Why did the Tukhashevsky case affect you so much?
INFORMANT: Because these people had great merit. They were great specialists in military affairs. My father often told me about Yakir. He had served in his division during the civil war. And what he told me about him was always good. He became indignant [about] how all this happened, and I was indignant with him.[27]

Thousands of miles away in the Molotov factory in Khabarovsk, a factory school teacher named O. B. Tsapenko apparently shared similar misgivings, publicly questioning the accusations against Tukhachevsky and Yakir and the details of the case against Zinoviev and Kamenev. Disbelief over the fate of these Old Bolsheviks, combined with the execution of dozens of "enemies" uncovered within the personnel of the nearby Amur railroad, then led Tsapenko to demonstratively resign from the party and surrender her party card.[28]

Of course if some reacted with disbelief to the charges, others succumbed to the social paranoia. Commoners in Leningrad were overheard commenting that "if the leading figures in the Red Army have turned out to be spies, it will be difficult to trust the Politburo"; "we should disband the entire Central Committee and elect a new government"; and so on.[29] Within the ranks, a soldier named Vasiliev in the 85th artillery regiment concluded that all the "bourgeois specialists" who had served under the old regime before joining the Red Army must be traitors. This assumption led him to announce to friends that "in my mind, all the former [tsarist] officers in the army need to be replaced. They are politically unreliable elements and the fascists will always try to find ways to buy their loyalty." Kondakov, the commander of a submarine in the Baltic fleet, made a similar comment when he claimed that "all the old officers and in general all the former [tsarist officers] who currently serve in the fleet and work dishonestly should be investigated, even if they have medals. After all, you can take the wolf out of the forest, but you cannot take the forest out of the wolf."[30]

As arrests in the summer and fall of 1937 spread to members of the command staff without an imperial pedigree, suspicions within the ranks ceased to discriminate between "reliable" and "unreliable" officers. The rumors apparently became such common knowledge that foreign military attachés in Moscow began to speculate on their overall effect on the Red Army itself. One of the best informed of this group, the Lithuanian Kasis Skuchas, became convinced that the Terror was undermining the Red Army's much-lauded esprit de corps. According to NKVD sources, Skuchas believed that "the purges have brought about a certain loss of faith among Red Army soldiers in the honesty and competency of their commanders."[31]

Word of this crisis in confidence and morale within the ranks reached the high command too frequently to be denied or written off as a temporary phenomenon. Even Voroshilov apparently experienced moments of despair, writing with unusual humility in an early outline of his speech to the June 1937 Central Committee party plenum that the revelations had undermined the Red Army not only as a fighting force, but as an institution as well:

> 6. How has the Army reacted to the arrests and the execution of the fascist band? The army's authority in the country [. . .] is crippled [*pokoleblen*], as is the high command in the army itself.
> [. . .]
> 11. The authority of the high command has been undermined [*podorvan*] [. . .].
> [. . .]
> 15. It's necessary to quickly restore the army's authority.
> [. . .]
> *Conclusions:* [. . .] This means that our method of work, our whole system for running the army, and my work as People's Commissar, has utterly collapsed.[32]

Unsurprisingly, Voroshilov excised such statements from the final text of his speech and probably never shared his sentiments with other members of the party hierarchy.[33] Nor did these doubts stop him from playing a key role in the ongoing purge of the Red Army's command staff.[34] Nevertheless, reports of restiveness in the ranks reached Stalin, perhaps through the party and secret police intelligence on popular morale that made its way to his desk. Apparently concerned, the general secretary took the issue to an August 1937 meeting of army political officers. There, he interrupted the speech of A. P. Prokofiev, a corps commissar and member of the military council of the North Caucasus military district, in order to have the officer address the crisis directly:

STALIN: And how have the Red Army soldiers related to the fact that they had commanders that they trusted, and then they were busted and arrested [ikh khlopnuli, arrestovali]? How did they react to that?

PROKOFIEV: As I reported, Com[rade] Stalin, at first in the ranks among an array of soldiers there were doubts, and they expressed these doubts by saying that such people like Gamarnik and Yakir, whom the party had trusted over a period of many years with high posts, had turned out to be enemies of the people, traitors.

STALIN: Well, yes, the party was caught napping [prozevala] . . .

PROKOFIEV: Yes, the party was indeed caught napping . . .

STALIN: Are there instances where the party has lost its authority, where the military leadership has lost its authority? Do they say to hell with you, you send us someone today and then arrest him tomorrow. Let God sort it out and decide who's to be believed? (Murmurs in the hall)

UNIDENTIFIED: Such conversations did take place. And such complaints were handed in.[35]

Apparently nervous about the implications of Prokofiev's frank assessment of the situation in the ranks, another officer, Kulikov, returned to the subject later in the conference. Reminding the audience of what they already knew—that "Comrade Stalin has asked whether the party's authority or the army's authority had been undermined"—he denied that any soldiers under his supervision had wavered in their faith in the system. Dissatisfied with such efforts to whitewash over the seriousness of the situation, Stalin reined the speaker in, calling out: "Well, it's a bit undermined."[36] Ya. V. Volkov, a divisional commissar and head of the Pacific Fleet's political directorate, agreed that the party hierarchy's concerns were indeed justified: "We also had some of those conversations that were reported in other military districts about how it's no longer possible to trust anyone. [Some said that] you can trust Stalin, Kaganovich, Voroshilov, and Kalinin. But there was distrust for the command staff."[37] Eager to resolve the vexing issue, Stalin seized on the distinction that Volkov drew between the party hierarchy and the command staff, joking: "Well, that's okay then. Let them try a bit harder. Let them win back their trust."[38]

But despite Stalin's bravado, problems with confidence in the ranks continued to make their presence felt for the remainder of the interwar period. Belorustsev, a soldier in the 7th special motorized armor brigade, revealed how little he trusted his superiors in 1938 in a conversation about vigilance:

> Now, if you notice or recognize an enemy, there's no one to report it to, because the higher the boss, the more likely that he's also an enemy of the people. It's possible that Stalin and some others are not enemies of the people, but the entire leadership of the army—Tukhachevsky, Yakir, and the others—had turned out to be enemies. You have to ask, whom can you trust and to whom can you report? Yagoda was in the organs of the NKVD, and he's also an enemy of the people.[39]

Nor were the party hierarchs exempt from this distrust within the ranks. A deputy political officer named Sharandin, for instance, questioned the loyalty of the country's leaders in the fall of 1938 as he denounced a memorization exercise in his party study circle. "Why do we have to know the membership of the Supreme Soviet presidium," he asked, "when half of them are probably enemies of the people?"[40] Even more damning were the comments of another soldier, Frantsishko, who expressed doubts over what he was reading in *Pravda*. When one of his interlocutors attempted to calm his fears by assuring him that the newspaper was the official organ of the party's Central Committee, Frantsishko replied dismissively: "What do I know? Perhaps there are wreckers there too?" In general, Frantsishko continued, the fact that so many traitors were being discovered in high office was upsetting and left him not knowing where to turn. "It's not at all clear who's the wrecker—the one who is hauled off or the one who uncovers and arrests him."[41]

Although such commentary's only immediate result was Frantsishko's own arrest, over time it came to haunt high officials, especially in the military. For instance, according to the Lithuanian observer Skuchas:

every commander in the command staff now senses that he is being watched by those around him with suspicion. As a result, he no longer can consider only military factors as he is giving an order. He is now aware that before he give an order, he must meticulously consider whether the order could be politically interpreted in a way that would be unfavorable to him. As a result of this, a tendency has emerged among commanders to avoid giving certain orders until they have been given preliminary approval by senior military commanders. And their senior commanders, in turn, are inclined in the same way to shrug off the responsibility for giving orders, either by formulating draft orders for the review of the high command even when military interests demand immediate action, or by simply slipping such orders under their desk blotters and ignoring them.[42]

Indeed, there is substantial evidence of the disorganizing effect that the purges had on Red Army discipline and readiness.[43] As late as the fall of 1939, the aftershocks of this crisis were still being felt. When orders were given for Red Army reserves to mobilize (perhaps in connection with the coming Finnish campaign), a soldier named Shtylev denounced the directive. "This is a wrecker's command," he alleged. "Enemies of the people—Tukhachevsky and Uborevich—they also signed such commands. I don't believe this decree."[44]

Evidence of how these revelations affected mass agitational efforts outside army ranks is found in the testimony of people like that of a former peasant who witnessed the slaughter of the Soviet Olympus as a teenager. As he recalled to an interviewer in 1950,

in the 6th and 7th grade, we see the portraits of Stalin and his closest associates, Blucher [sic, Bliukher] and Egorov. We learn their biography by heart and repeat it over and over again. Then, two weeks pass, and every one of us is told that these people are the enemies of the people. They don't tell us exactly what they have done, but they simply affix this label to them and tell us that they are enemies who have had contact with foreign agents. Now, even 14- or 15-year-olds begin to wonder how the closest associates of Stalin who have been associated with him for 20 years suddenly become enemies of the people.

Particularly devastating, according to this informant, was the Terror's effect on those who had most readily obeyed calls to idolize individual members of the heroic pantheon. "As a child," he said, "I picked Voroshilov as my personal hero. But, say, another boy picked Tukhachevski.

All the boy's fantasies are destroyed. What should he think now, this boy, who believed so blindly before?"[45] Of course, this crisis of confidence was not limited to military heroes. Kruzhin notes in his memoirs that as young Komsomol activists, he and his friends found the late 1938 arrest of Kosarev very disconcerting.[46]

Dozens of accounts by other eyewitnesses confirm the degree of anxiety and despair that mounted in society as each successive wave of the Terror swept away heroes who had long personified the Soviet system. After the Third Moscow Trial in early March 1938, a teacher in Vyborg was reported as exclaiming: "it's just not possible to believe that Bukharin and Rykov could have done those heinous things." A collective farmer named Oboenkov was even more outspoken in this regard, saying: "Soviet power has executed the best people, calling them enemies, but all they were guilty of struggling for was a good life for the peasantry."[47] Eventually, some began to lose track of the arrests on the local, regional, and all-union levels—one confused worker in Leningrad, for instance, was reported to have inquired whether there were any party leaders who *hadn't* been accused of treachery.[48] The merchant marine sailor quoted above recalled later that the purges caused him to lose his faith in official propaganda while still a school child. Discovery of enemies of the people throughout the party, state, and Red Army was shocking, as were "the shootings, the trials [of] people like Tukhachevsky, Bukharin, and Sinoviev [*sic*, Zinoviev]." Even for school children, the sudden fall of such iconic individuals provoked feelings of disbelief: "One day, their pictures are on the walls in school and in the textbooks. The next day, all of a sudden we were told they're enemies of the people." "How could one believe that?"[49]

Occasionally, the shock of the pantheon's purge was simply too great for the society's most impressionable, driving them to romanticize the fallen heroes as martyrs to an imagined cause. For instance, when the diary of a cadet named Diachonov was discovered at a flying school near Odessa, it was found to contain a fascinating mélange of idolatry mixed with wishful thinking and paranoiac anti-Semitism. "Some of the best people," he wrote, "who wanted to support the working people [. . .] are being slandered [. . .]. People like Trotsky, Kamenev, Zinoviev, Bliukher, and Yegorov. You died serving the workers' interests, but your words did not die, nor did your ideas or the plans you laid down. Believe me that although you didn't succeed in realizing them, we will continue the struggle against the kikes and Soviet power or at least our children will."[50] Others, like the Komsomol member A. Krukun near Kharkov, went even further. He and a group of friends were caught in 1937 distributing pamphlets celebrating the fallen for their service to an entirely different community of people: "Let us pray for the newly martyred Kamenev and Zinoviev, killed for the Russian Orthodox faith and the Russian Orthodox fatherland. May God save the souls of all those killed by the hand of the antichrist."[51]

Of course, such reactions were far from the norm. Remembering back to the years of the Terror in his memoirs, the musician Yu. Yelagin wrote of how ordinary Soviets reacted to how "overnight, the idols of yesterday turned out to be fascists, Trotskyites, spies, Bukharinites, traitors, saboteurs, and enemies of the people," stripping the Soviet Olympus of its heroes and patriots. "The average person looked on in horror and confusion as generals, writers, members of the government, Marxist philosophers, engineers, and scientists were consumed by Yezhov's meat grinder." According to Yelagin, people panicked over who would now serve as role models for inspiration and emulation. Stalin, of course, remained a popular locus of attention, but his example was too static and unwavering to function as an example for everyday conduct. Who else did not seem at risk? Yelagin notes somewhat self-servingly that the society found its new idols far from the shop floor, the guard tower, and the party headquarters: "only flyers, musicians, and chess players seemed to have their feet on solid ground." Generalizing on the basis of personal experience, Yelagin concluded that in the wake of the purges, "the popular masses shifted their sympathies to representatives of these three professions."[52]

As elections to the Supreme Soviet approached in October 1937, Leningrad resident Ye. A. Fokina was asked by one of her acquaintances whom she planned to vote for. "I'll vote for Voroshilov," she replied. "But," she added, "if I could vote for Tukhachevsky, I'd vote for him." A remarkably candid statement, it was far from the only comment of its kind recorded by the NKVD during that election cycle. As noted above, elections played an important symbolic role in the Soviet system, affording average people an opportunity to express themselves in political terms. But while electoral campaigns during the mid-1930s had celebrated unity through examples of heroism and patriotic sentiment, now public opinion was much more confused. A collective farmer named Voronov, for instance, nominated Bukharin as a candidate, despite his recent disappearance from public life. S. Popov, a worker in Slutsk, took a much more fatalistic approach, declaring the elections to be an exercise in futility. "There's no point in voting Stalin and Molotov into the Supreme Soviet," he claimed, "as they're sure to be executed soon."[53] Popov's sentiment that the system was turning against its heroes was echoed in an anonymous leaflet that circulated in Leningrad during elections the following spring:

> Comrades!
>   This regime of unheard-of terror is not coming to an end.
>   Hundreds of thousands of people have been arrested, banished, or killed.
>   The "untouchable" deputies—Postyshev, [L. M.] Zakovsky, Yegorov, Dybenko, [K. P.] Ushakov, and others—have been arrested. The hero of the civil war, Dybenko, has been killed. The families of these enemies of the people are being persecuted with a savagery that surpasses by far that of the tsarist hangmen.[54]

Although remembered today as hardliners within the party, NKVD, and Red Army, these individuals were the focus of considerable popular admiration and affection during the mid-1930s. Their "unmasking" as enemies during the Great Terror, therefore, undermined not only official propaganda, but public opinion itself.

As much as the outcry of people like Fokina, Voronov, and Popov can help characterize public reactions to the purge of Soviet heroes during the Great Terror, their sentiments can also aid in a broader reassessment of the period as well. Historically, there's been considerable debate over the degree to which the Terror interfered with ordinary people's lives. If many scholars have argued that the purges affected almost all Soviets in society in one way or another, others have persuasively contended that arrests were too targeted and, ultimately, too few in number, to unnerve the whole society.[55] According to this latter school of thought, personal experience during the Terror depended on an individual's proximity to specific societal groups. Elites were vulnerable, whether party, Komsomol, bureaucratic, military, diplomatic, technical, or cultural; similarly at risk were former members of Bolshevik factions and non-Bolshevik parties, former kulaks and clergy, recidivists, and members of diaspora nationalities living in border regions.

Most others, according to this literature, survived the purges unscathed, often entirely unaware of the orgy of bloodletting transpiring around them.

This chapter's analysis of propaganda and indoctrinational efforts during the Terror identifies a way in which the purges cast a shadow over societal groups that did not experience repression or the loss of loved ones firsthand. Many of these people sensed the instability of the official line through the fates of their idols and role models; many otherwise untouched by the Terror were profoundly shaken by its destruction of the Soviet Olympus. Ultimately, it was the Terror that gave rise to doubts about the propaganda state itself during these years. Put more bluntly, it was the regime's murder of its own usable past between 1936 and 1938 that undermined popular confidence within a significant cross section of Soviet society.[56]

10 Ossification of the Official Line

THE GREAT TERROR'S murder of the usable past between 1936 and 1938 hamstrung propaganda and agitational efforts as it consumed many of the iconic figures and famous personalities of the Soviet Olympus. Merciless and unpredictable, the Terror can ultimately be said to have slaughtered not only specific heroes within the party, Komsomol, and Red Army ranks, but also the motif of individual heroism itself. What were the propaganda state and its ideologists to do in such circumstances? Clearly, new material had to be issued for the printed page, the stage, and the movie house screen in order to replace what had been consumed by the Terror. But on a more systemic level, new themes and motifs were also needed to structure this new propaganda in order to avoid relying on what had been compromised during the recent bloodletting. This chapter examines how historians, ideologists, and their patrons within the party hierarchy attempted to salvage the propaganda state toward the end of this brutal period.

At the very height of the Terror in early 1938, Yaroslavsky delivered to Stalin a new version of his manuscript—now retitled *History of the ACP(b): A Short Textbook*—that he, Pospelov, and a team of IMEL researchers had been working on since the fall of 1937. Although in some senses routine, inasmuch as the historian regularly submitted his work to the general secretary for approval during these years, this event was by no means inevitable. The Terror had consumed many within the ideological establishment during the previous year, including Knorin and many of Yaroslavsky's other colleagues. Yaroslavsky's family had been hit by the purges as well, as his son-in-law's arrest in late 1937 was quickly followed by his wife's expulsion from the party and dismissal from her position in the Comintern. Most threateningly, Yezhov had begun keeping a file on Yaroslavsky himself and—according to Khrushchev—intended to arrest him.[1]

Yaroslavsky cheated fate, however, perhaps because of his involvement in the project at hand. His manuscript—now in its second incarnation—traced the party's revolutionary origins back to the populism and legal Marxism of the 1860s–1890s before narrating its early struggle with Menshevism and the long years of underground agitation. Devoting a whole chapter to the party's dramatic seizure of power in 1917, the manuscript then cast attention upon its dogged struggle to construct and defend socialism during the first twenty years of Soviet power. Although the *Short Textbook* contained a fairly narrow, selective cast of protagonists and malefactors, it was otherwise a surprisingly rich and detailed account. Predictably, Lenin and Stalin loomed particularly large, partly because they animated an otherwise impersonal narrative and partly because Yaroslavsky still apparently harbored dreams of writing the general secretary's biography.[2]

Stalin judged the manuscript to be worth looking at and circulated it among members of his inner circle shortly after receiving it. He also began to edit the introduction to the text, quickly rejecting first Yaroslavsky's version and then a newer one written by Pospelov.[3] Early that March, he and Zhdanov found time to meet with Pospelov, despite the fact that the ongoing Third Moscow Trial was about to decide the fates of Bukharin, Rykov, and their "co-conspirators."[4] Stalin then spent many hours poring over the text during the next few weeks, issuing a number of recommendations in the form of handwritten notes and marginalia scribbled onto the manuscript itself. Many of these corrections and suggestions have not survived, but those that do remain—concerning the manuscript's conclusion—contain all the hallmarks of the omnipresent conspiracy that dominated Soviet ideology during the spring of 1938:

1) All non-com[munist] parties in the working class—the SRs, Mensheviks, Anarcho-Syndicalists, *and so on*—became counter-rev[olution-

ary] <u>bourgeois</u> parties even before the Oct[ober] Revolution and *thereafter turned into* agents of intern[ational] espionage agencies.

2)   All *oppositionist* currents within our party ~~turned~~—the Trotskyites, ~~"leftists,"~~ rightists (Bukharin-Rykov), "leftists" ([V. V.] Lominadze, [L. A.] Shatskin), "work[ers'] oppos[ition]" (Shliapn[ikov], Medvedev, and o[thers]), "democr[atic] centralists" (Sapronov), and nationalists of every stripe and republic of the USSR—became enemies of the people and agents (spies) of intern[ational] espionage agencies in the course of the struggle.

3)   How did this come about?

a)   These oppositionist currents were in [*illegible*].

b)   Then, having been defeated in an ideological sense and having lost their footing within the working class, they turned for aid to the imperialists and became spies in pay of their espionage agencies.

As is visible from these directives, Stalin was most troubled by the textbook's inadequate treatment of the party's struggle with opposition, within both the socialist camp and the party itself. The treachery of the Mensheviks, SRs, and other socialists needed to be given a greater sense of historicity: if at first, before October 1917, they had secretly served the Russian bourgeoisie, after the revolution they switched their allegiance to foreign paymasters abroad. This explained the persistence of their double-dealing and resistance to the Bolshevik movement even after their cause became hopeless. Equally disconcerting was the textbook's failure to make sense of the opposition movements within the Bolshevik party. Referring obliquely to the paranoiac results of the now-complete Third Moscow Trial, Stalin instructed Yaroslavsky to focus on how all dissenting Bolshevik factions on the left and the right had joined together after their defeat to resume their struggle with the party's leadership. Lacking popular support, this unholy alliance then entered into a conspiracy with the enemies of the USSR abroad, revealing the full extent of its ideological and moral bankruptcy.[5] Taken together, these themes were to define Yaroslavsky's revisions to his textbook's conclusions; Stalin also clearly expected the historian to work back through the rest of the manuscript, interpolating details that would foreshadow the unmasking of the entire conspiracy in early 1938.

Although demanding, these instructions were much more specific than Yaroslavsky had ever received in the past, and the historian responded energetically to the task, apparently with the help of his new brigade of assistants. As he later recalled: "they said, 'You need to redo

Fig. 16: Stalin at his writing desk, late 1930s. RGASPI, f. 558, op. 11, d. 1650, l. 20.

it again.' Comrade Stalin provided a whole array of directions. A whole group took responsibility for these issues. Comrade Zhdanov even said along the way that 'a whole collective farm' had taken shape around the project."[6] Focusing closely on the task at hand, they spent late March and early April attempting to accommodate Stalin's objections. Pospelov's contributions during this time played such an important role that Yaroslavsky added his name to the title page as co-author. As they completed the revisions and submitted their third version the manuscript—now entitled *The History of the ACP(b): A Short Course*—to the party hierarchy, many associated with the project appear to have believed that it was, corrections not withstanding, ready for publication.[7] This was also visible in Stalin's own reactions to the developments on the textbook front. First, he steered a resolution through the Politburo in April 1938 calling for a similar set of advanced "short courses" to be written on geography, world history, party history, and the history of the USSR. Second, in the same resolution, he appointed an editing commission to proof what was expected to be the *Short Course*'s final draft.[8] Finally, he began editing the last chapters and conclusion on the margins of his copy of the third version's galleys.[9] Perhaps tipped off to some of the leader's initial editorial concerns, Yaroslavsky and Pospelov submitted yet another lightly revised set of galleys—now known as the textbook's fourth version—to the party hierarchs on April 26.[10]

Stalin turned to proofreading the *Short Course* galleys in a systematic way in late May, probably expecting the task to be relatively straight-forward. Instead, what he found left him deeply frustrated. Perhaps he had been too hurried that spring to read the manuscript attentively, pre-occupied first by the Bukharin-Rykov trial and then by rumors that the purges were beginning to take on a life of their own.[11] Perhaps Stetsky's arrest as the galleys were being handed in on April 26 gave him pause. Whatever the reason, he now judged the text to be fundamentally mis-conceived. According to Yaroslavsky, Stalin cursed that "no 'collective farm' will ever be able to get this right"—something that left him with no other choice than to get involved himself.[12]

Stalin thus sat down and rewrote major sections of the book over the course of several weeks that summer.[13] As he explained to his inner cir-cle in a letter later that August:

> Of the *History of the ACP(b)*'s 12 chapters, it turned out to be necessary to fundamentally revise 11 of them. Only the 5th chapter ended up not needing fundamental revisions. I did this in order to underscore and em-phasize theoretical moments in party history in view of our cadres' weak-ness in the area of theory and in view of the pressing need to begin eliminating this weakness. It was this reasoning that led to the need to fundamentally revise the book. Were it not for this reasoning, the book, of course, would not have demanded such revisions.[14]

As mild and almost apologetic as Stalin was, the new draft that he now sent to his colleagues and to Yaroslavsky and Pospelov made it very clear that he had objected to a lot more than just the previous draft's treatment of Marxist-Leninist theory.[15] Finding the narrative to be over-encumbered with historical minutia, Stalin ruthlessly struck out details, descriptions, and even entire pages that did not contribute directly to their respective chapters. He also strengthened the role of the central party apparatus throughout the text, crediting key events to this insti-tution and toning down Yaroslavsky and Pospelov's attribution of his-

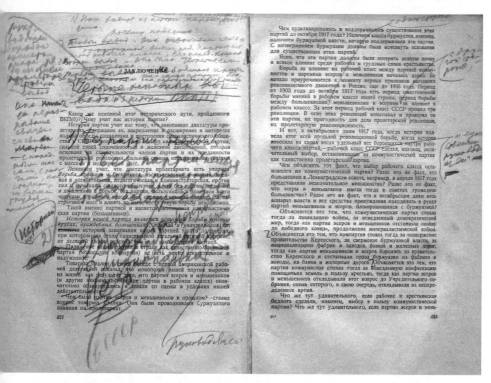

Fig. 17: The first pages of the conclusion to Yaroslavsky and Pospelov's third variant of the *Short Course* with Stalin's marginalia. RGASPI, f. 558, op. 3, d. 77, ll. 322–323.

torical agency to leading Bolshevik personalities.[16] This systematic revision to the narrative was fundamental enough to cause him to cut entire pages, dozens of subsections, and scores of parenthetical references relating to his own career—changes that did not eliminate the personality cult from the text, but did prevent it from eclipsing the leading role of the party in the Bolshevik historical saga.[17]

Perhaps most famously, Stalin rewrote the fourth chapter of the text in order to introduce a long subsection on the philosophical underpinnings of dialectical materialism. Simplifying Marx's, Engels', and Lenin's work on the subject into a schema that he judged to be appropriate for mass audiences, Stalin contended that dialectical materialism should be regarded in both theory and practice as the basic paradigm governing all of human experience, covering everything from the development of society to the makeup of individual identity and consciousness. Nature, humanity, economic relations, and philosophical thought were held to exist in a constantly changing state of symbiosis within which slow, insignificant, quantitative changes (catalyzed by the internal, dialectical contradictions found in all natural phenomena) regularly precipitated sudden, fundamental, qualitative transformations. Dialectical materialism, according to Stalin, provided the theoretical framework necessary for a thorough understanding of the historical process in general and the party's historical experience in particular. It also provided grounds upon which to reject other historical paradigms based on idealism, evolution, or cause-and-effect contingency.

Aside from this major theoretical intervention in the text, Stalin also reworked much of the other narrative red thread that he had long held to run through party history: the struggle with internal opposition.[18] As noted above, Stalin had instructed Yaroslavsky, Pospelov, and their team in March 1938 to interpolate evidence of an omnipresent left-right conspiracy back into the narrative, developing a longstanding theme of hidden double-dealing and wrecking in order to explain all of the complications the country had experienced during collectivization, industrialization, and the party's consolidation of power. Examples of poor agricultural policy, kulak resistance, industrial wrecking, consumer shortages, and factional activity were in this way tied to leading members of the Trotskyite-Bukharinite opposition and their capitalist paymasters abroad. Ultimately, this recourse to conspiracy as a way of explaining domestic shortcomings created a claustrophobic story of tension, vulnerability, and fear in the face of a highly capable, relentless enemy.

As Stalin began to work through this narrative a few months later, however, he appears to have found the omnipresent conspiracy paradigm inexpedient, if not totally unpersuasive. Reversing himself from earlier that spring, he now cut vast stretches of text from the manuscript (over 10,000 words from the final four chapters alone) in order to reduce the intensity and immediacy of the threat presented in Yaroslavsky and Pospelov's manuscript. Not only did the general secretary strike out much of the detail and discussion devoted to the crises in agriculture, industry, and party life, but he also blurred the attribution of these crises to a well-organized, centralized opposition at home or hostile enemies abroad. Stalin also cut discussion of the Comintern and class struggle in places like Germany and Spain, stifling the contention that there was a worldwide assault underway against socialism.[19] What Yaroslavsky and Pospelov had cast as a revealing exposé of pervasive wrecking and foreign-sponsored terrorism and insurrection was disassembled by Stalin into a more generalized story of the struggle for socialism.

This is not to say, of course, that Stalin completely repudiated the *Short Course*'s thesis that the threat of internal opposition was to be treated on par with the danger posed by hostile powers abroad. Indeed, all these forces—internal and external—were described in the book's final chapter as having banded together in a broad opportunistic cabal in order to topple Soviet power and reincorporate the lands of the USSR back into the capitalist system. But Stalin's editing reduced the actuality of this plot by decoupling it from the specific crises that the regime had faced in industry and agriculture during the early-to-mid-1930s, effectively transforming a tangible, concrete threat into an abstract menace. He also rolled back the immediacy of the crisis by suggesting that any malevolent plans already in motion had been arrested by the Third Moscow Trial. Stalin then completed this narrative by quickly segueing into an uplifting discussion of Soviet electoral democracy, denying his readers any opportunity for hand-wringing or doubt. In aggregate, these revisions not only displaced the omnipresent conspiracy from the center of the party's historical experience, but literally foreshadowed the end of the purges.

This new view of the Terror, combined with Stalin's new focus on the grand dynamics, themes, and patterns of party history—"theory," as he termed it—ultimately had an enormous effect on the *Short Course*'s narration of the usable past. Even more than before, Stalin's new "teaching on the party" required the organization and its leaders to be described as having never wavered in their pursuit of the revolutionary cause. Dating the origins of the movement back to the agrarian populists of the 1860s, the *Short Course* charted how these rural agitators had given way to the Marxist social democrats and their focus on the nascent working class two decades later. By the mid-1890s, Lenin had emerged to navigate this movement through the shoals of police persecution and internal division (versus the Mensheviks, "Legal Marxists," Economists, and others). Even as these rivals succumbed to "opportunism," the Bolsheviks remained true to their radical calling, leading Lenin to conclude in 1912 that his organization was now the only truly revolutionary party within the European social-democratic tradition. In the lead-up to October 1917, Lenin's leadership, along with his refusal to cooperate with less radical parties, gave the Bolshevik movement a sense of popular legitimacy that allowed it to seize power in the name of the workers, soldiers, and poor peasants. Lenin, being the visionary that he was, plotted a course through civil war and foreign intervention toward the construction of a socialist economy even before the forces of the ancien régime and bourgeois provisional government had been completely defeated. After Lenin's death in 1924, Stalin assumed the helm of the party and state and steered the USSR first through NEP-era reconstruction and then, after 1928, through shock industrialization, agricultural collectivization, and the struggle with internal enemies. A new constitution in 1936 celebrated the ostensible attainment of a full-fledged socialist economy and proclaimed the USSR to be the most democratic and egalitarian society in the world. Thanks to the party and its leadership, averred the *Short Course*, theory had become manifest reality and the Soviet Union now stood as a bastion of socialism and an inspiration for oppressed workers across the globe.

This new focus on the grand dynamics, themes, and patterns of party history replaced Yaroslavsky and Pospelov's complex—at times even subtle—treatment of historical causality with a dehistoricized assembly of crude postulates, platitudes, and explanatory paradigms. Attention to individual agency likewise vanished in a sweeping depersonalization of the text that explains Stalin's otherwise unexplainable purge of most of the remaining heroes from the narrative—names like Bliukher, Yezhov, the Cheliuskinites (Molokov, Vodopianov, Levanevsky, Liapidevsky, Doronin, Kamanin, Slepnev), the Papaninites (Papanin, P. P. Shirshov, E. T. Krenkel, Ye. K. Fedorov), and the famous flyers of the late 1930s (Chkalov, Gromov, G. F. Baidukov, A. V. Beliakov, A. B. Yumashev, S. A. Danilin).[20] By the time he finished editing the text, Stalin had eliminated mention of well over half of the book's protagonists and malefactors, signaling a return to the ahistorical, bloodless schematicism and anonymous social forces that party historians had been struggling to overcome since the early 1930s. Perhaps the last major explosion of political violence during the Terror, Stalin's purge of the *Short Course* effectively terminated the party's search for a usable past.[21]

These revisions to the text were distributed chapter-by-chapter to the members of the Politburo for a final round of editing between mid-August and early September.[22] For the most part, the party hierarchs reported only favorable impressions as they read through the manuscript; among the objections that were registered, virtually all related to minor questions of style and mechanics.[23] True, Molotov, Kalinin, Petrovsky, and A. I. Mikoian proposed a handful of more substantial corrections (and Molotov twice asked not to be credited with other people's accomplishments), but such commentary was largely ignored.[24] Yaroslavsky and Pospelov also enthusiastically participated in this round of editing, even though Stalin had replaced their names on the book's title page with an anonymous formula attributing the text to "a commission of the ACP(b) Central Committee."[25] In their first notes to the general secretary, both reported excitement over the general secretary's transformation of the manuscript's early chapters and only raised concerns about Stalin's removal of detail on his own career.[26] They followed up these initial letters with a series of corrections and clarifications that Stalin found quite useful while finishing the text.[27] That said, the general secretary proved unwilling to reconsider his decision to downgrade the role of the personality cult in the text. Once this round was complete, Stalin summoned Molotov, Zhdanov, Yaroslavsky, Pospelov, and L. Ya. Rovinsky, an editor from *Pravda,* to his Kremlin office for a series of nightly editorial meetings between September 8 and 18, during which time the *Short Course* was proofed, chapter by chapter.[28] Final endorsement at the end of each exhausting session cleared the way for *Pravda* to serialize the *Short Course on the History of the All-Union Communist Party (Bolsheviks)* in eleven full-page centerfold installments. Dozens of other papers printed the text for local audiences within days of its initial publication, both in Russian and other languages.

Unsurprisingly, these papers and a variety of leading journals celebrated the appearance of the *Short Course* in commentary that was both breathless and highly prescriptive. *Pravda* declared that "the duty of every Bolshevik, no matter whether a party member or not, is to commit to the serious, attentive, dogged study" of the new volume, described parenthetically as "an irreplaceable guide for mastering Bolshevism." Hints in the press of Stalin's personal involvement in the project—"the enormous theoretical work accomplished by the Central Committee and personally by the party's chief and genius of humanity,

Comrade Stalin"—guaranteed it unquestionable authority. *Pravda* called upon the entire party to immerse itself in the book, redoubling its efforts to master Bolshevik history.[29] Massive hardcover printings of the *Short Course* in 1938 confirmed the investment that the party hierarchy was making in the text.[30]

Despite the initial fanfare, propagandists quickly found the *Short Course* frustrating when they attempted to use it in party study circles and on the shop floor. Although conceptually striking, the text lacked the attention to heroic individuals and local color that had made Soviet propaganda effective since the early-to-mid-1930s. Many had come to regard these emphases as key to the official line's accessibility and were unsure about how else to popularize the new text. Such concerns were serious enough to surface at a propagandists' conference that was convened in late September 1938 to discuss the *Short Course*'s role in indoctrinational efforts. A specialist named Shlensky, for instance, noted that although the textbook was "an encyclopedia of everything known about issues concerning Marxism-Leninism," it paid insufficient attention to important individuals in party history. Auxiliary material or a formal curriculum, Shlensky said, would probably be needed to structure readers' work and guarantee its accessibility.[31]

Stalin responded impatiently to such suggestions when he took the floor, reminding the audience that the *Short Course* was intended to focus on large, theoretical questions rather than minutia. More strikingly, he criticized the party's longstanding approach to popular mobilization—an approach he had not only endorsed, but helped develop:

> Until now, party history has been written from a different perspective. I don't want to insult or hound [*khaiat'*] the authors of these history textbooks—they are people who've worked conscientiously and done much for the good of our party—but all the same, the path they've taken, the path which our textbooks have taken, just won't do. They've attempted to train and educate people by example [*na litsakh*], by celebrating exemplary individuals. Not everyone did this, but most did. And even now, Comrade Shlensky notes that the book gives insufficient treatment to the role of specific individuals. But since when is this what is at stake? We were presented with this sort of a draft text and we fundamentally revised it. [Originally,] this draft textbook was for the most part based on exemplary individuals—those who were the most heroic, those who escaped from exile and how many times they escaped, those who suffered in the name of the cause, etc., etc.

But should a textbook really be designed like this? Can we really use such a thing to train and educate our cadres? We ought to base our cadres' training on ideas, on theory. What is theory? Theory is knowledge of the laws of historical development. If we possess such knowledge, then we'll have real cadres, but if the people don't possess this knowledge, they won't be cadres—they'll be just empty spaces.

What do exemplary individuals really give us? I don't want to pit ideas and individuals against one another—sometimes it's necessary to refer to individuals, but we should refer to them only as much as it is really necessary. It's ideas that really matter, not individuals—ideas, in a theoretical context.[32]

Stalin also dealt a similar rebuff to the perceived need for more local color in indoctrinational efforts.[33] Unwilling to compromise on either issue during the conference, he reiterated his position again at the Politburo in early October as the party hierarchy formalized the reorganization of indoctrinational efforts around the *Short Course*.[34] Needless to say, Stalin's was the final word on the subject.

Part of Stalin's dismissal of concerns raised by the likes of Shlensky, Pospelov, and Yaroslavsky focused on his frustration with the excesses of the personality cult, which periodically threatened to eclipse more sophisticated forms of party propaganda.[35] But Stalin also could not have been unaware of the degree to which the Terror had hamstrung propaganda efforts based on famous reputations drawn from the ranks of the party, Komsomol, and Red Army. Shlensky and others seem to have hoped that the *Short Course* would correct the damage done by the purges and introduce a new pantheon of heroes that would revive the patriotic pageantry of the mid-1930s. Stalin's shrill, hypocritical dismissal of such an idea after so many years of encouragement reads like a tacit admission of the fact that Soviet propaganda would no longer be able to rely on popular heroism, famous personalities, and related motifs.

Although the Terror was directly responsible for this fiasco, Yaroslavsky, Pospelov, and even Knorin probably share at least some of the blame for the resulting ossification of party propaganda. They had been slow, after all, to embrace the new focus on popular heroism and patriotism after 1934, and had failed to do for party history what Gorky and Averbakh had done for Soviet industry, what Gorky and Mints had done for the civil war, and what Beria and Barbusse had done for Stalin's biography. By the time that they finally grasped the usefulness of this populist approach to mass mobilization, the purges were already underway and all they could do to animate their narrative was to fall back on the personality cult.

Part of Stalin's confidence in reorganizing party education and indoctrination around "theory" in 1938 stemmed from the fact that he had originally intended the party's flagship text to be used by only the best-educated members of the party elite. Such people could understand abstract material and were good enough Marxists to appreciate a text that was structured around historical patterns and dynamics rather than more populist appeals focusing on famous individuals or patriotic sloganeering. A different set of textbooks, based on older editions of Yaroslavsky's and Knorin's readers, was to cater to the needs of everyone else through a more conventional repertoire based on heroes, patriotism, and the personality cult. Knorin's arrest in the summer of 1937, however, forced the party hierarchy to scuttle these plans and hurriedly retarget its efforts from a bifurcated system to one that would embrace both the party elite and lower- and mid-level cadres.[36] The end result was an uneven, incompletely hybridized text that was to somehow satisfy both audiences. Historical accident, then, built the new party canon around a difficult, inaccessible text that returned party propaganda to the abstraction, materialism, and schematicism of the 1920s.[37]

If a majority of Soviet citizens ultimately attempted to learn at least parts of the *Short Course,* others tried to alert party authorities to the text's deficiencies. I. Sharbarov, a collective farmer from Rostov, wrote to party authorities that the book would be more engaging if it provided more biographical detail on Stalin—a comment that unintentionally reveals the degree to which he and his contemporaries had come to conflate party history and the personality cult. A. Serebrianskaia agreed that the text could be more animated and recommended that sections be added in the next printing that would detail the heroism and patriotic valor of Soviet troops in action on the Manchurian border and in Poland, Finland, and the Baltics.[38] O. Pugachev, a school teacher, complained that the *Short Course*'s fourth chapter was so convoluted and choked with obscure philosophical references that it simply had to be rewritten; failure to do so would result in misunderstandings and perhaps even unintentional heresy during class discussions. I. Gerbichenko and A. Timofeev, too, complained about the complexity of the text and recommended that state publishing houses produce a set of auxiliary texts that would supply readers with help on terminology and excerpts from vital primary sources. Similarly flustered, I. Gamma confessed that the text was so difficult that he doubted his generation would be able to master it without special classes.[39] Somewhat later, ranking officials at Agitprop also submitted recommendations for revisions to the *Short Course*.[40] But although all these suggestions were diligently filed away for safe keeping in the Central Committee archives, there is no evidence that the ideological establishment ever seriously contemplated altering this canonical text.

As flawed as it was, the *Short Course* had a profound effect on Soviet propaganda after its publication in the fall of 1938. Agitators who had longed for an officially endorsed textbook since the early 1930s finally had one; within months, the *Short Course* was structuring historical accounts of the revolutionary and postrevolutionary periods for anyone nervous about running afoul of the authorities, whether propagandist, pedagogue, scholar, censor, playwright, director, or museum curator. But perhaps because it was so schematic and bloodless, the *Short Course* also stimulated calls for additional, more accessible material on ideology as well—something only heightened by the conclusion of the Terror in late 1938. Even before the end of the purges, people like Shlensky, Gerbichenko, and Timofeev were already requesting curricular supplements, and it is in this vein that Karpinsky, the director of the State Political Publishing House, revived the idea producing an official Stalin biography.[41]

At first glance, such a call would seem to have been terribly risky. After all, not only had the *Short Course* just delivered an officially endorsed interpretation of Stalin's service to party and state, but the country's leading ideologists had also been explicitly warned against further investment in the celebration of exemplary individuals. And yet even a passing glance at the front page of *Pravda* during the fall and winter of 1938 suggests that the personality cult remained as ubiquitous as ever. So was there an opening for a biography or wasn't there? Yaroslavsky, at the height of his career between 1938 and 1939, concluded that there was, sensing correctly that Stalin's strange inconsistency in regard to the cult was actually a reflection of the party's failed attempt to launch a bifurcated educational system alongside the *Short Course*. Put most simply, although Stalin had very clear reservations regarding the role of the cult of personality in elite party schools, these same concerns did not apply to mass media or popular culture within society at large, where the general secretary was perfectly willing to allow his image to serve as the personification of Soviet power.

Although Yaroslavsky had been thinking of resuming his work on Stalin's biography since the final stages of the *Short Course*'s preparation, his return to the subject took shape around an invitation from the *Minor Soviet Encyclopedia* for a celebratory piece on Stalin to mark the leader's sixtieth jubilee in December 1939. Intimately acquainted with party publishing priorities since the *Short Course* ordeal, he felt that he could write something about Stalin that would fill a gaping hole in the existing literature. "The need for a biography is colossal," he confided to Zhdanov later that year, "especially in the newly liberated regions of Poland, the army, the schools, and the collective farms."[42] Favorable initial reviews of Yaroslavsky's manuscript faded that fall, however, as the editors of the encyclopedia began to express concern over its bulk and density. The biography's flowery, literary style may also have seemed inappropriate for an encyclopedia entry. With the deadline nearing, they demanded that Yaroslavsky streamline the piece to make it more telegraphic and reserved; stalemate ensued when his revisions proved unsatisfactory.[43] Frustrated, Yaroslavsky appealed to Stalin for permission to publish his manuscript separately as a short book. Stressing the importance of getting a biography into circulation, he denied that the text was inaccessible and assured his erstwhile patron that it had been written in a "simple style accessible to the masses."[44]

If the biography—*On Comrade Stalin*—did ultimately appear in print in late 1939, Yaroslavsky's triumph was short-lived, insofar as his book was immediately upstaged by another project bursting onto the scene at the same time.[45] Unbeknownst to Yaroslavsky, his old partner Pospelov had been secretly at work on another biographical narrative at the IMEL with M. B. Mitin, G. F. Aleksandrov, and Mints, where they enjoyed all of Agitprop's resources as well.[46] The end result of this brigade's efforts was a biographical narrative as different from Yaroslavsky's as night is from day. Structured around a simple, chronological storyline, the IMEL text often offered little more than a series of quotations from Stalin's major speeches and articles. It also focused almost exclusively on the general secretary and his relationship with Lenin, offering little independent insight into the leader's own life (in either a personal or a professional sense) or his relationship with other leading Bolsheviks. Much like the *Short Course,* the IMEL manuscript mentioned only two dozen other Bolsheviks by name, most of whom were long dead. Even close associates such as Zhdanov, Kaganovich, and Beria merited just a single, passing mention on the text's second-to-last page; Molotov's name appeared only twice in the entire manuscript and Voroshilov's just five times.[47] A biography in the sense that it focused on a single individual, the IMEL text was really more of a summary of Stalin's career highlights than it was a narrative—a curriculum vita in prose.[48]

Completed just weeks before Stalin's jubilee, the IMEL proofs were hurriedly circulated for review within the party hierarchy.[49] When a copy of the biography was sent to Yaroslavsky, the latter realized in horror that he had been outflanked again. His protest, addressed to Mitin, was both bitter and maudlin:

> I am saddened that the IMEL has taken such a wrongful position in regard to me and that *only at the last moment,* 9 days before Com[rade] Stalin's 60th birthday, I receive an invitation to make some comments— all the more because long ago I wrote to you personally and said that I have been working in this area and could take part in the compilation of a biography. This isn't [just] a personal insult, as I look upon the writing of Stalin's biography as *a serious party affair.*

After making a number of recommendations, Yaroslavsky begged the IMEL brigade to go over the text "again and again . . . as it is going to the masses." Objecting to the biography's terse, emotionless prose, he stressed the need for populism and accessibility, writing: "the masses must sense in every line a deep love for Comrade Stalin."[50] While Yaroslavsky was scribbling away, another copy landed on Stalin's desk, as was typical for the prewar years with manuscripts of this importance. Stalin, however, returned it to the IMEL unread, a note jotted on the cover page stating bluntly: "no time to look at it."[51]

Gambling on its acceptability, the IMEL advanced the biography into production, to be published a day before Stalin's birthday in *Pravda, Bolshevik, Proletarskaia revoliutsia,* and *Partiinoe stroitelstvo* under the title "Joseph Vissarionovich Stalin: A Short Biography." Attributed anonymously to the IMEL, the piece was a staid institutional history of Stalin's party career, based on Tovstukha's 1927 prototype and the materials that he had collected before his death. Released in hardcover dur-

ing the last week of 1939 and printed throughout 1940, the book enjoyed a run of 1.2 million.[52] Already prominent due to its visibility in libraries, bookstores, and the central press, the IMEL biography ended up
being reprinted in the *Minor Soviet Encyclopedia* as well, displacing
Yaroslavsky's piece yet again. Its appearance also required the reissuing
of recommended reading lists for the study of the *Short Course*.[53] Supplying a much-needed component of the party catechism, this text ef-
fcctively ended the search for an official Stalin biography.

Although Yaroslavsky's *On Comrade Stalin* was superior to the
IMEL biography in literary terms, it was also too complicated and detailed to remain current in the shifting geopolitical context of the early
1940s.[54] The *Short Biography,* by contrast, skirted controversial issues
with remarkable dexterity and remained in print alongside the *Short
Course* until it went into a second edition in 1947. Such staying power
and durability came at considerable cost, of course. Anecdotal evidence
indicates that although it succeeded in harnessing the personality cult to
discuss party history and ideology, it was read rather selectively. Contrary to official expectations, familiarity with Stalin's revolutionary
tenure did not automatically translate into a broader sense of Soviet patriotism or a new-found appreciation of the official line. Worse, the halting inclusion of only a handful of other Soviet heroes and role models
seems to have undermined the book's didactic role and its ability to engage audiences. As a result, when Soviets talked about the party and
Stalin's service therein during the late 1930s, they expressed themselves
in formulaic, clichéd terms that hint at a rather equivocal pattern of
popular reception.[55]

There are several explanations for this grassroots ambivalence in regard to the biography. Despite its fundamentally populist agenda, the
IMEL biography was written in remarkably turgid, stultifying prose.
This shortcoming was compounded by the dogmatism and rote learning that marred political education efforts in party study circles. But
popular ambivalence vis-à-vis the cult may have also stemmed from the
inability of Stalin's ideologists, party historians, and biographers to
emplot their account of the general secretary's life as a socialist realist
Bildungsroman—something which inhibited the book's potential to intrigue and inspire.[56] Unable to diverge from the static, canonical depiction of Stalin as monolithic and infallible, his biographers failed to

harness their genre's potential to describe the general secretary in more accessible, "literary" terms.[57]

But if the *Short Biography* was dull and unevocative, the *Short Course* was virtually impenetrable for all but the best-educated, most devout members of the party. Yaroslavsky and Pospelov had found it impossible to emplot their narrative as a sweeping, heroic epic, and this, combined with Stalin's desperate eleventh-hour return to abstract theory and schematicism, produced a textbook that was not only inaccessible, but confusing and inconsistent as well. And although it is understandable why the party hierarchy lacked the resolve to commission any follow-up work on party history once the *Short Course* made it into circulation, the lack of more accessible materials had a predictable effect on mobilizational efforts within Soviet society at large. By the end of the 1930s, the party canon—once envisaged as a powerful, dynamic catalyst of public opinion and popular support for the regime—had instead ossified into a gray amalgam of stultifying theory, cultish hagiography, and dogmatic catechism.

11 Stalinist Mass Culture on the Eve of War

IN THE FALL OF 1938, Emma Gershtein was granted a vacation at a Sevastopol sanatorium on the Crimean peninsula and bought a ticket in Moscow for the 40-odd hour train trip south. Such journeys were often animated times for socializing and drinking with traveling companions and new acquaintances from nearby sleeping berths, but Gershtein opted instead to pass the time alone, catching up on her reading. Soon, however, she began to feel a bit uneasy, as if she were somehow breaking some unspoken rule. "My nearest neighbor began looking at me suspiciously," Gershtein noted. "Finally, he said contemptuously: 'Is it really appropriate to be reading that book while lying down? One ought to study and outline it. It's a profound repository of thought.' The fact was that I had decided to spend those two wasted days reading obligatory literature. I had brought along the only-just-published history of the ACP(b)."[1] After the war, a former Soviet citizen remembered with embarrassment a similar scene from her teenage years, when she had dared to reproach her own mother for what she judged to be careless treatment of the same textbook.[2] For all its inaccessibility, the *Short Course* was a nearly sacred symbol of the party and state during the Stalin period.

The *Short Course* was, of course, officially just a textbook. But its impenetrability, combined with its canonical status, conferred upon the book an air of unchallengeable authority—something enhanced by widespread rumors that it had been written by Stalin himself. Possessing a copy of the *Short Course* was a sign of loyalty and status, and studying its contents was considered to be a solemn act, to be done only under the most sober of conditions. Interpretation or extension of the text's argumentation was a privilege granted only to a small circle of elite ideologists and central publishing houses;[3] for everyone else, mastery of the text was to be demonstrated by the ability to quote its platitudes and postulates word for word. Citation of the *Short Course* became a key part of authoritative commentary on an array of subjects, from history and philosophy to art, literature, and the sciences. Ultimately, its narrative would define the arrangement of thematic and chronological exhibits in Moscow's Museum of the Revolution and the Central Lenin Museum; its contents likewise defined what knowledge was necessary to possess for membership in the party and Komsomol.[4]

Such influence and reverence indicates that the *Short Course* served as no less than the party's central catechism from its introduction in 1938 until its denunciation in 1956. This chapter surveys the impact of the textbook on Soviet life, both in political education courses and in mass culture as a whole. Key in this examination is evidence of how people like Gershtein's traveling companion read and reacted to the *Short Course,* as such sources can speak to the popular resonance that the text enjoyed during the last years of the prewar period.

Few events in Soviet mass culture can compare with the celebrations surrounding the release of the *Short Course* during the fall of 1938. Official statements amid the fanfare conceded, of course, that the textbook was not designed for everyone, but refrained from styling it as an advanced reader. Instead, it was said to be a text primarily intended for upwardly mobile party members and managerial cadres. The party bosses attempted to be fairly consistent in this definition of the *Short Course*'s intended readership after its release, and officials like Stalin are known to have objected to commentary in *Pravda, Izvestia,* and *Komsomolskaia pravda* that advocated study of the textbook among unprepared stretches of society. At the same time, they also tended to succumb to the temptation to prescribe the book to audiences who were unlikely to be able to appreciate it. For instance, when Stalin tried to specify precisely who was expected to be able to master the textbook at the aforementioned September 1938 propagandists' conference, his answer proved to be surprisingly vague:

> So to whom is this book addressed? To our cadres and not to ordinary workers on the shop floor, nor to ordinary employees in institutions, but to the cadres whom Lenin described as professional revolutionaries. This book is addressed to our administrative cadres. They, most of all, need to go and work on their theory; after that, everyone else can go. One cannot forget, you know, that in our plants and factories we have youth who are studying [in addition to working], and that these people are the future leaders of our state.[5]

Such statements, prioritizing mid-ranking party members but wavering about who else was to work with the textbook, left the situation confusing. Apparently aware of the ambiguity, Stalin returned to the subject at an October Politburo meeting where these issues were to be formalized in a resolution on future indoctrinational efforts:

> To whom is this book addressed? To cadres, to our cadres. And who are our cadres? Cadres are our command staff, the low, middle, and high level command staff of our entire state system, including those working in the economy, cooperatives, trade, industry, culture, health—generally, all those who are critical for the functioning of the state and who allow the state to manage the economy and society at large.
>
> We are generally accustomed to referring to higher party cadres as simple cadres. This is not seen as insulting. And as for the rest, we refer to them, somewhat patronizingly, as employees. But you know, without these employees, without this intelligentsia, without these people who work with their minds, the state would cease to exist.[6]

Such a definition, which apparently included everyone from bureaucrats to bookkeepers, was elastic enough to include all members of the party or state administration above the shop floor in the study of the *Short Course*. "Even Comrade Khrushchev" should be included, quipped Stalin, teasing the Ukrainian party boss for his folksy lack of sophistication. Khrushchev, in actual fact, was probably a better illustration of Stalin's "cadres and employees" than the general secretary even knew. After all, like Khrushchev, many members of the party and state administration had had just a few years of formal schooling and were, for all intents and purposes, only functionally literate.[7] A survey of party administrators at the provincial, regional, city, and local level in 1937 revealed that three-quarters had the equivalent of only an elementary school education.[8] So even if they were technically members of the Soviet intelligentsia, they would still have to struggle to understand the *Short Course*, much less master it.[9]

Ostensibly, study of the *Short Course* was to proceed independently, rather than through organized reading circles and courses. This would eliminate the remaining weak link in the party's education system—the grassroots instructor—and empower the rank-and-file to "master Bolshevism" on their own.[10] Quickly, however, local and regional party organizations were flooded with requests for help with the text, as was the all-union press. As a result, party authorities began organizing consultations and lectures on the textbook that for all intents and purposes replicated the former study circles and courses.[11] These unofficial meetings were, in turn, flanked by an array of new courses in political economy and economic geography, within which the *Short Course* also played a leading role. Just as each chapter of the textbook began with an overview of Russo-Soviet history and economics, now the party's educational system was to reflect a similar hybridity. This is visible in a resolution of the Komsomol Central Committee issued in late 1938 reminding all teaching cadres that "a profound mastery of Marxism-Leninism demands a high level of schooling and knowledge of general history and the history of the peoples of the USSR." Nor were they to neglect "regular lectures on the foreign and domestic policies of the USSR and the history of our country."[12]

Similar priorities governed the Red Army's indoctrinational system. Initially, official syllabi and curricular plans within the ranks complemented the *Short Course* with auxiliary texts like *Our Motherland, The USSR and the Capitalist Countries,* and Shestakov's elementary history of the USSR in order to meet this objective.[13] This awkward collection of materials was replaced only in late 1939 by *The Red Armyman's Political Textbook,* which combined elements of these texts with the *Short Course* in a much more coherent framework.[14] Perhaps symptomatic of this curriculum's focus on state history, the discussion of internationalism, nationality policy, and the Friendship of the Peoples faded from the political educational system between 1938 and 1940. This tendency was exacerbated by supplementary book series like "The Red Armyman's Library," which were dominated by prerevolutionary russocentric themes that emphasized etatism or martial values. Feature films and newsreels shown in military garrisons during these years likewise em-

Fig. 18: Cover of a popular magazine featuring a young woman studying the *Short Course*. Note that a collection of primary sources has been crudely montaged into the foreground. *Ogonek* 31 (1938).

phasized statist and geopolitical issues at the expense of material relating to internationalism and the non-Russian republics. Never justified by any explicit rationale, political instruction on the eve of the war consisted almost entirely of the *Short Course,* etatist, russocentric sloganeering, and the Stalin cult.[15]

Frustration with the difficulty of the *Short Course* forced local party organizations to scramble to provide their consultants and lecturers with material to improve the text's accessibility. This led to the publication of a wave of auxiliary materials—cherry-picked primary sources and commentary—in order to aid in the study of specific chapters of the book. Although these volumes typically republished material drawn from the central press and ideological journals, they nevertheless enjoyed a poor reputation for political reliability.[16] In particular, they tended to accidentally allow mention of enemies of the people into print, either in the primary sources themselves or the commentaries' bylines. Ultimately, the quality of these auxiliary materials varied so widely that the Central Committee was forced to step in and ban the production of unauthorized materials. Even so, demand remained high, and "illegal" volumes of this sort continued to be printed and distributed on the sly until the start of the war.[17]

Student performance reveals something fascinating about the accessibility of the *Short Course* and its various curricular supplements. Although students appear to have grasped the statist dimensions of the indoctrinational line, they did quite poorly with the rest of the *Short Course*. In theory, they were supposed to combine their study of the book with select primary sources—the writings of Lenin and Stalin, the text of party and state decrees, etc. In practice, however, study circles typically got so bogged down in the *Short Course*'s first chapters that they failed to finish the book, much less other sorts of readings.[18] As one former Soviet citizen chuckled after the war, his study circle's slow, halting work on the text's fourth chapter—Stalin's famous contribution on dialectical materialism—ultimately assumed a chronic character:

> In one way or another we always managed to stop at the fourth chapter as summer approached. Then we stopped for vacations. In the fall we would start again from the beginning. I never did understand the fourth chapter. The head of the seminar was the head of the Party cell and the deputy Director of the Library. He was, however, pretty lazy, and did not insist on more energy on our part [. . .]. The discussion was [always] on a low level. No one would ever dream of asking a real question. Everything was just a matter of rehashing what was said in the book.[19]

Despite the reforms, then, formalism—the encouragement of rote memorization, the orchestration of pro forma question-and-answer drills, etc.—continued to plague the party educational system as it had before 1938. Internal reports, a Central Committee resolution, and a number of articles in *Bolshevik* dedicated to improving party education suggest that the situation did not improve before the onset of war in 1941.[20] Because of the canonical status of the *Short Course,* neither these reports nor the press could blame the textbook for its failings. That said, the fact that students and instructors alike proved more comfortable with Russo-Soviet history and current events than party history, political theory, or dialectical materialism indicates where the most serious curricular problems lay.[21]

There were, of course, other obstacles aside from the *Short Course*'s readability and the quality of the instruction that complicated its reception on the mass level. Particularly important was a dearth of other books, journals, newspapers, and brochures in study circles, clubs, and libraries in the wake of the Terror. Much of the problem stemmed from the censor's repeated purging of these collections between 1935 and 1938—something that is difficult to assess in its entirety due to the loss of most of Glavlit's interwar archives.[22] Nonetheless, it is possible to quantify the censor's impact in general terms, thanks to the survival of several major reports summarizing its activities during the late 1930s. According to these reports, between 1938 and 1940 Glavlit enjoyed jurisdiction over an average of 7,635 separate newspapers (a figure that does not include military publications), 1,665 journals, and 40,753 new book titles (totaling about 577 million books) per year. Glavlit also supervised the activities of about 1,500 radio stations, 4,500 presses, and 70,000 libraries.[23] In 1937 and 1938, the censor added 1,860 names to its list of politically unacceptable authors and withdrew 16,453 titles from circulation, all-in-all totaling about 24 million books.[24] Figures for 1939 and 1940 are incomplete, but include approximately 600 more authors and upwards of 20 million more books.[25] As high as these figures are, it bears repeating that they include only those authors and titles officially condemned by Glavlit between 1937 and 1940 and thus exclude not only those officially banned between early 1935 and late 1936, but all those that were chaotically removed by local Glavlit censors and library administrators on an ad hoc basis over the course of this entire period.

Such limitations on assessing Glavlit's overall impact on political education and mass culture mean that while it is possible to generally quantify the enormous destruction of books and other media on the all-union level, such figures fail to capture how wildly the purge varied

from locale to locale. Internal party, Komsomol, and military reports indicate that investigators never knew what to expect when they surveyed
library collections in the wake of the Terror. Often, inventories revealed
library shelves to have been denuded of almost everything of value. In
the Red Army's Irkutsk garrison, for instance, excessively broad interpretation of Glavlit orders during the mid-to-late 1930s resulted in the
library's collection being stripped of all material containing even inci-
dental references to enemies of the people, a methodology that left the
base without essential materials like party congress protocols and back
issues of important journals. The situation in Moscow's Central House
of the Red Army was no better; there Frunze's collected works and
many of Voroshilov's articles and speeches were missing for the same
reason. Other libraries had withdrawn texts as basic as *The USSR and
the Capitalist Countries* and *Our Motherland*.[26]

At the same time, however, there were many libraries where the
shelves remained rife with blacklisted titles. Over the span of just one
month in March 1939, 314 volumes had to be removed from Red Army
libraries. As late as January 1941, books about Trotsky and by Pokrovsky were still being uncovered in division libraries.[27] Ultimately, the
USSR's total loss of books and periodicals during these years was most
likely much higher than any extrapolation based on Glavlit's surviving
figures would indicate—so much so that it is probably only a slight ex-
aggeration to conclude that almost as many books were removed from
circulation during these years as were added. Literature concerning
party history, heroes, and patriotism was particularly hard hit. Indeed,
although the publishing campaign surrounding the *Short Course* was
in many senses unprecedented, many millions of volumes would have to
be printed to repair the damage done by the Terror.[28]

The difficulty of the *Short Course*, combined with the shortcomings
of the party educational system, inevitably affected popular morale
within party, Komsomol, and Red Army ranks. While it was possible to
memorize the textbook by rote, a more articulate command of the
material was a lot more elusive.[29] Some took the task of "mastering Bolshevism" so seriously that they sought out their own sources of information when official channels proved unable to satisfy demand. As
noted in previous chapters, such people borrowed whatever other books
and pamphlets they could get their hands on or bought them second-
hand—a practice that caused hundreds of loyal but naïve communists

to be caught with taboo texts by the likes of Trotsky, Zinoviev, and Nevsky during the late 1930s.[30] Others deliberately sought out this sort of literature, aware that it would supply information and points of view otherwise unavailable in the USSR. As one former Soviet citizen recalled after the war, there was considerable underground demand for books that had been banned as politically harmful:

> For example, take [the early editions of] the history of the Party written by Emilin Yaroskavsky [sic]. In these books you could see the deviationists with their portraits. This kind of book circulated, although it might get someone ten years in jail. We often saw such books in the school. Also there was a book by Popov called a political grammar. Everybody tried to get these books[—]the more they were forbidden, the more they were interesting[—]although everyone was afraid of being reported. Each one was interested in finding out how life was before, why this or that person was arrested, and they tried to compare what was written yesterday with what was written today and they attempted to find reasons for the differences.[31]

While this informant probably exaggerated how widespread the circulation of such literature was, the fact that there was any demand at all is quite revealing.

Others, frustrated with political education in general and the *Short Course* in particular, lashed out at the canonical text and the system it represented. I. N. Tsybin, for instance, a cadet and Komsomol member in the Ordzhonikidze garrison infantry school, got so exasperated with the *Short Course* that he reportedly declared: "If I knew who put this history together, I would hit him over the head [*pobil by ego po golove*]."[32] Others more articulately questioned whether mastering Bolshevism was really necessary for the rank-and-file. An army captain named Somov, for instance, apparently announced in 1939 that "I am not going to do the party-political work because the regulations don't require me to. Let the political officer do it—it's his bread and butter." Bessonov, a pilot in the air force, voiced similar emotions: "I can't get my head around the study of Lenin's works [*izuchenie trudov Lenina ne lezet v golovu*]. We're draftees—let the commanders study the history of the ACP(b)." A. Alekseev, a cadet at the Kirov infantry school in Leningrad, apparently felt no differently, asking "why are they forcing the study of party history on us? Anyone who wants to should study, but for me there's no point—we're just wasting time." His classmate

Tomachev echoed these sentiments, asking "why are they forcing us to study party history? I've never studied it and get along fine without it." Civilians too voiced similar objections, one former Soviet citizen commenting after the war that dialectical materialism—"diamat"—was an "unnecessary subject" that distracted him from more important work. "What did I need diamat for?" he continued. "It was nothing but a heavy burden on my shoulders [. . .]. Such subjects which had no relation to my professional training I hated very much. Especially I could not stand diamat, the history of the communist party, and military training."[33]

Forced indoctrination ultimately led some to reject not only party history, but the regime's whole approach to popular mobilization, contending that it added little to the Red Army's readiness to defend the USSR. When a deputy political officer in Chita asked a cadet named Kaiukov to spend more time preparing for class, the soldier replied with a hint of menace that "you can't kill me with politics, but I can kill you with my rifle. We need military training more [. . .] than political literacy." Vorov, a soldier in a rifle regiment, was reported for complaining to his comrades about the same thing: "They're teaching us these politics, and for what? It's not necessary. We're not going to fight with politics. It's not necessary in battle. We already know that before the revolution, Russia was hungry, swollen, and dressed in rags, and it's pretty much the same now."[34] Although the authorities viewed such statements as evidence of the need to redouble the fight against political illiteracy, they can also be read as a profound rejection of a system of political education that asked too much of people with too few years of schooling.

As in previous years, party authorities and propagandists attempted to bolster the everyday relevance of party history by incorporating the *Short Course* and its themes into mass culture. It was quoted routinely in the press and scholarly literature, and its likeness was displayed in public so frequently that it acquired an air of virtual ubiquity. A statue of a worker holding the *Short Course* aloft even towered over the Publishing Pavilion at the 1939 All-Union Agricultural Exhibit, which unsurprisingly featured a whole gallery devoted to the textbook and its various republican- and foreign-language incarnations. As noted above, the *Short Course* also supplied the background narrative for much of the Museum of the Revolution and the Central Lenin Museum after

Fig. 19: Statue of a worker raising a copy of the *Short Course* up to the sky. An installation at the Publishing Pavilion of the 1939 All-Union Agricultural Exhibition, Moscow. From *Pavilon Pechat': Putevoditel'* (Moscow: Sel'khozgiz, 1940), 5.

these institutions' hurried reorganization in 1938 and 1939. During these same years, the *Short Course* likewise came to play a major role in literary criticism and repertoire decisions for the theatrical stage and silver screen.[35]

As well as scripting the Soviet arts and letters, the *Short Course* had a massive effect on research in history, philosophy, and the social sciences. Much as with Gorky's *History of the Civil War in the USSR,* the appearance of this new text provided an officially sanctioned template for everything from textbooks to more specialized articles and monographs. Many historians, philosophers, and social scientists greeted the appearance of the *Short Course* with enthusiasm, as it finally provided a clear indication of the party hierarchy's official line on key factual and interpretive controversies concerning agency and causality that had long stymied work in these fields.[36] Within this new framework, historians and social scientists used the *Short Course* as a way of returning to scholarship, empirically "proving" its postulates, applying its lessons to other times, places, and national cultures, or rewriting other textbooks to conform to its analysis. Official decrees quickly appeared supporting such work.[37]

But if the *Short Course*'s appearance was in a certain sense liberating for many historians and social scientists, it had a much more restrictive effect on writers, artists, and other members of the creative intelligentsia interested in historical subjects from the recent past. Fundamentally, the problem was the *Short Course*'s tendency to credit Lenin, Stalin, and a handful of their close associates with all the historical agency behind the Russian revolutionary movement and the events of 1917, the civil war, and the postwar reconstruction. This straitjacketed imaginative and dramatic work on these crucial years by limiting writers' and artists' choice of potential protagonists and forcing them to participate in the highly regulated personality cult.[38] Even mention of purge survivors like Voroshilov and Budenny was complex, both because these "heroes" were sensitive about the portrayal of their careers on the page, stage, and screen and because they were difficult to cast without mentioning the names of comrades-in-arms who had literally disappeared from the historical record between 1936 and 1938. Although the artistic community had had to deal with restrictions of various sorts for years, the impact of the *Short Course*'s definitive statement on history, coming on the heels of the Terror's murder of the usable past, is hard to exaggerate.

Literaturnaia gazeta obliquely acknowledged this crisis at the height of the purges, proposing that the creative intelligentsia focus either on the distant past or the Soviet present, leaving recent decades to historians and social scientists. According to the paper, topics particularly ripe for literary and artistic exploitation included Aleksandr Nevsky, the medieval Battle on the River Kalka, contemporary arctic explorers, and the border guards.[39] Both chronological periods presented attractive possibilities—the early centuries of "Russian" state history, focusing on prerevolutionary traditions of political leadership, valor, and creativity, offered nearly a millennium of options that could easily be reconciled with the official line. Modern subjects concerning popular heroism in aviation, science, industry, agriculture, and defense also offered an array of potential protagonists who (hopefully) would not run afoul of the ongoing party purges.

As this editorial makes clear, despite the *Short Course*'s nominal stance against the celebration of individual heroes, the ideological establishment and the press encouraged this sort of creative work after 1938.[40] Identification of a new array of distinctive but uncomplicated heroes offered officials a chance to repopulate the Soviet Olympus and restore the effectiveness of their mobilizational propaganda. As a result, journalists devoted hundreds of column inches in the press to champion workers, flyers, arctic explorers, and border guards, combining mention of surviving reputations from the early 1930s with new names from the present. Thus in industry and agriculture, M. N. Mazai, I. P. Inochkin and A. A. Sokolov joined Stakhanov, Izotov, and the Vinogradov sisters; in aviation, Chkalov, Beliakov, Baidukov, P. D. Osipenko, V. S. Grizodubova and M. M. Raskova joined Gromov, Liapidevsky, and Levanevsky; on the border, N. F. Karatsupa and his dog Indus joined V. S. Kotelnikov and S. Lagoda; and in arctic exploration, the Papaninites joined the Cheliuskinites. Publications like *Flyers—A Collection of Stories* and *Our Transpolar Flight: Moscow—North Pole—North America* continued the celebration of aviation begun earlier in the decade. *Nine Months Adrift on the "North Pole" Station, Four Comrades,* and *Life on the Ice* popularized the polar exploits of Papanin and his team. And collections like *Patriots, The Heroes of Khasan, How We Beat the Japanese Samurais,* and *Everyday Heroism: Sketches about the Red Army* republished dozens of newspaper articles and feuilletons on border guards and their skirmishes on the Polish frontier and in the Far East at Khalkhin Gol and Lake Hasan.[41] Not accidentally, these publications frequently echoed the dramatic war reportage popularized in Koltsov's *Spanish Diary*, which *Pravda* had published in 1937–1938 before its author's arrest.[42]

Such pragmatic publishing was complemented by more ornate volumes like *Motherland: An Illustrated Reader, The Creative Work of the*

Peoples of the USSR, and *The Creative Work of the People's of the USSR About Stalin and the Red Army,* which wove prose, poetry, ethnographic folklore, visual art, and photography together in an interdisciplinary montage of celebratory material. Other volumes, like *Motherland of the Happy* and *Red Army Songs,* supplied collections of patriotic poetry, lyrics, and musical scores. Art exhibits like The Industry of Socialism and The Red Army at Twenty Years depicted this new array of heroes in ink, oil, plaster of Paris, and clay.[43] And all this verbal and visual propaganda was complemented by a new series of fictional heroes in novels such as G. Butkovsky's *The Motherland of Rainbows,* S. Koldunov's *The Hero's Craft,* and M. L. Slonimsky's *Border Guards,* as well as anthologies like *Guarding the Soviet Borders— Conversations with a Pioneer Troop* and *Guarding the Motherland: A Literary-Theatrical Collection.*[44] Perhaps best known of these literary works was *Patriots: A Tale About the Border Guards,* by S. Dikovsky, which follows an intertwined narrative focusing on a Soviet machine-gunner on the Manchurian boarder named A. N. Korzh and his Japanese counterpart across the frontier, Sato. According to one review of the book in *Znamia, Patriots* excelled in depicting its protagonists "in their struggle with the enemy." Dikovsky, according to *Znamia,*

> paints a portrait of the border guards, whose lives and struggles may serve as an example for every Soviet person. Especially notable in the tale is the figure of Andrei Korzh, whose characteristic traits resemble those of other representatives of Soviet youth. He is a collective image, within which the reader will easily recognize Kotelnikov, Lagoda, and other heroes whom we've also read about in the pages of the press. Andrei Korzh passionately loves his motherland and aims with all his being to protect the Soviet country from all kinds of spies and saboteurs.[45]

Korzh, as is clear from this description, is largely a stock figure, designed to heighten the contrast between Soviet life and the miserable everyday existence of ordinary people under Japanese rule. As such, it is only the secondary characters in the novel who offer readers a modicum of drama and interiority. Perhaps most engaging is Korzh's commander, Dubakh, who combines Chapaev's charisma with Klychkov's ideological mentoring, as illustrated in the following passage:

> Like any military leader, Dubakh was both a commander and a teacher. He marked the stray bullet holes in his troops' targets with the same red pencil that he used to circle the mistakes in their dictations.

There was so much that a young fighter had to know in 1935. How does the wind affect a bullet's flight and how big is the harvest this year in the Kuban? How many bullets can a Degtiarev machine gun fire per minute and what are the tactical characteristics of the Japanese infantry? [. . .]

It was necessary to know more now, if you please, than commanders in the civil war had known. All the same, however, according to Dubakh there was something missing from the training courses. What precisely that was he didn't know for sure. It wasn't the basics, and it wasn't the new ideas [. . .]. It was probably some sort of simple and wise formula that would draw together everything that his seventeen fighters were to defend in that sector—the people of all the union republics, their land, sea, grain, iron, ships, and cities [. . .].

It was the party that provided a word for this: motherland. You couldn't think up something stronger, shorter, or clearer.

Dubakh began to cut out all newspaper editorials on the subject of patriotism. Then he turned to articles describing the feats of Soviet patriots. He then decided to create a *Book of Heroes,* a detailed chronicle of the feats performed by Soviet patriots in the wake of the Cheliuskinite era, when millions of people developed a clear sense of the motherland's might [. . .].

In town, he found a massive photo album with a picture of Shishkin's bears on the cover and began to glue into it the newspaper clippings and heroes' portraits.

It turned out to be an anthology of twenty-line stories about the bravery, resourcefulness, and modesty of hundreds of poorly known Soviet people. It was entirely unsystematic. A doctor who injected herself with the plague during an experiment was flanked on one page with the crew of a stratospheric flight. Female skiers appeared alongside a student who saved a woman from a burning building; gold prospectors who discovered a wondrous lode flanked a shepherd who defended his herd from wolves [. . .]. There were flyers who had flown millions of kilometers, the best snipers in the USSR, professors who devised ways of giving birth painlessly, a pioneer who had captured a bandit, Soviet steelers, musicians, tank drivers, actors, firemen, scholars [. . .].

Day after day, this book would explain to his soldiers who Kokkinaki, Demchenko, [B. A.] Babochkin, [T. D.] Lysenko, and [M. M.] Botvinnik were [. . .]. They quoted it in their political classes and read it aloud each evening.

Dubakh was proud of this. He reported with all seriousness to the commandant of the sector that since the appearance of the *Book of Heroes,* his soldiers had begun to group their bullets more tightly together during target practice.[46]

Fig. 20: Advertisement for *Daughter of the Motherland,* dir. V. Korsh-Sablin (Belgoskino, 1937). From *Vecherniaia Moskva,* February 20, 1937, 4.

As is visible from this focus on Dubakh, Dikovsky was very conscious of the role his celebration of valor would play in the party's mobilizational propaganda. Writing in a realistic mode, Dikovsky reinforced the plausibility of his story by weaving mention of actual Soviet heroes into the narrative, suggesting that his protagonists were just as real. After

Fig. 21: Advertisement for *The Border under Lock-and-Key,* dir. V. Zhu-ravlyov (Soiuzdetfilm, 1938). From *Vecherniaia Moskva,* February 10, 1938, 4.

Korzh is martyred at the end of the novel in mortal combat with Sato, Dubakh memorializes him at their base by hanging his portrait on the wall alongside other famous members of the Soviet Olympus, complet-ing this fusion of fiction and reality.[47]

Cinema also fueled popular interest in contemporary heroism with a series of films on national defense, such as *Daughter of the Motherland,* *On the Border,* and *The Border under Lock and Key.*[48] Espionage also took center stage in a pair of spy films from the same years: *A High Decoration* and *Engineer Kochin's Mistake.*[49] But perhaps the most famous film of the period was Dzigan's *If Tomorrow There's War,* which followed Macheret's 1936 *The Motherland Is Calling* and a whole array of other literary and dramatic works in its exploration of the Soviet response to an imaginary surprise attack.[50] As Dzigan's co-director L. Antsi-Polovsky explained to *Literaturnaia gazeta,* their film aimed "to depict the first 3–4 days in our country in the event of an attempt by aggressors to violate our borders and our peaceful construction." They attempted to heighten the realism of the film by creating an entirely new genre of cinema that combined brief, staged scenes with actual newsreel. This literal montage of fantasy and reality—epitomized by the depiction of Vodopianov, Gromov, Yumashev, and M. S. Babushkin leading a bombing run on Nazi airfields—indeed caught the attention of audience members and film critics alike. Equally eye-catching was the fact that in contrast to previous years' material on martial thematics, *If Tomorrow There's War* featured a strikingly triumphalist emplotment in which the Red Army not only heroically rebuffs the invading force, but stages an immediate counterattack, leading the USSR into a brief, just, and victorious war of retribution. *Krasnaia zvezda* hailed this depiction of the USSR's ability to defend itself as a testament to both the society's resolve and the party leadership's foresight: "this good, patriotic film is able to show that we have something to defend, that we have the means to defend it, and that we have the people to handle the defense."[51]

Boasting a popular theme song, *If Tomorrow There's War* enjoyed considerable success during 1938 and early 1939. Several short stories, propaganda posters, and a canvas by the artist S. Perevyshin all played off the popularity of Dzigan's film.[52] It also inspired a reenactment of the film's enemy air attack at Moscow's Tushino airfield in August 1938 during the annual celebration of Aviation Day, in front of the Politburo and a crowd of thousands.[53] Articles in the press demanded more such films, but the sheer number of analogous pictures in production makes it clear that such requests were merely rhetorical. Projects underway matured shortly thereafter into films like *The Long-Range Raid, The Tankers, Naval Post, The Fourth Periscope, The Fifth Squadron,* and the surprisingly martial *Tractor Drivers.*[54] Discussion of work on an-

Fig. 22: Advertisement for *If Tomorrow There's War,* dir. Ye. L. Dzigan and L. Antsi-Polovsky (Mosfilm, 1938); iconic still of pilot A. B. Yumashev on a bombing raid in a Tupolev TB-3. Advertisement from *Vecherniaia Moskva,* February 15, 1938, 4.

other project in 1939, *Sailors,* allowed for its release just a few months before *The Fifth Ocean, Chkalov, Behind Enemy Lines,* and others made it to the screen between 1940 and 1941.[55]

As popular as these new newspaper articles, novels, films, and exhibits were, they suffered from a number of major shortcomings. For one, many of the new candidates for inclusion in the pantheon of heroes were no longer ordinary, rank-and-file Soviets—instead, they were now specially trained and equipped to make headlines. And while this in itself was not necessarily a bad thing, it had the effect of diminishing the heroism of their actions. For instance, during Papanin's mission to the North Pole in 1937, newspaper coverage of the harsh conditions that his group faced met with irritation as well as praise. In some circles, the Papaninites' feat even became a symbol of what was wrong with social conditions in the USSR. A. S. Arzhilovsky, for instance, decried the expedition as pure hype in a diary entry from that June:

> Our pilots have landed at the North Pole and now we are making a great show of our pride. They'll slide around on the ice up there, pocket their extra travel money, run up an incredible expense account, and fly on home, where fools will shower them with flowers, and as a result the state will have to increase its budgeted expenses for scientific discoveries and add a kopeck or two to what they charge the poor slobs who don't even go up in airplanes. What is there to gain from sliding around on the thick polar ice? If you ask me, not a thing. But bragging, portraits, the names of great men in the newspapers—no shortages here. Well, let them amuse themselves.[56]

Arzhilovsky's bitterness was echoed in 1938 by a Komsomol member in the Red Army named Zaglodin, who was overheard complaining about being stationed on the Mongolian steppe: "What did the Papaninites do to become Heroes of the Soviet Union that was so special? We're suffering more here and there's not a word about us in the press." His comrade-in-arms, a party member named Captain Tiulin, agreed, cursing the fact that "all they do is go on about the Papaninites when they have good conditions and are well provided for—all they do is yell about the Papaninites."[57]

In another case, after the crash of A. K. Serov and the famous female flyer Osipenko during an overcast training mission in May 1939, the Soviet press was filled with stories of the pilots' heroism and self-sacrifice. At least some ordinary Soviets, however, reacted cynically to their deaths. In the Red Army, a junior commander and Komsomol member named Ignatiev was reported as sneering: "these so-called heroes—we have so many of them that their places will be taken by others."[58] Parkhomenko, another fellow in the ranks, was even less respectful, reportedly saying:

> Oh, stop going on and on about them. You know, if a collective farmer dies, no one will say a word about him, and these so-called heroes—we have a lot of this sort. Their fate could have been predicted, as Osipenko was flying with a man when her plane crashed. If they hadn't been fooling around up there [esli by oni tam shashni ne zavodili], they would have made it back alive.[59]

As is clear from such commentary, for some, the press's giddy coverage of these heroes had not only ceased to persuade, but had unintentionally transformed its subjects into objects of ridicule.

Thematic complications with arctic exploration and aviation also undermined key dimensions of this heroic propaganda. As is visible from glimpses of the public reaction to the Papaninites' arctic expedition quoted above, planned research missions—even to places as inhospitable as the North Pole—were considerably less moving than the suspense-filled rescue to the Cheliuskinites a few years earlier. Postponement of the establishment of a permanent arctic base and the marginal results of the icebreaker Sedov's mission between 1937 and 1940 did little to stoke popular enthusiasm for such adventures. John McCannon puts it well: "Polar exploits were losing their relevance. All fads come to an end, and, with the passage of time, the USSR's Arctic craze was dying a natural death. More important, the threat of war was looming larger with every month [. . . and] there was little room for adventures in the Arctic as the USSR made its mental and emotional preparations for continental conflict."[60] Aviation too saw its popularity wane in the late 1930s, thanks to a series of major disasters. Levanevsky disappeared while on a transpolar flight from Moscow to Fairbanks in August 1937, and his loss was compounded by Babushkin's fatal crash during the fruitless search that followed. Osipenko, Grizodubova, and Raskova's ANT-37 "Motherland" crashed in October 1938 as they attempted to set a women's distance record, and although the three survived this ordeal, Osipenko died shortly thereafter in the accident described above with Serov. Perhaps most bitterly felt was Chkalov's death in December 1938, when he failed to land a new fighter that he was testing in a spectacular accident at Moscow's Central Airfield. When Kokkinaki attempted to redeem Soviet aviation's world reputation in April 1939 via a non-stop flight from Moscow to the New York World's Fair, his emergency crash landing in New Brunswick cast a deep pall over the theme of aviation in mobilizational propaganda.[61]

Although some heroic names and reputations remained in circulation after the decline of arctic- and aviation-oriented propaganda, their ability to win hearts and minds was hamstrung by their extraordinary one-dimensionality. Undeniably talented, these heroes were characterized in the press, popular fiction, and film as almost impossibly straitlaced and freshly scrubbed—Boy Scout–like qualities that critics labeled "officialese" (*shtamp*).[62] Chkalov (the test pilot) was as fearless as he was talented; Osipenko, Grizodubova, and Raskova (the "Motherland" flyers) were both feminine and competent; Karatsupa (the famous border-guard) loved his country and his dog; Korzh (from *Patriots*) was a simple and kind-hearted peasant draftee; Mikhailov (from *A High Award*) was an eagle-eyed NKVD agent; Lartsev (from *Engineer Kochin's Mistake*) was a tireless investigator; Tarasov (from *On the Border*) was a quick-witted border guard, and so on. According to the official line, they neither grew nor matured, nor did they act foolishly, make rash decisions, or commit even innocent mistakes. In aggregate, such characterizations had the effect of stripping these heroes' life stories of any sense of suspense or dramatic tension and compromised them as compelling and believable role models. The situation ultimately became serious enough for complaints about such hack films and plays to make it into the press.[63] Even more telling was the fact that when asked, few postwar Soviet refugees remembered reading about Korzh and Osipenko or recalled watching *A High Award* or *On the Border*. Needless to say, no one even thought to compare any of these works to *How the Steel Was Forged* or *Chapaev*.[64] Even Dikovsky, who was known to traffick in such predictable, overdetermined storylines himself, spoke out against this sort of artistic work when it was displayed at the Industry of Socialism exhibit in April 1939. "Of all of this huge collection of canvases, engravings, and sculpture," he declared, "only 20–25 are pleasing in a human way. This beautiful idea [. . .] has been realized in pale and even false terms." "The vast majority of these pictures," he continued, "are striking only in terms of their thoughtless, passive reflection of reality." This same complaint also was leveled at the formu-

Fig. 23: Advertisement for *The Long-Range Raid,* dir. P. Malakhov (Mosfilm, 1938). From *Vecherniaia Moskva,* February 21, 1938, 4.

laic art displayed during the Red Army at Twenty Years exhibit.[65] As is visible from such criticism, the new post-purge political and aesthetic orthodoxy had totally denuded Soviet heroes of their spontaneity, subjectivity, and spark.

But perhaps the most serious problem to affect Soviet mass culture in the wake of the Terror and *Short Course* was the new emphasis placed on the inevitability of victory. According to Stalin's new catechism, the party's past, present, and future followed an unwaveringly straight line of policy- and decision-making, informed by revolutionary theory. Defeat of the party's enemies and realization of the communist dream was now just a matter of time. Journalists, writers, and artists went to such lengths to avoid ambiguity and indeterminacy in regard to this official sense of confidence that their work often devolved into little more than bald boosterism and sloganeering—something referred in Russian as "hurrah-patriotism" or *shapkozakidatel'stvo* (an untranslatable expression for the myth of easy victory).[66] Often giddy enough to violate even the tenets of Socialist Realism, this pro forma work drove critics like P. Kuplevatsky to complain publicly in *Pravda* during April 1939. Hailing *Chapaev, Peter the First, The Man with a Gun,* and even *Lenin in October,* Kuplevatsky contrasted the believability and realistic tension of these films against the smug triumphalism of *If Tomorrow There's War, Naval Post, The Fearless,* and others. He justified his reservations by ridiculing Dzigan's film, noting:

> When the enemy squadron attempts to complete a mission over our territory, our air force completely destroys the enemy squadron in the air, losing only one or two planes. This is unbelievable! In the same film, when the opponents' tanks attempt to break through the front, our artillery destroys them without any losses on our side. And when our forces go on the counterattack, the enemy is unable to knock out a single tank. Again, this is unbelievable—losses are inevitable in wartime.[67]

Other critics assailed *Squadron No. 5* and *The Tankers* with similar intensity. Ordinary audience members also spoke out about the lack of realism in such films, especially in *If Tomorrow There's War.*[68] A common trope in the mass culture of the late 1930s, the myth of easy victory was certainly an odd way of mobilizing the society for a war that was commonly viewed as just over the horizon. Unsurprisingly, the bravado did not succeed in comforting popular misgivings. Perhaps it is for this reason that the schoolgirl Yevgenia Rudneva walked out of the comedy *The Tractor Drivers* in the fall of 1939 after the onset of hostilities in Europe, uneasy with the film's happy-go-lucky attitude toward the threat of war.[69] Ultimately, this "hurrah patriotism" ought to be traced back to the *Short Course*'s overconfident claims about its mastery of the laws of history. And tellingly, neither won the hearts and minds of Soviet audiences.[70]

Of course, this genre of propaganda and its implausible heroes, easy victories, and general escapism did appeal to some members of Soviet

Fig. 24: Advertisement for *The Fearless*, dir. L. Antsi-Polovsky (Tekhfilm, 1937). From *Vecherniaia Moskva*, October 19, 1937, 4.

society.[71] Voroshilov and the Red Army high command certainly encouraged these beliefs through massive displays of military might on Red Square and blustery speeches about victorious wars on foreign soil requiring minimal loss of life.[72] But did this barrage of official mass culture compensate for the inaccessibility of the monolithic *Short Course*? Soviet mobilizational propaganda was put to the test on November 27, 1939, when *Pravda* announced that Finnish forces had just shelled the frontier village of Mainila, killing several Red Army servicemen. A Soviet-engineered pretext to allow the USSR to declare war on its Scandinavian neighbor, the attack was represented in the press as a reflection of the threat posed by the capitalist world abroad. Finland, according to this line, was the forepost of a coalition of foreign bourgeois governments intent on undermining the Soviet experiment. Within days, the Soviet press announced that the Red Army had counterattacked, penetrating into Finnish territory. A general mobilization was announced and the Finnish communist O. V. Kuusinen—a functionary in the Comintern since the early 1920s—was proclaimed the head of a new Finnish Democratic Republic and People's Army based in the Karelian border town of Terijoki. Kuusinen's fighting force would apparently assist the Red Army in its liberation of the Finnish working class from the yoke of the reactionary Mannerheim regime in Helsinki. Press coverage predicted that the war would be a short one.[73]

Initial popular reactions to the declaration of war in early December 1939 appear to have been generally positive.[74] Private correspondence with Red Army soldiers at the front reveals support for the troops in the field as well as a broad consensus on the need for the USSR to aggressively defend its territorial integrity. I. Tarasov, for instance, wrote an ungrammatical letter to his brother on December 3, 1939, in which he declared:

> I ask you to be on guard and if necessary, not to hesitate to give your life, in which case I will go to defend our great socialist motherland and give my life, if necessary[;] our whole country is presently in a tense position and if it becomes necessary, our Soviet people will defend our motherland with their lives and sweep away any enemy who tries to attack our holy free country. Dear brother, I ask you not to panic and to be a hero as always [. . .] Brother, please describe what sort of preparatory work you're doing to get ready to defend our fatherland's motherland [*nasha otechestvennaia rodina*].

At about the same time, Antonia Kireeva wrote to her husband Aleksandr that she had heard about how "on the 30th you went into battle to defend our motherland and attack the Finns. It is of course good that you have gone to defend the motherland." A week later, Vasily Stulov wrote to his brother: "I wish you luck and good health as you finish your campaign against the White Finns[,] the savage enemies of the people."[75] Instinctively patriotic, such letters demonstrate a strong belief in an easy victory over Finland even as they express concern over the well-being of loved ones.

Unsurprisingly, heroism proved to be one of the most common themes in this correspondence, as Tarasov's letter above suggests. Just after the start of hostilities, Yelena Nikolaeva wrote to her brother Vladimir at the front: "we can see in the newspapers how our valiant and brave troops, commanders, and pilots are making it hot for the White Finns[;] our pilots are valiantly completing their missions, treating the White Finnish 'nests' to their Voroshilov 'butterflies.'"[76] Much more rarely did letter writers refer to the "internationalist" dimensions of the Red Army's mission in Finland, and even then, only in the most formulaic of ways. Yegor Filimonov concluded a letter to his brother Mikhail at the start of the war by writing: "Be an honest and loyal Red Armyman fighting for the working class." A schoolgirl named Nina wrote to a relative at the front in late December: "I'm very glad that you are advancing so quickly and victoriously into Finland, freeing the country from the White Guards."[77] A mixture of clichés and formulaic phrases drawn from the Soviet press and mass culture, this correspondence demonstrated few genuinely socialist values and little awareness of the USSR's grander territorial designs in Finland.

Popular support for the war faltered as the conflict dragged into 1940 without news of victory. Reversals and considerable loss of life in Finland created significant morale problems as the army struggled for the upper hand against an enemy that had not been expected to pose a serious challenge.[78] Grassroots attempts to make sense of the conflict are visible in the diary of a schoolgirl named Liudmila Ots in February 1940:

> I haven't written about the most important thing—the war. We are at war with Finland. It all began quite unexpectedly. At first, we assimilated parts of what used to be Poland: W[estern] Ukraine and W[estern] Belorussia. The remaining portion went to Germany. After that, we con-

cluded a friendship pact with the Baltic states. But Finland, or more likely, its government, did not like this and attacked us. And we decided that aside from this it was necessary to help the Finns create a democratic republic for themselves. Many people have been called up into the Red Army. The war is dragging on, but our guys are fighting very bravely and will doubtlessly win. If only that would come as soon as possible.[79]

Much like the troubled schoolgirl, Soviet soldiers had been indoctrinated into believing that ordinary Finns pressed into service by their bourgeois government would lay down their arms once they realized that the Red Army intended to set them free. When such rosy forecasts were not borne out in fact, many began to doubt other aspects of the ideological line framing the conflict. A soldier named Balashov, for instance, announced to his comrades that "the war that we are waging with Finland is an unjust war. The Finnish people do not want us to rule Finland and therefore they run away into the forest and don't greet us as liberators." Others were confused by the degree to which the situation on the ground deviated from what they were told to expect by Red Army agitators. Why were working-class Finns ignoring Kuusinen's call to lay down their arms? Why were they resisting the Soviet advance? If the Finnish toilers were defending the "bourgeois" Helsinki government, whom did the Soviet campaign aim to liberate? Such questions proved exasperating to a soldier named Grishnev near the front, who exclaimed in frustration: "What is the point of fighting? We don't know who we are defending and what we are fighting for."[80]

Ultimately, after the loss of several hundred thousand troops, the USSR conceded that "liberating" Finland was going to be a very costly endeavor and signed a peace treaty with Helsinki in early March 1940. Embarrassed by the fiasco, Stalin and the Red Army high command immediately searched for an explanation for why the USSR had been unable to defeat such a small and poorly equipped fighting force. Military doctrine, strategic planning, and battle tactics were subjected to review; propaganda and agitation within the ranks were also examined in order to explain what everyone agreed was low morale.[81] Stalin began the discussion of the latter, first at a Central Committee plenum in mid-March 1940 and a month later at a Central Committee meeting convened to assess the war's shortcomings.[82] Focusing much of the latter speech on military preparedness, he parenthetically assailed the "hurrah-patriotism" that reigned within the Red Army's command staff as a result of brief clashes with the Japanese in the Far East and more recently during the partitioning of Poland with Nazi Germany in September 1939: "the Polish campaign did us a lot of harm—it spoiled us. Entire newspaper articles and speeches were written around the idea that the Red Army was invincible, that it had no equal, that it had all the necessary equipment, that nothing was in short supply, nor had it ever been, and that our army was invincible. Historically speaking, there has never been such a thing as an invincible army." Stalin then continued, assailing the "cult of the civil war" within the command staff that was ultimately responsible for overconfidence within the ranks. "The civil war," he declared, "was not a real war, because it was a war without artillery, without aviation, without tanks, without mortars. It was a unique war, not a modern one." The magnitude of this crisis, according the Stalin, was compounded by the fact that the high command ought to have known better. After all, the imperial Russian army had waged four difficult wars in Finland and this experience ought to have been regarded as highly relevant—certainly more central to military planning than the civil war.[83] The general secretary repeated this line of argumentation at a planning commission of the High Military Council five days later, indicating the seriousness with which he regarded the issue.[84]

The question of political education and indoctrination returned to center stage at the next meeting of the High Military Council on May 10, 1940. There, Mekhlis, chief of the military's political directorate, delivered a keynote address in which he contended that a number of alterations had to be made in Red Army mobilizational strategy. First, changes had to be made to the "hurrah-patriotism" that flamboyantly described the Red Army as an invincible "army of heroes." Such boastfulness about the inherent superiority of the USSR's proletarian army and the expectation that all future wars would be offensive ones requiring only minimal loss of life had undermined military training and discipline. Worse, it had given rise to a rather superficial and inarticulate sense of patriotic identity that was incapable of weathering setbacks and reversals of fortune. Such giddiness, according to Mekhlis, had to be replaced by a more sober attitude toward military service and mobilization.[85]

Mekhlis's second corrective stemmed from his observation that indoctrination had become inaccessibly abstract and estranged from everyday life within the ranks. "We've gotten distracted by propagandizing only the *Short Course on the History of the ACP(b)*," Mekhlis confessed, "and have forgotten about propaganda that will work in all contexts. Propaganda focusing on military culture has yet to become an intrinsic part of Red Army training. It's imperative to help the command staff study military history, master specialized historical literature, and get a firm grasp on the military arts." Although a diehard Stalinist, Mekhlis had begun to doubt whether the *Short Course* deserved a priori precedence within the Red Army's political education system.[86]

Third, it was necessary to further deemphasize internationalist sloganeering within the ranks in favor of a more patriotic, statist orientation. Red Army soldiers, according to Mekhlis, were not finding ideological discussions of their "internationalist duty" very compelling. Even before the Winter War, at Khalkhin Gol, agitational sloganeering that styled Soviet participation in the conflict as "aid to the friendly Mongolian people" had been found to resonate poorly within Red Army ranks. Improvement in soldiers' performance was noted, however, once propagandists began to equate the defense of the Mongolian People's Republic with the defense of the USSR.[87] Similarly, internationalist propaganda during the Winter War—calls for the liberation of the Finnish people, the toppling of the reactionary Mannerheim regime, and the installation of a popular government—were not found to inspire Red Army soldiers. When agitation instead characterized the conflict as one designed to secure a defensive corridor around Leningrad, strengthen Soviet positions along the northwestern border, and launch a preemptive strike against an emerging capitalist threat, Red Army troops responded much more positively.[88]

Finally, Mekhlis attacked the "cult of the civil war" for having only marginal value in the geopolitical context of the early 1940s.[89] Basing his commentary on Stalin's statements during the previous month, Mekhlis declared the "experience of the old army" to be more relevant to Soviet troops than the Red cavalry romanticism of the revolutionary era. "We have a lot of unfair ridiculing of the old army despite the fact that we had such notable tsarist army generals as Suvorov, Kutuzov, and Bagration, who will always remain in the minds of the people as great Russian military leaders and who are revered in the Red Army as a legacy of the finest military traditions of the Russian soldier." According to Mekhlis, it was unpardonable that agitation during the recent campaign had been based on the civil war when Russia had won four conflicts in the region during the 18th and 19th centuries. Ignoring this history had denied the Red Army valuable experience and, more important, a practical vocabulary of inspirational rallying calls.[90]

Some of Mekhlis's suggestions were immediately adopted in the aftermath of the conference. Prerevolutionary Russian history, which had been undergoing a slow but steady rehabilitation since 1937, became a central aspect of mobilizational propaganda within the ranks. Mekhlis's advice on how to frame the war was also seriously discussed by other party and military authorities. Ye. A. Boltin, an executive editor at *Krasnaia zvezda,* repeated Mekhlis's conclusions almost word-for-word to a group of *litterateurs* associated with the Soviet Writers' Union that spring, explicitly noting the need to frame military action in defensive terms and tone down unpersuasive talk of "internationalist duty."[91] In the wake of this intervention, official communiqués issued that summer about the incorporation of Bessarabia and the Baltic states into the USSR stressed how these territories would contribute to the USSR's ability to defend itself alongside more conventional sloganeering about the liberation of these regions' inhabitants.[92] Attempts were also made to break with the myth of easy victory in literature, cinema, and the press, as visible in the example of the 1940 documentary film *The Mannerheim Line.*[93]

In many respects, however, Mekhlis's recommendations either fell on deaf ears or proved too radical for quick implementation. The experience of the civil war and its heroes—Voroshilov, Budenny, Chapaev, Shchors, S. G. Lazo, G. I. Kotovsky—continued to play a large role in military political education. The *Short Course* continued to form the central core of the military's indoctrinational program.[94] And Soviet mass culture continued to release books, plays, and films characterized by "hurrah-patriotism," as did the press in its editorials.[95] True, some effort was made to popularize recent heroes from the Soviet-Finnish conflict, but this military experience had been so mixed that it produced few scenes unambiguous enough to find a permanent place in the popular mind.[96]

With such halting reform, it should come as no surprise that the popular resonance of this clumsy ideological line did not improve substantially in the fourteen months or so that remained before the outbreak of hostilities with Nazi Germany. After the war, former Soviet citizens remembered regarding cinema in the late interwar period as dull and pre-dictable—little more than "a propaganda machine." The press and of-ficial communiqués were regarded with similar distrust. According to an NKVD report from February 1941, a military engineer on the Volga named N. I. Diabin was caught expressing near-universal doubts in re-gard to the propaganda state: "it's not possible to believe anything now (while saying this, Diabin mentioned the leaders of the party by name) or the party as a whole [. . .]. Everything that is written in the news-papers is a lie and shouldn't be believed." Similar misgivings caused an-other soldier named Kremenetsky to contradict official statements about Red Army service as a patriotic endeavor with the heretical declaration that "I have no fatherland nor anyone to defend." Even senior political officers were reported to have lost faith in the system after the fiasco with Finland and succumbed to trafficking in anti-Soviet agitation.[97]

Further indication of the degree to which the official line had ceased to work is reflected in the statements of otherwise loyal members of Soviet society. When called upon to explain the country's seizure of Bessarabia and the Baltics in 1940, Red Army soldiers described these campaigns in terms which were much more *realpolitik* than they were either internationalist or defensist. A. L. Grebinchenko, for instance, explained to his comrades in his rifle regiment what factor really pre-cipitated the USSR's annexation of a portion of Romania in 1940: "It's not the liberation of the Bessarabian people—our government needs land and that's why it's acting in this way." A soldier in another rifle regiment, A. M. Krivobokov, gave voice to similar skepticism regarding official justifications for the seizure of Lithuania, Latvia, and Estonia, of-fering a much more simple explanation for the annexation in their stead: "we don't know whether or not they wanted to enter into the Soviet Union, but facts are facts: when states are strong, we don't meddle in their internal affairs. In this case, we took them because we could han-dle them."[98] Almost neo-imperialist in character, these statements re-veal how little Grebinchenko, Krivobokov, and their fellow comrades had learned about the supposedly "distinguishing characteristics" of the USSR in their political literacy courses.

As is clear by now, the *Short Course* was hardly the first Soviet party history to confuse and frustrate its audiences. But it did preside over a new era in party education and indoctrination that differed significantly from the years when Popov, Knorin, Yaroslavsky, and Ingulov competed for readers. Unlike its predecessors, the *Short Course* enjoyed the official endorsement of the party hierarchy and reigned unchallenged over political education in the USSR. And unlike its predecessors, the *Short Course* was spared the need to compete with the more popular and accessible narrative of patriotic heroism that had been developed by journalists, writers, playwrights, and screenwriters earlier in the decade.

Ironically, however, the monopoly that the *Short Course* enjoyed did not allow it to resolve the ongoing crisis with political education and indoctrination. The Terror's murder of the usable past limited both what the *Short Course* could say and how it could say it, and in turn, the *Short Course* hampered Soviet mass culture's ability to repopulate the society's pantheon of heroes with names and reputations from the recent past. Ultimately, mobilizing the society was left up to a handful of iconic, infallible leaders (Lenin, Stalin), long-dead martyrs (Sverdlov, Chapaev, Dzerzhinsky), two-dimensional stuntmen (Chkalov, Gromov, Vodopianov, Papanin), and a number of overdetermined border guards (Karatsupa, Kotelnikov, Lagoda)—suitors who were ill equipped to woo the hearts and minds of a society that had fallen in love with more colorful patriots and heroes just a few years earlier.

Soviet society did not reject the *Short Course* and its teachings, of course, as it was too authoritative for such a dramatic gesture. Nor did it reject the new array of heroes offered up by Soviet mass culture between 1938 and 1941. But it did adopt a more routine, formal relationship to political indoctrination that lacked the idealism, passion, and engagement of the mid-1930s. Patriotism and the motherland remained evocative concepts, of course, but they now were much harder to personify in concrete, heroic terms than before the advent of the Terror. Ultimately, by purging the Old Guard and upwardly mobile cadres within the party, state, and armed forces, Stalin and his entourage had unintentionally crippled the party's ability to mobilize their society. This forced party ideologists to intensify both their embrace of the personality cult and their search for non-Soviet forms of mobilizational propaganda.

Conclusion:
The Propaganda State in
Crisis

DESPITE THE PARTY hierarchy's confidence in the *Short Course* after its appearance in 1938, word soon reached the ideological establishment that even advanced discussion circles and well-educated individuals were finding the text difficult to grasp. Prominent ideologists faced uncomfortable questions from all angles. What was to be prioritized as one studied the book? What were the red threads that were to be traced throughout the narrative? Or did the fact that the *Short Course* had been termed an "encyclopedia of Bolshevism" indicate that readers had to somehow master the entire text?

No less than Yaroslavsky himself tried to play down this confusion in early January 1939 while addressing a Komsomol Central Committee conference. "It seems to me," he began, "that many here have gotten mixed up and exaggerate the difficulties to be found in the study of the history of the party, Bolshevism, Marxism, and Leninism." This stemmed from a basic misunderstanding among grassroots-level propagandists over how key texts like the *Short Course* were to be made accessible to mass audiences. According to Yaroslavsky, party personnel involved in educational activities were asking the most basic questions —for instance, "what should be done in order to present what is needed from all 12 chapters in a form that is both maximally popularized and condensed? And, comrades are asking, what does *condensed* really mean? Does it mean there are certain places in the *Short Course* that aren't necessary to study and that should be crossed out?"[1] Such queries, according to Yaroslavsky, represented a profound failure to grasp how pedagogues and propagandists were to lead indoctrinational activities. Discouraging any inclination to abridge the canonical text, Yaroslavsky urged his audience to paraphrase the textbook's contents to their students in more colloquial terms. If that were done correctly, instructors would be able to devise ways of presenting the text in "more popularized and more simple" terms without ever actually simplifying the overarching content of the book.[2]

Perhaps unsatisfied with the vagueness of this answer himself, Yaroslavsky returned to the subject in a subsequent speech to another conference of specialists later that year. Speaking anecdotally, he noted that when he taught party history, he found it useful to communicate to his students a sweeping vision of the era: "You need to provide a living, representative picture of the period surrounding the subjects under examination, to recreate the epoch's aroma, if it's possible to say that, so that the listener can get a sense of the epoch." This approach to popularization apparently demanded two things. First, Yaroslavsky complemented the *Short Course* with an array of supplemental materials and visual aids. Second, he provided details and perspectives not covered in the official narrative. These pedagogical methods, Yaroslavsky averred, opened up the historico-philosophical world of the *Short Course* to even the least prepared of audiences.[3]

As reasonable as such a pedagogical strategy may seem, it was considerably less effective than Yaroslavsky believed. According to G. V. Shumeiko, an Agitprop staffer and one-time assistant to Pospelov, the Central Committee received numerous complaints from Yaroslavsky's students after the publication of the *Short Course*. These students found his broad approach to party history disconcerting and couldn't understand why his lectures strayed so far from the official curriculum. Unaware of Yaroslavsky's central role in the writing of the *Short Course*, they speculated that he might be speaking from old, out-dated lecture notes. Perhaps he hadn't fully appreciated the sea change in the party educational system that the *Short Course* had precipitated? Some requested that he be told to base his lectures more explicitly on the new orthodoxy. Others went further out of a sense of political vigilance and denounced the historian for deviating from the party line. As Shumeiko explains,

Yaroslavsky's position as lecturer was complicated by the fact that he often got sidetracked with stories about the various stages of party history and filled these stories with mention of great names, which intentionally or unintentionally equated Stalin with other participants of the revolutionary past. I myself witnessed quite a dramatic scene [while investigating these reports] at a lecture of Yaroslavsky's in the Lenin auditorium of the Miusskaia Square party school. Comments could be heard echoing from the audience during the lecture such as: "Illustrate the facts according to the *Short Course*—what you are saying is not depicted there!"

The old man, trying to remain calm, answered that he had personally witnessed the events that he was describing.

"So what?" echoed from the hall. "There is an official interpretation."
[. . . .]

I would say that such incidents undermined Yaroslavsky's prestige, as well as that of his Central Committee lecturers' group. And the aging old man began to give lectures less and less frequently.[4]

As is visible from this stunning turnabout, Yaroslavsky's grand vision of party history and his invocation of famous names and reputations unnerved his students in the wake of the purges. Although perplexed by the *Short Course*'s narration of party history, they knew enough to fear unofficial interpretations—even those of a leading party historian. Forced to choose between an interpretation that they could understand but not fully trust and another that they could trust but not fully understand, most chose the latter.

Such an example indicates that after nearly a decade of searching for a usable past, party history had ossified into a schematic, lifeless paean to Stalin's unerring leadership of the Bolshevik movement. As detailed in the preceding chapters, first the Great Terror and then the launch of the *Short Course* hobbled the party's ability to indoctrinate and mobilize as its historical actors, themes, and symbols atrophied from a broad cast of heroic patriots to Stalin and a few members of his entourage. Hesitation within the party hierarchy over how to replace the fallen names and reputations—whether with theory, the personality cult, or the veneration of martyrs from the military conflicts of the late 1930s —resulted only in further indecision and half-hearted experiments.

Surviving diaries and memoirs from these years suggest that the inability of the ideological establishment to maintain its focus on heroism and patriotic valor had a dramatic effect on the society even as the much-prophesized threat of armageddon loomed ever larger. Soviets who had spent the early and mid-1930s attempting to model their everyday lives, aspirations, and dreams on famous reputations struggled to maintain a sense of direction as the heroic was replaced by the formulaic. Even the most devout, who had struggled for years with the confusing and inaccessible nature of the Soviet past in order "to align themselves with history and to achieve a historically-grounded sense of selfhood,"[5] now found themselves confronting a new chronicle of party consciousness and identity that was unprecedented in its bloodless, impersonal style of narration. Convention, taboo, and the censor straitjacketed the evocative nature of the revolution, civil war, and socialist construction, whether in history, literature, poetry, art, or film, and this inhibited the individual dreams and flights of fancy that led ordinary citizens to identify with the Soviet experiment during the mid-1930s.

Worse, Soviets who had idealized Red Army commanders as their protectors and saviors only a few years earlier were now forced to confront fears of war without Tukhachevsky, Yegorov, Bliukher, and others. This was unnerving because if impressions of the USSR's defensive capabilities had long been based on popular confidence in concrete commanders, now they could only draw upon the example of ordinary Soviets like Korzh and Karatsupa. True, Soviet propaganda's continuing emphasis on "hurrah-patriotism" and its new attempts to publicize the valor and heroism of average soldiers and border guards filled part of the void left behind by the fallen commanders. But this new focus on ordinary heroes also forced Soviet citizens to identify much more intimately with the defense of the motherland. Diaries and memoirs of the late 1930s are rife with grim discussions not only of the winds of war and the eroding international situation, but also of the inevitability of military service, personal loss, and self-sacrifice.[6]

At first glance, this new focus for popular opinion might seem to be a positive one, as it would prepare ordinary citizens for the total war that would engulf the society just a few years later.[7] But it also imbued popular mobilization with a grossly romantic and fatalistic air that probably contributed only marginally to popular confidence. After all, the fearless heroes of this new line and their selfless acts of courage were so overdetermined as to be entirely unaffected by hesitation or self-doubt. Their mastery of the weapons of war and their composure under fire were instinctive, rather than acquired through everyday military training. And perhaps most glaring was these figures' selfless readiness to sacrifice their lives in order to defend the inviolability of the Soviet motherland. Such exceptionalism was impressive in nominal, propagandistic terms, but presented a very difficult model for ordinary Soviets to emulate in their personal lives. True, some diarists responded to this propaganda with the determination to display a similar sort of courage in the event of war. That said, the hyperbole of these accounts and their stark juxtaposition against mention of more prosaic hopes and dreams suggest considerable internal struggle, anguish, and anxiety.[8] Other diarists sought solace and comfort in another new propaganda development of these prewar years—the celebration of Russian national heroes, myths, and legends from the prerevolutionary period. Aleksandr Nevsky, Dmitry Donskoy, and Peter the Great, it seems, essentially replaced Tukhachevsky, Yegorov, and Bliukher in the popular imagination.

Although memories of Korzh and his compatriots may have flashed through ordinary Soviets' minds as they reacted to news of the German invasion of the USSR on June 22, 1941, these associations were quickly forgotten amid the deluge of worrisome reports and rumors that accompanied the Nazi surprise attack. Within a matter of days, *Pravda* and the all-union press began to offset distressing official communiqués from the front with commentary devoted to a new generation of rank-and-file heroes.[9] Whether the garrison of the Brest fortress, the Panfilovtsy at the gates of Moscow, or partisans like Zoia Kosmodemianskaia, these new martyrs to the Soviet cause exemplified honor, valor, and self-sacrifice.[10] Cast against the backdrop of a thousand years of Russian martial history, they were hailed as "the grandchildren of Suvorov and the children of Chapaev," a strategy that fused the two propaganda lines together.[11]

Amid this mobilizational populism, Stalin's *Short Course* and *Short Biography* faded from public life. Although these volumes' eclipse might seem to be a function of the personality cult's reduced profile during the war, it also stemmed from their schematic nature and interwar focus, which contributed little to the new emphasis on animated heroes of the present and distant past. In the end, only 250,000 copies of the *Short Course* and a half-million copies of the official biography were published between 1941 and 1945—symbolic numbers when compared to their prewar print runs. The volumes' place in Soviet society was largely symbolic as well, insofar as they made no mention of the ongoing conflict and therefore could do little to aid the war effort.[12] In March 1944, however, Agitprop head Aleksandrov prepared a major report on party propaganda in which he proposed to revive the study of the *Short Course*. The exigencies of the early wartime period had resulted not only in the curtailing of the text's print runs, but the disappearance of articles on history and philosophy in the party's main theoretical journals. Grassroots agitation revolving around party history had atrophied as well—a development that could no longer be tolerated as the party hierarchy began to think about a return to normalcy and domestic order. Aleksandrov proposed that party presses reprioritize the *Short Course* and supplement the book with a new generation of auxiliary pedagogical literature. Aleksandrov's opinion was seconded later that year by Volin, another ranking member of the ideological establishment.[13]

In 1945, as Stalin's cult of personality reclaimed its position in Soviet mass culture, ten million new copies of the *Short Course* were printed in a wave of cheap editions designed to return the textbook to the center of the party's indoctrinational efforts. Somewhat more slowly, major party journals and the all-union press also resumed publication of articles aiding those struggling with the *Short Course* by explaining arcane concepts and reprinting obscure primary sources. Regional publishing houses extended the impact of this latter initiative by releasing a new generation of brochures that assembled the best of these pieces together for even broader dissemination.[14] It was also at this time, during preparations for the publication of Stalin's collected works, that authorship of the *Short Course* was publicly reassigned from an anonymous Central Committee commission to the general secretary himself. Something only alluded to in public between 1938 and 1945, this announcement speaks volumes about the party hierarchy's continuing commitment to the text.[15]

Of course, the knowledge that Stalin had written the *Short Course* did not make the text any easier to grasp, and Soviet citizens struggled with it during the early postwar years in many of the same ways that they had between 1938 and 1941.[16] Grassroots activists were again forced to dedicate huge amounts of time to work with confused readers; party education courses were again forced to follow the text's agenda, periodization, and teachings; and party presses were again forced to expend huge amounts of paper and ink on the publication of auxiliary materials and study aids. Perhaps the only consolation was that the *Short Course* was now but one of several elements in a much broader indoctrinational repertoire. Russocentric propaganda, for instance, played an enormous role in postwar education and mass culture, supplying the society with an array of highly recognizable heroes, symbols, and epic events. This imagery was, in turn, complemented by mythmaking oriented around the war and the newly revived personality cult.[17] In other words, despite the *Short Course*'s shortcomings, postwar propaganda proved to be quite dynamic, animated, and accessible.

Stalin's claim of authorship of the *Short Course* and party publishing's return to printing mass editions of the book suggest that the leadership may have been planning to tie the book more squarely into postwar indoctrinational efforts. As early as 1946, the IMEL supplied the general secretary with new galleys of the original 1938 text, now reformatted as the fifteenth volume in his forthcoming *Works*.[18] Aleksandrov and a colleague at Agitprop also returned to the *Short Course* at this time in order prepare a second edition, complete with new chapters to frame the Molotov-Ribbentrop treaty and recent war within the overall narrative.[19] These efforts were complemented by the preparation of a second edition of the *Short Biography* that was likewise designed to accompany the general secretary's *Works* into print. Although Stalin took an initial dislike to this latter manuscript, he eventually allowed its publication after extensive revision.[20]

The appearance of a second edition of the *Short Biography* in 1947 begs the question as to why something similar wasn't done for the *Short Course*. After Stalin's death on March 5, 1953, a copy of the textbook was found at his dacha containing marginalia indicating that the general secretary had at least considered the idea of a second edition.[21] Why, then, didn't he follow through with it? Upon rereading the *Short Course*, perhaps Stalin found himself confounded by the scale of the revisions needed to update the ten-year-old text to suit the new postwar context. Perhaps the experience with the *Short Biography* had been so time-consuming that he hesitated to reopen the books on the *Short Course*. Perhaps he was simply preoccupied with other ideological priorities.[22] Whatever the explanation, the *Short Course* was fated to remain as it was, in its prewar edition; by 1953, over 40 million copies had been printed in some 67 languages.[23] Even more surprising is the fact that virtually nothing changed after Stalin's death ushered in a new period of collective leadership. Indeed, party officials were concerned enough about preserving the book's position in the canon that they began exploring ways to distance it from the personality cult.[24]

Ultimately, the *Short Course* remained in circulation until 1956, when Khrushchev denounced the book as a symbol of the personality cult during his Secret Speech at the 20th Party Congress.[25] In its place, a new generation of textbooks soon emerged that credited the party as a whole with what had previously been attributed solely to Stalin, effectively cutting the general secretary out of the annals of party history in much the same way that his *Short Course* had deleted all mention of the fallen heroes of the 1930s. Aside from this mechanistic shift in historical agency, however, the new texts followed much of the rest of the narrative that originally had been developed by Yaroslavsky, Pospelov, and Stalin himself.[26] What can explain this strange affection for the fundamental lessons of the *Short Course*? Was further innovation deemed unnecessary? Were more thoroughgoing changes seen as potentially disruptive? Perhaps the party hierarchy couldn't bear to pulp the entire party canon and start over again from scratch?[27]

Whatever the rationale, readers responded little better to the party's new histories that they did to the *Short Course*'s schemata. True, audiences were well-enough educated during the postwar years not to be confused by the texts in the way that their predecessors had been. But their approach to the subject—characterized by conformity, rote learning, and scripted question-and-answer drills—betrayed a similar lack of enthusiasm.[28] Ultimately, this mind-numbing routine and regimentation precluded the subject from ever serving as a usable past except for the legion of timeservers and careerists who committed the "History of the CPSU" to memory in their quest for promotion within the party nomenclatura.

Ronald Grigor Suny contends that ideology "gravitates between two poles of meaning"—one of which can be thought of as "discourse or culture" and the other which resembles "dogma or doctrine." If he is right, this paradigm offers a useful way of mapping Soviet ideological dynamics over the course of the 1928–1941 period.[29] Between 1917 and the late 1920s, the party attempted to inculcate in Soviet society a new, ideologically defined discourse and culture. Initially arcane and inaccessible, this ideology shed some of its schematic, materialist trappings during the early 1930s in order to embrace more populist forms of mobilizational propaganda without compromising its commitment to core Marxist-Leninist values. Inspirational and appealing, this new ideological line's focus on accessible discursive practices and role models for popular emulation gave rise to a surprisingly inclusive ideological culture midway into the decade. But as the Great Terror cast a pall over this new vision's ability to personify heroism and loyalty, the ideology itself ossified back into schematic dogma. Ultimately, it was this doctrinaire vision of party ideology that would reign supreme for over fifty years, paralyzing the evocative nature of the propaganda state.

This turnabout in ideology had a profound effect on Soviet indoctrinational efforts devoted to popular mobilization. Scholars have long been aware of the party hierarchy's encouragement of individualism, economic stratification, and gender inequality, as well as its heretical flirtation with Russian nationalism and the Orthodox church. These initiatives have often been viewed as a sign of either the regime's waning interest in revolution or its reversion to more conservative, neotraditional forms of governance and social organization. This book argues by contrast that these various measures were introduced into the repertoire of the propaganda state over the course of the mid-1930s in order to ease the continuing crisis affecting more orthodox indoctrinational efforts. Initially little more than ad hoc exigencies necessitated by what were expected to be only temporary difficulties, these mobilizational strategies were never intended to play anything more than an auxiliary, stop-gap role in party propaganda. Over time, however, the chronic nature of the dysfunction affecting the ideological establishment led to the expansion and regularization of these measures, ultimately transforming the very way in which the Soviet experiment represented itself. Far from intentional, premeditated ideological compromises, these initiatives were essentially the by-product of the party's failure to develop and promote a more orthodox rallying call. Historical contingency, in other words, determined the changing contours of interwar Soviet propaganda, rather than more intentional, long-term ideological dynamics.

This crisis's effect on Soviet identity formation was no less resounding. During the past decade, many scholars have focused on identity in Soviet society, demonstrating that ordinary citizens were remarkably pragmatic and savvy about the nature of the Stalinist system.[30] Some commentators see a recalibration of socialist values during these years.[31]

Others see a growth of ethnic self-identification, first among non-Russians and then among the Russians themselves.[32] Still others have traced identity formation during these years to a variety of other factors, from generational cohort and the party press to more prosaic issues.[33] Exceptional experiences like that of the Great Terror and the Second World War are also described as having been key to social identity in the USSR.[34] Calls have even been made to develop an entirely new approach to the study of individual subjectivity and collective identities in the USSR in light of the differences between the Soviet experience and that of more traditionally liberal societies.[35] But absent throughout all of these studies is attention paid to the party's failure to promote a more revolutionary sense of ideological identity, grounded in the tenets of class consciousness, socialist construction, and proletarian internationalism.[36] Even halting success in this area would have allowed for greater ideological consistency and revolutionary radicalism and alleviated the need to indulge particularistic, non-Marxist sorts of identity politics. But as this book has revealed, the propaganda state's crisis of the mid-to-late 1930s undermined all the gains made earlier in the decade through the inculcation of a heroic, patriotic sense of Soviet identity. Worse, the crisis repeatedly forced the party to resort to ad hoc mobilizational drives that sapped popular interest away from surviving elements of the official line.

Against the backdrop of such an ideological fiasco, the Bolsheviks' revival of ethnic and gender differentiation, variable wage scales, and a return to rank and privilege seems less like a pragmatic reinterpretation of Marxist-Leninist values than it does a panicky, stop-gap form of populist pandering. This is confirmed by Stalin's revival of Russian national heroes, the Russian national past, and Orthodox church during the second half of the 1930s when the circumstances were most dire. A product of weakness rather than strength, such a scenario reveals the propaganda state to have been trapped in the throes of a deep ideological crisis during these years—a crisis from which it never fully recovered.

Archival Repository Abbreviations

Arkhiv RAN	Arkhiv Rossiiskoi Akademii Nauk (Archive of the Russian Academy of Sciences)
GANO	Gosudarstvennyi arkhiv Novosibirskoi oblasti (State Archive of Novosibirsk Province)
GAOPIKO	Gosudarstvennyi arkhiv politicheskoi istorii Kaluzhskoi oblasti (State Archive of the Political History of Kaluga Province)
GARF	Gosudarstvennyi arkhiv Rossiiskoi Federatsii (the former Central State Archive of the October Revolution and the former RSFSR Central State Archive, presently the State Archive of the Russian Federation)
HPSSS	Harvard Project on the Soviet Social System
NA IRI RAN	Nauchnyi arkhiv Instituta Rossiiskoi istorii Rossiiskoi Akademii Nauk (Scholarly Archive of the Russian Academy of Sciences' Institute of Russian History)
OR GTG	Otdel rukopisei Gosudarstvennoi Tret'iakovskoi gallerei (Manuscript Division of the State Tret'iakov Museum)
OR RNB	Otdel rukopisei Rossiiskoi natsional'noi biblioteki (Manuscript Division of the Russian National Library)
RGALI	Rossiiskii gosudarstvennyi arkhiv literatury i iskusstva (Russian State Archive of Literature and Art)

RGANI	Rossiiskii gosudarstvennyi arkhiv noveishei istorii (the former "Current" Archive of the Central Committee, presently the Russian State Archive of Recent History)
RGASPI	Rossiiskii gosudarstvennyi arkhiv sotsial'no-politicheskoi istorii (the former Central Party Archive, presently the Russian State Archive of Social and Political History)
RGVA	Rossiiskii gosudarstvennyi voennyi arkhiv (Russian State Military Archive)
TsA FSB RF	Tsentral'nyi arkhiv Federal'noi sluzhby bezopasnosti Rossiiskoi Federatsii (the former central archive of the secret police, presently the Central Archive of the Federal Security Service)
TsAODM	Tsentral'nyi arkhiv obshchestvennykh dvizhenii Moskvy (the former Moscow party archive, presently the Central Archive of Social Movements of the City of Moscow)
TsDNA	Tsentr dokumentatsii "Narodnyi arkhiv" (the "People's Archive" Documentation Center, presently affiliated with RGANI)
TsGA SPb	Tsentral'nyi gosudarstvennyi arkhiv goroda Sankt-Peterburga i Leningradskoi oblasti (Central State Archive of the city of St. Petersburg and Leningrad Region)
TsGAIPD SPb	Tsentral'nyi gosudarstvennyi arkhiv istoriko-politicheskikh dokumentov goroda Sankt-Peterburga (the former Leningrad party archive, presently the Central State Archive of Historical and Political Documents of the City of St. Petersburg)
TsGALI SPb	Tsentral'nyi gosudarstvennyi arkhiv literatury i iskusstva goroda Sankt-Peterburga i Leningradskoi oblasti (Central State Archive of Literature and the Arts for St. Petersburg and Leningrad Region)
TsKhDMO	Tsentr khraneniia dokumentov molodezhnykh organizatsii (the former central archive of the Komsomol, now integrated into RGASPI)

Notes

INTRODUCTION

1. For examples of this literature, see Merle Fainsod, *How Russia Is Ruled* (Cambridge: Harvard University Press, 1953); Barrington Moore, *Terror and Progress in the USSR: Some Sources of Change and Stability in the Soviet Dictatorship* (Cambridge: Harvard University Press, 1954); Carl Friedrich and Zbigniew Brzezinski, *Totalitarian Dictatorship and Autocracy* (Cambridge: Harvard University Press, 1956); Alex Inkeles and Raymond Bauer, *The Soviet Citizen: Daily Life in a Totalitarian Society* (Cambridge: Harvard University Press, 1959); Brzezinski, *Ideology and Power in Soviet Politics* (New York: Praeger, 1962).

2. See, for example, *Stalinism: New Directions,* ed. Sheila Fitzpatrick (New York: Routledge, 2000); *Contending with Stalinism: Soviet Power and Popular Resistance in the 1930s,* ed. Lynne Viola (Ithaca: Cornell University Press, 2002); Yoram Gorlizki and Oleg Khlevniuk, *Cold Peace: Stalin and the Soviet Ruling Circle, 1945–1953* (New York: Oxford University Press, 2004); *Stalin: A New History,* ed. Sarah Davies and James Harris (Cambridge: Cambridge University Press, 2005).

3. Sheila Fitzpatrick, *Everyday Stalinism—Ordinary Life in Extraordinary Times: Soviet Russia in the 1930s* (New York: Oxford University Press, 2000); her anti-ideology manifesto is Fitzpatrick, "Politics as Practice: Thoughts on a New Soviet Political History," *Kritika* 5:1 (2004): 27–54.

4. For examples of recent literature on Stalin and ideology, see Erik van Ree, *The Political Thought of Joseph Stalin: A Study in Twentieth-Century Revolutionary Patriotism* (London: RoutledgeCurzon, 2002); David Priestland, *Stalinism and the Politics of Mobilization: Ideas, Power, and Terror in Inter-war Russia* (Oxford: Oxford University Press, 2006); Evgeny Dobrenko, *The Political Economy of Socialist Realism* (New Haven: Yale University Press, 2007).

5. See, for example, Vladimir Brovkin, *Russia after Lenin: Politics, Culture, and Society, 1921–1929* (New York: Routledge, 1998). The classic expression of this thesis is Leon Trotsky, *The Revolution Betrayed: What Is the Soviet Union and Where Is It Going?* (London: Faber and Faber, 1937).

6. On the revision of Marxist principles, see Roman Szporluk, "History and Russian Ethnocentrism," in *Ethnic Russia in the USSR: The Dilemma of Dominance*, ed. Edward Allworth (New York: Pergamon, 1980), 44–45; Szporluk, *Communism and Nationalism: Karl Marx versus Friedrich List* (New York: Oxford University Press, 1988), esp. 219–220; Dmitry Pospelovsky, "Ethnocentrism, Ethnic Tensions, and Marxism/Leninism," in *Ethnic Russia in the USSR*, 127; Yuri Y. Glazov, "Stalin's Legacy: Populism in Literature," in *The Search for Self-Definition in Russian Literature*, ed. Ewa Thompson (Houston: Rice University Press, 1991), 93–99; E. A. Rees, "Stalin and Russian Nationalism," in *Russian Nationalism Past and Present*, ed. Geoffrey Hosking and Robert Service (New York: St. Martin's, 1998), 77, 97, 101–103.

On the emergence of domestic etatism, see C. E. Black, "History and Politics in the Soviet Union," in *Rewriting Russian History: Soviet Interpretations of Russia's Past* (New York: Praeger, 1956), 24–25; K. F. Shteppa, *Soviet Historians and the Soviet State* (New Brunswick: Rutgers University Press, 1962), 124, 134–135; M. Agurskii, *Ideologiia natsional-bol'shevizma* (Paris: YMCA Press, 1980), 140–142; Agursky, "The Prospects for National Bolshevism," in *The Last Empire: Nationality and the Soviet Future*, ed. Robert Conquest (Stanford: Stanford University Press, 1986), 90; Moshe Lewin, *The Making of the Soviet System: Essays in the Social History of Inter-War Russia* (New York: Pantheon Books, 1985), 272–279; M. Heller and A. Nekrich, *Utopia in Power: The History of the Soviet Union from 1917 to the Present*, trans. Phyllis Carlos (New York: Summit Books, 1986), 269; Hugh Seton Watson, "Russian Nationalism in Historical Perspective," in *The Last Empire*, 25–28; Alain Besançon, "Nationalism and Bolshevism in the USSR," in *The Last Empire*, 4; Gerhard Simon, *Nationalismus und Nationalitätenpolitik in der Sowjetunion: Von der totalitären Diktatur zur nachstalinschen Gesellschaft* (Baden-Baden: Nomos, 1986), 172–173; Robert Tucker, *Stalin in Power: The Revolution from Above, 1928–1941* (New York: Norton, 1990), 50–58, 319–328, 479–486; G. Kostyrchenko, *V plenu u krasnogo faraona: Politicheskie presledovaniia evreev v SSSR v poslednee stalinskoe desiatiletie* (Moscow: Mezhdunarodnye otnosheniia, 1994), 7–8; Ronald Grigor Suny, "Stalin and His Stalinism: Power and Authority in the Soviet Union," in *Stalinism and Nazism: Dictatorships in Comparison*, ed. Ian Kershaw and Moshe Lewin (Cambridge: Cambridge University Press, 1997), 39; Maureen Perrie, "Nationalism and History: The Cult of Ivan the Terrible in Stalin's Russia," in *Russian Nationalism Past and Present*, 107–128; Timo Vihavainen, "Natsional'naia politika VKP(b)/KPSS v 1920-e—1950-e gody i sud'by karel'skoi i finskoi natsional'nostei," in *V sem'e edinoi: Natsional'naia politika partii bol'shevikov i ee osushchestvlenie na Severo-Zapade Rossii v 1920–1950-e gody* (Petrozavodsk: Izd-vo Petrozavodskogo universiteta, 1998), 15–41.

On eroding prospects for world revolution, see Klaus Mehnert, *Weltrevolution durch Weltgeschichte: Die Geschichtslehre des Stalinismus* (Kitzingen-Main: Holzner Verlag, 1950), 11, 72–73.

On the triumph of administrative power, see Roman Szporluk, "Nationalities and the Russian Problem in the USSR: An Historical Outline," *Journal of International Affairs* 27:1 (1973): 30–31; John Dunlop, *The Faces of Contemporary Russian Nationalism* (Princeton: Princeton University Press, 1983), 10–12; George Liber, *Soviet Nationality Policy, Urban Growth, and Identity Change in the Ukrainian SSR, 1923–1934* (Cambridge: Cambridge University Press, 1992), 51–52, 158–159, 178–179; Yuri Slezkine, "The USSR as a Communal Apartment, or, How a Socialist State Promoted Ethnic Particularism," *Slavic Review* 53:2 (1994): 415–452; G. Bordiugov and V. Bukharev, "Natsional'naia istoricheskaia mysl' v usloviiakh sovetskogo vremeni," in *Natsional'nye istorii v sovetskom i poslesovetskom gosudarstvakh* (Moscow: AIRO-XX, 1999), 21–73, esp. 39; Timo Vihavainen, "Nationalism and Internationalism: How Did the Bolsheviks Cope with National Sentiments?," in *The Fall of an Empire, the Birth of a Nation: National Identities in Russia*, ed. Chris Chulos and Timo Piirainen (Aldershot: Ashgate, 2000), 75–97; Terry Martin, "Modernization or Neo-Traditionalism? Ascribed Nationality and Soviet Primordialism," in *Stalinism*, 348–367; Martin, *The Affirmative Action Empire: Nations and Nationalism in the Soviet Union, 1923–1939* (Ithaca: Cornell University Press, 2001), esp. chap. 11; Andreas Kappeler, *The Russian Empire: A Multiethnic History* (New York: Longman, 2001), 378–382; Geoffrey Hosking, *Russia and the Russians* (Cambridge: Harvard University Press, 2001), 432–433.

On the emergence of nationalist sympathies, see Nicholas Timasheff, *The Great Retreat: The Growth and Decline of Communism in Russia* (New York: Dutton, 1947), chap. 7; Frederick Barghoorn, *Soviet Russian Nationalism* (New York: Oxford University Press, 1956), 28–34, 148–152, 233–237, 260; Barghoorn, "Four Faces of Soviet Russian Ethnocentrism," in *Ethnic Russia in the USSR: The Dilemma of Dominance*, 57; Barghoorn, "Russian Nationalism and Soviet Politics: Official and Unofficial Perspectives," in *The Last Empire*, 35; Ivan Dzyuba, *Internationalism or Russification: A Study of the Soviet Nationalities Problem*, ed. M. Davies (London: Weidenfeld & Nicolson, 1968), 65; Hans Kohn, "Soviet Communism and Nationalism: Three Stages of a Historical Development," in *Soviet Nationality Problems*, ed. Edward Allworth (New York: Columbia University Press, 1971), 57; Kostyrchenko, *V plenu u krasnogo faraona*, 7; Stephen Blank, *The Sorcerer as Apprentice: Stalin as Commissar of Nationalities, 1917–1924* (Westport: Greenwood, 1994), 211–225.

7. On increasing threats from the outside world, see Mehnert, *Weltrevolution durch Weltgeschichte*, 12–14; P. K. Urban, *Smena tendentsii v sovetskoi istoriografii* (Munich: Institut po izucheniiu SSSR, 1959), 9–11; Dunlop, *The Faces of Contemporary Russian Nationalism*, 10–12; S. V. Konstantinov, "Dorevoliutsionnaia istoriia Rossii v ideologii VKP(b) 30-kh gg.," in *Istoricheskaia nauka Rossii v XX veke* (Moscow: Skriptorii, 1997), 226–227; Suny, "Stalin and His Stalinism," 39; Jeffrey Brooks, *"Thank You, Comrade Stalin": Soviet Public Culture from Revolution to Cold War* (Princeton: Princeton University Press, 1999), 76.

On the exigencies of war, see Lowell Tillett, *The Great Friendship: Soviet Historians on the Non-Russian Nationalities* (Chapel Hill: University of North Carolina Press, 1969), 49–61; Christel Lane, *The Rites of Rulers: Ritual in Industrial Society—the Soviet Case* (Cambridge: Cambridge University Press, 1981), 181; Vera Dunham, *In Stalin's Time: Middleclass Values in Soviet Fiction* (Durham: Duke

University Press, 1990), 12, 17, 41, 66; John Barber and Mark Harrison, *The Soviet Home Front, 1941–1945: A Social and Economic History of the USSR in World War II* (London: Longman, 1991), 69; Victoria Bonnell, *Iconography of Power: Soviet Political Posters under Lenin and Stalin* (Berkeley: University of California Press, 1997), 255–257; Kees Boterbloem, *Life and Death under Stalin: Kalinin Province, 1945–1953* (Montreal: McGill-Queen's University Press, 1999), 257.

8. See James Harris, "Was Stalin a Weak Dictator?" *Journal of Modern History* 75:2 (2003): 375–386.

9. See, for instance, David Hoffmann, *Stalinist Values: The Cultural Norms of Soviet Modernity, 1917–1941* (Ithaca: Cornell University Press, 2003).

10. Stephen Kotkin, *Magnetic Mountain: Stalinism as a Civilization* (Berkeley: University of California Press, 1995), 357.

11. See Van Wyck Brooks, "On Creating a Usable Past," *Dial* 64 (1918): 337–341; Henry Steele Commager, *The Search for a Usable Past and Other Essays in Historiography* (New York: Knopf, 1967), 3–27.

12. Published continuously between 1938 and 1953 in 67 languages, the textbook enjoyed a record-setting print run of over 40 million copies—see T. Zelenov, "Bibliografiia," *Bol'shevik* 23 (1949): 89–90.

13. For early use of this term, see Harold Lasswell, "The Garrison State," *American Journal of Sociology* 46:4 (1941): 45; Alvin Johnson, "Politics and Propaganda," *American Journal of Economics and Sociology* 8:4 (1949): 424; etc.

14. *Politicheskii slovar'*, ed. G. Aleksandrov, V. Gal'ianov, and N. Rubinshtein (Moscow: Gos. izd-vo politicheskoi literatury, 1940), 204–205. Equally important, however, is the following nuance: "official ideology is not simply a determinant of the Soviet political process, but rather a construct whose changing nature reflects the varying impact of groups, institutions and individuals within the Soviet system." See the preface to Stephen White and Alex Pravda, eds., *Ideology and Soviet Politics* (Basingstoke: Palgrave Macmillan, 1988), vii. There is a large social science-informed literature addressing ideology as a broader historico-cultural factor in liberal societies (e.g., Clifford Geertz, "Ideology as a Cultural System," in *The Interpretation of Cultures: Selected Essays* [New York: Basic Books, 1973]), but little of it is directly applicable to the doctrinaire, top-down approach to political ideology practiced under Stalin.

15. Italics in original. Terry Eagleton, *Ideology* (New York: Verso, 1991), 5–6.

16. Ronald Grigor Suny, "On Ideology, Subjectivity, and Modernity: Disparate Thoughts about Doing Soviet History," *Russian History/Histoire Russe* 35:1–2 (2008): 251–258, here 253–255; also Steve Smith, "Two Cheers for the 'Return of Ideology,'" *Revolutionary Russia* 17:2 (2004): 119–135.

17. Garth Jowett and Victoria O'Donnell, *Propaganda and Persuasion*, 4th ed. (London: Sage, 2006), 2–7.

18. These differing modes of propaganda are stressed in the analysis of a former member of the Stalinist ideological establishment: A. M. Karmakov, *Reaktsiia sovetskogo naseleniia na propagandu*, no. 13, *Issledovaniia i materialy: Seriia II* (Munich: Institut po izucheniiu istorii i kul'tury SSSR, 1954).

19. V. I. Lenin, "Chto delat'?" (1902), in *Sochineniia*, 3rd ed., 30 vols. (Moscow:

Partizdat, 1937), 4: 359–510. Some dismiss the relevance of this distinction for contemporary analysis, while others contend that it remains salient—compare Peter Kenez, *The Birth of the Soviet Propaganda State: Soviet Methods of Mass Mobilization, 1917–1929* (New York: Cambridge University Press, 1985), 7–8; and Matthew Lenoe, *Closer to the Masses: Stalinist Culture, Social Revolution, and Soviet Newspapers* (Cambridge: Harvard University Press, 2004), 26–29.

20. For recent objections to this area of study, see Rogers Brubaker and Frederick Cooper, "Beyond 'Identity,'" *Theory and Society* 29:1 (2000): 1–47. For a refutation, see James Fearon, "What Is Identity (as We Now Use the Word)?" unpublished ms., 1999.

CHAPTER 1. THE PROPAGANDA STATE'S FIRST DECADE

1. V. I. Lenin, "O tverdoi revoliutsionnoi vlasti" (1917), in *Sochineniia*, 3rd ed., 30 vols. (Moscow: Partizdat, 1935), 20:342.

2. Lenin, "Detskaia bolezn' 'levizny' v kommunizme" (1920), 25:189.

3. Lenin, "Chto delat'?" (1902), 4:446–458. On this work, see Lars Lih, *Lenin Rediscovered: What Is to Be Done? In Context* (New York: Haymarket, 2008); Anna Krylova, "Beyond the Spontaneity-Consciousness Paradigm: 'Class Instinct' as a Promising Category of Historical Analysis," *Slavic Review* 62:1 (2003): 1–23.

4. Lenin, "Detskaia bolezn' 'levizny' v kommunizme," 190.

5. Lenin, "Gosudarstvo i revoliutsiia" (1917), 21:386.

6. Lenin, "Detskaia bolezn' 'levizny' v kommunizme," 197; I. V. Stalin, "K voprosam leninizma" (1926), in *Sochineniia*, 13 vols. (Moscow: Gos. izd-vo politicheskoi literatury, 1948), 8:52.

7. Stalin, "K voprosam leninizma," 46. Examples of this debate include Lenin and L. D. Trotsky's 1920–1921 dispute and a 1926 clash between Stalin and G. Ye. Zinoviev. The author is grateful to Erik van Ree for his advice regarding these debates.

8. Lenin, "Rech' o professional'nykh soiuzakh" (1921), in *Sochineniia*, 26:235. This passage is quoted prominently in Stalin, "K voprosam leninizma," 53.

9. Resolution of the Eighth Party Congress of March 18–23, 1919 "O politicheskoi propagande i kul'turno-prosvetitel'noi rabote v derevne," published in *KPSS v rezoliutsiiakh i resheniiakh s"ezdov, konferentsii i plenumov TsK* (Moscow: Izd-vo politicheskoi literatury, 1983), 2:111–113. See resolution of the Tenth Party Congress of March 1–16, 1921 "O Glavpolitprosvete i agitatsionno-propagandistich-eskikh zadachakh partii"; resolution of the Twelfth Party Congress of April 17–25, 1923 "Po voprosam propagandy, pechati i agitatsii"; resolutions of the Thirteenth Party Congress of January 23–31, 1924 "O kul'turnoi rabote v derevne," "O pechati," "Ob agitproprabote," "O rabote sredi molodezhi"; resolution of the Fourteenth Party Congress of December 18–21, 1925 "O rabote profsoiuzov," "O rabote komsomola," all ibid., 2:357–360, 3:111, 251–283, 444–461; etc.

10. Lenin, "Rech' na Vserossiiskom soveshchanii politprosvetov gubernskikh i uezdnykh otdelov narodnogo obrazovaniia" (1920), in *Sochineniia*, 25:448–456.

11. For the official narrative, see "Agitprop," "Tsentral'nyi komitet," in *Bol'shaia sovetskaia entsiklopediia*, 65 vols. (Moscow: Sovetskaia entsiklopediia, 1926–1948), 1:420–432; 55:551–554.

12. Peter Kenez, *The Birth of the Soviet Propaganda State: Soviet Methods of Mass Mobilization, 1917–1929* (New York: Cambridge University Press, 1985), 143–144, etc.

13. For party hierarchs like A. V. Lunacharsky, the combining of political and nonpolitical subjects was completely natural: "We cannot imagine how it would be possible to conduct popular schooling without conveying a Marxist worldview to everyone who is supposed to become a conscious citizen of the RSFSR." See A. V. Lunacharskii, "Znachenie sovpartshkol v sisteme narodnogo obrazovaniia," in *Problemy narodnogo obrazovaniia,* 2nd ed. (Moscow: Rabotnik prosveshcheniia, 1925), 84.

14. The basic dimensions of this system were established at the All-Russian Meeting of Directors of Regional Agitprop Departments in June 1921. Generally, see F. G. Krotov, *Shkola ideinoi zakalki: Ocherki istorii marksistsko-leninskogo obrazovaniia v KPSS* (Moscow: Izd-vo politicheskoi literatury, 1978), 9–88.

15. See, for instance, "Rezoliutsiia Vserossiiskogo soveshchaniia zaveduiushchikh agitotdeliami," *Vestnik agitatsii i propagandy* 16 (1921): 43. Interest in multidisciplinary approaches to teaching of Marxism-Leninism was reiterated at an Agitprop-convened conference of representatives from Glavpolitprosvet, the Commissariat of Education, the Komsomol Central Committee, and the All-Union Central Trade Union Council. See RGASPI, f. 17, op. 60, d. 259, l. 38.

16. On the dubious results of early reading circles and party courses, see, for instance, Anne Gorsuch, *Youth in Revolutionary Russia: Enthusiasts, Bohemians, and Delinquents* (Bloomington: Indiana University Press, 2000), 74–75.

17. On the eve of the third anniversary of the revolution, the Central Committee asked party leaders such as Stalin, Bukharin, Ye. A. Preobrazhensky, M. P. Tomsky, A. I. Rykov, M. N. Pokrovsky, A. S. Bubnov, Yu. M. Steklov, I. I. Skvortsov-Stepanov, V. P. Miliutin, Yu. Larin, L. N. Kritsman, and V. V. Vorovsky to write an array of short textbooks and brochures on party history and policy. See "Izveshchenie TsK," *Pravda,* October 10, 1920, 1. Bukharin and Preobrazhensky's *ABCs of Communism (Azbuka kommunizma)* was probably the most famous text to emerge from this effort. By the mid-1920s, textbooks by established party historians—Pokrovsky, V. I. Nevsky, Ye. M. Yaroslavsky, and N. N. Popov—had begun to appear in mass editions. For a discussion of these texts that is unfortunately choked with errors, see A. V. Guseva, "Kratkii kurs istorii VKP(b): istoriia sozdaniia i vozdeistviia na obshchestvennoe soznanie" (Candidate's diss., Moscow State Pedagogical University, 2002), 60–112; on Istpart, the Central Committee's party history committee, see Frederick Corney, *Telling October: Memory and the Making of the Bolshevik Revolution* (Ithaca: Cornell University Press, 2004).

18. Jochen Hellbeck, *Revolution on My Mind: Writing a Diary under Stalin* (Cambridge: Harvard University Press, 2006), 6.

19. I. Kuznetsov, "Razvitie ustnoi rechi v sisteme kompleksnogo prepodavaniia," *Sputnik politrabotnika* 3 (1924): 69–70, cited ibid., 24.

20. Valentina Kamyshina, "A Woman's Heart," in *Thirteen Who Fled,* ed. Louis Fischer (New York: Harper and Brothers, 1949), 103.

21. On the construction of communist autobiographies in the 1920s, see Igal

Halfin, *From Darkness to Light: Class, Consciousness, and Salvation in Revolutionary Russia* (Pittsburgh: University of Pittsburgh Press, 2000).

22. Hellbeck, *Revolution on My Mind*, 351.

23. While fascinating, Halfin's sample of autobiographies likely exaggerates this genre's propensity to display romanticism, idealism, and internal conflict. Most were too formulaic to indulge in these emotions.

24. See, for instance, A. S. Bubnov, *Osnovnye voprosy istorii RKP* (Moscow: Gos. izd., 1924); V. Iudovskii, *Istoriia VKP(b): Programma-konspekt dlia pervonachal'nykh kruzhkov samoobrazovaniia* (Moscow: Gos. izd., 1926); V. Volosevich, *Samaia kratkaia istoriia VKP(b) (dovedennaia do XIV s"ezda partii vkliuchitel'no)* (Moscow: Gos. izd., 1926); G. E. Zinov'ev, *Istoriia RKP(b): Populiarnyi ocherk* (Leningrad: Priboi, 1924); V. I. Nevskii, *Ocherk po istorii RKP* (Leningrad: Priboi, 1924); N. N. Popov, *Ocherk istorii VKP(b)* (Leningrad: Priboi, 1926); V. I. Nevskii, *Istoriia RKP(b)—Kratkii ocherk* (Leningrad: Priboi, 1925); E. Iaroslavskii, *Kratkie ocherki po istorii VKP(b) v dvukh chastiakh*, 2 vols. (Moscow: Gos. izd., 1926); *Istoriia VKP(b)*, ed. E. Iaroslavskii, 4 vols. (Moscow: Gos. izd., 1926, 1929–30); P. M. Kerzhentsev, *Stranitsy istorii RKP(b)* (Leningrad: Priboi, 1925); D. I. Kardashev, *Osnovnye istoricheskie etapy v razvitii VKP* (Khar'kov: Proletarii, 1927); E. Iaroslavskii, *Kratkaia istoriia VKP(b)* (Moscow: OGIZ, 1930); A. S. Bubnov, *VKP(b) v dvukh tomakh* (Moscow: Gos. sots. ekon. izd-vo, 1931). For an account of the party authorities' attempt to rein in this literature, see Brian Kassof, "The Knowledge Front: Politics, Ideology, and Economics in the Soviet Book Publishing Industry, 1925–1935" (Ph.D. diss., University of California at Berkeley, 2000), 359–367.

25. Generally, see Robert Maguire, *Red Virgin Soil: Soviet Literature in the 1920's* (Princeton: Princeton University Press, 1968); Edward Brown, *The Proletarian Episode in Russian Literature, 1928–1932* (New York: Columbia University Press, 1950).

26. Kenez, *The Birth of the Soviet Propaganda State*, 255; also 133, 140–144, 250–255.

27. See, for instance, Irina Davidian, "Mass Political Consciousness in Soviet Russia in the 1920s," in *Politics and Society under the Bolsheviks,* ed. Kevin McDermott and John Morison (New York: St. Martin's, 1999), 90–99; Olga Velikanova, *The Myth of the Besieged Fortress: Soviet Mass Perception in the 1920s–1930s*, working paper no. 7, *The Stalin Era Research and Archives Project* (Toronto: Centre for Russian and East European Studies, 2002).

28. *Golos naroda: Pis'ma i otkliki riadovykh sovetskikh grazhdan o sobytiiakh 1918–1932 gg.* (Moscow: Rosspen, 1998); *Krest'ianskie istorii: Rossiiskaia derevnia 1920-kh godov v pis'makh i dokumentakh* (Moscow: Rosspen, 2001).

29. See the April 1925 OGPU all-union report at TsA FSB RF, f. 2, op. 3, d. 1047, ll. 153–200, published in *Sovershenno sekretno: Lubianka Stalinu o polozhenii v strane, 1922–1934,* 10 vols. (Moscow: IRI RAN, 2002), 3: 236.

30. See Vladimir Brovkin, *Russia after Lenin: Politics, Culture, and Society, 1921–1929* (New York: Routledge, 1998), 57–80, 155–172; and scores of references to the movement after 1924 in the OGPU all-union reports published in *Sovershenno sekretno.*

31. See, for instance, the January 1925 OGPU all-union report at TsA FSB RF, f. 2, op. 3, d. 1047, ll. 116–200, published in *Sovershenno sekretno,* 3:73; RGASPI, f. 17, op. 85, d. 19, ll. 300–301; also A. Rozhkov, "Internatsional durakov," *Rodina* 12 (1999): 61–66.

32. See the OGPU all-union reports published in *Sovershenno sekretno,* vols. 1–3.

33. See the March and April 1925 OGPU all-union reports in TsA FSB RF, f. 2, op. 3, d. 1047, ll. 116–200, published ibid., 3:320, 198.

34. RGASPI, f. 17, op. 87, d. 200a, l. 42.

35. RGASPI, f. 17, op. 87, d. 200a, l. 940b.

36. RGASPI, f. 17, op. 87, d. 200a, l. 42.

37. Generally, see N. S. Simonov, "'Krepit' oboronu Strany Sovetov' ('voennaia trevoga' 1927 goda i ee posledstviia)," *Otechestvennaia istoriia* 3 (1996): 155–161; L. N. Nikolaev, "Ugroza voiny protiv SSSR (konets 20-kh—nachalo 30-kh gg.): Real'nost' ili mif?" in *Sovetskaia vneshniaia politika, 1917–1945* (Moscow: Mezhdunarodnye otnosheniia, 1992), 63–90; L. N. Nezhinskii, "Byla li voennaia ugroza SSSR v kontse 20-kh—nachale 30-kh godov?" *Istoriia SSSR* 6 (1990): 14–30; Alfred G. Meyer, "The Great War Scare of 1927," *Soviet Union/Union soviétique* 5:1 (1978): 1–27; John Sontag, "The Soviet War Scare of 1926–1927," *Russian Review* 34:1 (1975): 66–77.

38. "Podgotovka imperialisticheskoi ataki," *Kommunisticheskii internatsional,* September 24, 1926, 3; "Rezoliutsiia TsK Frantsuzskoi kompartii po russkomu voprosu," *Izvestiia,* November 11, 1926, 2; "Zaiavlenie Pol'skoi kompartii," in *Dokumenty i materialy po istorii sovetsko-pol'skikh otnoshenii,* 13 vols. (Moscow: Nauka, 1967), 5:63–68; *XV konferentsiia Vsesoiuznoi kommunisticheskoi partii (Bol'shevikov): Stenograficheskii otchet* (Moscow: Gos. izd-vo, 1927), 91–92, 55; "VII rasshirennyi plenum IKKI: Mezhdunarodnoe polozhenie i zadachi Kominterna (Doklad tov. Bukharina)," *Pravda,* November 25, 1926, 1–2; etc.

39. "XV moskovskaia gubernskaia partiinaia konferentsiia," *Pravda,* January 9, 1927, 3; N. Bukharin, "O mezhdunarodnom i vnutrennem polozhenii SSSR, *Pravda,* January 13, 1927, 2–5; "Preniia po dokladu tov. N. I. Bukharina," *Pravda,* January 14, 1927, 3–4; "Zakliuchitel'noe slovo tov. N. I. Bukharina," *Pravda,* January 20, 1927, 3; "Tov. Stalin na sobranii rabochikh Stalinskikh zh.-d. masterskikh Oktiabr'skoi dorogi," *Pravda,* March 3, 1927, 3.

40. On the popular alarm, see the spring 1927 OGPU all-union reports at TsA FSB RF, f. 2, op. 5, d. 385, ll. 80–255, published in *Sovershenno sekretno,* 5:147–148, 253–254, 320–322, 352–353.

41. *Pravda*'s lead editorial on May Day declared "the danger of war" to be "the most important international question" of the day—"Pervoe maia," *Pravda,* May 1, 1927, 1; also the Central Committee's June 1, 1927 announcement "Ob ugroze voennoi opasnosti," in *Spravochnik partiinogo rabotnika,* issue 6, part 1 (Moscow: Gosizdat, 1928), 470–474. Generally, see Velikanova, *The Myth of the Besieged Fortress,* 15.

42. See, for instance, the Central Committee resolution of March 7 and August 26, 1927 "Ob organizatsii i provedenii prazdnovaniia 10-letiia Oktriabr'skoi revoliutsii" and "O podgotovke k prazdnovaniiu 10-letiia Oktiabr'skoi revoliutsii," in *Spravochnik partiinogo rabotnika,* issue 6, part 1, 706–707, 703.

43. P. Klevstov, "Chto dala 'Nedelia oborony?'" *Sputnik agitatora* 17 (1927): 71–72. This event was discussed in the press as early as mid-May—see "2-aia vsesoiuznaia lotereia Osoaviakhima," *Pravda*, May 20, 1927, 3.

44. See, for instance, Sheila Fitzpatrick, *The Russian Revolution, 1917–1932* (Oxford: Oxford University Press, 1982), 111.

45. See May, June, July, August, and September 1927 OGPU all-union reports at TsA FSB RF, f. 2, op. 5, d. 385, ll. 256–361, 422–481; op. 4, d. 386, ll. 45–84; op. 5, d. 394, ll. 99–108; op. 6, d. 394, ll. 109–112, published in *Sovershenno sekretno*, 5:362–378, 401–408, 411–483, 484–584, 855–906.

46. June-August OGPU information and special reports at TsA FSB RF, f. 2, op. 5, d. 394, ll. 71–890b, published in *Tragediia sovetskoi derevni—kollektivizatsiia i razkulachivanie: Dokumenty i materialy, 1927–1939*, vol. 1, *Mai 1927—Noiabr' 1929*, ed. V. Danilov et al. (Moscow: Rosspen, 1999), 73–75, 80–81, 84–85; May all-union OGPU report at TsA FSB RF, f. 2, op. 5, d. 385, ll. 256–302, published in *Sovershenno sekretno*, 5:367; also RGASPI, f. 17, op. 85, d. 289; d. 19, ll. 138–140, 180–182. See also A. V. Baranov, "'Voennaia trevoga' 1927 g. kak faktor politicheskikh nastroenii v nepovskom obshchestve (po materialam Iuga Rossii)," in *Rossiia i mir glazami drug druga: iz istorii vzaimovospriiatiia*, 4th issue (Moscow: RAN IRI, 2007), 175–193.

47. May 1927 OGPU all-union report at TsA FSB RF, f. 2, op. 5, d. 385, ll. 256–302, published in *Sovershenno sekretno*, 5:363–364; May 1927 report to the Leningrad adminstration at TsGA SPb, f. 1000, op. 11, d. 558, ll. 72–78, published in *Piterskie rabochie i 'Diktatura proletariata,' Oktiabr' 1917–1929: ekonomicheskie konflikty i politicheskii protest—sbornik dokumentov*, ed. V. Iu. Cherniaev et al. (St. Petersburg: Blits, 2000), 369; June 1927 OGPU all-union report at TsA FSB RF, f. 2, op. 5, d. 385, ll. 303–361, published in *Sovershenno sekretno*, 5:420.

48. M. M. Kudiukina, "Krasnaia armiia i 'voennye trevogi' vtoroi poloviny 1920-kh godov," in *Rossiia i mir glazami drug druga*, 153–174.

49. See Terry Martin, "Obzory OGPU i sovetskie istoriki," in *Sovershenno sekretno*, 1:21–26; David Brandenberger, "Interrogating the Secret Police: Methodological Concerns Surrounding the Use of NKVD Svodki in Discussions of Stalin-Era Popular Opinion" (paper delivered at the Thirty-Fifth National Conference of the American Association for the Advancement of Slavic Studies, Salt Lake City, November 3–6, 2005).

50. Local reports on morale present a somewhat more optimistic interpretation of popular opinion than the all-union OGPU reports—see Kudiukina, "Krasnaia armiia i 'voennye trevogi' vtoroi poloviny 1920-kh godov"; Baranov, "'Voennaia trevoga' 1927 g. kak faktor politicheskikh nastroenii v nepovskom obshchestve," 175–193. See also Kenneth Slepyan, "The Limits of Mobilisation: Party, State, and the 1927 Civil Defense Campaign," *Europe-Asia Studies* 45:5 (1993): 851–868.

51. V. P. Danilov, "Collectivization, Dekulakization, and the 1933 Famine in Light of New Documentation from the Moscow FSB Archive" (paper delivered at the Davis Center for Russian and Eurasian Studies, Harvard University, April 29, 1999); *Tragediia sovetskoi derevni*, 1:21–22, 25–27.

52. The war scare also led the party hierarchy to launch reforms in other areas —see Simonov, "Krepit' oboronu Strany Sovetov."

53. Central Committee resolution of October 3, 1927 "Ob uluchshenii partru-kovodstva pechat'iu," in *Spravochnik partiinogo rabotnika,* issue 6, 2 pts. (Moscow: Gosizdat, 1928), 1:743–44.

54. Resolution of the Fifteenth Party Congress of December 2–19, 1927 "Po otchetu Tsentral'nogo komiteta," ibid., 4:263, 310.

55. "Iz materialov Vsesoiuznogo soveshchaniia po voprosam agitatsii, propa-gandy i kul'turnogo stroitel'stva," in *Spravochnik partiinogo rabotnika,* issue 7, 2 pts. (Moscow: Gosizdat, 1930), 1:415.

56. Ibid., 427. For more on this conference, see "Bol'shevistskaia partiia i sove-tskaia pechat'," *Novyi mir* 5 (1947): 133.

57. *Spravochnik partiinogo rabotnika,* issue 7, 1:414.

58. *Sotsialisticheskoe stroitel'stvo, samokritika i zadachi pechati—Sbornik ma-terialov Vsesoiuznogo soveshchaniia redaktorov pri TsK VKP(b), 22–27 sentiabria 1928 g.* (Moscow: Gos. izd-vo, 1928), 65. For more on this priority shift in the press, see Matthew Lenoe, *Closer to the Masses: Stalinist Culture, Social Revolution, and Soviet Newspapers* (Cambridge: Harvard University Press, 2004), chaps. 5–6.

59. A surprising number of these resolutions were published, indicating the ex-tent to which the party hierarchy intended to publicize its reformist efforts—see *Spravochnik partiinogo rabotnika,* issue 7, part 1, 394–399, 402–403, 438–439, 442–443, 456–460, 506–514; issue 7, part 2, 254–257, 260–272; issue 8, 320–324, 329.

60. Central Committee resolution of December 28, 1928 "Ob obsluzhivanii knigoi massovogo chitatelia," ibid., 400–402. For more on this transformation, see Kassof, "The Knowledge Front," chaps. 3, 5–7.

61. See, for instance, Jeffrey Rossman, *Worker Resistance under Stalin: Class and Revolution on the Shop Floor* (Cambridge: Harvard University Press, 2005).

62. Moshe Lewin, "Social Crises and Political Structures in the USSR," and "State, Society, and Ideology during the First Five-Year Plan," in *The Making of the Soviet System: Essays in the Interwar History of Soviet Russia* (New York: Pan-theon, 1985), 39–41, 209–240; K. B. Litvak, "K voprosu o partiinykh perepisiakh i kul'turnom urovne kommunistov v 20-e gody," *Voprosy istorii KPSS* 2 (1991): 79–92; John Barber, "Working Class Culture and Political Culture in the 1930s," in *The Culture of the Stalin Period,* ed. Hans Günther (New York: St. Martin's, 1990), 3–14.

63. Witnessing this confusion firsthand, John Scott commented later that "to give students of a very limited general education 'Anti-Duehrung,' [*sic*] 'The Di-alectics of Nature,' or 'Materialism and Empiro-Criticism' to read was only to in-vite blatant superficiality." See John Scott, *Behind the Urals: An American Engineer in Russia's City of Steel,* ed. Stephen Kotkin (Bloomington: Indiana University Press, 1989), 45.

64. The term is Stalin's—see I. Stalin, "God Velikogo pereloma," *Pravda,* No-vember 7, 1929, 2.

65. *Trudy Pervoi vsesoiuznoi konferentsii istorikov-marksistov 28/XII 1928–4/I 1929,* 2 vols. (Moscow: Kommunisticheskaia akademiia, 1930); *Voprosy pre-podavaniia leninizma, istorii VKP(b), Kominterna: stenogrammy soveshchaniia, sozvannogo Obshchestvom istorikov-marksistov 9 fevralia 1930 g.* (Moscow:

Kommunisticheskaia akademiia, 1930). Generally, see George Enteen, "Marxist Historians during the Cultural Revolution: A Case-Study in Professional Infighting," in *Cultural Revolution in Russia, 1928–1931,* ed. Sheila Fitzpatrick (Bloomington: Indiana University Press, 1978), 154–179; Enteen, "Intellektual'nye predposylki utverzhdeniia stalinizma v sovetskoi istoriografii," *Voprosy istorii* 5–6 (1995): 149–155; Serhii Plokhy, *Unmaking Imperial Russia: Mykhailo Hrushevsky and the Writing of Ukrainian History* (Toronto: University of Toronto Press, 2005), esp. chap. 6.

66. On the press and state publishing during these periods, see Lenoe, *Closer to the Masses,* chap. 5–6; Kassof, "The Knowledge Front," chaps. 3, 5–7.

67. Brown, *The Proletarian Episode in Russian Literature, 1928–1932.*

68. Oleg Ken, "'Alarm wojenny' wiosną 1930 roku a stosunki sowiecko-polskie," *Studia z Dziejów Rosji i Europy Środkowo-Wschodnej* 35 (1999): 41–74; Kudiukina, "Krasnaia armiia i 'voennye trevogi' vtoroi poloviny 1920-kh godov"; A. V. Golubev, *"Esli mir obrushitsia na nashu respubliku": sovetskoe obshchestvo i vneshniaia ugroza v 1920–1940-e gg.* (Moscow: Kuchkovo pole, 2008).

CHAPTER 2. THE SEARCH FOR A USABLE PARTY HISTORY

1. For a portion of the resolutions, see *Spravochnik partiinogo rabotnika,* issues 6–8 (Moscow: Gosizdat, 1928–1934); Alex Inkeles, *Public Opinion in Soviet Society: A Study in Mass Persuasion* (Cambridge: Harvard University Press, 1950), 77.

2. Central Committee resolution of September 13, 1930 "O zadachakh partprosveshcheniia," published in *Pravda,* September 16, 1930, 4.

3. This shift in priorities was first visible in the press—see Matthew Lenoe, *Closer to the Masses: Stalinist Culture, Social Revolution, and Soviet Newspapers* (Cambridge: Harvard University Press, 2004), chaps. 5–7; see also Chapter Four.

4. On the historian in question, A. G. Slutsky, see Robert Tucker, "The Rise of Stalin's Personality Cult," *American Historical Review* 84:2 (1979): 353–357.

5. I. V. Stalin, "O nekotorykh voprosakh istorii bol'shevizma," *Proletarskaia revoliutsiia* 6 (1931): 3–21.

6. Some argue that the affair was triggered by tensions within the party establishment; others suggest that Stalin initiated the turmoil to nurture his own personality cult. Compare John Barber, "Stalin's Letter to the Editors of Proletarskaya Revolyutsiya," *Soviet Studies* 28:1 (1976): 39–41; and Tucker, "The Rise of Stalin's Personality Cult," 355–358.

7. "'Za bol'shevistskoe izuchenie istorii partii': rech' tov. Kaganovicha L. M., proiznesennaia 1 dekabria na sobranii, posviashchennom 10-letiiu Instituta Krasnoi professury," *Pravda,* December 13, 1931, 2.

8. Longtime rivalries within the discipline contributed to the firestorm. See George Enteen, "Marxist Historians during the Cultural Revolution: A Case-Study in Professional Infighting," in *Cultural Revolution in Russia, 1928–1931,* ed. Sheila Fitzpatrick (Bloomington: Indiana University Press, 1978), 154–179; Enteen, "Intellektual'nye predposylki utverzhdeniia stalinizma v sovetskoi istoriografii," *Voprosy istorii* 5–6 (1995): 149–155; A. N. Artizov, "Kritika M. N. Pokrovskogo i

ego shkoly," *Istoriia SSSR* 1 (1991): 103–106. The party did attempt to rein in some of the criticism of Yaroslavsky—see, for instance, "Partiinye massy obsuzhdaiut pis'mo tov. Stalina," *Pravda,* December 26, 1931, 3.

9. George Enteen puts it well: "the writing of history had turned into an instrument of state-building. The preparation of party cadres in the spirit of Bolshevism and its moral principles was an issue that demanded attention. Historical facts themselves were not important in-and-of-themselves, but were instead a method of explaining and implementing approved rules of conduct. The essence of the matter apparently now revolved around the inculcation of party mindedness into new party members and those who may have felt lost in the wake of collectivization and other unexpected about-faces." Enteen, "Intellekual'nye predposylki utverzhdeniia stalinizma v sovetskoi istoriografii," 151–52.

10. See RGASPI, f. 17, op. 114, d. 277, ll. 1–15. Stalin personally reorganized the editorial brigade that Kaganovich assembled for this task—see f. 81, op. 3, d. 94, ll. 198.

11. RGASPI, f. 17, op. 114, d. 277, ll. 1–15; Politburo resolution of January 7, 1932 "O sostavlenii 'Istorii VKP(b),'" op. 3, d. 867, l. 11; Central Committee resolution of January 17, 1932 "Ob usilenii Kul'tpropotdela TsK rabotnikami i o perestroike raboty Kul'tpropa v dukhe sistematicheskoi propagandy marksizmaleninizma," in *Spravochnik partiinogo rabotnika,* 8th issue, 288.

12. Em. Iaroslavskii, "Za vysokii uroven' marksistsko-leninskogo vospitaniia," *Pravda,* August 29, 1933, 2; more generally, see TsGAIPD SPb, f. 24, op. 5, d. 1889, l. 30, etc. The results of the 1933 party purge were so vexing that new recruiting was suspended until November 1936.

13. Orgburo resolution of April 17, 1932 "Ob uchebnikakh dlia seti partprosveshcheniia," RGASPI, f. 17, op. 114, d. 295, ll. 4–5; I. L. Man'kovskaia and Iu. P. Sharapov, "Kul't lichnosti i istoriko-partiinaia nauka," *Voprosy istorii KPSS* 5 (1988): 62, 66, 68.

14. "Razvernut' rabotu po izucheniiu istorii partii," *Proletarskaia revoliutsiia* 4 (1934): 9. P. N. Ponomarev, the director of the Moscow party committee's Institute of Party History, wrote this editorial with I. P. Tovstukha, V. G. Knorin, K. F. Sidorov, and Ye. I. Korotky. See RGASPI, f. 72, op. 3, d. 344.

15. RGASPI, f. 17, op. 3, d. 867, l. 11.

16. RGASPI, f. 71, op. 2, d. 120, ll. 3–10; Tovstukha to Stalin (March 15, 1932), f. 558, op. 1, d. 3012, l. 1; f. 155, op. 1, d. 77, ll. 2–30b.

17. Aside from the leading party historians, other more minor members of the brigade included M. S. Volin, A. P. Kuchkin, L. I. Ryklin, V. B. Sorin, N. L. Rubinshtein, S. I. Avvakumov, M. A. Shachnev, A. Ye. Frug, A. M. Pankratova, A. I. Sereda, I. V. Volkovicher, K. I. Rozenblium, and Ya. B. Ronis, as well as the Leningrad-based scholars I. P. Vavilin, K. G. Sharikov, O. A. Lidak, V. I. Kotovich, N. A. Kornatovsky, and Z. B. Pindrik. See RGASPI, f. 89, op. 8, d. 604, ll. 43–44; f. 81, op. 3, d. 9, l. 198; f. 71, op. 3, d. 58, ll. 191–196.

18. M. Orakhelashvili to editorial board (November 29, 1934), RGASPI, f. 71, op. 3, d. 58, l. 196. Orakhelashvili took over adminstration of the brigade in 1933 as Tovstukha declined in health.

19. For Stalin's letter as a "turning point," see Nadezhda Mandel'shtam, *Vospo-minaniia* (New York: Izd-vo im. Chekhova, 1970), 277. Mandelshtam apparently read a reprint of the letter in *Bolshevik*.

20. RGASPI, f. 17, op. 114, d. 295, ll. 4–5.

21. N. Popov, *Ocherk istorii VKP(b)*, 15th ed. (Moscow: Moskovskii rabochii, 1932), 4; S. V. Sukharev, "Predtecha 'Kratkogo kursa' v litsakh i dokumentakh," *Voprosy istorii KPSS* 8 (1991): 113–114. The influence of this text is exaggerated in Frederick Giffin, "The Short Course: Stalin's History of the Communist Party of the Soviet Union," *International Review of History and Political Science* 23:3 (1988): 41. For mention of its persistent problems with complexity, see N. Ya. Koniaev to Yaroslavsky (March 28, 1933), RGASPI, f. 89, op. 8, d. 814, l. 47; Yaroslavsky to A. I. Stetsky (May 31, 1933), d. 828, l. 1.

22. *Istoriia VKP(b)*, 4 vols., ed. E. Iaroslavskii (Moscow: Gos. izd-vo, 1926, 1929–30); Iaroslavskii, *Kratkaia istoriia VKP(b)*, 3rd ed. (Moscow: Gos. izd-vo., 1931).

23. Kaganovich, "Za bol'shevistskoe izuchenie istorii partii," 2; Man'kovskaia and Sharapov, "Kul't lichnosti i istoriko-partiinaia nauka," 63–64; "Protiv falsifikatsii istorii bol'shevizma, protiv trotskistskoi kontrabandy, protiv gnilogo liberalizma," *Bol'shevik* 1–2 (1932): 125.

24. For evidence of Yaroslavsky's state of mind, see the February 3, 1932 diary entry in *Dnevnik istorika S. A. Piontkovskogo*, ed. A. L. Litvin et al. (Kazan': Kazan' State University Press, 2009), 451; Sandra Dahlke, "Emelian Iaroslavskii: Acteur dans le monde des historiens," *Communisme: Revue d'histoire, de sociologie et de science politique* 70 (2002): 213–244.

25. Stalin saw Yaroslavsky in his Kremlin office on December 9, 1931 and January 20, 1932—see *Na prieme u Stalina: tetradi (zhurnaly) zapisei lits, priniatykh I. V. Stalinym (1924–1953 gg.)* (Moscow: Novyi khronograf, 2008), 54, 58.

26. Em. Iaroslavskii, "V redaktsiiu 'Pravdy,'" *Pravda*, December 10, 1931, 4; Man'kovskaia, Sharapov, "Kul't lichnosti i istoriko-partiinaia nauka," 64; Yaroslavsky to Stalin ([late 1931]), RGASPI, f. 89, op. 7, d. 72, l. 6. For a fascinating account of his battle for rehabilitation, see George Enteen, "Stalin's Letter to *Proletarskaia Revoliutsiia* and the Agony of E. M. Iaroslavskii: Birth of a Fiction," unpublished ms., 1994.

27. Yaroslavsky made this announcement in a December 1931 speech to the Society of Old Bolsheviks. He claimed to have made the same recommendation to his editorial board, although the extant draft of his November 27, 1931 advisory letter does not contain this key passage. Compare RGASPI, f. 89, op. 7, d. 66, ll. 30 and 67 to 5.

28. See E. Iaroslavskii, *Partiia bol'shevikov v 1917 godu* (Moscow: Gos. izd-vo, 1927), 24, 32–34, 50, 71.

29. See P. Sevruk, "Pis'mo v redaktsiiu," *Pravda*, January 27, 1932, 4; Man'kovskaia, Sharapov, "Kul't lichnosti i istoriko-partiinaia nauka," 65.

30. Lenin's widow N. K. Krupskaia signaled her displeasure with this revisionist view by referring to the Prague conference as one among many important party meetings in her memoirs. P. N. Pospelov rebuked her for this "inadequate treat-

ment." Compare N. K. Krupskaia, *Vospominaniia o Lenine,* 3 vols. (Moscow: Gosizdat, 1933–1934), 2:178; and P. N. Pospelov, "K vospominaniiam o Lenine," *Pravda,* May 9, 1934, 4.

31. Yaroslavsky to Stalin (February 26, 1933), RGASPI, f. 89, op. 8, d. 827, l. 1. Yaroslavsky had won official permission to resubmit this text in September 1932; when his first set of revisions failed to satisfy the party hierarchy, he was forced to petition Stalin repeatedly for correctives. See the correspondence at f. 89, op. 3, d. 255, ll. 79–82; f. 17, op. 3, d. 989; f. 89, op. 12, d. 2, ll. 227, 229–238; also f. 17, op. 120, d. 62, l. 103.

32. See Yaroslavsky to Kaganovich (March 9, 1933), RGASPI, f. 89, op. 8, d. 827, l. 3; also George Enteen, "The Writing of Party History in the USSR: The Case of E. M. Iaroslavskii," *Journal of Contemporary History* 21:2 (1986): 327; I. L. Man'kovskaia, "Kommunisticheskaia partiia Sovetskogo Soiuza: Istoriografiia," in *Sovetskaia istoricheskaia entsiklopediia,* 14 vols. (Moscow: Sovetskaia entsiklopediia, 1965), 7:717. See also Yaroslavsky to Stetsky (June 26, 1933), d. 828, l. 16 and *passim;* Yaroslavsky to Koniaev (April 5, 1933), d. 814, l. 45. The meeting did not occur in Stalin's Kremlin office, as it is not registered in his calendar.

33. Em. Iaroslavskii, *Istoriia VKP(b),* 2 vols. (Moscow: Partizdat, 1933).

34. Some party historians no longer had the reputation to publish mass texts; others were reluctant to try because they "feared unjust criticism" from the authorities. See Yaroslavsky to Stalin (November 25, 1931), RGASPI, f. 89, op. 12, d. 2, l. 204.

35. On the dialectical materialism text, see *Dialekticheskii i istoricheskii materializm v 2-kh chastiakh: uchebnik dlia komvuzov i vuzov,* ed. M. B. Mitin and I. Razumovskii (Moscow: Partiinoe izd-vo, 1932). For complaints about this text, see diary entry from January 7, 1934 in A. G. Man'kov, "Iz dnevnika riadovogo cheloveka," *Zvezda* 5 (1994): 166. The party activist L. A. Potemkin was frustrated enough by this text to write his own—see Jochen Hellbeck, *Revolution on My Mind: Writing a Diary under Stalin* (Cambridge: Harvard University Press, 2006), 267.

On the political grammars, see B. Volin, *Politgramota: uchebnik dlia kandidatskikh partiinykh shkol* (Moscow: Partizdat, 1932, 1933, 1934); S. Ingulov, *Uchebnik politgramoty: uchebnik dlia kandidatskikh partiinykh shkol,* 2 vols. (Moscow: Partizdat, 1932, 1933, 1934). Each of these texts originated as an 1932 Orgburo commission—see RGASPI, f. 17, op. 114, d. 295, ll. 4–5.

36. Central Executive Committee resolution of March 14, 1933, "Ob otvetstvennosti sluzhashchikh v gosudarstvennykh uchrezhdeniiakh i predpriiatiiakh za vreditel'skie akty," *Pravda,* March 15, 1933, 1; I. Luppol, "Piatnadtsat' let sistemy gosudarstvennykh izdatel'stv," *Pravda,* May 19, 1934, 3.

37. PAINSPI Gruzii, f. 18, op. 8, d. 148, l. 24, cited in Sukharev, "Predtecha 'Kratkogo kursa' v litsakh i dokumentakh," 111.

38. Although Yenukidze's fall in the spring of 1935 was officially attributed to a lack of political vigilance and inappropriate personal conduct, his clash with L. P. Beria and L. Z. Mekhlis over their criticism of his memoirs in *Bolshevik* and *Pravda* in January 1935 left him very vulnerable. See S. V. Sukharev, "Litsedeistvo na poprishche istorii [Beriia—apologet kul'ta lichnosti Stalina," *Voprosy istorii KPSS* 3

(1990): 108–111; RGASPI, f. 558, op. 11, d. 206, l. 111; d. 728, ll. 108–124. More generally, see A. Enukidze, *Bol'shevistskie nelegal'nye tipografii,* 3rd ed. (Moscow: Gosizdat, 1934); Enukidze, "K voprosu ob istorii zakavkazskikh partiinykh organizatsii," *Pravda,* January 16, 1935, 7. Mensheviks in Parisian exile assumed Yenukidze's fall was due to his memoiristic activity—see P., "Deistvitel'nye prichiny raspravy s Enukidze," *Sotsialisticheskii vestnik,* August 25, 1935, 16.

39. GARF (TsGAOR), f. 5216, op. 1, d. 45, ll. 2, 15, 22, 68; d. 89, ll. 5, 90b-10.

40. The first brigade was composed of Bubnov, Kuchkin, Shachnev, Sereda, A. F. Abramov, M. V. Radkov, F. A. Anderson, N. M. Voitinsky, A. V. Soloveichko, A. S. Shcherbakov, G. Krovitsky, I. M. Volkov, F. Pauzer, A. A. Melkumov, and Ye. Ye. Shteinman—see GARF (TsGAOR), f. 5216, op. 1, d. 45, l. 22. The second consisted of Ponomarev, Kuchkin, Anderson, Voitinsky, Krovitsky, Melkumov, and A. I. Urazov—see d. 89, ll. 90b-10.

41. *Kratkaia istoriia VKP(b),* ed. V. Knorin (Moscow: Partiinoe izdatel'stvo, 1934). The first edition was submitted to the publisher in late 1933 and printed in January 1934.

42. See, in particular, Central Committee resolution of May 15, 1934 "O prepodavanii grazhdanskoi istorii v shkolakh SSSR," *Pravda,* May 16, 1934, 1.

43. V. Knorin, "Zamechaniia k uchebniku 'Kratkaia istoriia VKP(b),'" *Propagandist* 21 (1934): 41.

44. Ibid., 44.

45. "Razvernut' rabotu po izucheniiu istorii partii," 5–6.

46. See, for example, RGASPI, f. 71, op. 3, d. 57, ll. 41–420b; op. 1, d. 28, ll. 90, 157–158.

47. RGASPI, f. 558, op. 11, d. 1122, ll. 35–36.

48. Curiously, the Red Army's political directorate was more successful than the party's ideological establishment in adapting to the new mode of propaganda. This is clear from an early text celebrating heroes within the ranks and two editions of a civil war history textbook by S. Ye. Rabinovich. Especially the latter book was an improvement over the party histories, inasmuch as even the 1933 edition paid attention to individual heroism and charisma—particularly that of Stalin, Voroshilov, Budenny, Frunze, Gamarnik, Yakir, and Yegorov. It remained rather schematic, however, and was superseded by a second edition less than two years later that Rabinovich reworked in light of 1934's calls for animated, engaging historical narratives. This edition epitomized the new line's approach to mobilizational indoctrination, as it supplied an inspirational, accessible, Stalin-centric account of the civil war that also accommodated mention of dozens of lesser-known heroes— G. Gai, I. S. Kutiakov, V. M. Primakov, I. P. Uborevich, R. P. Eideman, G. I. Kotovsky, V. N. Bozhenko, A. I. Kork, and so on. See *Armiia Oktiabria,* ed. V. Borgens et al. (Moscow: Gosudarstvennoe voennoe izdatel'stvo, 1932); S. E. Rabinovich, *Istoriia grazhdanskoi voiny (kratkii ocherk): uchebnoe posobie dlia voennykh shkol RKKA* (Moscow: Partiinoe izdatel'stvo, 1933); Rabinovich, *Istoriia grazhdanskoi voiny (kratkii ocherk): uchebnoe posobie dlia voennykh shkol RKKA,* 2nd ed., ed. I. I. Mints (Moscow: Sotsekgiz, 1935).

49. Khlevniuk has also noticed a difference between the party hierarchy's con-

ciliatory line toward society after collectivization and its continuing efforts to root out political unreliability within the party ranks. See O. V. Khlevniuk, *Politbiuro: mekhanizmy politicheskoi vlasti v 1930-e gody* (Moscow: Rosspen, 1995), 148.

50. L. M. Kaganovich, "O perestoike massovoi raboty i partiinykh organizatsii," in *XVII s"ezd Vsesoiuznoi Kommunisticheskoi partii (b): Stenograficheskii otchet* (Moscow: Partizdat, 1934), 551–552.

51. L. V. Nikolaev's motive for killing Kirov remains a mystery to the present day. His bitterness may have stemmed from his expulsion from the party and dismissal from a local institute; rumors of an affair between Kirov and Nikolaev's wife (who was the boss's personal secretary) have never been substantiated. See Alla Kirilina, *Rikoshet, ili skol'ko chelovek bylo ubito vystrelom v Smol'nom* (St. Petersburg: Znanie, 1993), 48–49, 104.

52. "Zakrytoe pis'mo TsK VKP(b): Uroki sobytii, sviazannykh s zlodeiskim ubiistvom tov. Kirova" [January 18, 1935], *Izvestiia TsK KPSS* 8 (1989): 96, 100; "Obvinitel'noe zakliuchenie," *Pravda*, January 16, 1935, 6; "Zavershennyi krug prestupleniia," *Pravda*, January 17, 1935, 1. See also Peter Konecny, *Builders and Deserters: Students, State, and Community in Leningrad, 1917–1941* (Montreal: McGill-Queen's University Press, 1999), 128–189.

53. For a discussion of how local party organizations reacted to this letter, see Sadik Alimov, "Through the Eyes of my Youth," in *Soviet Youth: Twelve Komsomol Histories* (Munich: Institute for the Study of the USSR, 1959), 87–88. Unsurprisingly, the Leningrad party organization launched its own investigation earlier in December 1935, producing a fascinating array of reports on the popular mood analyzed in Lesley Rimmel, "The Kirov Murder and Soviet Society: Propaganda and Popular Opinion in Leningrad, 1934–1935" (Ph.D. diss., University of Pennsylvania, 1995), esp. chaps. 1–3.

54. Two files in the former central party archive contain reports dating to February-March 1935 from transportation-sector party organizations on local political dissidence—see RGASPI, f. 17, op. 120, dd. 174, 176. Dozens of similar files in the former Leningrad party archive used by researchers during the mid-1990s were no longer accessible when the present author sought them out a decade later.

55. RGASPI, f. 17, op. 120, d. 174, ll. 116, 78, 140; d. 176, l. 28; d. 174, l. 17.

56. "Vospitanie molodezhi—tsentral'naia zadacha komsomola," *Pravda*, March 6, 1935, 1; "Komsomol i shkola," *Pravda*, March 11, 1935, 1.

57. "Anketa shakhtnogo propagandista," *Pravda*, March 28, 1935, 3. Even the most devoted activists confessed that they struggled to convey basic information in these study circles—see W. I. Hyrshki, "An Interloper in the Komsomol," in *Soviet Youth*, 99–102.

58. "Nepodgotovlennogo propagandista ne dopustili k zaniatiiam," *Pravda*, April 6, 1935, 3. See also B. Gorelik, "Prokhodiat mimo glavnogo," *Pravda*, March 27, 1935, 3; S. Rozental', "Tri propagandista," *Pravda*, April 4, 1935, 3.

59. S. Rozental', "Obezlichka i bezotvetstvennost'," *Pravda*, March 24, 1935, 3; "Kak rabotali s aktivom," *Pravda*, April 4, 1935, 3; "Reshitel'no uluchshit' partiinuiu rabotu," *Pravda*, March 29, 1935, 1; A. Davidiuk, "Vyrashchivat' kul'turnykh rabochikh-propagandistov," *Pravda*, March 29, 1935, 3; V. Shirin, "Moi opyt vospitaniia sochuvstvuiushchikh," *Pravda*, March 11, 1935, 2; "Milliony trebuiut

politicheskii slovar'," *Pravda,* April 19, 1935, 3; "Pochemu skuchno na zaniatii?" *Pravda,* April 6, 1935, 3.

60. RGVA, f. 9, op. 29, d. 12, l. 41; TsGAIPD SPb, f. 24, op. 5, d. 2688, l. 9; Rozental', "Obezlichka i bezotvetstvennost'," 3; V. Filatov, "Opyt raboty vechernei partshkoly," *Propagandist* 23–24 (1936): 103–106.

61. Rozental', "Obezlichka i bezotvetstvennost'," 3.

62. RGASPI, f. 17, op. 120, d. 174, l. 80.

63. RGASPI, f. 17, op. 120, d. 174, ll. 79, 1290b.

64. RGASPI, f. 17, op. 120, d. 174, l. 17. For a former Komsomol member who admits to not knowing the correct answer to this question during a party exam, see Abdy Kurmanbekov, "When the Paths of the Fathers Are Narrow," in *Soviet Youth,* 161, 180; on the persistence of this debate, see Wendy Goldman, *Terror and Democracy in the Age of Stalin: The Social Dynamics of Repression* (New York: Cambridge University Press, 2007), 221–225.

65. RGASPI, f. 17, op. 120, d. 176, l. 28. See similar discussions at TsGAIPD SPb, f. 24, op. 5, d. 2687, ll. 14–1-20; B. Rokhlind, "Politicheskie besedy s bespartiinym aktivom," *Pravda,* March 31, 1935, 3.

66. RGASPI, f. 17, op. 120, d. 176, l. 28.

67. RGASPI, f. 17, op. 120, d. 174, ll. 12–13.

68. "O bditel'nosti i bezotvetsvennosti," *Pravda,* March 25, 1935, 1; "Zabotlivo vyrashchivat' partiinye kadry," *Pravda,* March 26, 1935, 1; "Protiv nedootsenki raboty s sochuvstvuiushchimi," *Pravda,* March 27, 1935, 1; B. Ponomarev, "Ob izuchenii istorii partii sovetskogo perioda," *Pravda,* April 10, 1935, 2.

69. "Glubzhe izuchat' istoriiu partii," *Pravda,* March 7, 1935, 1; "'O nekotorykh zadachakh Marksistsko-Leninskogo obrazovaniia': iz rechi tov. P. Postysheva na plenume Kievskogo gorodskogo partiinogo komiteta 22 fevralia 1935 goda," *Pravda,* March 5, 1935, 2. On the need for agitators to be well read, see Shirin, "Moi opyt vospitaniia sochuvstvuiushchikh"; G. Samarodin, "Sam rukovozhu kruzhkami po istorii partii," *Pravda,* March 28, 1935, 3; on the need for them to connect past and present, see Rozental', "Tri propagandista"; Ortenberg, "Tekushchaia politika i skholasticheskie spory," 3.

70. So many records from Kultprop have been lost that the only evidence of this meeting is found in Yaroslavsky's diary entry from March 10, 1935, cited in Sandra Dahlke, *Individuum und Herrschaft im Stalinismus: Emel'jan Jaroslavskij (1878–1943)* (Munich: Oldenbourg, 2010), 332–333.

71. Yaroslavsky to Stalin (March 11, 1935), RGASPI, f. 89, op. 1, d. 84, ll. 9–10. Pospelov confirmed the seriousness of this proposal in a discussion with a former colleague in 1972—see D. Rudnev, "Kto pisal 'Kratkii kurs,'" *Politika* 9 (1991): 63.

72. RGASPI, f. 558, op. 11, d. 1118, l. 99.

73. Central Committee resolution of March 27, 1935 "O sozdanii v gorkomakh VKP(b) otdelov partkadrov," *Pravda,* March 28, 1935, 2; "O zadachakh partiino-organizatsionnoi i politicheski-vospitatel'noi raboty: Postanovlenie plenuma Leningradskogo gorodskogo komiteta VKP(b) ot 29 marta 1935 goda," *Pravda,* March 30, 1935, 2–3; "Zabotlivo vyrashchivat' partiinye kadry"; "Reshitel'no uluchshit' partiinuiu rabotu."

74. The connection between the murder and the verification campaign is questioned in J. Arch Getty, *Origins of the Great Purges: The Soviet Communist Party Reconsidered, 1933–1938* (New York: Cambridge University Press, 1991), 58; and *The Road to Terror: Stalin and the Self-Destruction of the Bolsheviks, 1932–1939*, ed. J. Arch Getty and O. V. Naumov (New Haven: Yale University Press, 1999), 150, while a direct connection is posited in Khlevniuk, *Politbiuro: mekhanizmy politicheskoi vlasti v 1930-e gody*, 146–147; and Fabio Bettanin, *La Fabrica del Mito: Storia e politica nell'Urss staliniana* (Naples: Edizioni Scientifiche Italiani, 1998), 133–134. While the verification campaign was announced before Kirov's murder, its objectives and tenor were clearly shaped by the December crisis—see, for instance, RGASPI, f. 558, op. 11, d. 1118, ll. 101–102.

75. See undated Central Committee resolution "O reorganizatsii Kul'tpropa TsK VKP(b)," *Pravda*, May 14, 1935, 1. Stetsky retained control of the new agitprop department; B. M. Tal was to supervise the press and publishing, A. S. Shcherbakov was to oversee cultural enlightenment work, Volin was to curate school policy, and K. Ya. Bauman was to monitor the sciences.

76. Central Committee resolution of June 13, 1935 "O propagandistskoi rabote v blizhaishee vremia," *Pravda*, June 15, 1935, 1. This resolution is discussed in N. Rubinshtein, "Nedostatki v prepodavanii istorii VKP(b)," *Bol'shevik* 8 (1936): 32–42.

77. See Stetsky to Stalin (June 8, 1935), RGASPI, f. 17, op. 163, d. 1066, ll. 118–119; Stetsky to Stalin (June 15, 1935), f. 71, op. 3, d. 62, ll. 287–285; Yaroslavsky to Stalin (June 2, 1935), f. 558, op. 11, d. 843, ll. 7–8; f. 89, op. 8, d. 604, ll. 43–44. Stesky's first letter, which Stalin transformed into a Politburo resolution entitled "O populiarnom uchebnike," revealed that the collectively written, popular textbook was to be compiled by a brigade including Knorin, Yaroslavsky, Pospelov, Ponomarev, Rabinovich, Kuchkin, Anderson, Voitinsky, M. A. Moskalev, and L. M. Guliaev; its manuscript was due in early August. Orakhelashvili's IMEL brigade working on the four-volume academic history now included Volin, Avvakumov, Shachnev, Frug, Pankratova, Sereda, Volkovicher, Rosenblium, Ronis, and Ryklin in Moscow and Vavilin, Sharikov, Lidak, Kotovich, Kurnatovsky, and Pindrik in Leningrad. The new IMEL brigade assigned the two-volume text for propagandists and activists included Sorin, Volin, Kuchkin, Frug, Ryklin, Bystriansky, Rubinshtein, and M. S. Zorky under the supervision of Popov, Stetsky, Adoratsky, Piatnitsky, and Yaroslavsky; its manuscript was due December 1. See f. 17, op. 163, d. 1066, ll. 116–119; f. 71, op. 3, d. 57, ll. 41–420b; op. 1, d. 9, ll. 10–14, 18; d. 28, ll. 157–158, 178–193.

78. See, in particular, Adoratsky to Stalin (June 17, 1935), RGASPI, f. 71, op. 3, d. 62, l. 187. Stetsky noted to Stalin on June 15 that it was necessary to spur the new popular party history brigade into action—see Stetsky to Stalin (June 15, 1935), ll. 287–285. In the wake of this reminder, Yaroslavsky, Knorin, and Pospelov apparently opted to revise and expand Knorin's 1934 *Short History* rather than write a new text from scratch.

79. Yaroslavsky's private disapproval of this co-option is visible in his marginalia on a newspaper clipping of Beria's speech—see RGASPI, f. 89, op. 8, d. 155, l. 1. He hailed the speech in public in exclusively enthusiastic terms, of course—see his review of Beria's book in *Molodaia gvardiia* 10 (1935): 136–142.

80. See *Pravda,* July 29 to August 5, 1935; L. P. Beriia, *K voprosu ob istorii bol'shevistskikh organizatsii v Zakavkaz'e* (Moscow: Partizdat, 1935). S. V. Sukharev considers the speech to have been prepared as a surprise for Stalin while other scholars believe it to have been composed on the general secretary's orders, even including him in the editing process. That the production of the manuscript took place behind Stalin's back is doubtful, if only because it was preceded by several public speeches in Tbilisi and Beria's 1934 article in *Bolshevik.* Likewise, the notion that Stalin personally participated in the book's editing is unlikely, as the paper trail at the central party archive is relatively sparse. The manuscript was likely prepared independently with Stalin's tacit consent. See Sukharev, "Litsedeistvo na poprishche istorii," 113–14; A. T. Rybin, "Riadom so Stalinym," *Sotsiologicheskie issledovaniia* 3 (1988): 88; A. Antonov-Ovseenko, "Beriia," *Iunost'* 12 (1988): 69–70; Amy Knight, *Beria: Stalin's First Lieutenant* (Princeton: Princeton University Press, 1993), 58. For the archival paper trail, see RGASPI, f. 558, op. 11, dd. 704–705.

81. "Vsem zav. otdeleniiami kul'tury i propagandy leninizma," *Propagandist* 16 (1935): 39.

82. On these purges, see Merle Fainsod, *Smolensk under Soviet Rule* (Boston: Unwin Hyman, 1958), 374–377; on Politburo attempts to rein in these purges, see RGASPI, f. 17, op. 3, d. 965, ll. 30, 63–64. Archival evidence testifies to a blanket ban on some forty authors in 1935, enforced by a total mobilization of Glavlit, NKVD, and party personnel. See A. Samokhvalov to A. N. Vinokurov (January 28, 1938), GARF, f. r-9425, op. 1, d. 6, ll. 34–39.

83. See the announcements in *Pravda* on May 26 and June 26, 1935, respectively; also Man'kovskaia and Sharapov, "Kul't lichnosti i istoriko-partiinaia nauka," 66.

84. "Partiinoi propagande—krepkikh organizatorov," *Pravda,* March 31, 1936, 2.

85. Adoratsky to Stalin (June 17, 1935), RGASPI, f. 71, op. 3, d. 62, l. 187.

86. B. Volin and S. Ingulov, *Politgramota* (Moscow: Partizdat, 1935); Ingulov, *Politbesedy,* 2nd ed. (Moscow: Partizdat, 1935).

87. "O partiinoi propagande," *Izvestiia,* June 16, 1935, 1; D. Ortenberg, "Tekushchaia politika i skholasticheskie spory," *Pravda,* September 19, 1935, 3; Rubinshtein, "Nedostatki v prepodavanii istorii VKP(b)"; V. Furer, "Zametki o propagande," *Pravda,* July 21, 1935, 3; A. Stetskii, "O propagandistakh i agitatorakh," *Pravda,* September 22, 1935, 2.

88. "Soveshchanie prepodavatelei institutov Krasnoi professury," *Istorik-Marksist* 12 (1935): 119–123; *Soveshchanie po voprosam partiinoi propagandy i agitatsii pri TsK VKP(b), 4–7 dekabria 1935 g.* (Moscow: Partizdat, 1936).

89. See "Muzei Lenina," *Izvestiia,* January 15, 1936, 6; M. Rabichev, "Tsentral'nyi muzei V. I. Lenina," *Pravda,* April 29, 1936, 2; "Pamiatnik geniiu chelovechestva i vozhdiu proletariata," *Pravda,* May 15, 1936, 1; N. Izgoev, "Muzei Lenina," *Izvestiia,* May 15, 1936, 1; E. Grigor'ev, "Shkola bol'shevistskoi istorii," *Komsomol'skaia pravda,* May 15, 1936, 4. The idea of establishing this museum appears to have originated with Krupskaia in August 1935—see RGASPI, f. 558, op. 11, d. 755, ll. 36–39. It was authorized by the Politburo resolution of September 27, 1935 "O muzee Lenina," f. 17, op. 163, d. 1081, ll. 43–44.

90. *Soveshchanie po voprosam partiinoi propagandy i agitatsii pri TsK VKP(b),* 10, 29, 135.

91. See the page proofs to the first volume at RGASPI, f. 558, op. 3, d. 74.

92. Little evidence is available at the former central party archive that can characterize the circumstances surrounding this fiasco. Hints about the volume's shortcomings are visible in "O partiinoi propagande: rech' sekretaria TsK VKP(b) tov. A. Andreeva na otkrytii Vysshei shkoly propagandistov im. Ia. M. Sverdlova pri TsK VKP(b), 7 fevralia 1936 g.," *Pravda,* February 26, 1936, 2; A. I. Stetskii, "Ob institutakh Krasnoi professury," *Bol'shevik* 23–24 (1935): 54–55.

CHAPTER 3. PERSONIFYING THE SOVIET 'EXPERIMENT'

1. "'O kul'te lichnosti i ego posledstviiakh': Doklad Pervogo sekretaria TsK KPSS tov. Khrushcheva N. S. XX s"ezdu Kommunisticheskoi partii Sovetskogo Soiuza," *Izvestiia TsK KPSS* 3 (1989). Despite the influential nature of Khrushchev's analysis, it is doubtful that he actually subscribed to such a view. Pospelov, his ghostwriter, certainly understood the cult's function, having been one of its chief architects.

2. See Immanuel Wallerstein, *Africa—The Politics of Independence: An Interpretation of Modern African History* (New York: Vintage, 1961), 99; Clifford Geertz, *Local Knowledge: Further Essays in Interpretive Anthropology* (New York: Basic Books, 1983), 121–148.

3. Max Weber, *Economy and Society: An Outline of Interpretive Sociology,* ed. Guenther Roth and Claus Wittich, vol. 3 (New York: Bedminster, 1968), 1111–1126.

4. J. Arch Getty, "The Politics of Stalinism," in *The Stalin Phenomenon,* ed. Alec Nove (London: Weidenfeld & Nicolson, 1993), 119.

5. April 25, 1935 diary entry published in *Iosif Stalin v ob"iatiiakh sem'i: iz lichnogo arkhiva (Sbornik dokumentov),* ed. Iu. G. Murin and V. N. Denisov (Moscow: Rodina, 1993), 176.

6. Lion Feikhtvanger, *Moskva 1937 goda* (Moscow: Khudozhestvennaia literatura, 1937), 64–65, esp. 65. A longer, unedited transcript of their discussions is at RGASPI, f. 551, op. 11, d. 1120, ll. 8–10, and is discussed in Sarah Davies, "Stalin and the Making of the Leadership Cult in the 1930s," in *The Leadership Cult in Communist Dictatorships: Stalin and the Eastern Bloc,* ed. Balázc Apor et al. (New York: Palgrave, 2004), 37–38.

7. Stalin proposed this during a December 23, 1946 meeting with leading ideological cadres—see RGASPI, f. 629, op. 1, d. 54, l. 23.

8. Although a connection has long been posited between the cult and the idea of charismatic leadership, this analysis tends to address the cult's emergence as almost inevitable rather than historically contingent. Much like the crisis surrounding party propaganda discussed in the preceding chapter, the origins of the Stalin cult are best located in the party's inability to rally popular support by more orthodox Marxist-Leninist means during the late 1920s. Compare to Getty, "The Politics of Stalinism," 119; Moshe Lewin, "Stalin in the Mirror of the Other," in *Stalinism and Nazism: Dictatorships in Comparison,* ed. Ian Kershaw and Moshe

Lewin (Cambridge: Cambridge University Press, 1997), 107–134; Sarah Davies, *Popular Opinion in Stalin's Russia: Propaganda, Terror, and Dissent* (Cambridge: Cambridge University Press, 1997), 163, 167; Jeffrey Brooks, *"Thank You, Comrade Stalin": Soviet Public Culture from Revolution to Cold War* (Princeton: Princeton University Press, 1999), 59; Sheila Fitzpatrick, *Everyday Stalinism—Ordinary Life in Extraordinary Times: Soviet Russia in the 1930s* (New York: Oxford University Press, 1999), 24; etc.

9. Two models pervade the literature on the inner workings of the cult: George Orwell's depiction of an efficient, totalitarian monolith and Khrushchev's image of Stalin as the cult's meticulous editor-in-chief—see Roy Medvedev, *Let History Judge—The Origins and Consequences of Stalinism,* ed. and trans. George Shriver (New York: Columbia University Press, 1989), 817–819; D. A. Volkogonov, *Stalin: politicheskii portret,* 2 vols. (Moscow: Novosti, 1991), 1:387; Arkady Belinikov and Max Hayward in *The Soviet Censorship,* ed. Martin Dewhirst and Robert Farrell (Metuchen: Scarecrow Press, 1973), 17. The archives, however, reveal the Stalin cult to have been poorly organized, rife with political intrigue, and at least as ad hoc as other major projects of the era. Stalin's own participation in the cult was no more consistent—while his role is best described as supervisory, such a description fails to capture the arbitrariness of his involvement.

10. The arts may rival biography in this regard—see Evgenii Gromov, *Stalin: vlast' i iskusstvo* (Moscow: Respublika, 1998); Jan Plamper, "The Stalin Cult in the Visual Arts, 1929–1953" (Ph.D. diss., University of California at Berkeley, 2001).

11. For a rare exception to this rule, see the Stalin entry in *12 biografii,* ed. B. Volin (Moscow: Rabochaia Moskva, 1924), 46–51. The galleys of this volume are at RGASPI, f. 558, op. 11, d. 1277, ll. 27–61.

12. For drafts and galleys, see RGASPI, f. 558, op. 11, d. 1278, ll. 6–41; for Tovstukha's correspondence with Granat, see d. 1277, ll. 26, 67–670b, 123–1230b; d. 1278, ll. 1–5.

13. Iv. Tovstukha, "Stalin," in *Entsiklopedicheskii slovar' Granat,* vol. 41, sect. 3 (Moscow: Russkii biograficheskii institut Granat, 1927), 107–110; *Iosif Vissarionovich Stalin (Kratkaia biografiia),* ed. Iv. Tovstukha (Moscow: Gos. izd-vo, 1927).

14. "Iosif Vissarionovich Stalin (Biografiia)," *Pravda,* December 21, 1929, 4; "Knigi I. V. Stalina," *Pravda,* December 21, 1929, 8.

15. M. V. Vol'fson, "Stalin," in *Malaia sovetskaia entsiklopediia,* vol. 8 (Moscow: Sovetskaia entsiklopediia, 1930), 406–412; S. Ingulov, *Politgramota: uchebnik dlia kandidatskikh partiinykh shkol,* 2nd ed. (Moscow: Partizdat, 1933), 388–397; B. Volin and S. Ingulov, *Politgramota* (Moscow: Partizdat, 1935), 305–15. The only other biographical statements to be published before the end of the decade appeared in the collected works of prominent party leaders—see, for instance, M. A. Savel'ev, "Stalin," in V. I. Lenin, *Sochineniia,* vol. 15, 2nd/3rd ed. (Moscow: Partizdat, 1935), 714–15; RGASPI, f. 71, op. 10, d. 257, ll. 2–8.

16. Medvedev, *Let History Judge,* 817–818.

17. *XVII s"ezd Vsesoiuznoi Kommunisticheskoi partii (bol'shevikov) 26 ianvaria-10 fevralia 1934 g.: Stenograficheskii otchet* (Moscow: Partizdat, 1934), 620.

18. G. V. Plekhanov, "O roli lichnosti v istorii," in *Sochineniia,* 24 vols. (Moscow: Gos. izd-vo, 1925): 8:271–306; Plekhanov, *The Role of the Individual in History* (New York: International Publishers, 1940); Erik van Ree, *The Political Thought of Joseph Stalin: A Study in Twentieth Century Revolutionary Patriotism* (New York: RoutledgeCurzon, 2002), 161–162.

19. "Beseda s nemetskim pisatelem Emilem Liudvigom," *Bol'shevik* 8 (1932): 33. Stalin's view is reminiscent of Hegel's—see G. Hegel, *The Philosophy of History* (New York: Dover, 1956), 30.

20. Robert Tucker's conclusion that Stalin designed the process to promote the personality cult overestimates his foresight and ability to control events—see Chapter Two, n. 6.

21. "'Novaia, nevidannaia literatura': vystuplenie tov. P. Iudina," *Literaturnaia gazeta,* January 22, 1934, 3.

22. "Ot shestnadtsatogo k semnadtsatomu s"ezdu partii: doklad L. M. Kaganovicha o rabote TsK VKP(b) na Moskovskoi ob"edinennoi IV oblastnoi i III gorodskoi partiinoi konferentsii 17 ianvaria 1934 g.," *Pravda,* January 22, 1934, 4.

23. "Razvernut' rabotu po izucheniiu istorii partii," *Proletarskaia revoliutsiia* 4 (1934): 12. As noted above in Chapter Two, n. 14, this editorial was written by Tovstukha and Korotky, two insiders deeply involved in the efforts to develop a biography.

24. RGASPI, f. 17, op. 120, d. 176, l. 45. For other examples, see Davies, *Popular Opinion in Stalin's Russia,* 168–169.

25. RGASPI, f. 558, op. 1, d. 4572, l. 1. This monopoly regulated cult material on every level of the production process. All new images and representations of Stalin during the 1930s had to be approved by the general secretary's chancellery before being passed by the censor; publication of Lenin's and Stalin's writings was similarly monopolized by the Central Committee and IMEL. Even the technical side of such propaganda was regulated, leading regional presses to be scolded in early 1936 for printing poor-quality photos and pictures of "party and state leaders and distinguished locals from the region or factory" on linoleum, wood, cardboard, and other non-newsprint stock. See Plamper, "The Stalin Cult in the Visual Arts," 62–68; I. L. Man'kovskaia and Iu. P. Sharapov, "Kul't lichnosti i istoriko-partiinaia nauka," *Voprosy istorii KPSS* 5 (1988): 66–68; RGVA, f. 9, op. 29s, d. 265, l. 7.

26. Davies, "Stalin and the Making of the Leadership Cult in the 1930s," 33–37.

27. On Kirov, see Amy Knight, *Beria: Stalin's First Lieutenant* (Princeton: Princeton University Press, 1993), 57–58; Robert Tucker, *Stalin in Power: The Revolution from Above, 1928–1941* (New York: Norton, 1990), 335; Edvard Radzinskii, *Stalin* (Moscow: Vagrius, 1997), 13–15; on Gorky, see Lidiia Spiridonova, "'Ochen' sozhaleiu, chto delo razvalilos': kak ne byl napisan ocherk Gor'kogo o Staline," *Nezavisimaia gazeta,* March 27, 1998, 13; "'Zhmu vashu ruku, dorogoi tovarishch': perepiska Maksima Gor'kogo i Iosifa Stalina," *Novyi mir* 9 (1998): 163–168.

28. Beria's patronage over the Georgian Stalin cult included support for the collection of oral histories, the creation of a museum, and the erection of a marble pavilion over Stalin's humble childhood home. See S. V. Sukharev, "Litsedeistvo na poprishche istorii [Beriia—apologet kul'ta lichnosti Stalina]," *Voprosy istorii KPSS* 3 (1990): 105–106.

29. Willi Munzenberg, a German communist, had urged Tovstukha to return to the project in 1931, asking him to have the IMEL publish a "communist-written" biography in order to refute exposés being published abroad by renegades like B. G. Bazhanov. See Munzenberg to Tovstukha (April 13, 1931), RGASPI, f. 155, op. 1, d. 85, ll. 1, 3. For the vast materials Tovstukha assembled, see f. 71, op. 10, dd. 192–218, 364–373.

30. L. P. Beriia, "Bol'sheviki Zakavkaz'ia v bor'be za sotsializm," *Bol'shevik* 11 (1934): 24–37. Beria was not the only biographer to undermine his rivals—both Toroshelidze and Yaroslavsky eagerly attacked their competitors as well. See Sukharev, "Litsedeistvo na poprishche istorii," 105–107, 110–111, 116.

31. Yaroslavsky to F. Ye. Makharadze (February 1, 1935), RGASPI, f. 89, op. 8, d. 1001, ll. 7. See also l. 5 and more generally, dd. 1001–1014; Yaroslavsky to Tovstukha (January 19, 1935), f. 155, op. 1, d. 88, l. 1; Tovstukha to Yaroslavsky (January 28, 1935), f. 89, op. 8, d. 1001, ll. 23–24; f. 155, op. 1, d. 90, ll. 1–10b.

32. Yaroslavsky to Tovstukha ([February 1935]), RGASPI, f. 155, op. 1, d. 88, l. 2.

33. In early 1935, Tovstukha confidentially relayed to Adoratsky that "Stetsky recently proposed that I write a biography of Stalin. This is thus the *fourth* such offer I have received in the past year, suggesting that the issue is already fully mature." See Tovstukha to Adoratsky (January 13, 1935), RGASPI, f. 155, op. 1, d. 70, l. 28. Stetsky had apparently discussed the matter with Stalin a day after his fifty-fifth birthday on December 22, 1934—see *Na prieme u Stalina: tetradi (zhurnaly) zapisei lits, priniatykh I. V. Stalinym (1924–1953 gg.)* (Moscow: Novyi khronograf, 2008), 147.

34. Tovstukha to Adoratsky (April 14, 1935), RGASPI, f. 155, op. 1, d. 70, ll. 33–340b.

35. Yaroslavsky to Stetsky (March 11, 1935), RGASPI, f. 89, op. 1, d. 84, l. 15; Yaroslavsky to Stalin (June 2, 1935), f. 558, op. 11, d. 842, ll. 7–8, 9–10; Yaroslavsky to Stalin (August 1, 1935), ll. 11, 12; op. 1, d. 5089, l. 1.

36. Yaroslavsky misinterpreted this response to the Moscow party committee later that year—see RGASPI, f. 89, op. 8, d. 604, l. 43. It is both misinterpreted and miscited in Volkogonov, *Stalin: politicheskii portret*, 1:338–339.

37. "Zakrytoe pis'mo TsK VKP(b): Uroki sobytii, sviazannykh s zlodeiskim ubiistvom tov. Kirova" [January 18, 1935], *Izvestiia TsK KPSS* 8 (1989).

38. This quip, and those following it, are drawn from two files in the former central party archive containing correspondence from transportation-sector party organizations on local political dissidence in the wake of the Kirov assassination. All date to February and March 1935. See RGASPI, f. 17, op. 120, dd. 174, 176; here d. 176, ll. 135, 20, 125. For more sarcastic comments about Kirov's private life, see Lesley Rimmel, "The Kirov Murder and Soviet Society: Propaganda and Popular Opinion in Leningrad, 1934–1935" (Ph.D. diss., University of Pennsylvania, 1995), 58–63; also Sadik Alimov, "Through the Eyes of My Youth," in *Soviet Youth: Twelve Komsomol Histories* (Munich: Institute for the Study of the USSR, 1959), 88.

39. RGASPI, f. 17, op. 120, d. 176, l. 47.

40. RGASPI, f. 17, op. 120, d. 174, l. 79; d. 176, ll. 96, 26–27; also d. 174, ll. 68l; TsGAIPD SPb, f. 24, op. 5, d. 2681, l. 10.

41. RGASPI, f. 17, op. 120, d. 174, ll. 48, 68, 78; d. 176, ll. 25, 163; TsGAIPD SPb, f. k-598, op. 1, d. 5387, l. 93; d. 5407, l. 81, cited in Davies, *Public Opinion in Stalin's Russia,* 215.

42. RGASPI, f. 17, op. 120, d. 176, l. 96.

43. RGASPI, f. 17, op. 120, d. 174, l. 95.

44. RGASPI, f. 17, op. 120, d. 176, l. 115. On such vandalism, see TsGAIPD SPb, f. 24, op. 2v, d. 1843, l. 67.

45. RGASPI, f. 17, op. 120, d. 176, l. 27; d. 174, l. 18.

46. On weak indoctrination efforts in the public schools, see RGASPI, f. 17, op. 120, d. 174, ll. 710b, 91; on party study circles and their textbooks, see l. 710b. According to one report from Nikolaev, some circles were still using textbooks from the 1920s that treated Trotsky favorably—see d. 176, ll. 154–55. Libraries were offering such titles to patrons as well—see ll. 46–47, 94, 164–165; TsGAIPD SPb, f. 24, op. 2v, d. 1829, ll. 145–155.

47. RGASPI, f. 17, op. 120, d. 174, ll. 71, 48.

48. GARF, f. 9401, op. 1, d. 4157, ll. 201–203, 205, cited in Sarah Davies, "The Crime of 'Anti-Soviet Agitation' in the Soviet Union in the 1930s," *Cahiers du Monde Russe* 39:1–2 (1998): 153.

49. On this struggle with informal joke telling, see *Political Humor under Stalin: An Anthology of Unofficial Jokes and Anecdotes,* ed. David Brandenberger (Bloomington: Slavica, 2009), 1–26.

50. On the book's status as a biography rather than a historical narrative, see diary entry from November 14, 1936 in A. G. Solov'ev, "Tetradi krasnogo professora (1912–1941 gg.)," in *Neizvestnaia Rossiia—XX vek,* 4 vols. (Moscow: Istoricheskoe nasledie, 1993), 4:189.

51. See Chapter Two, n. 81.

52. RGASPI, f. 17, d. 120, d. 237, ll. 60–61. Dashniak, the Armenian Revolutionary Federation, was a leading socialist party in Armenia between 1917 and 1920.

53. Central Committee resolution of June 13, 1935 "O propagandistskoi rabote v blizhaishee vremia," *Pravda,* June 15, 1935, 1.

54. Sukharev, "Litsedeistvo na poprishche istorii," 106.

55. Medvedev, *Let History Judge,* 817–818; A. Kemp-Welch, *Stalin and the Literary Intelligentsia* (Basingstoke: Macmillan, 1991), 228.

56. Barbusse's biography and film were to reinforce one another: the biography would focus on Stalin and the struggle for industrial socialism while the film would depict Stalin as that struggle's personification. See G. B. Kulikova, "Iz istorii formirovaniia kul'ta lichnosti Stalina (A. Barbius i sozdanie biografii 'Ottsa narodov' v nachale 1930-kh godov)," *Otechestvennaia istoriia* 1 (2006): 98–107; RGASPI, f. 558, op. 11, dd. 699–700; on his earlier books, see Henri Barbusse, *Voici ce qu'on a fait de la Géorgie* (Paris: E. Flammarion, 1929); Barbusse, *Russie* (Paris: E. Flammarion, 1930).

57. See, for instance, Stalin's rejection of Mekhlis's concerns over a 1932 article that Barbusse wanted to publish in *Pravda:* RGASPI, f. 558, op. 11, d. 699, l. 60.

58. For Stetsky's critique, see RGASPI, f. 558, op. 11, d. 699, ll. 124–125; 126–135.

59. "Beseda s Anri Barbiusom," *Literaturnaia gazeta,* September 24, 1934, 1; Boris Frezinskii, "Velikaia illiuziia—Parizh, 1935," in *Minuvshee: Istoricheskii almanakh,* vol. 24 (St. Petersburg: Athenium-Feniks, 1998), 176.

60. Henri Barbusse, *Staline: un monde nouveau vu à travers un homme* (Paris: E. Flammarion, 1935). On the popular demand for a Russian translation, see M. Kol'tsov, "Barbius o Staline," *Pravda,* September 1, 1935, 2.

61. A. I. Stetskii, "Predislovie," in Anri Barbius, *Stalin: Chelovek, cherez kotorogo raskryvaetsia novyi mir* (Moscow: Khudozhestvennaia literatura, 1936), vii–x; see also D. Osipov, "Kniga Barbiusa o Staline," *Pravda,* March 11, 1936, 2.

62. Volkogonov, *Stalin: Politicheskii portret,* 1:391.

63. Plamper, "The Stalin Cult in the Visual Arts," esp. 71–113; HPSSS, no. 28/1745, schedule A, vol. 37, 43–46; no. 421, schedule A, vol. 21, 67.

CHAPTER 4. THE CULT OF HEROES AND HEROISM

1. "Charismatic Leadership," "Propaganda Techniques," "Symbols," in *Encyclopedia of Propaganda,* ed. Robert Cole, 3 vols. (New York: M. E. Sharpe, 1998), 1:106, 2:609–613, 3:757–761.

2. See A. Serafimovich, *Zheleznyi potok: epopeia* (Moscow: Mospoligraf, 1924).

3. See Jeffrey Brooks, "The Breakdown in the Production and Distribution of Printed Material, 1917–1927," in *Bolshevik Culture: Experiment and Order in the Russian Revolution,* ed. Abbot Gleason et al. (Bloomington: Indiana University Press, 1985), 151–174; Maurice Friedberg, *Russian Classics in Soviet Jackets* (New York: Columbia University Press, 1962).

4. Katerina Clark, "Little Heroes and Big Deeds: Literature Responds to the First Five-Year Plan," in *Cultural Revolution in Russia, 1928–1931,* ed. Sheila Fitzpatrick (Bloomington: Indiana University Press, 1978), 189–206.

5. S. V. Zhuravlev, *Fenomen "Istorii fabrik i zavodov": gor'kovskoe nachinanie v kontekste epokhi 1930-kh godov* (Moscow: IRI RAN, 1997), 4–5, 153–154, 180–181; Brian Kassof, "The Knowledge Front: Politics, Ideology, and Economics in the Soviet Book Publishing Industry, 1925–1935" (Ph.D. diss, University of California at Berkeley, 2000), esp. 226–234.

6. Gorky to Stalin (November 27, 1929), published in "Iz perepiski A. M. Gor'kogo," *Izvestiia TsK KPSS* 3 (1989): 183–187; M. Gor'kii, "Istoriia fabrik i zavodov," *Pravda,* September 7, 1931, 2. Gorky's interest in didactic heroes dates to his mid-1920s essay "On the Hero and the Crowd"—see Hans Günther, *Der sozialistische Übermensch: M. Gor'kij und der sowjetische Heldenmythos* (Stuttgart: J. B. Metzler, 1993), 92.

7. *Nashi dostizheniia* (1929–1937); *Zhizn' zamechatel'nykh liudei* (1931–); *Istoriia fabrik i zavodov* (1931–1938); *Istoriia grazhdanskoi voiny v SSSR* (1935–1942); *SSSR na stroike* (1930–1942). A fourth series, *Liudi vtoroi piatiletki,* resulted only in a single volume (*Tvorchestvo narodov SSSR,* ed. M. Gor'kii, L. Mekhlis, and A. Stetskii [Moscow: Pravda, 1937]); a number of other projects failed to advance past the planning stage, including elementary civics readers on the history of women, the international bourgeoisie, the Russian merchant class, and the

countryside. See Matthew Lenoe, *Closer to the Masses: Stalinist Culture, Social Revolution, and Soviet Newspapers* (Cambridge: Harvard University Press, 2004), 224–227; Erica Wolf, "When Photographs Speak, to Whom Do They Talk? The Origins and Audience of *SSSR na stroike* (*USSR in Construction*)," *Left History* 6:2 (2000): 53–82; Wolf, "Le statut de la photographie dans la revue *L'URSS en construction* (1930)," in *Caméra politique: cinéma et stalinisme*, ed. Kristian Fiegelson (Paris: Presses Sorbonne Nouvelle, 2005): 61–69; M. Gor'kii, "Istoriia derevni," *Pravda*, February 25, 1935, 3.

8. On this co-option of mass culture, see Chapter One, nn. 55–56. RAPP's service as the unofficial literary instrument of the party was neither consistent nor particularly willing—see Edward Brown, *The Proletarian Episode in Russian Literature, 1928–1932* (New York: Columbia University Press, 1950), chaps. 7–8.

9. Lenoe, *Closer to the Masses*, chaps. 5–7.

10. For the resolutions of the Sixteenth Party Congress, see *XVI s"ezd Vsesoiuznoi Kommunisticheskoi partii (bol'shevikov): stenograficheskii otchet* (Moscow: Partizdat, 1930), 714–715. Lenoe addresses many of these events from a slightly different perspective in *Closer to the Masses*, chap. 7. A number of commentators date the advent of Soviet heroism to 1934, missing the earlier debates and developments —see, for instance, Hans Günther, "The Heroic Myth in Socialist Realism," in *Traumfabrik Kommunismus: die visuelle Kultur der Stalinzeit / Dream Factory of Communism: The Visual Culture of the Stalin Era*, ed. Boris Groys and Max Hollen (Frankfurt: Schirn Kunsthalle, 2003), 108–109.

11. "Sotsialisticheskaia stroika i ee geroi," *Pravda*, May 18, 1931, 1. I. I. Oblomov, the protagonist of I. A. Goncharov's eponymous 1859 novel, typifies laziness and indecision.

12. See "Strana dolzhna znat' svoikh geroev," *Pravda*, May 18, 19, June 8, 9, etc.

13. "Luchshii zaboishchik i luchshii mashinist Donbassa," *Pravda*, May 11, 1932, 3; S. R. Gershberg, *Rabota u nas takaia: Zapisi zhurnalista—pravdista tridtsatykh godov* (Moscow: Gospolitizdat, 1971), 107–112.

14. Victoria Bonnell notes that if the generic "worker-icon" propaganda of the 1920s had attempted to inspire ordinary Soviets through abstract appeals to class consciousness, collectivism, and the spirit of 1917, the new line was much more concrete and calculating. Instead of appealing to Soviets' supposedly innate sense of class identity, "during the 1930s, the imagery of the worker in political propaganda had a different purpose. Now the image of the worker functioned as a model, an ideal type. Its purpose was to conjure up a vision of the new Soviet man, to provide a visual script for the appearance, demeanor, and conduct of the model Stalinist citizen." Abstract exhortation, then, had shifted to pragmatic, targeted mobilization and indoctrination. See Victoria Bonnell, *Iconography of Power: Soviet Political Posters under Lenin and Stalin* (Berkeley: University of California Press, 1997), 38.

15. See, for instance, I. S. Makar'ev, *Pokaz geroev truda—general'naia tema proletarskoi literatury* (Moscow: Gos. izd. khud. lit-ry, 1932), 5–6, 9, 15, 20–34.

16. According to Clark's widely accepted view, Socialist Realism's approach to literary, artistic, and cultural expression marked the end of both the previous decade's revolutionary literary movements and the avant garde itself. Breaking with the challenging, experimentalist genres of the 1920s, Socialist Realism embodied a

simple, highly readable style of narration that fused the realist prose of the nineteenth century with working-class values and the ideological didacticism of the party line. Thematically, this mode of expression excelled at promoting everyday tales of valor and self-sacrifice, within which heroic individuals struggled for the greater societal good under the watchful direction of the party. While not disputing Clark's analysis, Evgeny Dobrenko also finds a connection between Socialist Realism and the literary trends of the late 1920s, viewing the new literary method as a populist corrective to the often arcane and inaccessible literature of the avant garde. According to Dobrenko, many writers were aware that the cultural innovations of the first decade of Soviet rule had failed to win the hearts and minds of the USSR's poorly educated readership, and this led them away from the avant garde toward more conventional forms of literary expression. Such writerly instincts were reinforced by party insistence that literature embrace the tastes of the mass audience that it was courting. Matthew Lenoe takes this investigation still further, demonstrating that journalists were among the first to flirt with this revolutionary cooption of convention and sensation. See Clark, "Little Heroes and Big Deeds," 205–206; Clark, *The Soviet Novel: History as Ritual* (Chicago: University of Chicago Press, 1980), 34–5, 72, 119, 136–155, 148, 8–10; Evgeny Dobrenko, "The Disaster of Middlebrow Taste, or, Who 'Invented' Socialist Realism?" in *Socialist Realism without Shores*, ed. Thomas Lahusen and Evgeny Dobrenko (Durham: Duke University Press, 1997), 153–164; Lenoe, *Closer to the Masses,* chap. 7. Compare to interpretations that some sort of realist aesthetic inevitably would have emerged from the artistic free-for-all of the 1920s or that the avant garde's quest for state sponsorship and illiberal cultural hegemony actually facilitated the new mode of expression—Régine Robin, *Socialist Realism: An Impossible Aesthetic*, trans. Catherine Porter (Stanford: Stanford University Press, 1992), 192–296; Boris Groys, *The Total Art of Stalinism: Avant-garde, Aesthetic Dictatorship, and Beyond* (Princeton: Princeton University Press, 1992).

17. *The History of Plants and Factories* built upon a Soviet tradition of factory histories; it can also be traced to the German *Betriebsmonografie*—see Zhuravlev, *Fenomen "Istorii fabrik i zavodov,"* 19–29; Evgenii Dobrenko, "Moloko sovremennosti i tvorog istori: narrativ kak sposob proizvodstva sotsializma," *Voprosy literatury* 2 (2004): 32.

18. Especially lacking are planning documents from the main editorial board—see GARF, f. 7952; TsKhDMO, f. 1, op. 2–3; TsMAM, f. 665; Arkhiv A. M. Gor'kogo; Zhuravlev, *Fenomen "Istorii fabrik i zavodov,"* 13–27. For the remains of its Leningrad-based editorial board, see TsGA SPb, f. r-9618.

19. Gorky to Stalin (November 27, 1929), 183–187; "Zhmu vashu ruku, dorogoi tovarishch: perepiska Maksima Gor'kogo i Iosifa Stalina," *Novyi mir* 9 (1997): 167–192; Gor'kii, "Istoriia fabrik i zavodov," 2; N. G. Shushkanov, "Nachalo raboty," in *Rabochie pishut istoriiu zavodov,* ed. M. Gor'kii and L. Averbakh (Moscow: Istoriia zavodov, 1933), 116.

20. Central Committee resolution of October 10, 1931 "Ob izdanii 'Istorii zavodov,'" *Pravda*, October 11, 1931, 1.

21. Dobrenko, "Moloko sovremennosti i tvorog istorii," 27.

22. See, in particular, M. Gor'kii, "Za rabotu," *Pravda*, November 28, 1931, 2;

"Instruktsii Glavnoi redaktsii," *Pravda*, November 28, 1931, 2; Gorky to Shushkanov (March 12, 1932), published in A. M. *Gor'kii i sozdanie "Istorii fabrik i zavodov,"* ed. L. M. Zak et al. (Moscow: Izd-vo sotsial'no-ekon. lit-ry, 1959), 48.

23. M. Gor'kii, "Napishem istoriiu bor'by rabochego klassa," *Pravda*, November 7, 1931, 2.

24. On the marginal successes of the RAPP-inspired "production novel," see Clark, "Little Heroes and Big Deeds," 205–206.

25. Ia. Gruzinskii, "Litkruzhkovtsy—avtory 'Istorii zavodov,'" *Rost* 21 (1934): 44; Dobrenko, "Moloko sovremennosti i tvorog istorii," 32.

26. See, for instance, "Rabochim Uralmasha—avtoram 'Dela i liudi Mekhanicheskogo tsekha'" ([April 1933]), published in M. Gor'kii, *Pis'ma k rabkoram i pisateliam* (Moscow: Zhurgazob"edinenie, 1936), 35–36; Shushkanov, "Nachalo raboty," 125; An. L-in, "Kak ne nado pisat' istoriiu zavoda," *Na pod"eme* 12 (1931): 167–175; "Iz postanovleniia Glavnoi redaktsii" (April 10, 1932), in *Rabochie pishut istoriiu zavodov,* 17. See also M. Gor'kii, "Rabochie pishut istoriiu svoikh zavodov," *Pravda*, December 12, 1932, 2–3; N. Shushkanov, "Bol'she vnimaniia 'Istorii zavodov,'" *Na literaturnom postu* 4 (1932): 20; M. Smikhovich, "Khudozhestvennye problemy istorii zavodov," *Rost* 23–24 (1934): 55.

27. L. Averbakh, "Mozhet li byt' istoriia zavodov nauchnoi i khudozhestvennoi? (Rech' na vtorom Leningradskom soveshchanii po istorii zavodov, 28 ianvaria 1933 goda)," in *Rabochie pishut istoriiu zavodov,* 45. Some dismiss this professionalization—see Katerina Clark, "The 'History of the Factories' as a Factory of History: A Case Study in the Role of Soviet Literature in Subject Formation," in *Autobiographical Practices in Russia / Autobiographische Praktiken in Russland,* ed. Jochen Hellbeck, Klaus Heller (Gottingen: G&R Unipress GmbH, 2004), 23.

28. "Rech' sekretaria TsK VKP(b) A. A. Zhdanova," in *Pervyi vsesoiuznyi s"ezd sovetskikh pisatelei, 1934: Stenograficheskii otchet* (Moscow: Khudozhestvennaia literatura, 1934), 4. Zhdanov added: "in our country, the main heroes of our works of literature are those actually engaged in constructing our life—male and female workers, male and female collective farmers, party members, executives, managers, engineers, Komsomols, and pioneers. These are our chief categories and our chief literary heroes." Rooting this literature in the "heroic" realities of the 1930s, Zhdanov differentiated the new "revolutionary romanticism" of Socialist Realism from the "old kind of romanticism, which depicted imaginary life and imaginary heroes." For discussion in the press of heroism timed with the convening of this conference, see Jeffrey Brooks, "Socialist Realism in *Pravda*: Read All about It," *Slavic Review* 53:4 (1994): 978–979.

29. Central Executive Committee resolution of April 16, 1934 "Ob ustanovlenii vysshei stepeni otlichiia—zvaniia Geroia Sovetskogo Soiuza," *Pravda*, April 17, 1934, 1; see also John McCannon, *Red Arctic: Polar Exploration and the Myth of the North in the Soviet Union, 1932–1939* (Oxford: Oxford University Press, 1998).

30. "Mozhno zavidovat' strane, imeiushchei takikh geroev, i geroiam, imeiushchim takuiu rodinu," *Pravda*, June 19, 1934, 1. Alphonse Gabriel Capone (1899–1947) was a notorious Chicagoland gangster; John Herbert Dillinger (1903–1933) was a Robin Hood–like bank robber; Sherlock Holmes was Arthur Conan Doyle's

fictional nineteenth-century private detective; Mestrius Plutarchus (ca. 46–127) was a Greek historical biographer. Although some members of the Soviet pantheon distinguished themselves by struggle reminiscent of Capone and Dillinger, such similarities were misleading. If criminals defied the capitalist establishment in the name of individual exceptionalism, Soviet heroes challenged the establishment only when it was necessary to right anti-social wrongs. More often, they struggled with foreign enemies, technological challenges, or production targets. In so doing, they championed the establishment rather than its subversion, demonstrating the compatibility of individual-, societal-, and state-based values.

Pravda's statement appears to have inspired Ordzhonikidze to tell A. A. Mushpert: "Bathing individuals from among the people in glory—there's a critical significance to this sort of thing. In capitalist countries, nothing can compare with the popularity of gangsters like Al Capone. In our country, under socialism, heroes of labor ought to be the most famous." See S. R. Gershberg, *Rabota u nas takaia: Zapiski zhurnalista-pravdista tridtsatykh godov* (Moscow: Politizdat, 1971), 321.

31. *Pervyi vsesoiuznyi s"ezd sovetskikh pisatelei*, 126, 381, 388, 407, 444, 467, 526, 549, 557, 616. See also "Geroi nashei epokhi," *Literaturnyi kritik* 6 (1934): 3–12.

32. See "Rech' O. Iu. Shmidta," in *Pervyi vsesoiuznyi s"ezd sovetskikh pisatelei*, 57–63.

33. "Geroi Sovetskogo Soiuza" (1934), composed by A. Novikov, lyrics by T. Sikorskaia; *Geroi Arktiki (Cheliuskin)*, dir. Ia. M. Posel'skii (TsSDF, 1934). Stalin expressed enthusiasm for this newsreel on June 28, 1934—see RGASPI, f. 558, op. 11, d. 828, ll. 43–45. For a draft Central Committee resolution from June 22, 1934 calling for a pair of celebratory books about the heroes of the expedition and rescue effort, see f. 17, op. 163, d. 1028, ll. 77–82.

34. Ia. Il'in, "Vstuplenie," in *Liudi Stalingradskogo traktornogo*, ed. Ia. Il'in, L. Mekhlis et al. (Moscow: Istoriia fabrik i zavodov, 1933), 8; see also I. Savvin, *Cherty geroia vtoroi piatiletki: novaia tematika khudozhestvennoi literatury* (Moscow: MK VLKSM, 1934). Ilin's confidence in the hybridity of this genre is visible in his decision to write a lightly fictionalized novel in parallel with his volume in Gorky's series—see Il'in, *Bol'shoi konveier* (Moscow: Molodaia gvardiia, 1934).

35. S. M. Tsmyg, "Za chto my liubim zavod?" in *Liudi Stalingradskogo traktornogo*, 409.

36. G. Remizov, "No tut ne ostanavlivalsia parokhod," in *Liudi Stalingradskogo traktornogo*, 371. The party history textbooks mentioned are A. S. Bubnov, *VKP(b)* (Moscow: Gos. sots.-ekon. izd-vo, 1931); N. Popov, *Ocherki istorii VKP(b)* (Moscow: Partiinoe izd-vo, 1932).

37. L. Averbakh, "Literaturnye zametki," in *Liudi Stalingradskogo traktornogo*, 454.

38. G. Vasil'kovskii, "Liudi Stalingradskogo traktornogo," *Pravda*, August 7, 1933, 2; B. Kotin, "Liudi Stalingradskogo traktornogo," *Stalingrad* 5–6 (1933): 40.

39. *Rasskazy stroitelei metro*, ed. A. Kosarev et al. (Moscow: Istoriia fabrik i zavodov, 1935); *Bolshevtsy: Ocherki po istorii Bolshevskoi imeni G. G. Iagodi trudkommuny NKVD*, ed. M. Gor'kii et al. (Moscow: Istoriia fabrik i zavodov, 1936);

Rodina zavodov: literaturnyi sbornik po materialam istorii Ural'skogo zavoda tiazhelogo mashinostroeniia im. Sergo Ordzhonikidze (Sverdlovsk: n.p., 1935). For advance publicity, see A. Kosarev, "K 'Istorii metro,'" *Pravda,* September 26, 1934, 3; for reviews, see M. Popov, "Rasskazy stroitelei metro," *Pravda,* March 16, 1935, 4; A. Selivanovskii, "'Bolshevtsy," *Izvestiia,* August 4, 1936, 4.

40. *Peterburg-Moskva: postroika dorogi, 1842–1851,* ed. I. Velikin and I. Perepechko (Leningrad: Istoriia fabrik i zavodov, 1935); *Byt rabochikh Trekhgornoi manufaktury,* ed. S. M. Lapitskaia (Moscow: Istoriia fabrik i zavodov, 1935); *Krepostnoi Zlatoust: glavy iz istorii Zlatoustovskogo zavoda kontsa XVIII i pervoi poloviny XIX stoletiia,* ed. N. Shushkanov (Sverdlovsk: Sverdlovskoe obl. gos. izd-vo, 1935); *Rabochie Verkhisetskogo zavoda v grazhdanskoi voine 1918,* ed. Iu. Bessonov (Sverdlovsk: Sverdlovskoe obl. gos. izd-vo, 1935); also *Staraia Iuzovka 1869–1905: Stalinskii metalurgicheskii zavod,* ed. N. N. Popov (Moscow, Kiev: Istoriia fabrik i zavodov, 1937). More sweeping projects include *Fabrika "Krasnyi perekop": b. Iaroslavskaia bol'shaia manufaktura, 1722–1933,* ed. F. N. Samoilov et al., 2 vols. (Moscow: Istoriia fabrik i zavodov, 1935–1936).

41. *Belomorsko-Baltiiskii kanal imeni Stalina: Istoriia stroitel'stva,* ed. M. Gor'kii, L. Averbakh, S. Firin, et al. (Moscow: Istoriia fabrik i zavodov, 1934). For reviews, see A. Bolotnikov, "Kniga dostoinaia svoei temy," *Literaturnaia gazeta,* January 26, 1934, 2; S. Fin, "Kniga o 'chude' na Karel'skikh ozerakh," *Komsomol'skaia pravda,* January 24, 1934, 4; Iogann Al'tman, "Kniga o bol'shoi pobede," *Literaturnyi kritik* 6 (1934): 253–262. Generally, see Cynthia Ruder, *Making History for Stalin: The Story of the Belomor Canal* (Gainsville: University Press of Florida, 1998).

42. P., "'Liudi vtoroi piatiletki': kollektiv pisatelei pristupaet k etoi teme—M. Gor'kii rukovodit rabotoi," *Literaturnaia gazeta,* January 20, 1934, 4; M. Gor'kii, "Dve piatiletki," *Pravda,* April 9, 1935, 2–3. Official support for this project was more robust than that afforded to Gorky's proposal for a three-volume party history, the first volume of which was to concern Marxism and the party, the second the USSR's economic achievements, and the third the future of socialism in the USSR and abroad. Gorky was not a party member and was probably judged to lack the background to oversee such an undertaking. See Gorky to Stalin (November 12, 1931), published in *M. Gor'kii: Neizdannaia perepiska s Bogdanovym, Leninym, Stalinym, Zinov'evym, Kamenevym, Korolenko,* ed. S. V. Zaika (Moscow: Nasledie, 1998), 286–287.

43. Gorky to Stalin (February 27, 1929), in "Iz perepiski A. M. Gor'kogo," 187. This project was proposed to the Central Committee as early as 1927, apparently languishing there until Gorky revived the idea in 1929. See I. I. Mints, "Stalin v grazhdanskoi voine: mify i fakty," *Voprosy istorii* 11 (1989): 48.

44. Gorky to Stalin (November 12, 1931) and Gorky to Stalin (November 2, 1930), both published in "Zhmu vashu ruku, dorogoi tovarishch: perepiska Maksima Gor'kogo i Iosifa Stalina," 186, 174, and n. 6; Central Committee resolution of July 30, 1931 "Ob izdanii 'Istorii grazhdanskoi voiny,'" *Pravda,* July 31, 1931, 2. The main editorial board was initially composed of Gorky, Molotov, Voroshilov, Kirov, Zhdanov, Bubnov, and Gamarnik. Stalin was subsequently invited to join after showing interest in the project.

45. Gorky to B. P. Pozern (before August 10, 1931), RGASPI, f. 71, op. 36, d. 62, l. 2.

46. For a thorough account of the editorial process, see Justus Hartzok, "Children of Chapaev: The Russian Civil War Cult and the Creation of Soviet Identity, 1918–1941" (Ph.D. Diss., University of Iowa, 2009), 157–207.

47. Gorky to Mints (June 29, 1933), RGASPI, f. 71, op. 36, d. 62, ll. 4–7. He also conveyed these concerns to Stalin, who concurred—see Gorky to Stalin (June 29, 1933) and Stalin to Gorky (July 2, 1933), in "Zhmu vashu ruku, dorogoi tovarishch: perepiska Maksima Gor'kogo i Iosifa Stalina," 177.

48. Mints, "Stalin v grazhdanskoi voine: mify i fakty," 48.

49. Mints accompanied the draft with a letter outlining what was still missing (maps, chronological tables, index, etc.). He also asked if the volume didn't require more portraits and biographical sketches. Stalin agreed, scribbling onto the letter: "Needed portraits: Dzerzhinsky, Frunze, Uritsky, Volodarsky, Kuibyshev (in [the section on] Samara), Ioffe, Ordzhonikidze (he was in St. Petersburg at that time and played a major role), Slutsky (+), Antonov-Ovseenko. . . . Portraits are needed of Trotsky, who played a role in the Oct[ober] Rev[olution], Kamenev, Zinov'ev, Lashevich (he played a pos[itive] role), and Bubnov." Group portraits of the party's leadership in April and the Sixth Party Congress were also to be added. Mints recalled later that Kaganovich and Voroshilov protested against this decision, warning: "the people won't understand the inclusion of portraits of people who've undergone such sharp criticism." Ultimately, the pictures were included only in the book's deluxe edition. See Mints to Chief Editorial Board (December 8, 1934), RGASPI, f. 558, op. 1, d. 3164, ll. 1–10b; Mints, "Stalin v grazhdanskoi voine," 49.

50. Gorky to Stalin (November 12, 1934), RGASPI, f. 71, op. 36, d. 11, ll. 197–1970b.

51. See the page proofs to Istoriia grazhdanskoi voiny v SSSR at RGASPI, f. 558, op. 11, d. 3165, pages 217, 235, 299; 106, 145, 150; 134, 146, 158; 20–25, 78, 102, 124; 156; 127, 201, 45, 118, 247. A photocopy of these galleys is at f. 17, op. 120, d. 355.

52. See, for example, Mints to Gamarnik (August 19, 1935), RGASPI, f. 71, op. 36, d. 21, ll. 2820b-283. This letter is misdated to 1936 in T. Dubinskaia-Dzhalilova, "Velikii gumanist: po materialam perepiski M. Gor'kogo i I. V. Stalina," Novoe literaturnoe obozrenie 40:6 (1999): 236.

53. June 1977 interview with Mints, summarized in Robert Tucker, Stalin in Power: The Revolution from Above, 1929–1941 (New York: Norton, 1990), 531–532. On the editorial principles underlying the project, see I. I. Mints, "Podgotovka Velikoi proletarskoi revoliutsii: k vykhodu pervogo toma 'Istorii grazhdanskoi voiny v SSSR,'" Bol'shevik 21 (1935): 15–30; Mints, "Stalin v grazhdanskoi voine," 48.

54. Mints to Gamarnik (August 19, 1935), RGASPI, f. 71, op. 36, d. 21, ll. 283.

55. Istoriia grazhdanskoi voiny v SSSR, vol. 1, Podgotovka Velikoi proletarskoi revoliutsii (ot nachala voiny do nachala Oktiabria 1917 g.), ed. M. Gor'kii, I. I. Mints, et al. (Moscow: Istoriia grazhdanskoi voiny, 1935). On the release itself, see "'Istoriia grazhdanskoi voiny': vyshel pervyi tom," Izvestiia, November 4, 1935, 5.

56. Elaine MacKinnon, "Writing History for Stalin: Isaak Izrailevich Mints and the Istoriia grazhdanskoi voiny," Kritika 6:1 (2005): 22.

57. "Istoriia grazhdanskoi voiny," *Pravda,* November 6, 1935, 3; A. Starchakov, "'Istoriia grazhdanskoi voiny,'" *Izvestiia,* November 21, 1935, 6; E. Genkina, "Istoriia grazhdanskoi voiny v SSSR," *Istorik-Marksist* 1 (1936): 186–192.

58. Stalin's personal participation provided tremendous help to other authors, as such an officially sanctioned text offered a template upon which to base further work. See Boris Zaks, "Censorship at the Editorial Desk," in *The Red Pencil: Artists, Scholars, and Censors in the USSR,* ed. Marianna Tax Choldin and Maurice Friedberg (Boston: Unwin Hyman, 1989), 157.

59. N. A. Ostrovskii, *Kak zakalialas' stal'* (Moscow: OGIZ, 1932). Korchagin initially worries about his sexual virility (a metaphor for his political will), but sees these fears vanish from all editions published after 1934. Similarly, Korchagin's inability to reconcile marriage, family life, and commitment to the revolution is downplayed in later editions. Such developments dovetail with alterations to the character of the female Komsomol activist, who initially advocates free love before becoming more virtuous. Perhaps most significantly, beginning with the 1935 edition of the novel, Korchagin refrains from joining the 1921 Workers' Opposition, insofar as this misstep was no longer forgivable in the wake of the Kirov murder. See Herman Ermolaev, *Censorship in Soviet Literature, 1917–1991* (Lanham: Rowman and Littlefield, 1997), 92, 65, 66, 77, 79.

60. F. Gladkov, *Tsement* (Moscow: n.p., 1927). This analysis is based on a comparison of the book's 1932 edition against those issued in 1933, 1934, and 1935—see Ermolaev, *Censorship in Soviet Literature,* 66, 82, 92.

61. Compare F. V. Gladkov, *Energiia,* vol. 1 (Moscow: Sovetskaia literatura, 1932) to its second (1933) and third (1939) editions.

62. F. Panferov, *Bruski* (Moscow: Moskovskii rabochii, 1928–1937). Not only does Zdarkin cease to have doubts about the party's agricultural policy, but he demonstrates more control over his actions and libido. His relations with the local peasantry also improve, precluding the need to ever unholster his weapon. Panferov's peasants likewise appear much less hostile to Soviet power. See Ermolaev, *Censorship in Soviet Literature,* 62–63, 92, 65.

63. Iu. Libedinskii, *Kommisary* (Leningrad: Priboi, 1926). Initially, Libedinsky gentrified aspects of his characters' conduct in superficial terms, cleansing dialogues of offensive terms like "yid" in the book's 1933 edition. By 1935, the author had provided his characters with a more radical makeover, improving the physical appearance of the officer Lobichev and renaming him Lobachev for greater distinction. Even more radically, Libedinsky recast the short, swarthy Jewish party boss Sementovich as the tall, athletic Slav Grinev. See Ermolaev, *Censorship in Soviet Literature,* 81.

64. "Otriady nashi v atake, / Zheleznye liudi—bol'sheviki. / Lomaia kogti gidre-razrukhe. / Masshtabami del potriasaia ves' mir / Rosli Voroshilov, Budennyi, Bliukher / Chapaev, Parkhomenko, Shchors, Iakir / Za nimi proshli my ogon' i vodn / Svintsovyi potok i shrapnel'nyi ad." Al. Surkov, "Komandiry," *Pravda,* October 17, 1935, 4. Generally, see Surkov, *Rodina muzhestvennykh* (Moscow: Gosudarstvennoe izdatel'stvo khudozhestvennoi literatury, 1935).

65. *Khudozhestvennaia vystavka 15 let RKKA: zhivopis', grafika, skul'ptura, tekstil', dekorativnoe iskusstvo, iskusstvo Palekha i Mstery* (Moscow: Vsekhudozhnik, 1933), xxiii, 86, 271, 185, 341, 23, 7, 56, 73.

66. *Raboche-krest'ianskaia krasnaia armiia*, ed. F. E. Rodionov, des. El Lisitskii (Moscow: Izogiz, 1934).

67. *Arsenal*, dir. A. Dovzhenko (VUFKU, 1928); *Tri pesni o Lenine*, dir. Dz. Vertov (Mezhrabpom, 1934). See also *Bog voiny*, dir. E. Dzigan (Goskinoprom Gruzii, 1929); *Khleb*, dir. N. Shpikovskii (Ukrainfil'm, 1930), etc. For criticism, see B. Shumiatskii, "Bol'shoe iskusstvo," *Izvestiia*, January 11, 1935, 3; Shumiatskii, *Kinomatografiia milionov: opyt analiza* (Moscow: Kinofotizdat, 1935), 93–94.

68. See, for example, *Sovkinozhurnal 68/331* (Soiuzkinokhronika, 1930), *Na strazhe 10*, dir. V. Morgenstern (n.s., 1932), *15-ia godovshchina Oktiabria*, dir. Ia. M. Bliokh (Soiuzkinokhronika, 1932); *Strane sovetov 16 let*, dir. F. Kiselev (Soiuzkinokhronika, 1933).

69. *Chapaev*, dir. Vasil'ev "brothers" (Lenfil'm, 1934). G. N. and S. D. Vasiliev were not actually related.

70. Brat'ia Vasil'evy, "Zametki k postanovke," in *Chapaev—o fil'me* (Moscow: Kinofotizdat, 1936), 51–56; Jay Leyda, *Kino: A History of Russian and Soviet Film*, 3rd ed. (Princeton: Princeton University Press, 1983), 314; D. Pisarevskii, *Brat'ia Vasil'evy* (Moscow: Iskusstvo, 1981), 40–99. The Vasilievs added that by 1932, "the civil war had served so many times as the justification for the creation of shallow, primitive agitation plays and pseudo-adventure, pseudo-detective films. These works always left the audience disappointed and dissatisfied with their superficial depictions of this great and heroic stage in the struggle of the working class and toiling peasantry. The subject had been discredited in the eyes of the audience, handled with 'unclean hands,' bureaucratized and overdone. It had to be rehabilitated." See Vasil'evy, "Zametki k postanovke," 54–55. On the differences between the novel and screenplay, see Jeremy Hicks, "Educating Chapaev: From Document to Myth," in *Russian and Soviet Film Adaptations of Literature, 1900–2001: Screening the Word*, ed. Stephen Hutchings and Anat Vernitski (London: RoutledgeCurzon, 2005), 44–58. More generally, see Hartzok, "Children of Chapaev: The Russian Civil War Cult and the Creation of Soviet Identity, 1918–1941," 107–119.

71. Vasil'evy, "Zametki k postanovke," 58–59. In their preface to the screenplay, the Vasilievs expressed their motives more succinctly: "This is a film about *people.* . . . We want to inspire the audience and have the audience love our heroes and hate our enemies." See *Chapaev* (Moscow: Roskinoizdat, 1934), 12.

72. RGASPI, f. 558, op. 11, d. 828, ll. 55–60; 62–620b; 64–66; 67–68.

73. Stalin to Shumiatsky (January 10, 1935), published in *Pravda*, January 11, 1935, 1; M. Erlikh, "Ukrainskii Chapaev," *Pravda*, March 5, 1935, 6. Shumiatsky paraphrased Stalin's recognition of the role that individual heroes played in the overall narrative, noting that "in *Chapaev*, the heroism of the mass movement is shown alongside the fate of individual heroes, and it is through the latter that the masses are graphically and colorfully captured. . . . The film *Chapaev* has proven that in a dramatic work, it is the *individual figures*, the intensity of the tempo and the ideological breadth of the piece that are decisive." See Shumiatskii, *Kinematografiia millionov*, 154.

74. Official expectations were expressed clearly at a major meeting in March 1928—see *Puti kino: Pervoe Vsesoiuznoe soveshchanie po kinematografii* (Moscow: Tea-kino pechat', 1929), 429–444.

75. *Vstrechnyi*, dir. F. Ermler and S. Iutkevich (Rosfil'm, 1932); stenogram of a

1932 RosARRK presidium meeting at TsGALI, f. 166, op. 1, d. 373, ll. 5–70b, 23, 37–39, summarized in "Itogi diskussii o 'Vstrechnom,'" *Kino,* January 10, 1933, 1.
76. *Iunost' Maksima,* dir. G. Kozintsev and L. Trauberg (Lenfil'm, 1934).
77. Compare *Zemlia,* dir. A. Dovzhenko (VUFKU, 1930) to *Krest'iane,* dir. F. Ermler (Lenfil'm, 1934); *Aerograd,* dir. A. Dovzhenko (Mosfil'm/Ukrainfil'm, 1935). For reviews, see V. Ermilov, "'Krest'iane' F. Ermilera," *Pravda,* March 19, 1935, 4; B. Reznikov, "Zamechatel'nyi fil'm," *Pravda,* November 12, 1935, 4.
78. *Letchiki,* dir. Iu. Raizman (Mosfil'm, 1935); L. Trauberg, "'Letchiki: novyi fil'm Iu. Raizmana," *Izvestiia,* April 1, 1935, 6. Another positive review mourned the film's failure to invoke the Cheliuskin epic see B. Shumiatskii, "Otvechaem delom: o kartinkakh 'Letchiki' i 'Novyi Gulliver,'" *Pravda,* March 23, 1935, 2.
79. *Dzhul'bars,* dir. V. Shneiderov (Mezhrabpomfil'm, 1935); E. Vilenskii, "Dzhul'bars," *Izvestiia,* February 8, 1936, 6.
80. "Rekord zaboishchika Stakhanova," *Pravda,* September 2, 1935, 6; "Ot sorevnovaniia odinochek k sorevnovaniiu mass!" *Pravda,* September 8, 1935, 1; "Vazhnyi pochin v Donbasse," *Pravda,* September 11, 1935, 1.
81. Lewis Siegelbaum, *Stakhanovism and the Politics of Productivity in the USSR, 1935–1941* (Cambridge: Cambridge University Press, 1988), 76.
82. See the dozens of speeches published in *Pravda* November 15–22, 1935.
83. A. Stakhanov, "Moi opyt," *Pravda,* November 15, 1935, 2; "Rech' tovarishcha Stalina na Pervom vsesoiuznom soveshchanii stakhanovtsev," *Pravda,* December 22, 1935, 1; "Initsiatory velikogo dvizheniia," *Izvestiia,* December 9, 1935, 1.
84. See the runs of articles at "Soveshchanie peredovykh kombainerov i kombainerok SSSR s chlenami partii i pravitel'stva," *Izvestiia,* December 24, 1935; "Soveshchanie peredovikov urozhainosti po zernu, traktoristov i mashinistov molotilok s rukovoditeliami partii i pravitel'stva," *Izvestiia,* January 1–5, 1936; "Soveshchanie rukovodiashchikh rabotnikov MTS i zemel'nikh organov s rukovoditeliami partii i pravitel'stva," *Izvestiia,* January 8–10, 1936; "Soveshchanie peredovikov zhivotnovodstva s rukovoditeliami partii i pravitel'stva," *Izvestiia,* February 15–19, 21, 1936; "Soveshchanie peredovikov po l'nu i konople s rukovoditeliami partii i pravitel'stva," *Izvestiia,* March 16–18, 20–23, 1936.
85. See, for instance, L. Abramov, "Stalinskoe plemia pobeditelei," *Pravda,* January 15, 1936, 8; "Stalinskoe plemia stakhanovtsev," *Izvestiia,* January 15, 1936, 6.
86. N. Bukharin, "Geroi i geroini," *Izvestiia,* November 11, 1935, 2. Simeon Stylite (Semeon Stolpnik) was a fifth-century Syrian ascetic who sat on a pillar for 37 years in order to be closer to God.
87. "Polkovodtsy Krasnoi armii," *Pravda,* November 21, 1935, 1; Resolution of the Central Executive Committee of November 20, 1935 "O prisvoenii voennogo zvaniia Marshala Sovetskogo soiuza tovarishcham Voroshilovu K. E., Tukhachevskomu M. N., Egorovu A. I., Budennomu S. M., Bliukheru V. K.," *Pravda,* November 21, 1935, 1; M. Kol'tsov, "Nashi marshaly," *Pravda,* November 21, 1935, 3. The resolution, which was reprinted in *Izvestiia,* was accompanied by pictures of the command staff. See also celebratory articles in *Pravda* (N. Popov, "I. E. Iakir," F. Rodionov, "Komissary") and *Izvestiia* (K. Radek, "Krasnaia armiia i ee mar-

shaly"). This spectacle was preceded that month by a celebration of the civil war victory at Pcrckop, a tribute to Yegorov in connection with his 50th jubilee and the long-awaited release of the *History of the Civil War in the USSR*—see V. Bliukher, "Pobeda khrabrykh," and A. Kork, "Perekop," *Izvestiia*, November 14, 1935, 2, 3; "Piatidesiatiletie tov. A. I. Egorova" and N. Izgoev, "Nachal'nik genshtaba," *Izvestiia*, November 11, 1935, 2; "'Istoriia grazhdanskoi voiny': vyshel pervyi tom," *Izvestiia*, November 4, 1935, 5.

88. Central Executive Committee resolution of November 26, 1935 "O prisvoenii tov. Iagode G. G. zvaniia general'nogo komissara," *Pravda*, November 27, 1935, 1; "Na strazhe!" *Pravda*, November 27, 1935, 1.

89. "Soveshchanie peredovykh kolkhoznikov i kolkhoznits Tadzhikistana i Turkmenii s rukovoditeliami partii i pravitel'stva," *Pravda*, December 5, 1935, 2; December 6, 1935, 1–3; "Priem delegatsii trudiashchikhsia SSR Armenii v Kremle," *Pravda*, January 6, 1936, 2–3; "Priem delegatsii Sovetskogo Azerbaidzhana rukovoditeliami partii i pravitel'stva v Kremle," *Pravda*, January 24, 1936, 2–3; "Priem delegatov trudiashchikhsia Buriat-Mongol'skoi ASSR rukovoditeliami partii i pravitel'stva v Kremle," *Pravda*, January 30, 1936, 1; "Priem delegatsii Sovetskoi Gruzii rukovoditeliami partii i pravitel'stva v Kremle," *Pravda*, March 21, 1936, 1–5. These receptions followed earlier events like the Ashkhabad-Moscow horse race, which was described as on a par with the heroism of the civil war and first Five-Year Plan—see "Syny rodiny," *Izvestiia*, August 27, 1935, 1.

90. *Semero smelykh*, dir. S. Gerasimov (Mosfil'm, 1936); *Zakliuchennye*, dir. E. Cherviakov (Mosfil'm, 1936); *Partiinyi bilet*, dir. I. Pyr'ev (Mosfil'm, 1936). See also N. Izgoev, "Partiinyi bilet," *Izvestiia*, April 7, 1936, 6; B. Reznikov, "Partiinyi bilet (Kinokartina, proizvodstvo studii 'Mosfil'm' 1936 g.)," *Pravda*, March 14, 1936, 3. *Inmates* was based on Pogodin's 1935 play *Aristocrats;* for Stalin's advice to the director of *The Party Card*, see RGASPI, f. 558, op. 11, f. 829, ll. 84–85.

91. *Deputat Baltiki*, dir. I. Kheifits and A. Zarkhi (Lenfil'm, 1936); *My iz Kronshtadta*, dir. E. Dzigan (Mosfil'm, 1936); *Rodina zovet*, dir. A. Macheret and K. Krumin (Mos'film, 1936). Stalin considered *We Are from Kronshtadt* "good and extremely interesting"—see RGASPI, f. 558, op. 11, d. 829, ll. 86–90. On the original title of *The Motherland Is Calling*, see E. Margolit, "Kak v zerkale: Germaniia v sovetskom igrovom kino, 1920–1930-kh gg.," *Kinovedcheskie zapiski* 59 (2002): 61–80, here 80, n. 22.

92. *Podrugi*, dir. L. Arnshtam (Lenfil'm, 1935); RGASPI, f. 558, op. 11, d. 829, ll. 64–66.

93. B. Shumiatskii, "Za prostoe i poniatnoe kinoiskusstvo," *Izvestiia*, March 6, 1936, 3.

94. Vl. Nemirovich-Danchenko, "Prostota geroicheskikh chuvstv," *Pravda*, May 19, 1934, 5.

95. A. Afinogenov and V. Kirshon, "Temy, geroi, kharaktery: k itogam teatral'nogo sezona," *Pravda*, June 2, 1935, 4; A. Afinogenov and Ia. Boiarskii, "Zritel' sovetskogo teatra," *Pravda*, October 13, 1935, 4; B. Lavrenev, "Ne sdadimsia," *Izvestiia*, October 18, 1935, 6; "'Chapaev' v teatre LOSPS," *Izvestiia*, February 3, 1936, 4. Of course, much of this crisis was at least as attributable to the ongoing campaign against formalism as other factors. Soviet-themed theater did not recover

until the war—see V. Shcherbina, "Istoricheskaia tema v sovetskoi dramaturgii," *Teatr* 1 (1938): 71–84.

96. Diary entry from April 7, 1934 in Georgi Dimitrov, *Dnevnik (9 Mart 1933–6 Fevuari 1949)* (Sofia: Universitetsko izdatelstvo "Sv. Kliment Okhridski," 1997), 101.

CHAPTER 5. THE PAGEANTRY OF SOVIET PATRIOTISM

1. The best study of this overlooked subject is Erwin Oberländer, *Sowjetpatriotismus und Geschichte—dokumentation* (Köln: Wissenschaft und Politik, 1967), 15–33, 53–103; more derivative is Gerhard Simon, *Nationalismus und Nationalitätenpolitik in der Sowjetunion—Von der totalitären Diktatur zur nachstalinschen Gesellschaft* (Baden Baden: Nomos, 1986), 171–179.

2. See, for example, Lenin's 1918 statements on revolutionary defensism: I. V. Lenin, "Tiazhelyi, no neobkhodimyi," "Glavnaia zadacha nashikh dnei," in *Sochineniia*, 30 vols. (Moscow: Partizdat, 1930), 22:290–293; 374–378; K. B. Radek, *Razvitie mirovoi revoliutsii i taktika Kommunisticheskoi partii v bor'be za diktaturu proletariata* (Moscow: Gosudarstvennoe izdatel'stvo, 1920), 84–85. Note that this narrow definition of "defensism" calls into question the notion that the party leadership espoused "red patriotism" during the civil war. See M. Agurskii, *Ideologiia nastional-bol'shevizma* (Paris: YMCA Press, 1980).

Lenin's "revolutionary defensism," incidentally, coincides perfectly with Marx and Engels' views on the subject. After all, they never expected the workers of the world to immediately unite into a single revolutionary movement and believed that workers in certain countries would succeed in throwing off the capitalist yoke earlier than others. In such circumstances, they called for proletarian forces to consolidate power on the national level before continuing the cause of revolutionary internationalism. It is for this reason that *The Communist Manifesto* directs the proletariat in revolutionary societies to "rise to be the leading national class" and "constitute itself as the nation" once national elites are defeated. This support for revolutionary societies should be distinguished, however, from any endorsement of conventional patriotism. Although Austro-Marxists like Karl Renner and Otto Bauer advanced a socialist model composed along both class and national lines, Marx and Engels considered national cultures to be more or less illusory and expected them to decompose in the wake of a global social revolution. Thus while Marx and Engels encouraged the working class to defend revolutionary societies, this was really no more than instrumental defensism, insofar as they expected these societies to advance the cause of world revolution rather than national or cultural particularism.

3. "Kommunisticheskii manifest," in *Noveishii entsiklopedicheskii slovar'*, vol. 8 (Leningrad: P. P. Soikin, 1926–1927), 1951; P. Stuchka, "Patriotizm," in *Entsiklopediia gosudarstva i prava*, vol. 3 (Moscow: Izdatel'stvo Kommunisticheskoi akademii, 1925–1927), 252–254.

4. Samuel Harper, *Making Bolsheviks* (Chicago: University of Chicago Press, 1931), 18.

5. I. V. Stalin, "O zadachakh khoziaistvennikov: rech' na pervoi Vsesoiuznoi

konferentsii rabotnikov sotsialisticheskoi promyshlennosti, 4-go fevralia 1931," in *Voprosy Leninizma* (Moscow: Partizdat, 1934), 445.

6. M. Vol'fson, "Patriotizm," in *Malaia sovetskaia entsiklopediia,* 10 vols. (Moscow: Sovetskaia entsiklopediia, 1931), 6:356.

7. The 1928 Comintern program called upon its allies abroad to defend Soviet interests, as "in the USSR, the world proletariat has genuinely acquired for the first time its own fatherland [. . .] its only fatherland." See *Programma i ustav Kommunisticheskogo internatsionala (Priniata IV kongressom 1 sentiabria 1928 v Moskve)* (Moscow: Gosudarstvennoe izdatel'stvo, 1928), 66, 68. This statement appears in all subsequent editions of the program through 1936; it was reemphasized at a Comintern plenum after Stalin's historic address—see "Rezoliutsii XI plenuma IKKI po dokladu tov. Kashena," *Pravda,* April 24, 1931, 4.

8. For evidence of the shift toward a more etatist ideological worldview, see Stalin's unpublished speeches from the early 1930s reproduced in V. A. Nevezhin, *Zastol'nye rechi Stalina: dokumenty i materialy* (Moscow: AIRO-XX, 2003), 41–107, etc.

9. Compare *Polituchebnik krasnoarmeitsa: dlia peremennogo sostava territorial'nykh chastei 1-go goda sluzhby* (Leningrad: Gosvoenizdat, 1931) and *Polituchebnik dlia krasnoarmeitsev* (Moscow: Gosvoenizdat, 1931) to *Krasnoarmeiskii polituchebnik—nachal'nyi kurs,* ed. A. Kadishev (Moscow: Gosvoenizdat, 1931), 64; *Krasnoarmeiskii polituchebnik (kurs voenno-politicheskii): voiny v epokhu imperializma; podgotovka voiny protiv SSSR,* ed. M. Subotskii (Moscow: Gosvoenizdat, 1932), 45; *Krasnoarmeiskii polituchebnik: voennopoliticheskii kurs,* ed. M. Subotskii (Moscow: Gosvoenizdat, 1932), 66; *Na strazhe sotsializma: rabochaia kniga krasnoarmeitsa dlia politzaniatii,* ed. N. Kharitonov (Moscow: Gosvoenizdat, 1932), 255–260.

10. See, for instance, Central Committee resolution of September 5, 1931 "O nachal'noi i srednei shkole"; Central Committee resolution of April 21, 1931 "O rabote pionerskoi organizatsii"; Central Committee resolution of August 25, 1932 "Ob uchebnykh programmakh i rezhime v nachal'noi i srednei shkole"; etc., in *Direktivy VKP(b) i postanovleniia sovetskogo pravitel'stva o narodnom obrazovanii, 1917–1947 gg.,* 2 vols. (Moscow: Akademiia pedagogicheskikh nauk, 1947).

11. The telegram to Liapidevsky et al. is published in *Krasnaia gazeta,* April 14, 1934, 1.

12. Stalin's interpolations are rendered in italics and his excisions in strikeout—see RGASPI, f. 17, op. 163, d. 1020, ll. 57–59, 62.

13. Before 1934, the term motherland (*rodina*) was used in Soviet mass culture to refer to ethnically homogeneous home territories—see V. G. Fink, *Novaia rodina: p'esa v 4 deistviiakh* (Moscow: Sovetskaia literatura, 1933), about Jews and Birobaidzhan; *Izmennik rodiny,* dir. I. Mutanov (Mezhrabpomfil'm, 1933), about a Polish war hero experiencing second thoughts; *Moia rodina,* dir. A. Zarkhi and I. Kheifits (Lenfil'm, 1933), about a young Chinese patriot. The Hungarian political émigré and poet Antal Hidas published a book about his adopted motherland in early 1934 that anticipated the use of the term in regard to the USSR: Anatol' Gidash, *Moskva-rodina: izbrannye stikhi,* trans. A. Kochetkov and A. Romm (Moscow: Gosudarstvennoe izdatel'stvo khudozhestvennoi literatury, 1934).

14. "Lozungi k 1 maia 1934 goda," *Pravda,* March 19, 1934, 1.

15. "Geroicheskim synam sotsialisticheskoi rodiny—besstrashnym sovetskim letchikam i muzhestvennym Cheliuskintsam—vysshaia revoliutsionnaia nagrada," *Krasnaia gazeta,* April 21, 1934, 1; S. Kirov, "Budem dostoinymi synami nashei sotsialisticheskoi rodiny," *Krasnaia gazeta,* May 1, 1934, 1.

16. Little remains, for instance, of the voluminous paperwork generated by the Central Committee's various propaganda departments (Kultprop, Agitprop) and their denizens (Stetsky, etc.) during the 1930s. For further details, see pp. 6–7 of RGASPI's guide to inventory 125 of collection 17.

17. *Pravda* blamed the defeat of the workers' rebellion on both the bourgeoisie and the moderate Austrian socialists, who were described as traitors to the workers' cause. See "Proletarii vsekh stran!" *Pravda,* March 19, 1934, 1.

18. Personal communication with V. N. Khaustov, August 3, 2010; O. N. Ken, "Obyknovennaia tragediia: Leningrad 1935-i," *Delo,* January 23, 2006, 9.

19. *XVII s"ezd Vsesoiuznoi kommunisticheskoi partii (b): Stenograficheskii otchet* (Moscow: Partizdat, 1934), 13–14.

20. On March 4, 1934, the Politburo discussed the public schools' instruction of civic history and assigned Bubnov the task of preparing a set of proposals. He presented his report to the Politburo and an array of scholars, pedagogues, and officials on March 20. See RGASPI, f. 17, op. 163, d. 1013, l. 4; d. 1015, ll. 8–90b. Generally, see David Brandenberger, *National Bolshevism: Stalinist Mass Culture and the Formation of Modern Russian National Identity, 1931–1956* (Cambridge: Harvard University Press, 2002), 30–37; A. M. Dubrovskii, *Istorik i vlast': Istoricheskaia nauka v SSSR i kontseptsiia istorii feodal'noi Rossii v kontekste politiki i ideologii (1930–1950-e gg.)* (Briansk: BGU, 2005), 178–207.

21. Just before Stalin and his inner circle met with their invited guests on March 20 to discuss the public schools' civic history instruction, they discussed the crime of treason (*izmena rodine*) and asked Akulov, A. Ya. Vyshinsky, and N. V. Krylenko to prepare a report on the subject. Politburo records contradict one another over who initiated the discussion: Stalin or Voroshilov. See RGASPI, f. 17, op. 163, d. 1015, l. 4; d. 1020, l. 17; d. 1022, l. 62.

22. Joint Central Committee and Sovnarkom resolutions of May 15, 1934 "O prepodavanii grazhdanskoi istorii v shkolakh SSSR," "O prepodavanii geografii v nachal'noi i srednei shkole SSSR," *Pravda,* May 16, 1934, 1.

23. This agenda had been alluded to in the press—see D. Osipov, "Skelety v shkole," *Pravda,* April 5, 1934, 1; "Za podlinnuiu istoriiu—protiv skholastiki i abstraktsii," *Za kommunisticheskoe prosveshchenie,* April 10, 1934, 1; [A. Z.] Ionnisiani, "Bez ucheta istoricheskoi obstanovki, faktov i lits," *Za kommunisticheskoe prosveshchenie,* April 24, 1934, 3.

24. In particular, Vasilkovsky revived a long-forgotten thesis of Lenin's that argues that within every nation, there are progressive elements as well as reactionary ones. This allowed Vasilkovsky and others to selectively rehabilitate "progressive" Russians from the prerevolutionary period without legitimating the old regime itself. See Lenin, "O natsional'noi gordosti velikorossov," 18:80–83. Stalin associated 1917 specifically with the Russian working class frequently during the 1920s and early 1930s—see, for instance, I. V. Stalin, "K voprosu o strategii i taktike russkikh

kommunistov" (1923), reprinted in *Sochineniia*, 13 vols. (Moscow: Gos. izd-vo polit. lit-ry, 1952), 5:160–180. The fact that these russocentric views were not widely disseminated at the time indicates that they were difficult to reconcile with the reigning internationalist line.

25. G. Vasil'kovskii, "Vysshii zakon zhizni," *Pravda*, May 28, 1934, 4. This argument drew upon newspaper coverage of refugee Austrian workers present on Red Square for the May Day parade—see D. Zaslavskii, "Pis'mo s rodiny na chuzhbinu," *Pravda*, May 25, 1934, 4.

26. "Za rodinu," *Pravda*, June 9, 1934, 1. The latter reference to national defense alluded to a letter published a day earlier by a group of air force pilots vowing to sacrifice their lives in the name of the motherland: "Krasnye letchiki znaiut, za chto oni boriutsia: pis'mo semi letchikov—geroev Sovetskogo soiuza," *Pravda*, June 8, 1934, 1. This editorial was reprinted in other prominent papers, e.g., *Krasnaia gazeta*, June 10, 1934, 1.

27. E. Dobrenko, *Metafora vlasti: literatura stalinskoi epokhi v istoricheskom osveshchenii* (Munich: Verlag Otto Sagner, 1993), 171–201.

28. A few veteran Bolsheviks published pieces during the emergence of this patriotic line that asserted that "the motherland" was a place defined by the heroes it produced rather than by the territory it occupied. The latter position quickly prevailed. See A. Ershin, "Slovo o rodine [razgovor s F. Ia. Voitkanym]," *Krasnaia gazeta*, June 18, 1934, 3; K. Krivenia, "Moi zavod, moia rodina," *Kino*, June 18, 1934, 3; G. Kolosov, "Slava nashei rodiny," *Krasnaia zvezda*, June 20, 1934, 1.

29. For the Politburo resolution, see RGASPI, f. 17, op. 163, d. 1026, l. 138, published as Central Committee resolution of June 8, 1934 "O dopolnenii Polozheniia o prestupleniiakh gosudarstvennykh (kontrrevoliutsionnykh i osobo dlia Soiuza SSR opasnykh prestupleniiakh protiv poriadka upravleniia) stat'iami ob izmene rodine," *Pravda*, June 9, 1934, 1.

30. "Za rodinu," *Sotsialisticheskii vestnik*, June 25, 1934, 1–2.

31. N. I. Bukharin, "Rozhdenie i razvitie sotsialisticheskoi rodiny," *Izvestiia*, July 6, 1934, 3. See also his defense of state interests in that edition's unsigned editorial: "Velikaia derzhava proletariata," 1.

32. Mikhail Kol'tsov, "Naidennaia rodina," *Pravda*, June 19, 1934, 5.

33. Emphases in original. "Za rodinu," *Krasnaia zvezda*, July 6, 1934, 1.

34. K. Radek, "Moia rodina," *Izvestiia*, July 6, 1934, 2. See also the speech by Czechoslovak poet V. Nezval, "Rabochie imeiut otechestvo," *Literaturnaia gazeta*, September 3, 1934, 3.

35. "O rodine: ugolok propagandista," *Pravda*, August 7, 1934, 4.

36. A. Ugarov, "O sotsialisticheskoi rodine," *Bol'shevik* 19–20 (1934): 54–67, esp. 66. On defense of the socialist motherland, see the Komsomol boss's unusually eloquent conference speech—A. Kosarev, "Bespredel'no liubit' nashu rodinu," *Komsomol'skaia pravda*, October 21, 1934, 3.

37. "Ob izmeneniiakh v Sovetskoi konstitutsii (Doklad V. M. Molotova na VII s"ezde Sovetov, 6-ogo fevralia s.g.)," *Pravda*, February 7, 1935, 3.

38. "Sotsialisticheskoe otechestvo i ego zashchita," *Izvestiia*, February 1, 1935, 1.

39. "Sovetskii patriotizm," *Pravda*, March 19, 1935, 1; also "Rodina vsekh trudiashchikhsia," *Izvestiia*, May 1, 1935, 1; I. Ehrenburg, "Nasha rodina," *Izvestiia*,

May 1, 1935, 4; "Partiia i narod," *Pravda,* May 12, 1935, 1; D. Zaslavskii, "O liubvi k otechestvu," *Pravda,* November 7, 1935, 5; "'Delo Lenina pobedilo v SSSR okonchatel'no i bespovorotno'—doklad tov. A. I. Stetskogo v Bol'shom teatre, na torzhestvenno-traurnom zasedanii povsviashchennom 12-oi godovshchine smerti V. I. Lenina, 21 ianvaria 1936 g.," *Pravda,* January 24, 1936, 3–4. Zaslavsky elaborated on Radek's and Molotov's earlier arguments in order to suggest that the internationalist nature of Soviet patriotism left it uniquely compatible with local cultures and traditions, inasmuch as it was defined by the ethic of the revolution and socialist construction, not language or ethnicity. Zaslavskii, "O liubvi k otechestvu."

40. G. Glezerman, "Nashe otechestvo," *Komsomol'skaia pravda,* February 11, 1936, 2. See also P. Kogan, "Zashchita rodiny—internatsional'nyi dolg," *Komsomol'skaia pravda,* March 28, 1936, 2.

41. "Edinaia sem'ia narodov," *Pravda,* January 30, 1936, 1.

42. "Rech' tov. Stalina na soveshchanii peredovykh kolkhoznikov i kolkhoznits Tadzhikistana i Turkmenistana," *Pravda,* December 5, 1935, 3; "Priem delegatsii trudiashchikhsia SSR Armenii v Kremle," *Pravda,* January 6, 1936, 2–3; "Priem delegatsii Sovetskogo Azerbidzhana rukovoditeliami partii i pravitel'stva v Kremle," *Pravda,* January 24, 1936, 2–3; "Priem delegatov trudiashchikhsia Buriat-Mongol'skoi ASSR rukovoditeliami partii i pravitel'stva v Kremle," *Pravda,* January 30, 1936, 1; "Priem delegatsii Sovetskoi Gruzii rukovoditeliami partii i pravitel'stva v Kremle," *Pravda,* March 21, 1936, 1–5.

43. "Sovetskie kazaki," *Pravda,* February 18, 1936, 1; Resolution of the Central Executive Committee of April 20, 1936 "O sniatii s kazachestva ogranicheniia po sluzhbe v RKKA," *Pravda,* April 21, 1936, 1; "Kolkhoznoe kazachestvo," *Pravda,* April 24, 1936, 1; "Prikaz Narodnogo komissara oborony Soiuza SSR, no. 67, 23 aprelia 1936 goda," *Pravda,* April 24, 1936, 1; TASS, "'Sokolami sletimsia na zashchitu velikoi rodiny': sovetskoe kazachestvo goriacho privetstvuet postanovlenie TsIK SSSR," *Pravda,* April 24, 1936, 2. Alternately, see A. P. Skorik, "K istorii odnoi politicheskoi kampanii v 1930-e gg.," *Voprosy istorii* 1 (2009): 87–95.

44. Karl Radek, "Sovetskii patriotizm," *Pravda,* May 1, 1936, 6. Exiled Mensheviks labeled this explosion of patriotic rhetoric a betrayal of the revolution—see "Propavshii lozung," *Sotsialisticheskii vestnik,* May 10, 1936, 1–2. Radek's piece echoes an earlier attempt to historicize the notion of motherland found in P. Lapinskii, "Rodina: zametki na poliakh," *Izvestiia,* July 8, 1935, 2.

45. *Nasha sotsialisticheskaia rodina: sbornik statei k Chrezvychainomu VIII s"ezdu sovetov* (Leningrad: Leningradskoe oblastnoe izdatel'stvo, 1936).

46. See articles ranging from "Muzhestva, khrabost', geroizm," *Pravda,* June 1, 1936, 1 (perhaps also written by Radek) to A. Korneichuk, "Sovetskii patriotizm," *Literaturnaia gazeta,* January 15, 1938, 3.

47. TsKhDMO, f. 1, op. 23, d. 1253, ll. 36–37.

48. "Komsomol i shkola," *Pravda,* March 11, 1935, 1.

49. S. Rozental', "Tri propagandista," *Pravda,* April 4, 1935, 3.

50. *SSSR—strana sotsializma: Statisticheskii sbornik,* ed. L. Mekhlis, E. Varga, and V. Karpinskii (Moscow: Partizdat, 1936); L. P. Beriia, *K voprosu ob istorii bol'shevistskikh organizatsii v Zakavkaz'e* (Moscow: Partizdat, 1935); K. E. Voroshilov, *Stalin i Krasnaia Armiia* (Moscow: Partizdat, 1936). Generally, see TsKhDMO, f. 1, op. 23, d. 1253, ll. 3–100.

51. See B. M. Tal', "O zadachakh bol'shevistskoi pechati," *Izvestiia,* May 10, 1936, 3; B. Belen'skaia, "Pochemu trudiashchiesia nashei strany liubiat svoiu rodinu (Metodicheskaia rabota dlia III klassa)," *Istoriia v srednei shkole* 5 (1935): 125–141; see also "'Gotov'sia k zashchite svoei rodiny': metodicheskaia razrabotka dlia VI klassa," *Istoriia v srednei shkole* 5 (1935): 142–56.

52. "Znat' prekrasnuiu nashu rodinu," *Pravda,* July 24, 1935, 1.

53. "Vystavka '20 let RKKA,'" *Pravda,* October 29, 1935, 4; *Khudozhestvennaia vystavka 15 let RKKA: zhivopis', grafika, skul'ptura, tekstil', dekorativnoe iskusstvo, iskusstvo palekha i mstery* (Moscow: Vsekhudozhnik, 1933), xvii–xviii.

54. See L. Pervomaiskii, "Pesnia," trans. D. Shleiman, *Izvestiia,* June 12, 1935, 3; M. Ryl'skii, "Moia otchizna," trans. A. Volkovich, *Izvestiia,* July 6, 1935, 3.

55. Al. Surkov, "Otchizna," *Pravda,* July 5, 1935, 2; Surkov, "Pesnia molodosti," *Pravda,* October 20, 1935, 3; Surkov, *Rodina muzhestvennykh* (Moscow: Goslitizdat, 1935). Critics liked Surkov's ability to combine patriotic thematics with a more conventional celebration of class and revolutionary duty, but didn't care for his treatment of other subjects (nature, aviation, the Black Sea, etc.). See M. Serebrianskii, "Rodina muzhestvennykh," *Pravda,* January 28, 1936, 4.

56. N. Sidorenko, "Rodina Oktiabria," *Izvestiia,* November 7, 1935, 4; M. Sadri, "Rodine," *Pravda,* January 6, 1936, 4. Sadri's poem was apparently translated by the famous Gulag memoirist Ye. S. Ginzburg.

57. *Rodina muzhestvennykh,* ed. D. Ermilov (Moscow: Gosudarstvennoe izdatel'stvo po voprosam radio, 1936), 23–25, 21–22. The brochure's introduction quoted extensively from Kosarev's 1934 Komsomol congress speech.

58. The playwright A. M. Goldenberg, for instance, complained at a Writers' Union meeting in May 1936 about his confusion over the revival of "old values such as 'motherland,' 'patriotism,' and 'the people.'" RGALI, f. 631, op. 2, d. 177, ll. 32–33. O. D. Forsh moaned about similar feelings of confusion in November 1936: TsA FSB, f. 3, op. 3, d. 121, ll. 98–107, published in *Vlast' i khudozhestvennaia intelligentsiia: dokumenty TsK RKP(b)-VKP(b), ChK-OGPU-NKVD o kul'turnoi politike, 1917–1953 gg.,* ed. A. N. Iakovlev, A. Artizov, and O. Naumov (Moscow: Demokratiia, 1999), 338.

59. Iv. Kataev, "Vstrecha," in *Otechestvo* (Moscow: Sovetskii pisatel', 1935), 5–104; V. Ermilov, "Rodina i liudi," *Pravda,* June 16, 1935, 4.

60. A. Afinogenov, "Dalekoe," *Krasnaia nov'* 11 (1935): 3–26; Iogann Al'tman, "Rodina i ee synov'ia (P'esa A. Afinogenova v Teatre im. Vakhtangova)," *Izvestiia,* November 28, 1935, 4.

61. B. Levin, *Rodina: p'esa v trekh aktakh, vos'mi kartinakh* (Moscow: Goslitizdat, 1936). The play was sent to press in the last days of 1935 and premiered in early 1936: S. Tregub, "'Rodina': novaia postanovka Kamernogo teatra," *Komsomol'skaia pravda,* January 27, 1936, 4. For another example of a narrative revolving around conflicting visions of the motherland, see I. Shukhov, "Rodina," *Oktiabr'* 8, 9, 10 (1935). Favorable reviews (e.g., V. Novinskii, "Pisatel' i deistvitel'nost'," *Oktiabr'* 10 [1936]: 197–208) led to the novel's publication as a freestanding book in 1936.

62. "My krasnoe znamia podnimem vysoko, / Da zdravstvuet rodina-mat'! / Nad nashim nad krasnym nad Dal'nim Vostokom / Znamenam chuzhim ne byvat'!" See "Vstavaite, partizany," by D. Kabalevskii and V. Gusev (1935). Their

"Aerograd City" (1935) also invoked the issue of patriotism: "Good bye, mama, the plane is taking off. / Fly out to visit me, as I'm not coming back. / It's calling me, as the Motherland does, / The city of my heart—Aerograd. / The city, the city Aerograd." (Proshchai, mama, uletaet samolet. / Priletai ko mne, ne zhdi menia nazad. / On zovet menia, kak rodina zovet, / Gorod serdtsa moego—Aerograd. / Gorod, gorod Aerograd.)

63. *Aerograd,* dir. A. Dovzhenko (Ukrainfil'm, 1935); B. Reznikov, "Zamechatel'nyi fil'm," *Pravda,* November 12, 1935, 4; V. Potapov, "Aerograd," *Trud,* November 10, 1935, 3; see also N. Izgoev, "Aerograd," *Izvestiia,* November 3, 1935, 3. On the film, see George Liber, *Alexander Dovzhenko: A Life in Soviet Film* (London: British Film Institute, 2002), 140–146.

64. *Trinadtsat',* dir. M. Romm (Mosfil'm, 1936). The last names of the unit members mentioned in the film include Skuratov, Akchurin, Timoshkin, Sviridenko, Petrov, Levkoev, Balandin, Zhurba, Muradov, and Kuliev. Such comradeship, teamwork, and self-sacrifice were also identified as markers of Soviet patriotism in Gerasimov's film *The Courageous Seven.* According to one critic, such qualities could have been nurtured only in a non-bourgeois milieu like that offered by the USSR. See V. Molonov, "Semero smelykh," *Pravda,* February 4, 1936, 4.

65. *My iz Kronshtata,* dir. E. Dzigan (Mosfil'm, 1936); I. Erukhimovich, "'My iz Kronshtadta': zamechatel'nyi fil'm," *Pravda,* March 3, 1936, 3; N. Izgoev, "My iz Kronshtadta," *Izvestiia,* March 4, 1936, 4. The screenplay was written by Vs. V. Vishnevsky, whose diary repeatedly invokes the Bolshevik search for a usable past during the 1930s. See RGALI, f. 1038, op. 1, dd. 2071–2077.

66. *Rodina zovet,* dir. A. Macheret and K. Krumin (Mosfil'm, 1936); I. Erukhimovich, "Rodina zovet!" *Pravda,* May 12, 1936, 4; A. Macheret, "Rodina zovet," *Kino,* April 22, 1936, 2. See also V. Tairov, "Rodina zovet: novaia kartina Mosfil'ma," *Vecherniaia Moskva,* June 9, 1936, 3.

67. *Bor'ba za Kiev,* dir. L. Antsi-Polovskii et al. (Soiuzkinokhronika/Soiuzdetfil'm, 1935); also "Velikaia rodina i ee syny" and "Zheleznyi marsh: parad chastei Kievskogo voennogo okruga," *Izvestiia,* September 18, 1935, 1; A. Agranovskii, "'Bor'ba za Kiev' na ekrane," *Pravda,* November 23, 1935, 4.

68. *Belorusskie manevry* (TsSDF, 1936); also "Manevry voisk Belorusskogo voennogo okruga," *Izvestiia,* September 10–11, 1936.

69. *Manevry voisk Moskovskogo voennogo okruga* (TsSDF, 1936); also "Parad chastei Moskovskogo voennogo okruga," *Izvestiia,* September 26, 1936, 3.

70. *Takticheskie ucheniia v DVKA* (TsSDF, 1936); also "Boitsy OKDVA zakonchili takticheskie ucheniia," *Izvestiia,* September 29, 1936, 3.

71. Although stridently internationalist, *Circus* was framed in the press as being more about domestic unity and the Friendship of the Peoples that it was about foreign support for the revolution. See *Tsirk,* dir. G. Aleksandrov (Mosfil'm, 1936); Brat'ia Tur, "Tsirk," *Izvestiia,* May 24, 1936, 4; N. D., "Zhizneradostnyi fil'm," *Literaturnaia gazeta,* May 30, 1936, 5. For evidence that popular reactions to the film mirrored this coverage, see diary entry from March 9, 1937 in A. T. Mar'ian, *Gody moi, kak soldaty: dnevnik sel'skogo aktivista, 1925–1953 gg.* (Kishinev: Kartia Molodoveniaske, 1987), 108.

CHAPTER 6. THE POPULARITY OF THE OFFICIAL LINE

1. A. P. Mukhin et al., "Budem ravniats'ia po geroiam SSSR"; N. Rakitin et al., "Liudiam zheleznoi otvagi"; B. Levin, "Kem by ia khotel byt'," all in *Pravda,* June 19, 1934, 5.

2. For similar attempts to shape public opinion, see, for instance, "Molodye sovetskie patrioty," *Pravda,* April 16, 1936, 1.

3. Mapping popular opinion anywhere in the world before the mid-twentieth century is complicated by a lack of systematic, rigorously collected data. As elsewhere, the only profitable approach to the Soviet case involves the analysis and triangulation of as many impressionistic accounts from as great a variety of sources as possible. For a thorough problematization of secret police and party reports on the popular mood, see Lesley Rimmel, "Svodki and Popular Opinion in Stalinist Leningrad," *Cahiers du Monde russe* 40:1–2 (1999): 217–234.

4. RGVA, f. 9, op. 29, d. 244, l. 3.

5. Diary entry from April 15, 1936, in M. Molochko, *Zhil-byl mal'chishka* (Minsk: Belarus, 1965), 125.

6. See diary entries from January 9, 1933 and May 17, 1937 in A. T. Mar'ian, *Gody moi, kak soldaty: dnevnik sel'skogo aktivista, 1925–1953 gg.* (Kishinev: Kartia Molodoveniaske, 1987), 66, 110; diary entry from April 20, 1933 in A. G. Man'kov, "Iz dnevnika riadovogo cheloveka," *Zvezda* 5 (1994): 142; diary entry from February 24, 1938 in *Poka stuchit serdtse: Dnevniki i pis'ma Geroia Sovetskogo Soiuza Evgenii Rudnevoi* (Moscow: Moskovskii gos. universitet, 1995), 55.

7. Diary entry from early February 1935 in "Diary of Leonid Alekseyevich Potyomkin," in *Intimacy and Terror: Soviet Diaries of the 1930s,* ed. Véronique Garros, Natalia Korenevskaya, and Thomas Lahusen (New York: New Press, 1995), 260–261. Later, Potemkin commented after seeing a newsreel: "Com[rade] Stalin's speech impressed me deeply with its simplicity and intimacy[,] the familiar accent of his origins mobilizing me to social and political activism." Diary entry from April 1935, ibid., 273.

8. For an example of one such misunderstanding, consider Shildiakov, a Red Army study group leader, who attempted to explain several European states' new diplomatic entreaties to the Soviet Union in 1935 by claiming that they "do not want to fight with us as they see the USSR as a socialist fatherland." Others stressed the USSR's geopolitical primacy, noting with irony that "Our country is the richest country in the world. But the workers in the country of Soviets are poorer than anyone else on earth." RGVA, f. 9, op. 29, d. 191, l. 106; d. 243, l. 71.

9. See diary entries from February 24, March 9, and April 24, 1934, in Molochko, *Zhil-byl mal'chishka,* 64–65, 67, 85.

10. A. Likhachev, "Cheliuskintsy—vlasteli dum shkol'nikov," *Pravda,* June 19, 1934, 5.

11. D. Zaslavskii, "Geroicheskaia nauka," *Pravda,* June 19, 1934, 5.

12. See, for example, diary entries of June 20–21 and 23, 1934 in Nina Lugovskaia, *Khochu zhit': iz dnevnika shkol'nitsy* (Moscow: Glas, 2004), 162–164; Tatiana Poloz to Feoktista Miagkova et al. (June 24 and 28, 1934), cited in Orlando Figes, *The Whisperers: Private Life in Stalin's Russia* (New York: Metropolitan

Books, 2007), 220–221. Lugovskaia was a teenager heavily influenced by her father's SR-beliefs; Poloz, a Trotskyite, was writing to her mother from the Gulag. For a broader treatment of the society's reaction to these events, see John McCannon, *Red Arctic: Polar Exploration and the Myth of the North in the Soviet Union, 1932–1939* (Oxford: Oxford University Press, 1998), 134–140.

13. Oleg Krasovsky, "Early Years," in *Soviet Youth: Twelve Komsomol Histories* (Munich: Institute for the Study of the USSR, 1959), 143.

14. Anna Krylova, "Soviet Modernity in Life and Fiction: The Generation of the 'New Soviet Person' in the 1930s" (Ph.D. diss., Johns Hopkins University, 2000), esp. chap. 6. For an example of youthful excitement over being called up "to defend the motherland," see diary entries from July 27 and October 7, 1936 in Mar'ian, *Gody moi, kak soldaty,* 97, 105.

15. N. Verkhovtsev, "Literaturnyi minimum krasnoarmeitsa," *Pravda,* September 16, 1935, 4; *Byli gory Vysokoi: rasskazy rabochikh Vysokogorskogo zheleznogo rudnika—o staroi i novoi zhizni,* ed. M. Gor'kii and D. Mirskii (Moscow: Istoriia zavodov, 1935).

16. A. Bezborodova, "Beseda s chitateliami," *Pravda,* October 6, 1936, 4.

17. "Istoriiu grazhdanskoi voiny chitaiut massy," *Pravda,* October 6, 1936, 4.

18. Evgenii Dobrenko, *Formovka sovetskogo chitatelia: sotsial'nye i estetiteskie predposylki retseptsii sovetskoi literatury* (St. Petersburg: Akademicheskii proekt, 1997), 258–277.

19. For more general surveys, see Maurice Friedberg, "Russian Writers and Soviet Readers," *American Slavic and East European Review* 14:1 (1955): 114–119; Klaus Mehnert, *Russians and Their Favorite Books* (Stanford: Stanford University Press, 1983), 90–92, 238–243.

20. On *Quiet Flows the Don,* see HPSSS, no. 9, schedule A, vol. 1, 103; no. 20, schedule A, vol. 2, 35; no. 64, schedule B, vol. 23, 77; no. 72, schedule B, vol. 23, 27; no. 96/1493, schedule A, vol. 35, 40; no. 102/1011, schedule A, vol. 31, 56; no. 111, schedule A, vol. 9, 64; no. 118, schedule A, vol. 9, 30; no. 118/1517, schedule A, vol. 35, 51; no. 128, schedule A, vol. 10, 17; no. 134, schedule A, vol. 10, 31; no. 136, schedule A, vol. 11, 70; no. 147, schedule A, vol. 12, 76; no. 189, schedule A, vol. 14, 57; no. 260, schedule A, vol. 14, 25; no. 266/1313, schedule A, vol. 33, 71; no. 273, schedule A, 17, 29; no. 300, schedule A, vol. 15, 13; no. 302, schedule A, vol. 15, 33; no. 302/1728, schedule A, vol. 37, 48; no. 306, schedule A, vol. 16, 48; no. 308/1123, schedule A, vol. 32, 20–21; no. 331, schedule A, vol. 17, 37; no. 338/1390, schedule A, vol. 33, 40; no. 340, schedule A, vol. 18, 39; no. 344, schedule A, vol. 18, 37; no. 373, schedule A, vol. 19, 53; no. 386/1495, schedule A, vol. 35, 53; no. 415/1035, schedule A, vol. 31, 30; no. 420, schedule A, vol. 21, 18; no. 431, schedule A, vol. 21, 47; no. 446, schedule A, vol. 22, 61; no. 449, schedule A, vol. 22, 19; no. 451/1053, schedule A, vol. 31, 36; no. 454/1350, schedule A, vol. 33, 31; no. 468, schedule A, vol. 23, 42; no. 473, schedule A, vol. 24, 72; no. 481, schedule A, vol. 24, 70; no. 487/1693, schedule A, vol. 36, 45; no. 491, schedule A, vol. 25, 26; no. 493, schedule A, vol. 25, 63; no. 494/1434, schedule A, vol. 34, 34; no. 530, schedule A, vol. 27, 27; no. 532, schedule A, vol. 28, 64; no. 628, schedule A, vol. 29, 44; no. 644/1354, schedule A, vol. 33, 57; no. 1035, schedule A, vol. 31, 30, no. 1390, schedule A, vol. 33, 40; no. 1493,

schedule A, vol. 35, 40; no. 1693, schedule A, vol. 36, 45; no. 1705, schedule A, vol. 36, 48; no. 1706, schedule A, vol. 37, 34. On *Virgin Soil Upturned,* see HPSSS, no. 96/1493, schedule A, vol. 35, 40; no. 260, schedule A, vol. 14, 25; no. 308/1123, schedule A, vol. 32, 20–21; no. 355/1498, schedule A, vol. 35, 50; no. 340, schedule A, vol. 18, 39; no. 415, schedule A, vol. 20, 43–44; no. 456, schedule A, vol. 23, 35; no. 473, schedule A, vol. 24, 72; no. 1390, schedule A, vol. 33, 40; no. 1493, schedule A, vol. 35, 40. For another favorable account, see diary entry from October 19, 1934 in Mar'ian, *Gody moi, kak soldaty,* 82.

21. HPSSS, no. 308/1123, schedule A, vol. 32, 17; no. 473, schedule A, vol. 24, 72.

22. HPSSS, no. 308/1123, schedule A, vol. 32, 17, 20; no. 344, schedule A, vol. 18, 37; no. 420, schedule A, vol. 21, 18; no. 446, schedule A, vol. 22, 61; no. 452, schedule A, vol. 22, 38; no. 479, schedule A, vol. 24, 42; no. 519, schedule A, vol. 26, 28; no. 529, schedule A, vol. 27, 53.

23. On Avdeenko, see HPSSS, no. 67, schedule A, vol. 6, 4; no. 644/1354, schedule A, vol. 33, 57; on Fadeev, see no. 266, schedule A, vol. 14, 23; no. 301, schedule A, vol. 15, 44; no. 67, schedule B, vol. 6, 2; 301, schedule B, vol. 15, 44; no. 385, schedule B, vol. 20, 16; no. 503, schedule B, vol. 9, 5; on Ilf and Petrov, see no. 96 /1493, schedule A, vol. 35, 40; no. 102/1011, schedule A, vol. 31, 56; no. 331, schedule A, vol. 17, 37; no. 473, schedule A, vol. 24, 71; no. 479/1108, schedule A, vol. 31, 31.

24. On Gladkov, see HPSSS, no. 339, schedule A, vol. 18, 35; no. 494/1434, schedule A, vol. 34, 34; on Serafimovich, see HPSSS, no. 134, schedule A, vol. 10, 31; no. 644/1354, schedule A, vol. 33, 57; on Zoshchenko, see HPSSS schedule A, vol. 33, no. 266/1313, 71; no. 445, schedule A, vol. 31, 47; no. 445/1007, schedule A, vol. 31, 46; no. 519, schedule A, vol. 26, 28; on Mayakovsky, see HPSSS, no. 102/1011 schedule A, vol. 31, 56; no. 308/1123, schedule A, vol. 32, 21; no. 398, schedule A, vol. 20, 18; no. 445, schedule A, vol. 31, 47; no. 468, schedule A, vol. 23, 42; no. 481, schedule A, vol. 24, 70.

25. See, for instance, HPSSS, no. 1124, schedule A, vol. 32, 39.

26. Z. Kabalkina, "Chitatel' o romane N. Ostrovskogo," *Pravda,* January 31, 1936, 4. For more reader comments, see N. Liubovich, "N. Ostrovskii i ego chitateli," *Novyi mir* 7 (1937): 255–262; Ia. Roshchin, "Golos chitatelia," *Literaturnoe obozrenie* 11 (1939): 70.

27. Yevgenia Rudneva worshipped the novel's protagonist, writing that "Korchagin-Ostrovsky is deserving enough to be a model for many generations." See diary entry from January 18, 1938 in *Poka stuchit serdtse,* 51–52. See also Krasovsky, "Early Years," 143; and nearly a dozen HPSSS interviews: no. 118, schedule A, vol. 9, 30; no. 189, schedule A, vol. 14, 57; no. 240, schedule A, vol. 14, 14–15; no. 420, schedule A, vol. 21, 18; no. 449, schedule A, vol. 22, 19; no. 479/1108, schedule A, vol. 31, 31; no. 519, schedule A, vol. 26, 28; no. 624, schedule A, vol. 30, l. 42; no. 386/1495, schedule B, vol. 18, 24–25.

28. "Rabochie o khudozhestvennoi literature: 'Energiia' F. Gladkova," *Oktiabr'* 5 (1935): 207, 202, 206.

29. Ibid., 207.

30. See diary entries from May 8 and April 19, 1933, in Molochko, *Zhil-byl*

mal'chishka, 31, 22. The literary works under discussion are A. Kron, *Vintovka No. 492116: p'esa v 3-kh deistviiakh* (Moscow: Gos. izd-vo khudozh. lit-ry, 1931), and V. A. Shishkov, *Fil'ka i Amel'ka: povest' iz byta besprizornykh* (Paris: Biblioteka Illiustrirovannoi Rossii, 1933). Interestingly, Molochko also disliked Arnshtam's film *Podrugi*, probably because of its low emphasis on revolutionary consciousness. See diary entry from April 2, 1936 in Molochko, *Zhil-byl mal'chishka*, 123.

31. Dobrenko, *Formovka sovetskogo chitatelia*, 258–277. For other examples, see diary entries from September 30 and November 26, 1936 in Man'kov, "Iz dnevnika riadovogo cheloveka," 158, 163.

32. The book's ambiguity and dark interiority was excised from the narrative as it was adapted for the screen. For readers who were probably introduced to the book after the release of the film, see HPSSS, no. 134, schedule A, vol. 10, 31; no. 456, schedule A, vol. 23, 35; no. 481, schedule A, vol. 24, 70.

33. RGASPI, f. 558, op. 11, d. 828, ll. 64–66. For the "erroneous" reviews and Mekhlis's corrective, see S. S. Dinamov, "O groznykh dniakh bor'by: 'Chapaev,'" *Pravda*, November 3, 1934, 4; Kh. Kersonskii, "'Chapaev': novaia kartina 'Lenfil'ma,'" *Izvestiia*, November 10, 1934, 6; Kinozritel', "Kartinki v gazete i kartiny na ekrane (O retsenzii Khris. Kersonskogo v 'Izvestiiakh,')" *Pravda*, November 12, 1934, 3; "'Chapaeva' smotrit vsia strana," *Pravda*, November 21, 1934, 1.

34. Diary entry of February 23, 1935 in Mar'ian, *Gody moi, kak soldaty*, 94.

35. On ticket sales, see *Soviet Films, 1938–1939*, ed. M. Borodin, L. Chernyavsky et al., trans. J. Van Zant (Moscow: State Publishing House for Cinema Literature, 1939), 84; on colloquialisms and playgrounds, see B. Shumiatskii, "Tempy i ritm sotsialisticheskogo realizma," *Pravda*, March 16, 1935, 2–3; RGALI, f. 631, op. 2, d. 298, l. 110b. When *Dzhulbars* began generating fan mail in 1935, the film's actors played a trick on its director by sending him a note of their own, ostensibly written by a schoolboy: "Dear Uncle Shneiderov! I would like to ask your advice. First I saw *Chapaev* and decided to become a machine-gunner. Now I've seen your film *Dzhulbars* and would like to become a dog." As silly as this joke is, its humor stems from the common knowledge that many of this cinematic genre's heroes served as popular role models. See Andrei Fait, "Po gornym tropam," *Sovetskii ekran* 17 (1975): 20; also Brat. Grim, "Prazdnichnye tosty: druzheskie parodii," *Kino*, December 29, 1938, 3.

36. For discussion of how playing Chapaev occasionally turned into real war games, see *Stalinism as a Way of Life: A Narrative of Documents*, ed. Lewis Siegelbaum and Andrei Sokolov (New Haven: Yale University Press, 2000), 400, citing TsKhDMO, f. 1, op. 23, d. 1472, l. 620b; TsAODM, f. 1934, op. 1, d. 94, l. 12; also Justus Hartzok, "Children of Chapaev: The Russian Civil War Cult and the Creation of Soviet Identity, 1918–1941" (Ph.D. Diss., University of Iowa, 2009), 119–156, esp. 138–141, 151–153.

37. "'Kartina rozhdaet nenavist' k vragam': iz vystuplenii kolkhoznikov Reutovskogo raiona Moskovskoi oblasti," *Pravda*, March 20, 1935, 3.

38. A. Morov, "Kolkhozniki obsuzhdaiut fil'm 'Krest'iane,'" *Pravda*, March 20, 1935, 3. For similar evaluations, see E. P. Romanov to Ermler (May 7, 1935), and B. V. Khoroshilov to Ermler ([May 1935]), TsGALI SPb, f. 166, op. 1, d. 337, ll. 3, 11.

39. Morov, "Kolkhozniki obsuzhdaiut fil'm 'Krest'iane.'" For similar articles, see "Fil'm 'Krest'iane'—na kolkhoznyi ekran," *Izvestiia,* March 21, 1935, 3; "Kartina rozhdaet nenavist' k vragam (iz vystuplenii kolkhoznikov Reutovskogo raiona Moskovskoi oblasti)," *Pravda,* March 20, 1935, 3.

40. "Kolkhozniki o kartine 'Krest'iane," *Izvestiia,* March 20, 1935, 3. For similar evaluations of Nikolai Mironovich, see K. R. Fedorenko to N. I. Bogoliubov (May 7, 1935), TsGALI, f. 166, op. 1, d. 337, l. 7, and the stenographic record of a public discussion of the film in early 1935—d. 376, ll. 50b, 70b, 13.

41. "Uspekh fil'ma 'My iz Kronshtadta,'" *Pravda,* March 26, 1936, 6; "Uspekh kartiny 'My iz Kronshtadtda' v Minske," *Pravda,* March 24, 1936, 4; "Uspekh zamechatel'nogo fil'ma—pervyi den' demonstratsii 'My iz Kronshtadta,'" 6; *Soviet Films, 1938–1939,* 82.

42. Ia. Portnov and N. Tokarev, "Geroi fil'ma—v zritel'nom zale," *Pravda,* March 23, 1936, 3; December 4, 1936 letter to *Pionerskaia pravda,* RGALI, f. 3015, op. 1, d. 455, l. 1.

43. E. Dzigan, *My iz Kronshtadta: printsipy rezhisserskogo postroeniia fil'ma* (Moscow: Iskusstvo, 1937), 64.

44. RGALI, f. 1964, op. 1, d. 268, ll. 42, 44.

45. See, for instance, diary entries from September 4, 1933 and May 17, 1937 in Mar'ian, *Gody moi, kak soldaty,* 69, 110.

46. On *Happy-Go-Lucky Fellows,* he wrote on January 12, 1935: "its cheerfulness and musicality make for a pleasant spectacle, arousing cheerfulness in the spectator." On *Flyers,* he wrote in April 1935 that the film shows the "fervor and high spirits of the New Men" in Soviet society. On *The Courageous Seven,* he wrote on July 1, 1936 that it was "an interesting combination of the work of the northern expeditions with the participation of a geologist and a doctor." On *Circus,* he wrote in August 1936 that "the ideological-emotional contents of that film are beautiful. It fascinates the viewer and fills him with a sensation of good cheer. [Especially fascinating is] the psychological resurrection of Mary Dixon in the country of the new Mankind . . . [after having been ostracized in the United States for having a biracial child]. Her first free and confident joy in life filled my eyes with tears of sympathy and an excess of common joy." "Diary of Leonid Alekseyevich Potyomkin," 259, 273, 286, 288–289.

47. *S. M. Kirov,* dir. S. Gurov, Ia. M. Bliokh and I. Setkina (TsSDF, 1935); diary entry from January 26, 1935 in "Diary of Leonid Alekseyevich Potyomkin," 260; diary entry from late January, 1935, cited in Jochen Hellbeck, *Revolution on My Mind: Writing a Diary under Stalin* (Cambridge: Harvard University Press, 2006), 248–249.

48. RGVA, f. 9, op. 29, d. 237, l. 85.

49. I. Savvin, *Cherty geroia vtoroi piatiletki: novaia tematika khudozhestvennoi literatury* (Moscow: MK VLKSM, 1934), 57.

50. RGVA, f. 9, op. 29, d. 237, l. 86.

51. A loose translation of "Poi serdtse o velikoi rodine, / Okhraniai ee granitsy i doliny. / Net bol'shei vesti—o ne bylo donyne—/ Byt' patriotom velikogo Stalina." RGVA, f. 9, op. 29, d. 237, l. 86.

52. "2000 chelovek posetili Muzei I. V. Lenina," *Komsomol'skaia pravda,* May

16, 1936, 1. For similar comments, see diary entry from July 31 and August 3, 1939 in Mar'ian, *Gody moi, kak soldaty*, 121.

53. Apparently only eyewitnesses to the events themselves found fault with the museum's narrative. As N. I. Podvoisky, an Old Bolshevik and veteran revolutionary, sadly observed to a colleague: "the museum depicts the history of the party and its organizational role under Lenin's leadership beautifully. But C[omrade] Stalin's immodest self-advertisement interferes with the impression people get. . . . [W]e oldsters can see very well where there is falseness and distortion. But the young generation will accept all of it blindly [*za chistuiu monetu*] and will get an incorrect sense of the party's history. . . . [I] hope that in time, party historians will sort out the exaggerations and that the party will be cleansed of them. [They'll realize that] advertising is not important—it's important to stop the general line of the party from being distorted. But so far, that's not happening." Diary entry from May 15, 1936 in A. G. Solov'ev, "Tetradi krasnogo professora (1912–1941 gg.)," in *Neizvestnaia Rossiia XX vek*, vol. 4 (Moscow: Istoricheskoe nasledie, 1993), 187.

54. For accounts of visits to Lenin's tomb, see diary entry from December 31, 1936 in *Poka stuchit serdtse*, 41; diary entry from August 3, 1939 in Mar'ian, *Gody moi, kak soldaty*, 122.

55. Perhaps it is for this reason that these events often involved vast swaths of society including even the least politically engaged. On parades, see diary entries from May 1 and November 11, 1931 in Mar'ian, *Gody moi, kak soldaty*, 56, 72; diary entries from April 29, 1933 in Molochko, *Zhil-byl mal'chishka*, 27; diary entries from November 10, 1933 and May 1, 1934 in Man'kov, "Iz dnevnika riadovogo cheloveka," 162, 173; diary entry from October 25, 1937 (Old Style) in I. D. Frolov, "Chronicle of the Year 1937," in *Intimacy and Terror*, 48; commentary on Z. Denisevskaia in Hellbeck, *Revolution on My Mind*, 154–157; D. A. Shtange to G. V. Shtange (November 7, 1937), in "Diary of Galina Vladimirovna Shtange," in *Intimacy and Terror*, 202; Alexei Gorchakov, "The Long Road," and Tanya Senkevich, "A Soviet Girl's Diary," in *Thirteen Who Fled*, ed. Louis Fischer (New York: Harper and Brothers, 1949), 62–63, 116–117, 121.

On elections, see diary entries from July 31, 1936 and November 2, 1937 in Mar'ian, *Gody moi, kak soldaty*, 96–97, 112–113; diary entries from November 25 and December 12, 1937, and July 25, 1938 in *Poka stuchit serdtse*, 48, 57; diary entry from December 6, 1936 in "Diary of Galina Vladimirovna Shtange," 181; Peter Kruzhin, "A Young Communist," in *Thirteen Who Fled*, 92–93.

On funerals, see diary entries from June 21 and 26, 1933 in Molochko, *Zhil-byl mal'chishka*, 43–44; diary entry from December 28, 1933 in Man'kov, "Iz dnevnika riadovogo cheloveka," 165; diary entry from December 6, 1934 in "Diary of Leonid Alekseyevich Potyomkin," in *Intimacy and Terror*, 256; diary entries from December 30, 1936, February 21, 1937, and August 26, 1939 in "Dnevnik Niny Kosterinoi," *Novyi mir* 12 (1962): 39, 40, 79.

For rare expressions of disdain regarding these events, see diary entry from May 1, 1931 in Mar'ian, *Gody moi, kak soldaty*, 54; diary entries from May 1 and November 7, 1931, May 1 and November 8, 1932, and November 7, 1933 in A. A. Tsember, *Dnevnik*, ed. L. P. Roshchevskaia (Syktyvkar: n.p., 1997), 106, 113, 123,

126, 136; diary entry from November 5, 1932 in Lugovskaia *Khochu zhit'*, 51; diary entries from November 3, 7–9, December 8, 1936, and February 19, 1937 in "Diary of Andrei Stepanovich Arzhilovsky," in *Intimacy and Terror*, 117–121, 131, 147; diary entry from May 1, 1938 and March 23, 1939 in "Diary of Lyubov Vasilievna Shaporina," in *Intimacy and Terror*, 361, 367.

56. See diary entry from April 29, 1933 in Molochko, *Zhil-byl mal'chishka*, 27. A. S. Arzhilovskii, although usually a skeptic, was also impressed by May Day's martial show—see diary entries from May 1 and 5, 1937 in "Diary of Andrei Stepanovich Arzhilovsky," 159–160.

57. Diary entry from May 5, 1935, in diary of A. A. Aleksin, TsGA SPb, f. r-3394, op. 1, d. 57, l. 2.

58. Diary entry from April 3, 1933 in Molochko, *Zhil-byl mal'chishka*, 17. See also entries from April 21 and June 3, ibid., 24, 41.

59. On civilian excitement relating to the celebration of Red Armyman's Day, see diary entries from February 20, 1935 in Molochko, *Zhil-byl mal'chishka*, 94–95; February 21, 1937 in *Poka stuchit serdtse*, 44; March 1, 1938 in "Diary of Galina Vladimirovna Shtange," 213.

60. See diary entry from May 1, 1933 in Man'kov, "Iz dnevnika riadovogo cheloveka," 143; diary entries from June 20 and November 7, 1936 in "Dnevnik Niny Kosterinoi," 32, 38.

61. "Vstrecha s narodom," *Izvestiia*, September 18, 1935, 1.

62. Diary entry from May 20, 1933 in Molochko, *Zhil-byl mal'chishka*, 36. Note Molochko's excitement over an address of the Old Bolshevik S. A. Khasman to his Pioneer troop—see diary entry from April 21, 1933, ibid., 24, 26. Similarly, Marian mentioned a visit from Petrovsky, and Rudneva attended an address by Ivan Trunov, a Komsomol border guard known for catching 30 armed intruders at one time. See diary entry from July 31 and August 3, 1939 in Mar'ian, *Gody moi, kak soldaty*, 59; diary entry from August 3, 1937 in *Poka stuchit serdtse*, 47.

63. Sarah Davies, *Popular Opinion in Stalin's Russia: Propaganda, Terror, and Dissent, 1934–1941* (Cambridge: Cambridge University Press, 1997), chap. 10.

64. See, for instance, HPSSS, no. 531, schedule A, vol. 27, 45.

65. See, for instance, HPSSS, no. 27, schedule A, vol. 3, 36–37; Peter Gornev, "The Life of a Soviet Soldier," Alexei Gorchakov, "The Long Road," and Lidia Obukhova, "Two Evils," all in *Thirteen Who Fled*, 34, 67–68, 145–146.

66. In 1935, a worker at Leningrad's Bolshevik factory announced: "the Stakhanov movement is a clever invention of the Bolsheviks. Stakhanov, Busygin, and the others are frauds. Now the Stakhanovites are going to regret superseding the norms." For this and other examples of popular disdain for these labor heroes, see TsGAIPD SPb, f. 24, op. 2v, d. 1843, ll. 3–18; d. 1844, ll. 1–17; d. 2490, ll. 48–51.

67. Jeffrey Brooks, "Socialist Realism in *Pravda*: Read All about It," *Slavic Review* 53:4 (1994): 975, citing M. M. Bakhtin, *The Dialogic Imagination*, ed. Michael Holquist, trans. Caryl Emerson and Michael Holquist (Austin: University of Texas, 1981), 343–348. Hellbeck has made a similarly strong case for the near-total subordination of individual subjectivity to Stalinist discourse during this time period. Both differ with Stephen Kotkin, who stresses that the adoption of these

discursive norms—the act of "speaking Bolshevik"—was more indicative of conformity with the system than wholesale indoctrination. See Jochen Hellbeck, "Fashioning the Stalinist Soul: The Diary of Stepan Podlubnyi," *Jahrbücher für Geschichte Osteuropas* 44:4 (1996): 233–273; Stephen Kotkin, *Magnetic Mountain: Stalinism as Civilization* (Berkeley: University of California Press, 1995), chap. 5.

68. See diary entries from May 18, 1933, March 20, 1934, and March 3, 1935 in Molochko, *Zhil-byl mal'chishka*, 36, 77–80, 96.

69. RGVA, f. 9, op. 29, d. 244, l. 4.

70. Resolution of the Leningrad party committee of March 29, 1935 "O zadachakh partiino-organizatsionnoi i politicheski-vospitatel'noi raboty," *Pravda,* March 30, 1935, 2–3.

71. See, for example, RGVA, f. 9, op. 29, d. 244, l. 4; "Anketa shakhtnogo propagandista" and G. Samarodin, "Sam rukovozhu kruzhkami po istorii partii," both published in *Pravda,* March 28, 1935, 3; N. Verkhovtsev, "Literaturnyi minimum krasnoarmeitsa," *Pravda,* September 16, 1935, 4.

72. RGVA, f. 9, op. 29, d. 214, ll. 28–29.

73. RGVA, f. 9, op. 29, d. 214, ll. 55–57.

74. RGVA, f. 9, op. 9, d. 214, ll. 118, 103.

75. See W. I. Hyrshki, "An Interloper in the Komsomol," in *Soviet Youth,* 98. For a discussion of a similarly disposed worker whose "love for her factory is not a distracted love, like the patriotic love of the petty bourgeois for his 'fatherland,' but a concrete, living love, made of flesh and blood," see Savvin, *Cherty geroia vtoroi piatiletki,* 21.

76. Petr Kruzhin, "False Dawn," in *Soviet Youth,* 204, 205.

77. K. Simonov, *Glazami cheloveka moego pokoleniia: razmyshleniia o I. V. Staline* (Moscow: Novosti, 1988), 64–65; G. K. Zhukov, *Vospominaniia i razmyshleniia* (Moscow: Novosti, 1969), 143–146.

78. See, for instance, David Brandenberger, "Politics Projected into the Past: What Precipitated the 1936 Campaign against M. N. Pokrovskii?" in *Reinterpreting Revolutionary Russia: Essays in Honour of James D. White* (London: Macmillan, 2006), 202–214.

79. A. "Sovetskii patriotizm—legalizatsiia obyvatel'skogo patriotizma," *Sotsialisticheskii vestnik,* March 25, 1935, 24. This letter was sent on the eve of the French foreign minister's visit to Moscow. For a patriotic editorial anticipating this visit, see "Partiia i narod," *Pravda,* May 12, 1935, 1.

80. X, "Po Rossii," *Sotsialisticheskii vestnik,* December 28, 1935, 21.

CHAPTER 7. THE MURDER OF THE USABLE PAST

1. Garth Jowett and Victoria O'Donnell, *Propaganda and Persuasion,* 4th ed. (London: Sage, 2006), 2–7.

2. Central Committee resolution of March 27, 1935 "O sozdanii v gorkomakh VKP(b) otdelov partkadrov," *Pravda,* March 28, 1935, 2; Central Committee resolution of June 13, 1935 "O propagandistskoi rabote v blizhaishee vremia," *Pravda,* June 15, 1935, 1; etc. For articles that attempted to accelerate the implementation of these resolutions, see "O partiinoi propagande," *Izvestiia,* June 16,

1935, 1; V. Furer, "Zametki o propagande," *Pravda,* July 21, 1935, 3; "Geroicheskoe pokolenie Oktiabria," *Izvestiia,* July 28, 1935, 1; A. Stetskii, "O propagandistakh i agitatorakh," *Pravda,* September 22, 1935, 2; N. Rubinshtein, "Nedostatki v prepodavanii istorii VKP(b)," *Bol'shevik* 8 (1936): 32–42.

3. "Soveshchanie prepodavatelei institutov Krasnoi professury," *Istorik-Marksist* 12 (1935): 119–123; *Soveshchanie po voprosam partiinoi propagandy i agitatsii pri TsK VKP(b), 4–7 dekabria 1935 g.* (Moscow: Partizdat, 1936).

4. Such reluctance flew in the face of repeated calls for more attention to personal heroics. See, for example, G. Zaidel', "Litsom k izucheniiu istorii," *Krasnaia gazeta,* May 10, 1934, 2; "Razvernut' rabotu po izucheniiu istorii partii," *Proletarskaia revoliutsiia* 4 (1934): 11–12; "O partiinoi propagande: rech' sekretaria TsK VKP(b) tov. A. Andreeva na otkrytii Vysshei shkoly propagandistov im. Ia. M. Sverdlova pri TsK VKP(b), 7 fevralia 1936 g.," *Pravda,* February 26, 1936, 2; N. Rubinshtein, "Nedostatki v prepodavanii istorii VKP(b)," *Bol'shevik* 8 (1936): 32–42. Internal memos include Orakhelashvili to members of four-volume textbook brigade (August 28, 1934), RGASPI, f. 71, op. 3, d. 57, l. 42.

5. TsGAIPD SPb, f. 24, op. 2v, d. 1829, ll. 92–93.

6. "Znat' i liubit' istoriiu svoei rodiny," *Pravda,* March 7, 1936, 1. For the official announcement, see "Ob organizatsii konkursa na luchshii uchebnik dlia nachal'noi shkoly po elementarnomu kursu istorii SSSR," *Pravda,* March 4, 1936, 1. See also Charles Dickens, *A Child's History of England* (London: Chapman and Hall, 1929); H. G. Wells, *A Short History of the World* (London: Watts, 1929); A. S. Pushkin, *Istoriia Pugachevskogo bunta* (St. Petersburg: Tip. II otdeleniia sobstvennoi E. V. I. Kantseliarii, 1834); and Tolstoy's textbooks—*Azbuka, Novaia azbuka,* and several anthologies—which date to the 1870s.

7. As he read the competition announcement in *Pravda,* Bulgakov underlined its appeal for material that was "clear, interesting [and] artistic." Initially enthusiastic about the project, he drafted seven chapters before losing interest. See *Dnevnik Eleny Bulgakovoi,* ed. V. I. Losev and L. Ianovskaia (Moscow: Izd-vo "Knizhnaia palata," 1990), 116, 366–367; M. A. Bulgakov, "'Kurs istorii SSSR' (vypiski iz chernovika)," *Novyi zhurnal* 143 (1981): 54–88; Ia. S. Lur'e and V. M. Paneiakh, "Rabota M. A. Bulgakova nad kursom istorii SSSR," *Russkaia literatura* 3 (1988): 183–193. Bulgakov's manuscript is stored at RO RGB 552; for other professionals' manuscripts, see RGASPI, f. 17, op. 120, dd. 361–365; GARF, f. 2306, op. 70, d. 2421.

8. "'Za bol'shevistskoe izuchenie istorii partii': rech' tov. Kaganovicha L. M. proiznesennaia 1-dekabria na sobranii, posviashchennom 10-letiiu Instituta Krasnoi professury," *Pravda,* December 13, 1931, 2.

9. A. I. Stetskii, "Ob institutakh Krasnoi professury," *Bol'shevik* 23–24 (1935): 54–55; "O partiinoi propagande: rech' sekretaria TsK VKP(b) tov. A. Andreeva"; E. Grigor'ev, "Shkola bol'shevistskikh istorii," *Komsomol'skaia pravda,* May 15, 1936, 4; etc.

10. Yaroslavsky had been working on revisions to his *History of the ACP(b)* since mid-1935, when he began lobbying Stalin to keep it in print. Permission to publish it under a new title—*Sketches on the History of the ACP(b)*—was granted in May 1936 and resulted in a book printed that September which successfully com-

bined the party's demand for ideological orthodoxy with accessibility. See Yaroslavsky to Stalin (June 2, 1935), RGASPI, f. 558, op. 11, d. 842, ll. 7–8; Politburo resolution of May 28, 1936 "Ob izdanii kinigi tov. Iaroslavskogo 'Istoriia VKP(b),'" RGASPI, f. 17, op. 163, d. 1109, ll. 85–86; Iaroslavskii, *Ocherki po istorii VKP(b)*, 2 vols. (Moscow: Partizdat, 1936). Yaroslavsky apparently worked on the older, shorter text without explicit authoritization—see E. Iaroslavskii, *Kratkaia istoriia VKP(b)*, 3rd ed. (Moscow: OGIZ, 1931).

11. A few chapters by Volin, Ryklin, Rubinshtein, and Bystriansky are all that remain of this effort—see RGASPI, f. 71, op. 2, d. 139, ll. 1–335.

12. While it is possible that this brigade was decommissioned in light of its low productivity, its demise is more likely due to a loss of confidence in Orakhelashvili. Beria denounced the Old Bolshevik's memoirs on the Transcaucasian Bolshevik underground in July 1935, and when this appeared in *Pravda*, Orakhelashvili protested in a letter to the editor that the paper refused to print. When he appealed to Stalin for help, the latter sided with Beria and advised the former to confess his errors. Despite accepting this advice, Orakhelashvili failed to rehabilitate himself in the eyes of the party hierarchy. See RGASPI, f. 558, op. 11, d. 781, ll. 48–52, 42–43, 53; d. 3179, ll. 1–2; M. D. Orakhelashvili, "V Redaktsiiu 'Pravdy,'" *Pravda*, August 12, 1935, 6.

13. "Politicheski vospitat' kadry, likvidirovat' bespechnost'," *Pravda*, March 29, 1937, 1; "'O nedostatkakh partiinoi raboty i merakh likvidatsii trotskistskikh i inykh dvurushnikov'—Doklad t. Stalina na plenume TsK VKP(b)," *Pravda*, March 29, 1937, 2–4.

14. S. V. Zhuravlev, *Fenomen "Istorii fabrik i zavodov": gor'kovskoe nachinanie v kontektse epokhi 1930-kh godov* (Moscow: IRI RAN, 1997), 113, 73–77, 154. This crisis not only hamstrung the completion of the metro history, but led to a recall of *Rasskazy stroitelei metro*, ed. A. Kosarev et al. (Moscow: Istoriia fabrik i zavodov, 1935). The dimensions of arrests among Stakhanovites require quantification, as one specialist contends that few were ever purged—see Lewis Siegelbaum, *Stakhanovism and the Politics of Productivity, 1935–1941* (Cambridge: Cambridge University Press, 1988), 225.

15. Stephen Kotkin, *Magnetic Mountain: Stalinism as a Civilization* (Berkeley: University of California Press, 1995), 372; Kenneth Straus, *Factory and Community in Stalin's Russia* (Pittsburgh: Pittsburgh University Press, 1997), 332.

16. GARF, f. 4851, op. 1, d. 937, ll. 2–4, 41, 44; *Bolshevtsy: Ocherki po istorii Bolshevskoi imeni G. G. Iagodi trudkommuny NKVD*, ed. M. Gor'kii, K. Gorbunov, and M. Luzgin (Moscow: Istoriia fabrik i zavodov, 1936). The book circulated for less than a year.

17. *Liudi Stalingradskogo traktornogo*, ed. Ia. Il'in, L. Mekhlis, et al. (Moscow: Istoriia fabrik i zavodov, 1933). Aside from Averbakh and the NKVD officials mentioned in the *Belomorsko-Baltiiskii kanal imeni Stalina*, other enemies of the people appearing in the book included Postyshev, Koltsov, Kirshon, I. I. Makarov, V. Ya. Zazubrin, and G. K. Nikiforov. See Cynthia Ruder, *Making History for Stalin: The Story of the Belomor Canal* (Gainsville: University of Florida Press, 1998), 88–89, 207, 43.

18. The only book to emerge from the *Liudi vtoroi piatiletki* series focused on

concrete achievements rather than the individuals who contributed to them—a total reversal of the principles laid down by Gorky and Averbakh. See *Tvorchestvo narodov SSSR*, ed. M. Gor'kii and L. Mekhlis (Moscow: Pravda, 1937); TsGA, f. 9618, op. 1, d. 418, ll. 1–13, 121–142.

19. GARF, f. 7952, op. 1, d. 24, l. 74; d. 229, ll. 34–40, cited in Zhuravlev, *Fenomen "Istorii fabrik i zavodov,"* 76–77 and n. 140.

20. Man'kovskaia and Shaparov, "Kul't lichnosti i istoriko-partiinaia nauka," 66–68.

21. *Kratkii kurs istorii SSSR*, ed. A. V. Shestakov (Moscow: Gos. uchebno-pedagog. izd-vo, 1937), 157.

22. S. E. Rabinovich, *Istoriia grazhdanskoi voiny (kratkii ocherk): uchebnoe posobie dlia voennykh shkol RKKA*, 2nd ed. (Moscow: Partiinoe izdatel'stvo, 1935); L. A. Kassil', *Parad na Krasnoi ploshchadi* (Moscow: Detizdat, 1937).

23. *Raboche-krest'ianskaia krasnaia armiia*, ed. F. E. Rodionov, des. El Lisitskii (Moscow: Krasnaia zvezda, 1934); *Khudozhestvennaia vystavka 15 let RKKA: zhivopis', grafika, skul'ptura, tekstil', dekorativnoe iskusstvo, iskusstvo palekha i mstery* (Moscow: Vsekhudozhnik, 1933).

24. On the *Political Grammar*, see B. Volin and S. Ingulov, *Politgramota*, 2nd ed. (Moscow: Partizdat, 1937), 169–173. The second edition of Ingulov's *Politbesedy* likewise erred in mentioning party and military leaders who were disgraced between mid-1937 and 1938 such as V. Ya. Kosior, Chubar, Postyshev, Rudzutak, R. I. Eikhe, Yezhov, Kosarev, Stetsky, Gamarnik, A. I. Krinitsky, Antipov, Yegorov, Bliukher, Petrovsky, A. G. Cherviakov, G. M. Musabekov, F. G. Khodzhaev, N. Aitakov, and A. R. Rakhimbaev. See Ingulov, *Politbesedy*, 2nd ed. (Moscow: Partizdat, 1937), 205–209, 107, 95–99. Still anther well-known 1937 textbook had to be reissued after Ingulov's arrest: *Nasha rodina*, ed. A. Stetskii, S. Ingulov, and N. Baranskii (Moscow: Partizdat, 1937).

On Shestakov's history text, see *Kratkii kurs istorii SSSR*, 151, 177–178, 181–182, 188, 199. A copy of the textbook in the author's personal collection that circulated in Vologda in the late 1930s reveals both blackened-out names and newspaper clippings glued over the portraits of the unfortunates. Memoirists report similar phenomena from Moscow to the Caucasus—see Nadezhda Mandel'shtam, *Vospominaniia* (New York: Izd-vo im. Chekhova, 1970), 366; Nina Nar, "The Campaign against Illiteracy and Semi-Illiteracy in the Ukraine, Transcaucasus, and Northern Caucasus, 1922–1941," in *Soviet Education*, ed. George Kline (London: Routledge and Paul, 1957), 149. The Shestakov text was reissued without the offending text and illustrations in 1941.

25. See Kotkin, *Magnetic Mountain: Stalinism as a Civilization*, 583–584; RGVA, f. 9, op. 39, d. 79, l. 1.

26. Twenty-six were recast as traitors or stricken from the narrative entirely: Bubnov, Bukharin, Kosior, Piatakov, Piatnitsky, Rykov, Ya. A. Berzin, A. A. Bitsenko, G. I. Boky, M. P. Bronsky, N. P. Briukhanov, Yu. P. Gaven, P. F. Kodetsky, A. L. Kolegaev, N. N. Krestinsky, G. I. Lomov (Oppokov), Miliutin, N. Osinsky (V. V. Obolensky), A. N. Paderin, Ya. Ya. Peche, N. A. Pozharov, F. F. Raskolnikov, I. T. Smigla, G. Ya. Sokolnikov, G. F. Fedorov, and K. K. Yurenev. Compare the 1935 and 1938 editions of *Istoriia grazhdanskoi voiny v SSSR*, vol. 1,

Podgotovka Velikoi proletarskoi revoliutsii (ot nachala voiny do nachala Oktiabria 1917 g.).

27. "Zamechatel'nye dokumenty bol'shevizma," *Pravda*, November 21, 1937, 5.

28. Glavlit was originally subordinate to the Commissariat of Education; in 1933, it became an autonomous agency under Sovnarkom.

29. Few of the bulletins have survived—see, for instance, RGVA, f. 9, op. 35s, d. 92, ll. 37, 83; RGASPI, f. 82, op. 1, d. 991, ll. 1–67.

30. HPSSS, no. 306, schedule A, vol. 31, 5–6.

31. For an example of a librarian arrested for insufficient vigilance, see HPSSS, no. 1241, schedule A, vol. 32, 20–21.

32. See, for example, RGVA, f. 9, op. 35s, d. 92, ll. 103–107.

33. GARF, f. 5446, op. 22a, d. 29, ll. 12–18. The author is grateful for M. V. Zelenov's aid in analyzing this crisis. See also *Istoriia politicheskoi tsenzury: dokumenty i kommentarii*, ed. T. M. Goriaeva (Moscow: Rosspen, 1997), 72–75.

34. See the Orgburo resolution of December 9, 1937 "O likvidatsii vreditel'skoi sistemy iz"iatiia Glavlitom literatury," RGASPI, f. 17, op. 114, d. 834, l. 1. On Ingulov's fall, see d. 635, l. 55; GARF, f. 9425, op. 1, d. 5, l. 9. The author is grateful to M. V. Zelenov for his analysis of this crisis. See also APRF, f. 3, op. 34, d. 37, ll. 81–86, published in *Istoriia politicheskoi tsenzury: dokumenty i kommentarii*, 72–75.

35. See RGVA, f. 9, op. 35s, d. 92; op. 32s, d. 90.

36. Compare, for instance, the membership of the Bolshevik military organization in early 1917 as listed in the September 1936 and August 1937 printings of Em. Iaroslavskii, *Ocherki po istorii VKP(b)*, 2 vols. (Moscow: Partizdat, 1936, 1937), 1: 376 versus 1: 306.

37. Compare, for instance, the list of party members assisting Stalin during the 1917 revolution as listed in August 1937 and January 1938 printings of Iaroslavskii, *Ocherki po istorii VKP(b)*, 1: 335 versus 1: 323.

38. Yaroslavsky reports being asked repeatedly about new textbooks whenever he gave public talks during these years—see RGASPI, f. 89, op. 8, d. 807, l. 4.

39. See "Materialy fevral'sko-martovskogo plenuma TsK VKP(b) 1937 g.," *Voprosy istorii* 3 (1995): 11; Stalin, "O nedostatkakh partiinoi raboty," 2–4.

40. "Materialy fevral'sko-martovskogo plenuma TsK VKP(b) 1937 g.," *Voprosy istorii* 10 (1994): 13; *Voprosy istorii* 3 (1995): 14–15; Orgburo resolution of March 25, 1937 "O vypolnenii resheniia Plenuma TsK ob organizatsii partiinykh kursov, leninskikh kursov i kursov po istorii i politike partii," RGASPI, f. 17, op. 114, d. 800, l. 1. According to Stalin's proposal, the commission charged with overseeing the organization of these courses was to be chaired by Andreev and include Zhdanov, Stetsky, Yezhov, Gamarnik, Khrushchev, G. M. Malenkov, and Ya. A. Yakovlev.

41. RGASPI, f. 558, op. 11, d. 1219, ll. 1–6. The manuscript itself does not appear to have survived.

42. Draft Politburo resolution "Ob uchebnike istorii VKP(b)," RGASPI, f. 17, op. 163, d. 1144, ll. 1–50b.

43. At the Politburo meeting, the commission in charge of organizing the new party courses was reassigned to Zhdanov and expanded to include Stetsky, Yezhov,

Gamarnik, Khrushchev, Malenkov, Yakovlev, Akulov, Tal, Popov, Yaroslavsky, Knorin, Pospelov, Rubinstein, Mekhlis, and Ugarov. See Politburo resolution of April 16, 1937 "Ob organizatsii kursov usovershenstvovaniia dlia partkadrov, soglasno rezoliutsii poslednego plenuma TsK po punktu 4 poriadka dnia plenuma," RGASPI, f. 17, op. 114, d. 800, l. 2. Curiously, the only detailed material on the "Party" and "Leninist" courses is stored at RGVA. This file was apparently left behind after the suicide of its addressee—Gamarnik—on the eve of his arrest in late May 1937. Duplicate copies that should be at RGASPI apparently disappeared along with the Agitprop archives from the 1930s. See RGVA, f. 9, op. 29s, d. 323, ll. 110–119; RGASPI, f. 17, op. 3, d. 989, l. 16.

44. Politburo resolution of April 16, 1937 "Ob uchebnike po istorii VKP(b)," RGASPI, f. 17, op. 163, d. 1144, l. 5-50b; f. 558, op. 1, d. 3212, l. 27. It was published as "K izucheniiu istorii VKP(b)," *Pravda,* May 6, 1937, 4. Many of these provisions were developed further in Politburo resolution of May 11, 1937 "Ob organizatsii partiinykh kursov," f. 17, op. 114, d. 840, ll. 46–48.

45. Yaroslavsky signaled his frustration with Stetsky's critique of his *Kratkaia istoriia* in marginalia written on the typescript—see RGASPI, f. 558, op. 11, d. 1219, ll. 1–6. On *Ocherki po istorii VKP(b),* see n. 10 above.

46. V. Knorin, "K voprosu ob izuchenii istorii VKP(b)," *Bol'shevik* 9 (1937): 1–6; reprinted in *Propagandist* 10 (1937): 11–18; etc. Both Yaroslavsky and Knorin were to complete revisions to their older texts by July 1, 1937—see Politburo resolution of May 11, 1937 "Ob organizatsii partiinykh kursov," RGASPI, f. 17, op. 114, d. 840, ll. 46–48.

47. RGASPI, f. 629, op. 1, d. 10, ll. 21–97.

48. A. Litvin, *Bez prava na mysl': Istoriki v epokhu Bol'shogo Terrora—ocherki sudeb* (Kazan': Tatarskoe knizhnoe izd-vo, 1994), 20–21; A. N. Artizov, "Sud'by istorikov shkoly M. N. Pokrovskogo (seredina 1930-kh godov)," *Voprosy istorii* 7 (1994): 34–48; "1937 god: Institut Krasnoi professury (Stenograficheskii otchet 5–6 maia, 1937)," *Otechestvennaia istoriia* 2 (1992): 119–46. See also Peter Konecny, *Builders and Deserters: Students, State, and Community in Leningrad, 1917–1941* (Montreal: McGill University Press, 1999), 129–136.

49. RGASPI, f. 71, op. 1, d. 10, ll. 22–26.

50. See diary entry from November 7, 1937 in Georgi Dimitrov, *Dnevnik (9 Mart 1933–6 Fevuari 1949)* (Sofia: Universitetsko izdatelstvo "Sv. Kliment Okhridski," 1997), 128. Knorin was arrested on June 22, 1937; his deputies, Anderson and P. Ya. Viskne, met the same fate days later.

51. A Politburo resolution passed days after Knorin's arrest reassigned responsibility for the flagship textbook to Yaroslavsky and Pospelov. See Politburo resolution of June 28, 1937 "Ob uchebnikakh dlia leninskikh kursov," RGASPI, f. 17, op. 114, d. 840, l. 49.

52. Adoratsky to Andreev (November 28, 1937), RGASPI, f. 71, op. 3, d. 98, l. 232.

53. Yaroslavsky to Stalin (July 1, 1937), RGASPI, f. 558, op. 1, d. 1203, l. 1; Yaroslavsky's typescript is at op. 11, d. 1203–1208; the galleys are at op. 3, d. 381.

54. RGASPI, f. 558, op. 11, d. 1219, ll. 21, 22–35. Yaroslavsky's marginalia responding to this critique are at ll. 8–20.

55. Knorin's arrest also doomed an entire issue of *Proletarskaia revoliutsiia,* due to his involvement in its editing. See RGASPI, f. 71, op. 3, d. 98, l. 232.

56. Pospelov mentions this recommendation in an undated letter to Yaroslavsky and Stetsky that was written during late 1937—see RGASPI, f. 629, op. 1, d. 64, l. 73. The new chapter titles, authors, and projected lengths are at l. 78; new outlines to the introduction and several chapters are at ll. 74–77, 79–84.

57. RGASPI, f. 89, op. 8, d. 807, ll. 2–3. The speech was given in connection with Stalin's jubilee on December 21, 1939. An accompanying note from the Higher Party School reveals plans to publish the speech; the fact that it never appeared suggests that the party hierarchy was reluctant to publicize the *Short Course*'s chaotic evolution.

58. On Pospelov's editing of Yaroslavsky's manuscript, see Yaroslavsky to Pospelov (September 13 and 19, 1937), f. 629, op. 1, d. 5, ll. 5–6.

59. On the purges' chilling effects on arctic exploration, see John McCannon, *Red Arctic: Polar Exploration and the Myth of the North in the Soviet Union, 1932–1939* (Oxford: Oxford University Press, 1998), 149–168.

60. Scott Palmer, *Dictatorship of the Air: Aviation Culture and the Fate of Modern Russia* (New York: Cambridge University Press, 2006), 248–251.

61. RGASPI, f. 17, op. 3, d. 976, ll. 24–25. The playwrights were Tolstoy, Korneichuk, Afinogenov, Kirshon, Ivanov, Vishnevsky, Mikitenko, K. A. Trenev, and S. N. Dadiani. The directors and screenwriters were Pogodin, the Vasiliev brothers, Kapler, Dovzhenko, P. A. Pavlenko, A. G. Rzheshevsky, L. I. Slavin, M. Ye. Chiaureli, and V. Lavrenev. See op. 163, d. 1101, ll. 65–66; f. 82, op. 2, d. 959, ll. 58–60.

62. RGALI, f. 962, op. 3, d. 293, ll. 11–12, 5–6; RGASPI, f. 82, op. 2, d. 959, ll. 58–60.

63. *Lenin v Oktiabre,* dir. M. Romm (Mosfil'm, 1937). On the film, see Maia Turovskaia, "Mosfil'm—1937," in *Sovetskoe bogatstvo: stat'i o kul'ture, literature i kino: k shestidesiatiletiiu Khansa Giuntera,* ed. Mariia Balina, Evgenii Dobrenko, and Iurii Murashov (St. Petersburg: Akademicheskii proekt, 2002), 277–294. Chiaureli's *Velikoe zarevo* was the runner-up.

64. Karen Petrone, *Life Has Become More Joyous, Comrades: Celebrations in the Time of Stalin* (Bloomington: Indiana University Press, 2000), 163–164.

65. A. Davidiuk, "Volnuiushchaia kartina," *Pravda,* December 14, 1937, 4; B. Agapov, "Dragotsennyi obraz," *Izvestiia,* December 16, 1937, 4.

66. Although audiences were struck by any depiction of Lenin and Stalin on the screen, many found these disappointing. For evidence of the audience's critical reaction to the film—"Why was Lenin's speech at the Petrograd Soviet so short?" "Why is Stalin silent?" "Why does Stalin speak without an accent?"—see RGALI, f. 1966, op. 1, d. 268, ll. 46, 20b, 47; TsGAIPD SPb, f. 24, op. 8, d. 555, ll. 143,147, 226; d. 560, l. 45. Newspaper coverage may have elevated popular expectations for the film—see "'Lenin v Oktiabre': Blestiashchee dostizhenie sovetskogo kinoiskusstva," *Izvestiia,* November 5, 1937, 4; "Ogromnyi uspekh fil'ma 'Lenin v Oktiabre,'" *Izvestiia,* December 12, 1937, 4; "Fil'm 'Lenin v Oktiabre' v Leningrade," *Izvestiia,* December 13, 1937, 4. Generally, on the depiction of Lenin and Stalin in film between 1927 and 1953, see Nina Chernova, "'My govorim—partiia, podrazumevaem . . . ': Uskol'zaiushchii obraz stalinskogo kinematografa," *Svobodnaia mysl'* 12 (2005): 160–174.

67. See Politburo resolution of August 25, 1935, "O rabote Instituta Marksa-Engel'sa-Lenina," RGASPI, f. 558, op. 11, d. 1279, ll. 15–17; f. 71, op. 1, d. 9, ll. 3, 8, 10, 18.

68. On the text's popularity, see "Liubimye avtory magnitogortsev," *Magnitogorskii rabochii*, September 1, 1936, 4.

69. Barbius, *Stalin*, x, 17–19, 29, 20, 38, 66, 78, 102, 131, 186, 216–218, 222, 252, 260, 291, 346.

70. Beria's and Voroshilov's first and second editions had been removed from circulation on account of their mention of enemies; only the third editions would weather the purges.

71. Dimitrov's proposed series was apparently patterned after the "Lives of Remarkable People" series that Gorky had revived in 1929–1931. See Dimitrov to Tal (December 21, 1936), RGASPI, f. 17, op. 120, d. 258, ll. 28–30.

72. RGASPI, f. 71, op. 1, d. 9, ll. 3, 8, 10, 18; d. 10, l. 31; op. 4, d. 113, l. 36; op. 3, d. 98, ll. 245, 247; d. 117, l. 188. The ailing Saveliev finally managed to hand in his biography in 1939 after the end of the Terror and just weeks before he himself died. It was never published—see op. 10, d. 257, ll. 6–161.

73. RGASPI, f. 71, op. 1, d. 10, l. 45.

74. RGASPI, f. 558, op. 1, d. 3218, ll. 1–4, published in P. N. Pospelov, "Piat'desiat let Kommunisticheskoi partii Sovetskogo Soiuza," *Voprosy istorii* 11 (1953): 21. See also TsKhDMO, f. 1, op. 23, d. 1304, ll. 57–58; d. 1251, l. 126. On the rejection of another book on Stalin's childhood, see the documents surrounding A. M. Kurlina's *Detskie, iunosheskie gody i nachalo revoliutsionnoi deiatel'nosti I. V. Stalina, 1879–1904 gg.* at RGASPI, f. 17, op. 132, d. 471, ll. 44–82.

75. See Iu. Polevoi, "Chto chitat' o zhizni i deiatel'nosti tovarishcha Stalina," in *K shestidesiatiletiiu so dnia rozhdeniia Iosifa Vissarionovicha Stalina (V pomoshch' agitatoram)* (Ulan Ude: n.p., 1939), 36–67. Exceptions include *Stalin i Khashim (1901–1902 gody)* (Sukhumi: n.p., 1934); *Rasskazy starykh rabochikh Zakavkaz'ia o velikom Staline* (Moscow: Partizdat, 1937); *Batumskaia demonstratsiia 1902 goda* (Moscow: Partizdat, 1937).

76. For examples of the traditional view of the purges as crippling the Red Army, see Dmitri Volkogonov, *Stalin: Triumph and Tragedy* (London: Weidenfeld and Nicolson, 1991), 345, 364–371; Vojtech Mastny, *The Cold War and Soviet Insecurity: The Stalin Years* (Oxford: Oxford University Press, 1996), 14, 157. For skepticism over the terror's exclusive responsibility for Soviet military weakness, see Roger Reese, *Stalin's Reluctant Soldiers: A Social History of the Red Army, 1925–1941* (Lawrence: University Press of Kansas, 1996), 132–162; Reese, *The Soviet Military Experience* (New York: Routledge, 2000), 85–92.

77. R. W. Davies writes of economic disruption caused by the purges in the military-industrial complex, state statistics, the state bank, and economic planning. See R. W. Davies, "Industry," and Davies and S. G. Wheatcroft, "The Crooked Mirror of Soviet Economic Statistics," in *The Economic Transformation of the Soviet Union, 1913–1945*, ed. R. W. Davies, Mark Harrison, and S. G. Wheatcroft (Cambridge: Cambridge University Press, 1994), 147, 157, 29; Davies, "Making Economic Policy," in *Behind the Facade of Stalin's Command Economy: Evidence from the Soviet State and Party Archives*, ed. Paul Gregory (Stanford: Hoover Institution Press, 2001), 75–77. Jonathan Halsam's discussion of similar paralysis in the diplo-

matic corps is matched by Volkogonov's treatment of the Comintern—Jonathan Haslam, *The Soviet Union and the Struggle for Collective Security in Europe, 1933–1939* (New York: St. Martin's, 1984), chaps. 8, 10; Volkogonov, *Stalin: Triumph and Tragedy,* 345–346.

CHAPTER 8. MASS CULTURE IN A TIME OF TERROR

1. See, for instance, "Kul'tura sotsializma," *Oktiabr'* 11 (1935): 1–6.

2. RGALI, f. 631, op. 15, d. 223, l. 7, cited in Karen Petrone, *Life Has Become More Joyous, Comrades: Celebrations in the Time of Stalin* (Bloomington: Indiana University Press, 2000), 169.

3. See HPSSS, no. 179, schedule A, vol. 13, 67; no. 308/1123, schedule A, vol. 32, 21; no. 67, schedule B, vol. 7, 34; no. 308/1123, schedule A, vol. 32, 21; no. 495, schedule B, vol. 9, 33.

4. RGALI, f. 631, op. 2, d. 155, ll. 46–56.

5. RGALI, f. 631, op. 2, d. 177, ll. 32, 37, 46. On this atmosphere of dread, see also Petrone, *Life Has Become More Joyous, Comrades,* esp. 169.

6. See E. Kostrova, "Srok istekaet segodnia," *Literaturnaia gazeta,* May 15, 1937, 5. Few of the plays Boiarsky listed—Virta's *Zemlia,* Amaglobeli's *Master schast'ia,* Bill-Belotserkovsky's *Granitsa,* Vashentsev's *Nashi dni,* Kaverin's *Beleet parus odinokii,* Nikitin's *Baku,* Kataev's *Aktery,* Nikulin's *Port Artur,* or Yanovsky's *Duma o Britanke*—ever appeared on the stage.

7. Rumor held that Mikitenko's *Kogda vskhodilo solntse* not only valorized Gamarnik, but also juxtaposed Lenin against Stalin. See RGALI, f. 962, op. 3, d. 293, l. 4.

8. On Amaglobeli's arrest, see RGALI, f. 231, op. 15, d. 349, l. 65.

9. "Iubileinye p'esy v moskovskikh teatrakh," *Literaturnaia gazeta,* November 10, 1937, 6. I. V. Chekin's *Vecher v sentiabre* and L. N. Rakhmanov's *Bespokoinaia starost' (Professor Polezhaev)* were also staged, as was the Georgian version of Dadiani's *Iz iskry.* On the latter, see A. Andronikashvilli, "Obraz molodogo vozhdia," *Teatr* 11–12 (1939): 76.

10. RGASPI, f. 17, op. 120, d. 256, ll. 161–163. The internal critique contradicted initial reviews in the press, which waxed rhapsodic over the piece. See B. Belogorskii and D. Kal'm, "Chelovek s ruzh'em," *Izvestiia,* November 14, 1937, 4; A. Gurvich, "Zamechatel'nyi spektakl," *Literaturnaia gazeta,* November 26, 1937, 5.

11. Stalin described *Chudak* as a "remarkable" and "necessary" play—see Afinogenov to A. I. Goloshchanova (December 7, 1929), RGALI, f. 2172, op. 2, d. 49, l. 2.

12. Both Stalin and Gorky took a strong dislike to *Lozh',* the latter writing to the author that "a Bolshevik is interesting not for his faults, but for his virtues." Stalin or members of his entourage called for the closure of *Saliut, Ispaniia!* after attending a performance in late 1936. See Gorky to Afinogenov ([April 1933]), in *Literaturnoe nasledstvo,* vol. 17, *Gor'kii i sovetskie pisateli: neizdannaia perepiska* (Moscow: Izd-vo Akademii nauk, 1963), 31–34; diary entries from November 29 and December 12, 1936 at RGALI, f. 2172, op. 1, d. 119, ll. 256, 264.

13. On the April 27, 1937 meeting and Afinogenov's fall, see "Na sobranii

moskovskikh dramaturgov," *Komsomol'skaia pravda,* April 29, 1937, 4; "Iz zasedaniia partgruppy Pravleniia SSP," *Literaturnaia gazeta,* May 20, 1937, 1; diary entry from May 20, 1937 in A. Afinogenov, "Dnevnik 1937 goda," *Sovetskaia dramaturgiia* 2 (1993): 224; Del'man, "Bor'ba s averbakhshchinoi," *Literaturnaia gazeta,* May 30, 1937, 5; RGALI, f. 962, op. 3, d. 293, l. 1.

14. On this refashioning process, see Jochen Hellbeck, "Writing the Self in the Time of Terror: Alexander Afinogenov's Diary of 1937," in *Self & Story in Russian History,* ed. Laura Engelstein and Stephanie Sandler (Ithaca: Cornell University Press, 2000), 69–93; Hellbeck, *Revolution on My Mind: Writing a Diary under Stalin* (Cambridge: Harvard University Press, 2006), 285–346.

15. Herman Ermolaev, *Censorship in Soviet Literature, 1917–1991* (Lanham: Rowman and Littlefield, 1997), 69–70.

16. N. E. Virta, *Odinochestvo* (Moscow: Goslitizdat, 1935)—see "Index librorum prohibitorum russkikh pisatelei 1917–1991," *Novoe literaturnoe obozrenie* (hereafter *NLO*) 53:1 (2002): 442–443.

17. A. S. Serafimovich, *Zheleznyi potok* (Moscow: VTsSPS)—see *NLO* 62:4 (2003): 542.

18. D. A. Furmanov, *Krasnyi desant* (Moscow: Detizdat, 1937), 24, 15, 22, 30; D. A. Furmanov, *Chapaev* (Moscow: Gosizdat, 1929), 126, 128—see *NLO* 62:4 (2003): 547.

19. E. G. Bagritskii, *Odnotomnik* (Moscow: Sovetskaia literatura, 1934), 248 —see *NLO* 53:1 (2002): 436; E. D. Zozulia, *Dva portreta* (Moscow: Zhurgazob"edinenie, 1932)—see *NLO* 56:4 (2002): 419–420; M. M. Zoshchenko, *Istoriia odnoi zhizni* (Leningrad: Izd-vo pisatelei v Leningrade, 1934)—see *NLO* 56:4 (2002): 420; L. A. Kassil', *Budenyshi* (Moscow: Detizdat, 1934), 7; *Parad na Krasnoi ploshchadi: al'bom* (Moscow: Detizdat, 1937)—see *NLO* 56:4 (2002): 423.

20. F. I. Panferov, *Bruski,* vols. 1, 3 (Moscow: Moskovskii rabochii, 1927; Goslitizdat, 1930, 1933, 1937)—see *NLO* 61:3 (2003): 424; K. G. Paustovskii, *Marshal Bliukher* (Moscow: Partizdat, 1938)—see "Index librorum prohibitorum russkikh pisatelei 1917–1991," *NLO* 61:3 (2003): 425; M. A. Svetlov, *Khleb: poema* (Moscow: Molodaia gvardiia, 1928)—see *NLO* 62:4 (2003): 540; K. I. Chukovskii, *Ot dvukh do piati* (Moscow: Detizdat, 1935, 1937)—see *NLO* 62:4 (2003): 550. Panferov sent a series of increasingly desperate letters to Stalin regarding *Bruski*'s problems with the censor—see RGASPI, f. 558, op. 11, d. 786, ll. 14–25.

21. F. V. Gladkov, *Energiia,* vol. 1 (Moscow: Sovetskaia literatura, 1933)—see *NLO* 53:1 (2002): 445.

22. *Stikhi i legendy Maksima Gor'kogo* (Moscow: Academia, 1932)—see *NLO* 53:1 (2002): 445–446.

23. See, for example, RGVA, f. 9, op. 35s, d. 92, ll. 103–107.

24. A major exception to this rule was a reprinting of the second and third editions of Lenin's *Sochineniia,* which were sent to press in 1938 after permission was secured from the party hierarchs to strip them of all mentions of enemies of the people. See RGASPI, f. 71, op. 3, d. 98, l. 239; d. 114, ll. 102–103; d. 117, ll. 165, 185–186, 191, 285–290.

25. Postwar interviews with Soviet refugees confirm the cultural profile of this

marginal film. See HPSSS, no. 61, schedule A, vol. 5, 37; no. 309, schedule A, vol. 16, 21; no. 148, schedule A, vol. 11, 45; no. 642/1109, schedule A, vol. 32, 38; no. 119, schedule A, vol. 9, 23; etc.

26. *Za Sovetskuiu rodinu* (sometimes referred to as *Za rodinu*), dir. R. Muzykant and Iu. Muzykant (Lenfil'm 1937); A. Sopodvizhnikov, "Fil'm o geroicheskom pokhode," *Pravda*, October 30, 1937, 6. See also G. S. Fish, *Padenie Kimas-ozera*, 4th ed. (Moscow: Sovetskii pisatel', 1935).

27. *Baltiitsy*, dir. A. M. Faintsimmer (Belgoskino, 1937); A. Levshin, "Baltiitsy," *Uchitel'skaia gazeta*, November 29, 1937, 4. See also M. Manuil'skii, "Geroicheskie dni," *Pravda*, November 20, 1937, 6; E. Kriger, "Baltiitsy," *Izvestiia*, December 25, 1937, 4; S. Gekht, "Vernyi skolok s prirody," *Literaturnaia gazeta*, January 27, 1938, 5.

28. *Volochaevskie dni*, dir. Vasil'ev brothers (Lenfil'm, 1937); E. Kriger, "Volochaevskie dni," *Izvestiia*, December 3, 1937, 4; E. Kriger, "O glavnom geroe," *Izvestiia*, December 12, 1937, 4; G. Voronov, "Volochaevskie dni," *Literaturnaia gazeta*, December 5, 1937, 4. Another in this genre of "defensist" films was the documentary *Neustrashimye*, dir. L. Antsy-Polovskii (Tekhfil'm, 1937)—see "Novyi fil'm 'Neustrashimye,'" *Izvestiia*, October 9, 1937, 4.

29. Brat. Vasil'evy, "Rozhdenie fil'ma," *Kino*, January 5, 1938, 2.

30. *Vozvrashenie Maksima*, dir. G. Kozintsev and L. Trauberg (Lenfil'm, 1937). This was the middle film of the trilogy between 1934's *Iunost' Maksima* and 1938's *Vyborgskaia storona*.

31. *Chelovek z ruzh'em*, dir. S. Iutkevich (Lenfil'm, 1938). A. G. Man'kov hated the film, especially its intimate portraits of Lenin and Stalin. See diary entry from November 29, 1938, in A. G. Man'kov, "Iz dnevnika, 1938–1941 gg.," *Zvezda* 11 (1995): 172–173. Generally, see N. Chernova, "'My govorim—partiia, podrazumevaem . . . ': uskol'zaiushchii obraz stalinskogo kinematografa," *Svobodnaia mysl'* 12 (2005): 160–174.

32. *Velikii grazhdanin*, dir. F. Ermler (Lenfil'm, 1937, 1939).

33. Stalin personally intervened in the editing of the screenplay to heighten the starkness of this standoff. His criticism of unrealistic details in the screenplay reveals that he regarded the film as more of a documentary than a work of fiction. See RGASPI, f. 71, op. 10, d. 127, ll. 188–189.

34. P. Gromov, "O khudozhestvennom metode fil'ma Ermlera 'Velikii grazhdanin,'" *Zvezda* 1 (1940): 168; Julie Cassiday, "Kirov and Death in *The Great Citizen*: The Fatal Consequences of Linguistic Mediation," *Slavic Review* 64:4 (2005): 800.

35. M. Kritsman, "Cherty novogo cheloveka v obrazakh kino," *Iskusstvo kino* 11 (1939): 18, 22; M. Mikhailov, "Velikii grazhdanin," *Sputnik agitatora* 6 (1938): 46; A. Milovidov, "Velikii grazhdanin," *Pravda*, February 17, 1938, 6.

36. Ermler's term was "razgovornyi kinematograf"—see M. Bleiman, M. Bol'shintsov, and F. Ermler, "Rabota nad stsenariem," *Iskusstvo kino* 4–5 (1938): 30. For analyses of the implications of this genre, see Cassiday, "Kirov and Death in *The Great Citizen*," 799–822; Oksana Bulgakova, "Sovetskoe kino v poiskakh 'obshchei modeli,'" in *Sotsrealisticheskii kanon*, ed. Hans Günther and Evgenii Dobrenko (St. Petersburg: Akademicheskii proekt, 2000), 146–165.

37. Screenwriter N. S. Tikhonov and director Arnshtam harnessed Kirov's reputation in a similar way to add weight to their protagonist "Comrade Aleksei," a Bolshevik revolutionary who unites the diverse peoples of the Caucasus around the cause in *Druz'ia,* dir. L. O. Arnshtam (Lenfil'm, 1938)—see "Kinopovest' o druzhbe narodov," *Izvestiia,* February 27, 1938, 4.

38. On the film's reception, see TsGALI SPb, f. 166, op. 1, dd. 338, 380–383; and a collection of articles entitled "Velikii grazhdanin: zritel' o novoi kartine" (*Vecherniaia Moskva,* March 2, 1938, 3). There, K. I. Bubenkov refers to Shakhov as the quintessential role model while O. G. Barshak predicts that the film will help "our youth and the breadth of the working class and peasant masses, as well as our propagandists and agitators, tell the story of the party's struggle with the cursed enemies of our socialist motherland." According to A. Danilov, the film "will serve as a visual aid for the study of party history."

39. For more on the purges' hamstringing of *Shchors,* see George Liber, *Alexander Dovzhenko: A Life in Soviet Film* (London: British Film Institute, 2002), chap. 7; Paul Babitsky and Martin Lutich, *The Soviet Movie Industry: Two Case Studies,* no. 31, *Research Program on the USSR Mimeograph Series* (New York: Praeger, 1953), 62, 27, 7; Paul Babitsky and John Rimberg, *The Soviet Film Industry* (New York: Praeger, 1955), 161.

40. Even before the purges, issues associated with party history held up dozens of film projects. According to one source, only 15 percent of the 102 films scheduled to be completed by November 1, 1936 were delivered. RSFSR studios fulfilled about 22 percent of their orders, while studios in Belorussia, Ukraine, and Georgia completed between 14 and 20 percent. Studios in Azerbaidzhan, Armenia, and Central Asia failed to release a single film. See "Kak realizuetsia plan vypuska fil'mov," *Iskusstvo kino* 11 (1936): 36–40. In their memoirs, two Soviet film industry insiders illustrate even more clearly the difficulty of shooting films with contemporary subject matter. Despite party directives that called for the majority of films shot in 1935 to concern the Soviet present, 75 percent ended up focusing on historical subjects because of difficulties encountered with contemporary themes. See Babitsky and Lutich, *The Soviet Movie Industry,* 51–52 (referring to D. Nikol'skii, "Siuzhety 1936 goda," *Iskusstvo kino* 5 [1936]: 21–26).

41. On the film, see A. Ivanov, *Ekran sud'by* (Moscow: Iskusstvo, 1971), 278–9; diary entry from May 10, 1935, in *"Iz pamiati vyplyli vospominaniia . . .": Dnevnikovye zapisi, putevye zametki, memuary Akademika AN SSSR I. I. Mintsa,* ed. V. L. Telytsin (Moscow: Sobranie, 2007), 9–10; TsGALI, f. 257, op. 16, d. 605, ll. 99–101. For mention of enemies in the screenplay, see ll. 33, 13–16, 73, 97.

42. Dzigan's film was deemed "thematically inexpedient" in 1941—see Nina Chernova and Vasilii Tokarev, "'Pervaia konnaia': kinematograficheskii reid v zavben'e—istoricheskii komentarii k kinoprotsessu, 1938–1941 gg." *Kinovedcheskie zapiski* 65 (2003): 280–313. For Voroshilov's and Budennyi's criticism and Stalin's line-editing of Vishnevsky's screenplay, see RGASPI, f. 558, op. 11, d. 165.

43. Diary entry from October 9, 1940 in Vs. Ivanov, *Perepiska s A. M. Gor'kim: iz dnevnikov i zapisnykh knizhek* (Moscow: Sovetskii pisatel', 1985), 315. See also *Aleksandr Parkhomenko,* dir. L. Lukov (Kiev film studios, 1942).

44. "Novaia istoriko-revoliutsionnaia kartina," *Kino,* January 11, 1940, 1; *Razgrom Iudenicha,* dir. P. Petrov-Bytov (Lenfil'm, 1941).

45. "V. I. Lenin," dir. Ia. Posel'skii (TsSDF, 1935); RGASPI, f. 17, op. 120, d. 257, ll. 73–74. For Stalin's endorsement, see f. 558, op. 11, d. 828, ll. 110–111.

46. RGALI, f. 2456, op. 4, d. 42, l. 65; d. 40, l. 39. The Glavlit orders for the removal of these films from domestic circulation do not seem to have survived, but they were subsequently banned from foreign distribution as well: RGASPI, f. 17, op. 120, d. 349, ll. 18–22; see also f. 82, op. 2, d. 959, ll. 8, 52–54. In the case of *Shakhtery,* the concern was that the protagonist, Primak, might be confused with the recently purged Primakov. See f. 17, op. 120, d. 256, l. 149.

47. *Tri pesni o Lenine* was rereleased in 1938 after editing out shots of enemies and adding new material, including a long speech by Stalin. See John MacKay, "Allegory and Accommodation: Vertov's *Three Songs of Lenin* (1934) as a Stalinist Film," *Film History* 18 (2006): esp. 378, n. 22; RGALI, f. 2091, op. 1, d. 48, ll. 24–28, 10, 16; f. 2456, op. 4, d. 42, ll. 7–70b, 14, 66; RGASPI, f. 17, op. 120, d. 349, ll. 18–25. On the film's rerelease, see "'Tri pes'ni o Lenine'—novyi vypusk fil'ma," *Kino,* January 22, 1938, 1.

48. In Vertov's *Lullaby (Kolybel'naia),* footage shot at the All-Union Conference of Red Army Commander and Command Staff Wives was partially blackened out in order to remove Gamarnik from view. He is clearly visible beside Stalin in a photograph from this conference published in *Izvestia* on December 23, 1936. For later editing of this film that removed images of Yezhov and G. M. Viatkin, see A. S. Deriabin, "*Kolybel'naia* Dzigi Vertova: zamysl—voploshchenie—ekrannaia sud'ba," *Kinovedcheskie zapiski* 51 (2001): 41–42. The author is grateful to John MacKay for his insights into Vertov's ordeal with the censor in 1936–1938.

49. See *Doklad I. V. Stalina o proekte konstitutsii SSSR* (n.s., 1936); *Rech' I. V. Stalina na predvybornom sobranii Stalinskogo izbiratel'nogo okruga* (n.s., 1937); *Na Severnom poliuse,* dir. I. Venzher and M. Troianovskii (Mos. studiia Kinokhroniki, 1937); *Papanintsy* (TsSDF, 1938); *Stalinskoe plemia* (Soiuzkinokhronika, 1937); *Strana sovetov,* dir. E. Shub (Mosfil'm, 1937); *Moskva-Volga,* dir. R. Gikov (Soiuzkinokhronika, 1937). For examples of the censorial instructions, See RGASPI, f. 17, op. 120, d. 257, l. 126; d. 349, ll. 18–22; f. 82, op. 2, d. 959, l. 75; RGALI, f. 2456, op. 4, d. 43, ll. 2–12.

50. *Geroi Arktiki (Cheliuskin),* dir. Ia. M. Posel'skii (TsSDF, 1934). See RGASPI, f. 82, op. 2, d. 959, ll. 52–54.

51. See *Sovkinozhurnal; Sotsialisticheskaia derevnia; SSSR na ekrane; Pobednyi marsh sotsializma; Na strazhe SSSR;* and *1-oe Maia v Moskve,* dir. Ia. Posel'skii (Soiuzkinokhronika, 1934); *Bor'ba za Kiev,* dir. L. Antsi-Polovskii (Soiuzdetfil'm, 1935), *Kavaleristy,* dir. V. Baikov (Soiuzkinokhronika, 1935); *Zamechatel'nyi god,* dir. N. Solov'ev (Soiuzkinokhronika, 1936); *Sergo liubimyi,* dir. A. Litvin (Soiuzkinokhroniki, 1937); *Bogatyri rodiny,* dir. L. Verlamov and F. Kiselev (Soiuzkinokhronika, 1937); *Prazdnik stalinskikh sokolov,* dir. R. Gikov (Mos. studiia kinokhroniki, 1938). On the censor's instructions, see, for example, RGALI, f. 2456, op. 4, d. 42, ll. 24, 35, 83; TsGAIPD SPb, f. 24, op. 8, d. 497, l. 42.

52. Instead, film studios appear to have focused on orders to identify, sequester, and destroy stock footage of enemies of the people in their archives—see RGALI, f. 2456, op. 4, d. 42, ll. 1–12, 14, 19, 28–34, 92.

53. On the purges' effect on the Red Army Museum, see Justus Hartzok, "Children of Chapaev: The Russian Civil War Cult and the Creation of Soviet Identity, 1918–1941" (Ph.D. Diss., University of Iowa, 2009), 253–264.

54. Although the Red Army exhibit was supposedly in dialogue with previous shows in 1928 and 1933, it displayed portraits of political leaders far more frequently than military leaders. In general, most of the 400 works of art displayed depicted anonymous members of the rank-and-file, rather than identifiable heroes. See A. Iumashev, "V otkrytii vystavki," *Izvestiia*, March 8, 1938, 3; E. Kriger, "Sekret uspekha," *Izvestiia*, May 5, 1938, 3; G. Savitskii, "Zametki o vystavke," *Izvestiia*, May 5, 1938, 3; "Khudozhestvennaia vystavka 20 let RKKA," *Izvestiia*, January 22, 1938, 3; E. Melikadze, "Vystavka 'XX let RKKA i VMF,'" *Novyi mir* 6 (1938): 270–279. The exhibit was well attended, drawing 2,000 people a day in search of the heroic and patriotic; ultimately, 265,000 saw the exhibition in 1938. "Na vystavke 'XX let RKKA i Voenno-Morskogo Flota,'" *Izvestiia*, May 10, 1938, 4; "265,000 posetitelei vystavki 'XX let RKKA i Voennomu Morskomu Flotu," *Sovetskoe iskusstvo*, December 5, 1938, 6.

On the industry exhibition, see *Vsesoiuznaia khudozhestvennaia vystavka "Industriia sotsializma": putevoditel'* (Moscow: Industriia sotsializma, 1939); Susan Reid, "Socialist Realism in the Stalinist Terror: The Industry of Socialism Art Exhibition, 1935–41," *Russian Review* 60:2 (2001): 68–69; E. Bekreeva, "Problemy sovetskoi zhivopisi v khudozhestvennoi kritike 30-kh godov" (Candidate's diss., Moscow State University, 1989), 129.

55. Well-known victims of the Terror are the Latvian-born G. G. Klutsis, P. Irbit, and V. Yakub.

56. Jan Plamper, "The Stalin Cult in the Visual Arts, 1929–1953" (Ph.D. diss., University of California at Berkeley, 2001), 1–2.

57. Ivanov, *Ekran sud'by*, 263; Reid, "Socialist Realism during the Stalinist Terror," 168; Bekreeva, "Problemy sovetskoi zhivopisi v kudozhestvennoi kritike 30-kh godov," 129; Matthew Cullerne Brown, "Aleksandr Gerasimov," in *Art of the Soviets: Painting, Sculpture, and Architecture in a One-Party State, 1917–1992*, ed. Matthew Cullerne Brown and Brandon Taylor (New York: St. Martin's, 1993), 131. See also A. Gerasimov, "Gruppovoi portret komandirov tiazheloi promyshlennosti," *Pravda*, October 21, 1936, 4.

58. HPSSS, no. 328/1745, schedule A, vol. 37, 47.

59. *XX let RKKA i VMF v politicheskom plakate i massovoi kartine: putevoditel'*, ed. N. Strugatskii (Leningrad: GPB, 1938), 7.

60. Visitors even left commentary to this effect in the comment book of a Tret"iakov Gallery exhibition of nineteenth-century Russian historical art. Students from Voronezh, for instance, wrote: "those on the tour would have liked to see pictures depicting the heroic work of the Soviet people of our day. This isn't displayed on the gallery walls at present. Wouldn't it be valuable to depict the life and struggle of the Red Army at Lake Khasan, the Stakhanovite movement . . . ?" A group from the Moscow Aviation Institute left a similar note, complaining about the poor coverage that the "revolutionary movement of the toilers" received at the exhibition. See OR GTG, f. 8.II, d. 995, 1l. 30, 1.

61. The best-known example is V. P. Efanov, who employed a brigade of artists in the creation of "The Notable People from the Country of Soviets," an enormous

panorama for the Soviet pavilion at the New York World's Fair. It depicted some 60 Soviet notables including flyers such as Chkalov, Yumashev, Gromov, Osipenko, Grizodubova, Raskova, Kokkinaki; polar explorers such as Shmidt and Papanin; Stakhanovites such as Stakhanov, Krivonos, the Vinogradova sisters; the bard Dzhambul; the musicians I. M. Moskvin, V. I. Nemirovich-Danchenko, and A. K. Tarasova; the writer Tolstoy, and so on. According to Efanov, the panorama was a collective portrait that embraced the "typical characteristics of the people of the Soviet era." See D. Shmarinov, "Kak sozdavalos' panno 'Znatnye liudi strany sovetov,'" *Tvorchestvo* 7 (1939): 4–5.

62. TsKhDMO, f. 1, op. 23, d. 1251, ll. 10–11; RGVA, f. 9, op. 29s, d. 321, l. 1; op. 35s, d. 92, ll. 34–35. When Knorin's text was removed from circulation, local propagandists telegraphed the authorities about what to do. Were they to make do with the text for the time being after blackening out all mention of enemies of the people, or were they to depart from the curriculum mandated earlier that year in "Programma po istorii VKP(b) dlia partiinykh kruzhkov (proekt)," *Bol'shevik* 11 (1937): 68–89?

63. M. I. Kalinin, *Chto dala sovetskaia vlast' trudiashchimsia?* (Moscow: Partizdat, 1937); *Nasha rodina,* ed. A. Stetskii, S. Ingulov, and N. Baranskii (Moscow: Partizdat, 1937); *Nasha rodina,* ed. N. Baranskii and P. N. Pospelov (Moscow: Partizdat, 1938). This book was criticized for offering virtually nothing on the republics' history, economics, culture, or people—see "Kniga o rodine," *Izvestiia,* October 19, 1937, 2.

64. V. M. Molotov, *K 20-letiiu Oktiabr'skoi revoliutsii* (Moscow: Partizdat, 1937); *20 let sovetskoi vlasti: Statisticheskii sbornik (tsifrovoi material dlia propagandistov)* (Moscow: Partizdat, 1937).

65. RGVA, f. 9, op. 29s, d. 355, ll. 15–20; d. 349, l. 69. The Komsomol and armed forces serialized this text and attendant supplements or printed them as booklets, e.g., *Komsomol'skii propagandist i agitator* 5 (1938); *Propagandist i agitator RKKA* 34 (1937); *Sozdanie russkogo natsional'nogo gosudarstva (v pomoshch' gruppovodam politzaniatii)* (Leningrad: KBF, 1938); *Kak rabochie i krest'iane zavoevali vlast' i postroili sotsialisticheskoe obshchestvo* (Moscow: Partizdat, 1937); etc.

66. See, for instance, RGVA, f. 9, op. 35s, d. 92, l. 120. The same crude sort of censorship was performed in public school classrooms as well.

67. David Brandenberger, *National Bolshevism: Stalinist Mass Culture and the Formation of Modern Russian National Identity, 1931–1956* (Cambridge: Harvard University Press, 2002), chaps. 2–4.

68. "Postanovlenie plenuma TsK VLKSM ob organizatsii propagandistskoi raboty," *Propagandist i agitator RKKA* 28 (1936): 1–5; TsKhDMO, f. 1, op. 23, d. 1253, ll. 36–37.

69. "O partiinoi propagande: rech' sekretaria TsK VKP(b) t. A. Andreeva na otkrytii Vysshei partiinoi shkoly propagandistov im. Ia. M. Sverdlova pri TsK VKP(b)," *Pravda,* February 26, 1936, 2; I. Bakulin, "O nedostatkakh komsol'skogo kruzhka po istorii partii," *Propagandist* 23–24 (1936): 90–99; V. Merzlinkin, "O komsomol'skoi polituchebe," *Propagandist i agitator RKKA* 31 (1936): 23; V. Sokolova, "Uluchshit' rukovodstvo propagandistami," *Propagandist* 18 (1936):

43–46; I. Bakulin, "O skhematizme v zaniatii odnogo kruzhka," *Propagandist* 19 (1936): 47–53; V. Chernoglazov, "Izuchenie oktiabr'skogo perioda v kruzhke po istorii VKP(b)," *Propagandist* 20 (1936): 57–59; I. Adam, "Iz opyta raboty seminara propagandistov," *Propagandist* 23–24 (1936): 99–103; N. Dedikov, "Propagandist, ego vospitanie i ucheba," *Propagandist* 22 (1936): 28–37.

70. RGVA, f. 9, op. 29s, d. 323, l. 100; RGASPI, f. 17, op. 120, d. 307, ll. 10, 38, 85–86, 122–125, 148–149, 289; Peter Konecny, *Builders and Deserters: Students, State, and Community in Leningrad, 1917–1941* (Montreal: McGill-Queen's University Press, 1999), 135–137, 138–141; [Anonymous], *Lenin Schools for [the] Training of Political Officers in the Soviet Army*, no. 12, *Research Program on the USSR Mimeograph Series* (New York: Praeger, 1952), 3–6.

71. RGASPI, f. 17, op. 120, d. 238, l. 1. See also d. 237, ll. 70–75.

72. RGASPI, f. 17, op. 120, d. 237, ll. 124–126.

73. "Dual power" refers to the Provisional Government's power-sharing agreement with the socialist-dominated Petrograd Soviet. On Lenin's orders, the Bolsheviks declined to participate in the arrangement. See RGASPI, f. 17, op. 120, d. 237, ll. 126–127. Similarly confused answers emerged from a study circle in the Voronezh region. For instance, when a propagandist asked his students about Lenin's view on peace with Germany in 1918, a student replied: "Trotsky was sent to Germany to conclude a peace agreement, but he said there that we would not conclude an agreement, in so doing betraying the party. He did this in order to support the slogan 'no peace, no war,' which meant that power would be given to Germany without a fight." See d. 238, l. 14. A follow-up investigation in Khar'kov six months later revealed little improvement—see d. 237, ll. 154–166.

74. RGASPI, f. 17, op. 120, d. 237, l. 60.

75. HPSSS, no. 1434, schedule A, vol. 34, 25, 28.

76. Irina Karsavina, "Secret Flight," in *Thirteen Who Fled*, ed. Louis Fischer (New York: Harper and Brothers, 1949), 44–45.

77. See, for instance, RGASPI, f. 17, op. 120, d. 237, ll. 126, 161; d. 238, ll. 3, 13–14; d. 326, ll. 2, 48–74; HPSSS, no. 1108, schedule A, vol. 31, 30; no. 1684, schedule A, vol. 36, 17; no. 1693, schedule A, vol. 36, 8; no. 128, schedule A, vol. 10, 17; no. 628, schedule A, vol. 29, 44; no. 1091, schedule A, vol. 31, 28.

78. RGASPI, f. 17, op. 120, d. 237, ll. 133–134.

79. For discussions of taboo political subjects, see RGVA, f. 9, op. 39s, d. 69, ll. 99, 102, etc.; on use of Trotsky's *Moia zhizn'*, see d. 48, l. 19; on Zinoviev's textbook, see op. 36s, d. 3594, l. 17. Lenin's testament was taboo on account of its questioning of Stalin's suitability for high office.

80. See "'O nedostatkakh partiinoi raboty i merakh likvidatsii trotskistskikh i inykh dvurushnikov'—Doklad t. Stalina na plenume TsK VKP(b)," *Pravda*, March 29, 1937, 2–4; "Materialy fevral'sko-martovskogo plenuma TsK VKP(b) 1937 g.," *Voprosy istorii* 3 (1995): 11, etc.

81. Politburo resolution of April 16, 1937 "Ob uchebnike po istorii VKP(b)," RGASPI, f. 17, op. 163, d. 1144, ll. 5–50b; Politburo resolution of May 11, 1937 "Ob organizatsii partiinykh kursov," op. 114, d. 840, ll. 46–48.

82. On the stillborn 1937 curriculum, see RGVA, f. 9, op. 29s, d. 349, ll. 2–4, 7, 165–171, 313–316; "Programma po istorii VKP(b) dlia partiinykh kruzhkov

(proekt)"; A. Fedorov, "O podgotovke mladshikh politrukov," *Propagandist i agitator RKKA* 12 (1938): 8–9.

83. "Politicheskoe vospitanie v srednei shkole," *Pravda*, May 10, 1937, 1.

84. RGASPI, f. 17, op. 120, d. 237, ll. 129–132; f. 88, op. 1, d. 803, ll. 7–8. According to the former report, the environment in Khar'kov became so unregulated during late 1937 that a student in School No. 5 was caught circulating leaflets proclaiming: "The USSR is the enemy of peace. Down with the USSR! Postyshev is a drunkard. Down with the Pioneer organization. Organize fascist youth organizations. Organize terrorist youth groups. Long live fascism!" Admittedly a rare occurrence, this sort of dissent was not totally unheard of during these years. Indeed, just across town in School No. 13, another student was caught at about the same time with "Down with the Bolsheviks! Hitler is the leader of the masses!" inscribed in his notebook. See f. 17, op. 120, d. 237, l. 34.

85. GAOPIKO, f. 1, op. 1, d. 2807, l. 14, cited in Catherine Merridale, *Ivan's War: Life and Death in the Red Army, 1939–1945* (New York: Metropolitan Books, 2006), 45. For similarly alarmist reports of the discovery of old newspapers displaying pictures of Zinoviev at a Leningrad bakery in 1936, see TsGAIPD SPb, f. 24, op. 2v, d. 1846, l. 89.

CHAPTER 9. PUBLIC OPINION IMPERILED

1. K. Simonov, *Glazami cheloveka moego pokoleniia: razmyshleniia o I. V. Staline* (Moscow: Novosti, 1988), 54–55. For evidence of the party hierarchy's conscious effort to rally popular opinion against Tukhachevsky and his comrades, see Stalin's June 11, 1937 circular to all provincial party committees, published in "Neskol'ko nedel' iz zhizni sekretaria TsK," *Rossiiskie vesti*, June 9, 1992, 2.

2. The opinion of a militant ex-SR, for instance, is visible in his daughter's diary —see diary entries from December 11 and 30, 1934, in Nina Lugovskaia, *Khochu zhit': iz dnevnika shkol'nitsy, 1932–1937* (Moscow: Glas, 2004), 206, 223–224.

3. Diary entry from June 10, 1935 in A. G. Solov'ev, "Tetradi krasnogo professora (1912–1941 gg.)," in *Neizvestnaia Rossiia—XX vek*, 4 vols. (Moscow: Istoricheskoe nasledie, 1993), 4:180. Solovyov had reported serving on a Central Committee brigade investigating Yenukidze's professional and personal conduct that April, but had not understood the point of the investigation.

4. Sarah Davies, "Us Against Them: Social Identity in Soviet Russia, 1934–1941," *Russian Review* 56:1 (1997): 78, citing TsGAIPD SPb, f. 24, op. 2v, d. 1367, ll. 71–72.

5. HPSSS, no. 220, schedule B, vol. 2, 7; no. 415/1035, schedule A, vol. 31, 13. "Impressive" in this source is likely a mistranslation of "striking" [*vpechatliaiushche*].

6. A different version of the same sentiment, circulating elsewhere in the same region, held that "It's a shame that they've shot the Zinovievites. During the coming elections, we might have voted for them." See "Spetssoobshchenie Upravleniia NKVD SSSR po Voronezhskoi oblasti o neudovletvoritel'nom provedenii otchetnoi kampanii sel'sovetov" (October 14, 1936), published in "Demokratiia . . . pod nadzorom NKVD: obsuzhdenie proekta Konstitutsii 1936 g.," in *Neizvestnaia Rossiia —XX vek*, 4 vols. (Moscow: Istoricheskoe nasledie, 1992), 2:276–281.

7. See, for instance, TsGAIPD SPb, f. 24, op. 2v, d. 2498, l. 146.

8. Nikolai Lunev, "Blind Faith in a Bright Future," in *Soviet Youth: Twelve Komsomol Histories* (Munich: Institute for the Study of the USSR, 1959), 36. Similar doubts are expressed in diary entries from February 7, March 25, August 22, and September 10, 1937 in "Dnevnik Niny Kosterinoi," *Novyi mir* 12 (1962): 40, 41, 45.

9. HPSSS, no. 34, schedule A, vol. 4, 22. Yagoda's reelection to the Central Executive Committee was announced in *Pravda* on February 7, 1935; his demotion to Commissar of Communications was publicized on September 27, 1936, and his arrest followed on March 4, 1937.

10. Abdy Kurmanbekov, "When the Paths of the Fathers Are Narrow," in *Soviet Youth,* 167; HPSSS, no. 46, schedule A, vol. 6, 48–49.

11. Petr Kruzhin, "False Dawn," in *Soviet Youth,* 205. Aspects of this account also appear in Kruzhin, "A Young Communist," in *Thirteen Who Fled,* ed. Louis Fischer (New York: Harper and Brothers, 1949), 85–86.

12. "'O nedostatkakh partiinoi raboty i merakh po likvidatsii trotskistskikh i inykh dvurushnikov'—Doklad t. Stalina na plenume TsK VKP(b)," *Pravda,* March 29, 1937, 2–4.

13. TsGAIPD SPb, f. 24, op. 2v, d. 2664, ll. 217, 207–209, 2, 7, cited in Olga Velikanova, *The Myth of the Besieged Fortress: Soviet Mass Perception in the 1920s–1930s,* working paper no. 7, *The Stalin Era Research and Archives Project* (Toronto: CREES, 2002), 15.

14. TsGAIPD SPb, f. 24, op. 2v, d. 2498, ll. 1–5.

15. RGVA, f. 9, op. 29, d. 340, ll. 445, 482. On morale problems in the ranks, see O. F. Suvenirov, *Tragediia RKKA, 1937–1938* (Moscow: Terra, 1998), 331–332.

16. Diary entry from June 12, 1937 in "Dnevnik A. A. Krolenko," OR RNB, f. 1120, op. 1, d. 230, l. 850b.

17. A. V. Gorbatov, *Gody i voiny* (Moscow: Voennoe izdatel'stvo, 1965), 122–123. These memoirs were originally published in 1964 in *Novyi mir.*

18. See HPSSS, no. 7, schedule A, volume 1, 24; also no. 11, schedule A, vol. 2, 36; no. 41, schedule A, vol. 4, 24. For another account of school children defacing Tukhachevsky's portrait, see that of Inna Shikheeva-Gaister, cited in Orlando Figes, *The Whisperers: Private Life in Stalin's Russia* (New York: Metropolitan Books, 2007), 298.

19. HPSSS, no. 534, schedule A, vol. 28, 59. See also no. 11, schedule A, vol. 2, 37.

20. Davies, "Us Against Them: Social Identity in Soviet Russia, 1934–1941," 79, citing TsGAPID SPb, f. 24, op. 2v, d. 2664, ll. 1–8; d. 2498, ll. 1–2, 150; d. 2286, l. 13; d. 2665, ll. 2–4; d. 3178, ll. 23, 28–29; d. 2499, l. 24; op. 10, d. 291, l. 78. For similar sentiments, see diary entry from February 3, 1937 in "Diary of Andrei Stepanovich Arzhilovsky," in *Intimacy and Terror: Soviet Diaries of the 1930s,* ed. Véronique Garros, Natalia Korenevskaya, and Thomas Lahusen (New York: New Press, 1995), 143–144.

21. HPSSS, no. 142/1664, schedule A, vol. 36, 30.

22. HPSSS, no. 25, schedule A, vol. 3, 48. This statement is fanciful—there is little evidence of any organized oppositional activity within the Red Army high command.

23. HPSSS, no. 526, schedule A, vol. 27, 36.

24. Gorbatov, *Gody i voiny,* 122–123. For similar accounts, see Peter Gornev, "The Life of a Soviet Soldier," Alexei Gorchakov, "The Long Road," and Lidia Obukhova, "Two Evils," in *Thirteen Who Fled,* 34, 67–68, 145–146.

25. Diary entries from June 8–9, 1937 in A. Afinogenov, "Dnevnik 1937 goda," *Sovetskaia dramaturgiia* 2 (1993): 227.

26. Kruzhin, "False Dawn," 208.

27. HPSSS, no. 531, schedule A, vol. 27, 45.

28. PAKhK, f. r-2, op. 1, d. 1303, ll. 108–114; and A. S. Suturin, *Delo kraevogo masshtaba* (Khabarovsk: Khabarovskoe knizhnoe izdatel'stvo, 1991), 67–74, both cited in Steven Merritt, "The Great Purges in the Soviet Far East, 1937–1938" (Ph.D. diss. University of California at Riverside, 2000), 320.

29. TsGAIPD SPb, f. 24, op. 2v, d. 2664, ll. 217, 207, 209, 2, 7, cited in Velikanova, *The Myth of the Besieged Fortress,* 15.

30. RGVA, f. 9, op. 29, d. 340, ll. 445, 482.

31. TsA FSB RF, f. 3, op. 5, d. 180, ll. 4–5, quoted in A. M. Demidov, "Krasnaia armiia nakanune i v period massovykh repressii po otsenkam inostrannykh razvedok," in *Istoricheskie chteniia na Lubianke 1999 god: Otechestvennye spetssluzhby v 20–30-e gody,* ed. V. M. Kommissarov (Novgorod: NovGU, 2000), 150.

32. RGVA, f. 33987, op. 3, d. 1023, ll. 22, 24, 36. Voroshilov appears to have been reading a devastating report on morale in the Moscow military district as he drafted the speech—see ll. 40–43.

33. For the actual text of Voroshilov's speech and supporting documents, see RGVA, f. 33987, op. 3, d. 1023, ll. 27–39, 13–19.

34. N. S. Chernyshev, *1937 god: Elita Krasnoi Armii na golgofe* (Moscow: Veche, 2003), 471–502.

35. RGVA, f. 9, op. 29, d. 318, l. 79. For examples of widespread distrust, see TsGAIPD SPb, f. 24, op. 2v, d. 2498, ll. 1–5.

36. RGVA, f. 9, op. 29, d. 318, l. 103.

37. RGVA, f. 9, op. 29, d. 318, ll. 220–221. For another official's acknowledgment of the frequency of such comments, see the speech of I. D. Vaineros quoted in Suturin, *Delo kraevogo masshtaba,* 35, cited in Merritt, "The Great Purges in the Soviet Far East," 321.

38. RGVA, f. 9, op. 29, d. 318, l. 221.

39. RGVA, f. 9, op. 39, d. 54, l. 119.

40. RGVA, f. 9, op. 39, d. 54, l. 114.

41. RGVA, f. 9, op. 39, d. 54, l. 154.

42. TsA FSB RF, f. 3, op. 5, d. 180, ll. 4–5, quoted in Demidov, "Krasnaia armiia nakanune i v period massovykh repressii po otsenkam inostrannykh razvedok," 150.

43. See, for example, V. S. Mil'bakh, *Osobaia krasnoznamennaia dal'nevostochnaia armiia—Politicheskie repressii komandno-nachal'stvuiushchego sostava, 1937–1938* (St. Petersburg: Izd-vo S-Peterburgskogo universiteta, 2007), 167–216.

44. RGVA, f. 9, op. 39, d. 79, ll. 93–94.

45. Idiosyncratic syntax and punctuation in the original. See HPSSS, no. 27, schedule A, vol. 3, 36–37. Paul Robeson's son recalled his Moscow school friends

being similarly dispirited by the arrests of such heroes—see Paul Robeson, Jr., *The Undiscovered Paul Robeson: An Artist's Journey, 1898–1939* (New York: Wiley, 2001), 290.

46. Kruzhin, "A Young Communist," 87.

47. TsGAIPD SPb, f. 24, op. 2v, d. 3027, l. 49; d. 3026, l. 118

48. See TsGAIPD SPb, f. 24, op. 2v, d. 3178, ll. 29, 19, 23, cited in Davies, "Us Against Them: Social Identity in Soviet Russia, 1934–1941," 79. Such questions were likely provoked by platitudes like that of another Vyborg teacher, A. S. Korobkov, who declared in June 1938: "Soviet power has executed all the good administrators." See d. 3027, l. 49.

49. See HPSSS, no. 7, schedule A, volume 1, 24; also no. 11, schedule A, vol. 2, 36; no. 41, schedule A, vol. 4, 24.

50. RGVA, f. 9, op. 39s, d. 95, l. 313. This NKVD report does not point out the irony of Diachonov's assumption that Trotsky, Zinoviev, and Kamenev—all Jews by birth—might be pursuing an anti-Semitic agenda.

51. RGASPI, f. 17, op. 120, d. 237, ll. 121–22. Like Diachonov above, Krukun seems to have been unaware that Zinoviev and Kamenev were Jews by birth and atheists by conviction.

52. Iu. Elagin, *Ukroshchenie iskusstv* (New York: Izd-vo imeni Chekhova, 1953), 302.

53. TsGAIPD SPb, f. 24, op. 2v, d. 2498, l. 152; d. 3026, l. 118.

54. TsGAIPD SPb, f. 24, op. 2v, d. 3023, l. 8.

55. See, for instance, Robert Thurston, "Social Dimensions of Stalin's Rule: Humor and Terror in the USSR," *Journal of Social History* 24:3 (1991): 541–562. For a firsthand account of how the Terror was assumed to be targeting mostly communists and Jews, see F. Beck and W. Godin, *Russian Purge and the Extraction of Confession* (New York: Viking Press, 1951), 146.

56. This explanation for the collapse of popular morale is more plausible than other potential explanations, e.g., that widespread talk of conspiracies resonated with age-old apocalyptic folk belief. See Gábor Rittersporn, "The Omnipresent Conspiracy: On Soviet Images of Politics and Social Relations in the 1930s," in *Stalinist Terror: New Perspectives*, ed. J. Arch Getty and Roberta Manning (Cambridge: Cambridge University Press, 1993), 115.

CHAPTER 10. OSSIFICATION OF THE OFFICIAL LINE

1. RGASPI, f. 671, op. 1, d. 265, ll. 29–41, 67, 71, cited in Nikita Petrov and Marc Jansen, *"Stalinskii pitomets": Nikolai Ezhov* (Moscow: Rosspen, 2008), 193; N. S. Khrushchev, *Vospominaniia* (Moscow: Vagrius, 1997), 252. Yaroslavsky's son-in-law was the diplomat M. I. Rozenberg; his wife was K. I. Kirsanova.

2. See the galleys at RGASPI, f. 558, op. 11, d. 1208, ll. 2–295. The manuscript was apparently delivered shortly after a firm deadline was set by the Orgburo resolution of February 16, 1938: "Voprosy 'Partiinykh kursov," f. 17, op. 114, d. 840, l. 32.

3. For Pospelov's typescript draft, the first part of which is dated February 26, 1937, see RGASPI, f. 558, op. 11, d. 1217, ll. 2–24. This typescript and other as-

pects of the editorial process have been published in part by M. V. Zelenov. See "I. V. Stalin v rabote nad 'Kratkim kursom istorii VKP(b),'" *Voprosy istorii* 11, 12 (2002); I. V. Stalin, *Istoricheskaia ideologiia v SSSR v 1920–1950-e gody: Perepiska s istorikami, stat'i i zametki po istorii, stenogrammy vystuplenii—sbornik dokumentov i materialov,* vol. 1, *1920–1930-e gody,* ed. M. V. Zelenov (St. Petersburg: Nauka-Piter, 2006), 316–328.

4. The three met on March 4 and 5, 1938. See *Na prieme u Stalina: tetradi (zhurnaly) zapisei lits, priniatykh I. V. Stalinym (1924–1953 gg.)* (Moscow: Novyi khronograf, 2008), 232.

5. RGASPI, f. 558, op. 11, d. 1217, ll. 25–46, here 26–28. Other surviving commentary reveals criticism of a more limited nature, e.g., the need for additional statements by Lenin on the inadequacy of small-holder agriculture. Such material was evidently to reinforce the case for full-scale collectivization presented in Chapter Eleven.

6. RGASPI, f. 89, op. 8, d. 807, l. 3.

7. Three copies of the third version's galleys are at RGASPI, f. 558, op. 3, dd. 75–77. The last chapters of d. 77 are covered with Stalin's marginalia; part of its title page with Stalin's marginalia was torn out and is now at op. 11, d. 1217, l. 1. On the confidence that the text was virtually ready, see f. 89, op. 8, d. 831, l. 1; f. 77, op. 1, d. 692, l. 175

8. The commission formally consisted of Stalin, Molotov, and Zhdanov. See RGASPI, f. 17, op. 125, d. 26, l. 29; op. 120, d. 383, l. 1; Politburo resolution of April 25, 1938 "Ob izdaniiakh 'Kratkikh kursov' i 'uchebnikov' dlia prepodavaniia v partiinykh i komsomol'skikh shkolakh, kursakh i kruzhkakh," op. 3, d. 998, l. 1.

9. For Stalin's April editing of the third version's galleys, see RGASPI, f. 558, op. 3, d. 77.

10. Four copies of the fourth version's galleys dating to April 24, 1938 are stored at RGASPI, f. 17, op. 120, d. 383; over a hundred pages of another copy (pp. 51–120, 141–177, 259–290), covered with Stalin's corrections, are at f. 558, op. 11, d. 1209–1211.

11. The party hierarchs do not seem to have experienced any one moment of epiphany about the destructiveness of the terror. Instead, concerns gradually emerged as the purges began to debilitate party and state institutions under their command. See Boris Starkov, "Narkom Yezhov," in *Stalinist Terror: New Perspectives,* ed. J. Arch Getty and Roberta Manning (Cambridge: Cambridge University Press, 1993), 36; *The Road to Terror: Stalin and the Self-Destruction of the Bolsheviks, 1932–1939,* ed. J. Arch Getty and O. V. Naumov (New Haven: Yale University Press, 1999), 528–546.

12. RGASPI, f. 89, op. 8, d. 807, l. 3.

13. Stalin did not receive visitors in his Kremlin office in late May, late June, or late July, indicating that he spent this time editing—see *Na prieme u Stalina,* 236–239; Zelenov, "I. V. Stalin v rabote nad 'Kratkim kursom istorii VKP(b).'"

14. Stalin to the Politburo and authors of the *Short Course* (August 16, 1938), RGASPI, f. 558, op. 11, d. 1219, ll. 36–37.

15. Three sets of Stalin's revisions survive, at least in part. The first round, composed of the last chapters to the third version's galleys and unbound pages of the

fourth version's galleys, typescript, hand-written pages, and interpolations, are at RGASPI, f. 558, op. 3, d. 77; op. 11, d. 1209, ll. 1–147; d. 1210, ll. 148–328; d. 1211, ll. 329–392. The early stages of Stalin's first revisions to chapters 6 and 8–10 appear to be missing; of his second round of revisions, only chapter 4 survives —see d. 1213, ll. 160–237. A complete copy of Stalin's last round of revisions—a typescript sent to members of his inner circle with additional marginalia added between August 16 and September 9—survives at d. 1212, ll. 1–157; d. 1213, ll. ll. 238–314; d. 1214, ll. 315–444; d. 1215, ll. 445–576; d. 1216, ll. 568–670.

16. This and the following paragraphs are based on a comparison of RGASPI, f. 17, op. 120, d. 383 and *Istoriia VKP(b): Kratkii kurs* (Moscow: Gos. izd-vo politicheskoi literatury, 1938). For a detailed analysis, see *Stalin's Catechism: A Critical Edition of* The Short Course on the History of the All-Union Communist Party (Bolsheviks), ed. David Brandenberger and M. V. Zelenov (New Haven: Yale University Press, forthcoming).

17. This undermines the notion that the *Short Course* can be regarded as Stalin's autobiography. See Jochen Hellbeck, "Introduction," in *Autobiographical Practices in Russia / Autobiographische Praktiken in Russland,* ed. Jochen Hellbeck and Klaus Heller (Gottingen: G&R Unipress GmbH, 2004), 23; Robert Tucker, *Stalin in Power: The Revolution from Above, 1929–1941* (New York: Norton, 1990), 539.

18. For a more detailed treatment of how this threat to the party was narrated during the purge, see David Brandenberger, "Ideological Zig Zag: Official Explanations for the Great Terror, 1936–1938," in *The Anatomy of Terror: Political Violence under Stalin,* ed. James Harris (Oxford: Oxford University Press, forthcoming).

19. Instead of an imminent attack on the USSR, Stalin stressed the growing strife *between* capitalist countries—tensions that he viewed as evidence of the start of "a second imperialist war" several months before the infamous September 1938 Munich accords.

The dramatic excision of the Comintern from party history likely stems from Stalin's increasingly low opinion of the organization. It was also apparently at this time that the general secretary decided to try its fallen officials (including Knorin) in camera rather than afford them the publicity of a fourth major show trial. See B. A. Starkov, "The Trial That Was Not Held," *Europe-Asia Studies* 46:8 (1994): 1297–1315.

20. See RGASPI, f. 558, op. 3, d. 77, ll. 252–253, 293, 294–295. Volkogonov implausibly asserts that Stalin personally removed mention of people from the text after condemning them to death—see D. A. Volkogonov, *Stalin: Politicheskii portret,* 2 vols. (Moscow: Novosti, 1991), 1:388. That said, the excision of Yezhov's name from the narrative does seem to have foreshadowed his fall by some six months (although several minor mentions were accidentally allowed into print and corrected only in 1940—see *Istoriia VKP(b): Kratkii kurs,* 197, 234, 313).

21. At first glance, this reassertion of the centrality of "theory" would seem to confirm many critics' assumptions about the general secretary's penchant for vulgar Marxism. But such a conclusion ignores the fact that Stalin had spent the first half of the 1930s *demanding* an animated, accessible, and heroic approach to party

ideology. It also ignores the circumstances under which this style of mobilization ground to a halt after 1936. Stalin's return to "theory," in other words, is impossible to disentangle from his regime's slaughter of its own Olympus.

22. RGASPI, f. 558, op. 11, d. 1219, ll. 36–37.

23. The recipients were Andreev, Yezhov, Kaganovich, Kalinin, Molotov, Petrovsky, Voroshilov, Zhdanov, Khrushchev, and A. I. Mikoian.

24. See RGASPI, f. 558, op. 11, d. 1219, ll. 54, 74, 79–80; 44, 83, 93; 50, 75; 45–48.

25. RGASPI, f. 558, op. 11, d. 1217, l. 1. Years later, Pospelov explained this change in authorship by apparently paraphrasing Stalin: "if the book comes out under the editorship of the Central Committee commission, this will give it a lot of weight and ensure it the trust of the mass reader. We need to indicate that the *Short Course* has the approval of the Central Committee. This will put to an end the differences in the evaluation of events that were found in the old party history texts." D. Rudnev, "Kto pisal 'Kratkii kurs,'" *Politika* 9 (1991): 64. He may have been paraphrasing a speech given to a propagandists' conference in late September 1938—see RGASPI, f. 558, op. 11, d. 1122, ll. 35–36.

26. Yaroslavsky to Stalin (August 17, 1938), RGASPI, f. 558, op. 11, d. 1219, l. 38; Pospelov to Stalin (August 17, 1938), ll. 39–40.

27. Most of the substantial comments were offered by Yaroslavsky and Pospelov. See RGASPI, f. 558, op. 11, d. 1219.

28. See *Na prieme u Stalina*, 239–240. Poskrebyshev is not listed in Stalin's office logbook as being present at these sessions, but Yaroslavsky remembered him as being involved. RGASPI, f. 89, op. 8, d. 807, l. 5.

29. "Gluboko izuchat' istoriiu partii Lenina-Stalina," *Pravda*, September 9, 1938, 1; see also "Vospityvat' molodezh' v dukhe bol'shevistskikh traditsii," *Pravda*, September 11, 1938, 1; "Obespechit' glubokoe izuchenie istorii VKP(b)," *Pravda*, September 17, 1938, 1.

30. The initial printing was quickly increased to eight million—see Politburo resolution of November 2, 1938 "O dopolnitel'nom izdanii knigi 'Kratkii kurs istorii VKP(b),'" RGASPI, f. 17, op. 3, d. 1003, l. 7.

31. RGASPI, f. 17, op. 120, d. 307, ll. 7–11. Others agreed—see ll. 68–72, 80–85, 113–114.

32. RGASPI, f. 558, op. 11, d. 1122, ll. 3–4.

33. RGASPI, f. 558, op. 11, d. 1122, ll. 19, 28–29, 41. For Stalin's notes on the speech, see ll. 112–123.

34. RGASPI, f. 17, op. 163, d. 1218, ll. 42–44.

35. Sarah Davies, "Stalin and the Making of the Leader Cult in the 1930s," in *The Leader Cult in Communist Dictatorship: Stalin and the Eastern Bloc*, ed. Balázs Apor, Jan Behrends, Polly Jones, and E. A. Rees (Basingstoke: Palgrave, 2005), 36–37.

36. Central Committee resolution of November 14, 1938 "O postanovke partiinoi propagandy v sviazi s vypuskom 'Kratkogo kursa istorii VKP(b),'" *Pravda*, November 15, 1938, 1–2.

37. Volkogonov claims the opposite—that the *Short Course*'s "simple style and primitive arguments made it accessible to everyone." See Volkogonov, *Stalin*, 1:388; 2:549–551.

38. RGASPI, f. 17, op. 125, d. 1, ll. 5, 94.

39. RGASPI, f. 17, op. 125, d. 1, ll. 47–470b, 17, 92–93, 103–104.

40. See RGASPI, f. 558, op. 11, dd. 1221–1222.

41. RGASPI, f. 17, op. 120, d. 307, l. 269.

42. RGASPI, f. 89, op. 8, dd. 996, 1017–1018; Yaroslavsky to Kaganovich (November 27, 1939), d. 1016, l. 1.

43. On Yaroslavsky's correspondence with the encyclopedia, see RGASPI, f. 89, op. 8, d. 1017, ll. 14–19.

44. Yaroslavsky to Stalin (December 7, 1939), RGASPI, f. 89, op. 8, d. 1020, ll. 2–3. The book's drafts are at d. 995.

45. Em. Iaroslavskii, O tovarishche Staline (Moscow: Gos. izd-vo polit. lit-ry, 1939). Print runs never exceeded 200,000.

46. Mitin, who had just replaced Adoratsky as the director of the IMEL, was likely trying to rehabilitate his institute with this project.

47. Although a large number of Stalin's comrades-in-arms appear in the text—Kalinin, Ordzhonikidze, Voroshilov, Molotov, Sverdlov, Dzerzhinsky, Budenny, Shchadenko, Kirov, Kaganovich, Mikoian, Andreev, Zhdanov, Khrushchev, Beria, N. M. Shvernik, V. Z. Ketskhoveli, A. G. Tsulukidze, V. K. Kurnatovsky, I. P. Vatsek, V. F. Saratovets, P. A. Dzhaparidze, S. G. Shaumian, S. S. Spandarian—all figure only fleetingly in the biography and only Voroshilov is mentioned more than twice. Ten enemies of the people figure in the narrative in equally minor ways; only Trotsky is mentioned more than twice or allowed any agency. Another unpublished biography developed at the IMEL in mid-1939 by Saveliev treated Stalin's entourage in the same way—see RGASPI, f. 71, op. 10, d. 257, ll. 6–161.

48. RGASPI, f. 71, op. 10, d. 258, ll. 124–211. Mitin added the name of one more long-dead Bolshevik—Frunze—to the biography's galleys on December 14. See l. 18.

49. The oldest draft of the IMEL biography dates to December 7, 1939—see RGASPI, f. 71, op. 10, d. 258, ll. 124–211. Mitin's galleys are at ll. 1–43; Aleksandrov's are at ll. 46–122. See also f. 558, op. 11, d. 1279.

50. Yaroslavsky to Mitin (December 13, 1939), RGASPI, f. 89, op. 8, d. 1022, ll. 1–2; f. 71, op. 10, d. 258, ll. 42, 44.

51. RGASPI, f. 558, op. 1, d. 3226, l. 1. Although Stalin is often described as a meticulous editor, his library is full of books in which the corrections fade after the first few pages, testifying to a lack of time or patience.

52. "Iosif Vissarionovich Stalin (Kratkaia biografiia)," Pravda, December 20, 1939, 2–6; reprinted in Bol'shevik 23–24 (1939): 12–56; Proletarskaia revoliutsiia 4 (1939): 9–64; Partiinoe stroitel'stvo 23–24 (1939): 7–41; Iosif Vissarionovich Stalin (Kratkaia biografiia) (Moscow: Gos. izd-vo polit. lit-ry, 1939). The text was written by Volin, M. S. Pozner, P. S. Cheremnykh, and V. D. Mochalov and edited by Mitin, Aleksandrov, Pospelov, and Mints. See RGASPI, f. 629, op. 1, d. 55, l. 52; R. Koniushaia, "Iz vospominanii ob izdanii sochinenii I. V. Stalina i ego kratkoi biografii," Edinstvo, January 19, 1995, 3. Ironically, Yaroslavsky has traditionally been credited with authoring the book along with Mitin and Pospelov—see A. Antonov-Ovseyenko, The Time of Stalin: Portrait of a Tyranny (New York: Harper & Row, 1981), 198, 201, 233.

53. "Iosif Vissarionovich Stalin (Kratkaia biografiia)," in Malaia sovetskaia

entsiklopediia, 10 vols. (Moscow: Sovetskaia entsiklopediia, 1940), 10:319–392; *Ukazatel' osnovnykh pervoistochnikov v pomoshch' izuchaiushchim "Kratkii kurs istorii VKP(b)," * ed. P. Pospelov and G. Aleksandrov (Moscow: Gospolitizdat, 1940), 25, 50, 61, etc. The only other biographical statement published in 1939 was in *Istoriko-revoliutsionnyi kalendar',* ed. A. V. Shestakov (Moscow: OGIZ, 1939), 631–49; reprinted in *K shestidesiatiletiiu so dnia rozhdeniia Iosifa Vissarionovicha Stalina* (Ulan Ude: n.p., 1939), 1–35.

54. Before a second edition could be released, Yaroslavsky had to adjust passages on Japan, the Molotov-Ribbentrop pact, and the Polish campaign and add new commentary on the Soviet-Finnish War and Soviet patriotism. See pp. 138, 145, and 113 at RGASPI, f. 89, op. 8, d. 995, l. 29, d. 1015.

55. See, for instance, RGASPI, f. 17, op. 125, d. 10, l. 72; f. 71, op. 10, d. 268, ll. 98, 103–109, 112–233; more generally, Sarah Davies, *Popular Opinion in Stalin's Russia: Terror, Propaganda, and Dissent, 1933–1941* (Cambridge: Cambridge University Press, 1997), 167–182.

56. See Katerina Clark, *The Soviet Novel: History as Ritual* (Chicago: University of Chicago Press, 1980), 14–15, 57. For a similar interpretation of the cult's aesthetic limitations, see Jan Plamper, "The Stalin Cult in the Visual Arts, 1929–1953" (Ph.D. diss., University of California—Berkeley, 2001), 11.

57. Bulgakov attempted to cast Stalin as a romantic hero in his 1939 play *Batum* —something which earned him a stinging rebuke from the authorities. See diary entry from August 17, 1939 in *Dnevnik Eleny Bulgakovoi,* ed. V. I. Losev and L. Ianovskaia (Moscow: Izd-vo "Knizhnaia palata," 1990), 279.

CHAPTER 11. STALINIST MASS CULTURE ON THE EVE OF WAR

1. Emma Gershtein, "Lishniaia liubov': stseny iz moskovskoi zhizni (Okonchanie)," *Novyi mir* 12 (1993): 146. The author is grateful to Jochen Hellbeck for this reference.

2. HPSSS, no. 14, schedule A, vol. 2, 58.

3. RGASPI, f. 17, op. 125, d. 26, ll. 51–56; RGANI, f. 6, op. 2, d. 147, ll. 6–29, 41–74; d. 172, ll. 99–122.

4. See Central Committee Resolution of August 7, 1939 "O Muzee V. I. Lenina," RGASPI, f. 17, op. 116, d. 12, l. 44; f. 71, op. 10, d. 374, ll. 20–23. This reorganization was originally proposed in September 1938—see f. 17, op. 120, d. 307, ll. 53, 150.

5. RGASPI, f. 558, op. 11, d. 1122, l. 10.

6. RGASPI, f. 17, op. 163, d. 1218, ll. 44–45.

7. RGASPI, f. 17, op. 163, d. 1218, l. 45. Barely literate, Khrushchev dictated everything he "wrote" to his staff. Personal communication with William Taubman, April 13, 2003.

8. RGASPI, f. 17, op. 2, d. 773, l. 127, cited in O. V. Khlevniuk, *1937-i: Stalin, NKVD i sovetskoe obshchestvo* (Moscow: Respublika, 1992), 78.

9. At least some of those best suited to work with the *Short Course* reacted negatively to the book's tendentiousness and singular focus on the general secretary. Solovyov reported right after the textbook's publication that S. Zhbankov was very

dissatisfied with how it turned out. Quoting Zhbankov, Solovyov wrote: "Com-[rade] Stalin gives himself too much credit. He doesn't deny that he wrote it and yet at the same time the textbook contains no less than a hundred mentions of himself and quotations [from his speeches and writing]. What's the point in this? It's not serious at all. Moreover, he credits himself with things that never happened. For instance, the leadership of the Bolshevik faction in the Fourth Duma. And there's a huge amount of attention cast on the recent show trials of the enemies of the people, as if he is trying to justify himself. No, there's no way you can say the textbook is high quality." Solovyov concluded later: "there is some truth to what Zhbankov is saying." See diary entry from October 13, 1938 in A. G. Solov'ev, "Tetradi krasnogo professora (1912–1941 gg.)," in *Neizvestnaia Rossiia: XX vek,* vols. 1–4 (Moscow: Istoricheskoe nasledie, 1993), 4:199. Later, Solovyov reported M. M. Litvinov's private rant about "Stalin's limited mind, his phenomenal sense of self-confidence and self-importance, his need for praise, his stubbornness, his careerism, and his unlimited power," which Litvinov explained as "the legacy of many centuries of ignorance and a lack of culture." See diary entry from June 22, 1939, ibid., 203.

10. Central Committee resolution of November 14, 1938 "O postanovke partiinoi propagandy v sviazi s vypuskom 'Kratkogo kursa istorii VKP(b),'" *Pravda,* November 15, 1938, 1–2; generally, see F. G. Krotov, *Shkola ideinoi zakalki: Ocherki istorii marksistsko-leninskogo obrazovaniia v KPSS* (Moscow: Izd-vo politicheskoi literatury, 1978), 91–101. Some commentators have mistakenly read this resolution as disbanding the party educational system in favor of individual study. See, for instance, V. V. Volkov, "Kontseptsiia kul'turnosti, 1935–1938 gody: Sovetskaia tsivilizatsiia i povsednevnost' stalinskogo vremeni," *Sotsiologicheskii zhurnal* 1–2 (1996): 210–211; Oleg Kharkhordin, *The Collective and the Individual in Russia: A Study of Background Practices* (Berkeley: University of California Press, 1999), 166.

11. TsGAIPD SPb, f. 24, op. 10, dd. 401, 406, 408, 443–447. See also "Otvety na voprosy chitatelei," *Pravda,* December 8, 10, and 24, 1938, 2.

12. TsKhDMO, f. 1, op. 23, d. 1342, ll. 22ob-24.

13. *SSSR i strany kapitalizma,* ed. L. Mekhlis, E. Varga, and V. Karpinskii, 2nd ed. (Moscow: Partizdat, 1938); RGVA, f. 9, op. 29s, d. 513, ll. 35–36, 48, 88, 98, 438; TsKhDMO, f. 1, op. 23, d. 1342, ll. 22ob-24; "Programmy eksternata za Voenno-politicheskoe uchilishche v 1939 godu," *Propagandist i agitator RKKA* 15 (1939): 38–40.

14. *Krasnoarmeiskii polituchebnik,* chap. 1–3 (Moscow: Voenizdat, 1939). By 1941, 14 chapters had been issued as separate booklets, the first three of which concerned Russo-Soviet history.

15. On the curriculum, see RGVA, f. 9, op. 29s, d. 513; "O politicheskoi uchebe krasnoarmeitsev i mladshikh komandirov RKKA v 1938–1939 uchebnom godu," *Pravda,* December 9, 1938, 3. On the reading lists, see S. Gurov, "Biblioteka Krasnoarmeitsa," *Pravda,* December 7, 1938, 6; B. Iakovlev, "Biblioteka patriotov," *Krasnaia zvezda,* September 16, 1939, 2. On film, see RGVA, f. 9, op. 29, d. 237. On the new line's russocentric etatism, see David Brandenberger, *National Bolshevism: Stalinist Mass Culture and the Formation of Modern Russian National Identity, 1931–1956* (Cambridge: Harvard University Press, 2002).

16. Dozens of books and pamphlets under the title *V pomoshch' izuchaiushchim istoriiu VKP(b)* were published between late 1939 and mid-1941 by regional party organizations' departments of propaganda and agitation. All of these publications republished articles and pieces from the central press, relying on *Pravda, Bolshevik, Pod znamenem marksizma,* as well as *Molodoi bolshevik* and *Sovetskaia Ukraina.* See, for instance, *Pomoshch' izuchaiushchim istoriiu VKP(b): Konsul'tatsiia k IV glave Kratkogo kursa istorii VKP(b)* (Odessa: Sotsialisticheskaia Moldaviia, 1939), 251–259; *Pomoshch' izuchaiushchim istoriiu VKP(b): K IV glave Kratkogo kursa istorii VKP(b)* (Stalingrad: Oblastnoe knigoizdatel'stvo, 1941), 42–81; TsGAIPD SPb, f. 24, op. 10, d. 418.

17. RGASPI, f. 17, op. 125, d. 26, ll. 53–55; d. 42, ll. 36–38.

18. HPSSS, no. 1434, schedule A, vol. 34, 34; RGVA, f. 9, op. 29s, d. 254, l. 57; GARF, f. 2303, op. 70, d. 2631, l. 188; RGVA, f. 9, op. 29s, d. 513, l. 135; Ts-GAIPD SPb, f. 24, op. 10, d. 443, ll. 206–207. Specialists at the September 1938 propagandists' conference predicted that the book's fourth chapter would be most difficult—see, for instance, RGASPI, f. 17, op. 120, d. 307, l. 38.

19. HPSSS, no. 306, schedule A, vol. 31, 31. According to this informant, much of his class preparation was similarly superficial: "Each one of us was supposed to prepare a lecture on an assigned chapter, with the assignments being handed out by a Party member in our Library cell. We all hated this, as it took time and we thought it pretty useless, especially as we had been exposed to all this in school and higher educational institutions. We tried to prepare the lectures as quickly as possible by making outlines and summaries which we would all lend to each other. This worked very well as we kept on repeating the same thing, year in and year out. I would get my lectures together from the summaries in some of the less well-known newspapers and also from periodicals."

20. RGVA, f. 9, op. 29s, d. 513, l. 135; op. 39s, d. 95, ll. 68, 98–104; op. 29s, d. 452, ll. 49–50; "O postanovke propagandy Marksizma-Leninizma v Belorusskoi SSR, Orlovskoi i Kurskoi oblastiiakh," *Bol'shevik* 15–16 (1939): 48–50; also "Protiv samoteka v propagande Marksizma-Leninizma," *Bol'shevik* 15–16 (1939): 51–58; "Bol'shevistskuiu propagandu—na vysshuiu stupen'," *Bol'shevik* 10 (1940): esp. 4–7.

21. TsKhDMO, f. 1, op. 23, d. 1304, l. 30; also ll. 46–47; *Poka stuchit serdtse: Dnevniki i pis'ma Geroia Sovetskogo Soiuza Evgenii Rudnevoi* (Moscow: Moskovskii gos. universitet, 1995), 71.

22. RGVA, f. 9, op. 29s, d. 452, ll. 192, 242–246, 334; d. 349, l. 1; d. 378, ll. 64, 89, 98; d. 90, l. 259; op. 35s, d. 90, ll. 212–213; d. 95, l. 509; also HPSSS no. 1, schedule A, vol. 1, 49; no. 66, schedule A, vol. 6, 23.

23. For the three reports, see GARF, f. 9425, op. 1, d. 5, ll. 4–94; d. 11, ll. 2–63.

24. GARF, f. 9425, op. 1, d. 5, l. 66; d. 11, l. 61.

25. GARF, f. 9425, op. 1, d. 5, ll. 87, 33.

26. RGVA, f. 9, op. 29s, d. 491, ll. 152–153; op. 35s, d. 92, l. 211. The situation was even worse in the non-Russian regions. For instance, vast amounts of literature in non-Russian languages was indiscriminately purged from Central Asian military district libraries in the late 1930s. See op. 32s, d. 90, l. 11.

27. See RGVA, d. 9, op. 32s, d. 90, ll. 241, 255, 260–261, 280; op. 35s, d. 92, ll. 70, 83–84, 226; op. 39s, d. 95, l. 326; op. 32s, d. 90, ll. 256–257, 261. Offending material remained in circulation despite Glavlit's demand that: "the directors of libraries, book warehouses, stores, clubs, exhibitions, photo libraries, museums, archives, theaters, publishing houses, and newspaper editorial boards are required to turn over to local Glavlit organs all printed or reproduced material that qualifies for seizure under Glavlit orders."

28. On the general shortage of textual materials after the emergence of the *Short Course*, see RGVA, f. 9, op. 35s, d. 3778, ll. 64, 89, 98; d. 90, ll. 212–213; op. 32s, d. 90, ll. 241, 255, 260–291, 280.

29. On rote learning, consider a 1939 incident from the Lenin military academy in which a cadet noted that Trotsky had spoken at the second party conference. His study partner responded naively: "Where did you read that? There's nothing about a speech by Trotsky in the textbook." RGVA, f. 9, op. 29s, d. 491, ll. 392–393.

30. See RGVA, f. 9, op. 35s, d. 92, l. 120; op. 36s, d. 3594, l. 17; HPSSS, no. 1124, schedule A, vol. 32, 39.

31. HPSSS, no. 417, schedule A, vol. 21, 29–30. On the circulation of a pamphlet by Tomsky, see Peter Kruzhin, "A Young Communist," in *Thirteen Who Fled*, ed. Louis Fischer (New York: Harper and Brothers, 1949), 87–88. For a party member's complaint about having to dispose of his taboo books, see diary entry from April 11, 1935 in Solov'ev, "Dnevnik krasnogo professora (1912–1941 gg.)," 179.

32. RGVA, f. 9, op. 39s, d. 95, l. 68. For more on frustration with the book, see Stephen Kotkin, *Magnetic Mountain: Stalinism as a Civilization* (Berkeley: University of California Press, 1995), 309, 331; HPSSS, no. 14, schedule A, vol. 2, 6–8; no. 17, schedule A, vol. 2, 35.

33. RGVA, f. 9, op. 39s, d. 75, l. 84; d. 95, l. 19; d. 75, l. 35; HPSSS, no. 1441, schedule A, vol. 34, 46, 44. See also no. 389/1204, schedule A, vol. 32, 7; no. 90/1441, schedule A, vol. 34, 44.

34. RGVA, f. 9, op. 39s, d. 75, l. 49; d. 89, l. 161.

35. *Vsesoiuznaia sel'skokhoziaistvennaia vystavka 1939*, eds. P. N. Pospelov, A. V. Gritsenko, and N. V. Tsitsina (Moscow: Sel'khozgiz, 1939), 516; *Pavil'on "Pechat'": Putevoditel'* (Moscow: Sel'khozgiz, 1940), 5; RGASPI, f. 17, op. 116, d. 12, l. 44; f. 71, op. 10, d. 374, ll. 20–23; P. Iudin, "Istoriia partii i literatura," *Literaturnaia gazeta*, November 7, 1938, 3; "Vooruzhit' bol'shevizmom khudozhestvennuiu intelligentsiiu," *Teatr* 12 (1938): 5–9.

36. A. M. Pankratova alludes to this relief in a 1939 speech at Arkhiv RAN, f. 1577, op. 2, d. 30, ll. 45–53, published in *Istorik i vremia: 20–50-e gody XX veka —A. M. Pankratova*, ed. Iu. S. Kukushkin (Moscow: Mosgorarkhiv, 2000), 217–220.

37. Central Committee resolution of November 14, 1938 "O postanovke partinoi propagandy v sviazi s vypuskom 'Kratkogo kursa istorii VKP(b),'" *Pravda*, November 15, 1938, 1–2. The *Short Course* also limited scholarship, of course. N. N. Maslov notes that "researchers were not able to step outside of the scope of the postulates and formulas advanced by the book; nor were they allowed to publish anything that would contradict the popular textbook or even expand outside of the tenets that it proposed. This acted as a brake on the development of a more

scholarly history of the CPSU in the decades that followed. . . ." See N. N. Maslov, "'Kratkii kurs istorii VKP(b)'—entsiklopediia kul'ta lichnosti Stalina," *Voprosy istorii KPSS* 11 (1988): 66. A good example of the way that the text shaped historical research is visible in M. V. Nechkina's work on Russian underdevelopment —see A. M. Dubrovskii, *Istorik i vlast': istoricheskaia nauka v SSSR i kontseptsii istorii feodal'noi Rossii v kontekste politiki i ideologii (1930–1950 gg.)* (Briansk: BGU, 2005), 361–407.

38. On the regulation of the Stalin cult, see Jan Plamper, "The Stalin Cult in the Visual Arts, 1929–1953" (Ph.D. diss., University of California at Berkeley, 2001), esp. 63–68.

39. "V poiskakh temy," *Literaturnaia gazeta*, April 10, 1938, 1. Note that the semi-mythical Battle on the Kalka is represented here as a historical event.

40. Of course, there were a few books that attempted to redirect readers' attention from heroes and emblematic individuals to more depersonalized institutions (the party, the military) and collectives (workers, peasants, ethnic Russians, the society as a whole). See E. Vesenin, *Sovetskii patriotizm* (Moscow: Gosudarstvennoe sotsial'no-ekonomicheskoe izdatel'stvo, 1938).

41. *Letchiki—sbornik rasskazov*, ed. A. I. Langfang (Moscow: Aeroflot, 1938); *Nash transpoliarnyi reis: Moskva—severnyi polius—Severnaia Amerika*, ed. V. Chkalov (Moscow: Gos. izd-vo polit. lit-ry, 1938); *Deviat' mesiatsev na dreifuiushchei stantsii "Severnyi polius,"* ed. I. D. Papanin et al. (Moscow: Gos. izd-vo polit. lit-ry, 1938); *Chetyre tovarishcha—dnevnik*, ed. E. T. Krenkel' (Moscow: Gos. izd-vo polit. lit-ry, 1940); *Zhizn' na l'dine—dnevnik*, ed. I. D. Papanin (Moscow: Gos. izd-vo polit. lit-ry, 1940); *Patrioty: sbornik rasskazov, ocherkov i zametok o geroizme sovetskih grazhdan, o predannosti nashei rodine, ob okhrane sotsialisticheskoi sobstvennosti* (Moscow: Molodaia gvardiia, 1937); *Geroi Khasana* (Leningrad: Lenizdat, 1939); *Kak my bili iaponskikh samuraev* (Moscow: Molodaia gvardiia, 1939); *Geroicheskie budni: ocherki o Krasnoi armii* (Moscow: Gos. izd-vo khudozhestvennoi literatury, 1938). Generally, see *Na strazhe rodiny: kratkii ukazatel' literatury dlia uchitelei i bibliotekarei k XX godovshchine RKKA i BMF* (Leningrad: LengorONO, 1939).

42. Ostensibly about the Spanish republicans' struggle against the Falangist right, Koltsov's *Ispanskii dnevnik* was regarded by many as concerning the coming conflict between the USSR and Nazi Germany—see D. Rudnev, "Kto pisal 'Kratkii kurs,'" *Politika* 9 (1991): 62; K. Simonov, *Glazami cheloveka moego pokoleniia: razmyshleniia o I. V. Staline* (Moscow: Novosti, 1988), 60.

43. *Rodina: illustrirovannaia kniga dlia chteniia* (Moscow: Molodaia gvardiia, 1939); *Tvorchestvo narodov SSSR*, ed. M. Gor'kii, L. Z. Mekhlis, and A. I. Stetskii (Moscow: Pravda, 1937); *Tvorchestvo narodov SSSR o Staline i Krasnoi armii* (Moscow: Gosudarstvennoe voennoe izdatel'stvo, 1939); *Rodina schastlivykh: sbornik stikhov posviashchennykh vyboram v Verkhovnyi Sovet SSSR*, ed. I. Utkin (Moscow: Gosudarstvennoe izdatel'stvo, 1937); *Krasnoarmeiskie pesni* (Moscow: Voenizdat, 1939); and Chapter Eight, n. 54.

44. G. Butkovskii, *Rodina radug* (Moscow: Sovetskii pisatel', 1938); S. Koldunov, *Remeslo geroia* (Moscow: Gos. izd-vo Khudozh. lit-ra, 1938); M. L. Slonimskii, *Pogranichniki* (Leningrad: Sovetskii pisatel', 1939); *Na strazhe sovetskikh*

granits: besedy s pionerskim otriadom (Moscow: Molodaia gvardiia, 1937); *Na strazhe rodiny: literaturno-estradnyi sbornik* (Moscow: Iskusstvo, 1939). For a thorough list of this literature, see *Na strazhe rodiny: kratkii ukazatel' literatury dlia uchitelei i bibliotekarei k XX godovshchine RKKA i VMF* (Leningrad: LengorONO, 1939).

45. V. Shiperovich, "O 'Patriotakh' S. Dikovskogo," *Znamia* 4 (1938): 264–269. V. S. Kotelnikov, a border guard commander, was killed in action on the Manchurian frontier in 1935; S. Lagoda was mortally wounded on the same border in 1936. For an earlier review printed after the story was first serialized, see Iu. Sevriuk, "'Patrioty': Povest' S. Dikovskogo—*Novyi mir* 11," *Krasnaia zvezda*, January 5, 1938, 3.

46. S. Dikovskii, *Patrioty: Povest'* (Moscow: Sovetskii pisatel', 1938), 58–61. "Shishkin's bears" refers to a series of canvases by the nineteenth-century painter I. I. Shishkin; B. A. Babochkin was the actor who played Chapaev on the screen; M. M. Botvinnik was a chess champion. Critics hailed the use of such everyday details as this album—see S. Gekht, "Patrioty," *Literaturnyi kritik* 1 (1938): 172–179, here 175.

47. Ironically, in the first edition, Dubakh hangs Korzh's picture next to Bliukher's—a mistake that required the book to be pulled and rereleased in 1939. Compare Dikovskii, *Patrioty: Povest'*, 67, 144, 187; Dikovskii, *Patrioty* (Moscow: Gos. lit. izdat, 1939).

48. *Doch' rodiny*, dir. V. Korsh-Sablin (Belgoskino, 1937); *Na granitse*, dir. A. Ivanov (Lenfil'm, 1938); *Granitsa na zamke*, dir. V. Zhuravlev (Soiuzdetfil'm, 1938). See also *Patriot*, dir. Ia. Frid and A. Apsolon (Lenfil'm, 1939); *Sovetskie patrioty*, dir. G. Lomidze (Ashkhabad film studio, 1939); *Pogranichniki* (Ashkhabad film studio, 1939); *Na dal'nei zastave*, dir. E. Briunchugin (Stalinabad film studio, 1940). The latter was apparently not released for "thematic reasons." A scene in *Na granitse* in which the border guard Tarasov interrogates the saboteur Volkov bears traces of hurried prerelease editing in order to cut shots of a portrait of Yezhov hanging in the room.

49. *Vysokaia nagrada*, dir. E. Shneider (Soiuzdetfil'm, 1939); *Oshibka inzhenera Kochina*, dir. A. Macheret (Mosfil'm, 1939); also *Shpion* (a.k.a. *Gost'*), dir. G. Rappaport and A. Minkin (Lenfil'm, 1939). An earlier film about the crash of a test plane was condemned as demoralizing just before its release in April 1937 despite receiving positive press from Ordzhonikidze, Vodopianov, and Liapidevsky. See *Bol'shie kryl'ia* (a.k.a. *Tebia liubit Rodina, Ispytaniia*), dir. M. Dubson and K. Gakkel' (Lenfil'm, 1937); "Fal'shivaia kartina," *Pravda*, April 12, 1937, 6.

50. See N. Iu. Kuleshova, "'Bol'shoi den': Griadushchaia voina v literature 1930-kh godov," *Otechestvennaia istoriia* 1 (2002): 181–191.

51. *Esli zavtra voina*, dir. E. Dzigan and L. Antsi-Polovskii (Mosfil'm, 1938); A. K. "Esli zavtra voina," *Literaturnaia gazeta*, February 17, 1938, 5; P. Korzinkin, "'Esli zavtra voina': kinoplakat Mosfil'ma," *Krasnaia zvezda*, February 17, 1938, 4.

52. "Esli zavtra voina," by V. Lebedev-Kumach and the Pokrass brothers (1938); G. F. Baidukov, "Razgrom fashistskoi eskadry (Fantaziia o budushchei voine)," *Pravda*, August 19, 1938, 3–4; V. Agureev, "Esli zavtra voina . . . vzgliad v budu-

shchee," *Krasnaia zvezda,* November 17, 1938, 4; N. N. Shpanov, "Pervyi udar," *Znamia* 1 (1939): 4–122; "Esli zavtra voina" (V. B. Koretskii, 1939). For an excited reaction to Baidukov's tale, see diary entry from August 19, 1938 in "Diary of Vladimir Petrovich Stavsky," in *Intimacy and Terror: Soviet Diaries of the 1930s,* ed. Véronique Garros, Natalia Korenevskaya, and Thomas Lahusen (New York: New Press, 1995), 232.

53. L. Brontman, "Vchera na Tushinskom aerodrome," *Pravda,* August 19, 1938, 1–2; Vs. Vishnevskii, "Vozdushnyi boi," *Pravda,* August 19, 1938, 2; diary entry from September 14, 1938 in "Diary of Vladimir Petrovich Stavsky," 239–240.

54. "Oboronnye fil'my—na ekran," *Kino,* February 5, 1938, 2; M. Gromov, "Sozdadim oboronnye fil'my," *Iskusstvo kino* 8 (1939): 4; *Glubokii reid,* dir. P. Malakhov (Mosfil'm, 1938); *Tankisty,* dir. Z. Drapkin and R. Maiman (Lenfil'm, 1939); *Morskoi post,* dir. V. Gonchukov (Odessa studios, 1939); *Chetvertyi periskop,* dir. V. Eisymont (Lenfil'm, 1939); *Eskadril'ia No. 5,* dir. A. Room (Kiev film studio, 1939); *Traktoristy,* dir. I. Pyr'ev (Mosfil'm, 1939). For an example of press coverage on these films, see V. Katinov, "Oboronnaia tema: Traktoristy," *Iskusstvo kino* 7 (1939), 7–9.

55. See, for instance, A. Zelenov, "Moriaki," *Iskusstvo kino* 7 (1939): 5–6; *Moriaki,* dir. V. Braun (Odessa studios, 1939); *Piatyi okean,* dir. I. Annenskii (Kiev studios, 1940); *Valerii Chkalov,* dir. M. Kalatozov (Lenfil'm, 1941); *V tylu vraga,* dir. E. Shneider (Soiuzdetfil'm, 1941).

56. Diary entry from June 6, 1937 in "Diary of Andrei Stepanovich Arzhilovsky," in *Intimacy and Terror,* 161–162. For more sarcasm, see diary entry from June 30.

57. RGVA, f. 9, op. 39, d. 54, ll. 8, 115.

58. RGVA, f. 9, op. 39, d. 79, l. 6.

59. RGVA, f. 9, op. 39, d. 79, l. 7.

60. John McCannon, *Red Arctic: Polar Exploration and the Myth of the North in the Soviet Union, 1931–1939* (New York: Oxford University Press, 1998), 80.

61. On these disasters, see Karen Petrone, *Life Has Become More Joyous, Comrades: Celebrations in the Time of Stalin* (Bloomington: Indiana University, 2000), 78–84; Scott Palmer, *Dictatorship of the Air: Aviation Culture and the Fate of Modern Russia* (New York: Cambridge University Press, 2006), 247–258. Kokkinaki's crash was so embarrassing that his name was removed from the second edition of *Patrioty*—see Dikovskii, *Patrioty,* 161.

62. I. Trauberg, "Odin iz mnogikh—po povodu stsenariia 'Sovetskie patrioty,'" *Kino,* 11 September 1938, 2; G. Brovman, "Literaturnye zametki o sovremennoi teme," *Novyi mir* 11 (1938): 199–210, esp. 204–206; RGALI, f. 631, op. 15, d. 336, ll. 62–63, 69–71; L. V., "'Oshibka inzhenera Kochina': na prosmotr v Dome kino," *Vecherniaia Moskva* November 19, 1939, 3; M. Romm, "Vozvrashchenie zhanra," *Kino,* November 23, 1939, 3; M. Liashenko, "Uspekhi i promakhi," *Kino,* November 23, 1939, 3.

63. B. Volgin, "Patrioticheskii fi'lm 'Glubokii reid' (studiia—Mostekhfil'm, stsen.—V. Shpanov, rezh.—P. Malakhov),'" *Kino,* February 5, 1938, 1; Trauberg, "Odin

iz mnogikh—po povodu stsenariia 'Sovetskie patrioty,'" 2; "'Tema' i 'kachestvo,'" *Teatr* 10 (1939): 5–7.

64. For mention of these novels and films, see HPSSS, no. 258, schedule A, vol. 14, 81–84 (*Vysokaia nagrada*); no. 286, schedule A, vol. 15, 11 (*Oshibka inzhenera Kochina, Chkalov*); no. 386, schedule A, vol. 20, 18 (*Tankisty*); no. 434, schedule A, vol. 22, 31 (*Esli zavtra voina*); no. 96/1493, schedule A, vol. 35, 17 (*Tankisty*); no. 380/1460, schedule A, vol. 34, 46 (*Granitsa pod zamkom*).

65. "Rech' tov. S. Dikovskogo (na obshchemoskovskom sobranii pisatelei)," *Literaturnaia gazeta*, April 20, 1939, 4; R. Kraev, "Disput prodolzhaetsia," *Sovetskoe iskusstvo*, December 4, 1938, 6. For background on the exhibit, see Justus Hartzok, "Children of Chapaev: The Russian Civil War Cult and the Creation of Soviet Identity, 1918–1941" (Ph.D. Diss., University of Iowa, 2009), 242–268.

66. For an example of party authorities' negative reaction to ambiguity, see the fallout from I. Sel'vinskii, "Cheliuskiniana: epopeia," *Novyi mir* 1 (1937): 114–169; Sel'vinskii to Molotov (November 30, 1937), RGASPI, f. 17, op. 120, d. 298, ll. 51–52; Mekhlis to Molotov et al. (December 28, 1937), f. 82, op. 2, d. 984, ll. 72–75.

67. P. Kuplevatskii, "Protiv shapkozakidatel'stva," *Pravda*, April 19, 1939, 4.

68. A. Zelenov, "Eskadril'ia No. 5," *Kino*, April 5, 1939, 3; L. Cherniavskii, "Oboronnaia lenta," *Kino*, June 5, 1940, 3; TsGAIPD SPb, f. 24, op. 8, d. 555, ll. 114, 159, 165–166; d. 560, ll. 45–46, 55.

69. Diary entry from between August 9 and October 17, 1939 in *Poka stuchit serdtse*, 80. This film's connection to war preparedness is discussed in O. Leonidov, "Traktoristy," *Kino*, March 23, 1939, 2; "Zriteli o fil'me 'Traktoristy,'" *Kino*, January 5, 1940, 4.

70. Although quick victory in the 1939 Polish campaign may have led some to embrace "hurrah-patriotism," this should not be exaggerated. Compare V. A. Tokarev, "Sovetskoe obshchestvo i Pol'skaia kampaniia 1939 g.: 'Romanticheskoe oshchushchenie voiny," in *Chelovek i voina: voina kak iavlenie kul'tury,*" ed. I. V. Narskii and O. V. Nikonova (Moscow: AIRO-XX, 2001), 410–413; N. A. Lomagin, "Nastroenie leningradtsev v zerkale politicheskogo kontrolia v preddverii napadeniia germanii na SSSR," in *Bitva za Leningrad: problemy sovremennykh issledovanii—sbornik statei* (St. Petersburg: Izd-vo S-Peterburgskogo universiteta, 2007), 5–13.

71. Schoolboy Yury Baranov found films of this genre appealing. Four days after raving about *Chkalov* in his diary, Baranov reports having seen the film *Moriaki*: "a typical film about national defense concerning a future naval war. An answer to 'Tsushima,' etc." Diary entry from April 14, 1941 in Iurii Baranov, *Goluboi razliv: Dnevniki, pis'ma, stikhotvoreniia, 1936–1942*, ed. E. Starshinov (Iaroslavl': Verkhne-Volzhskoe knizhnoe izd-vo, 1988), 109.

72. V. D. Soldatenkov, *Politicheskie i nravstvennye posledstviia usileniia vlasti VKP(b), 1928–1941* (St. Petersburg: Prosveshchenie, 1994), 127–141.

73. "Rech' po radio Predsedateliia soveta narodnykh komissarov SSSR tov. V. M. Molotova," *Pravda*, November 30, 1939, 1; "Deklaratsiia Narodnogo pravitel'stva Finliandii," *Pravda*, December 2, 1939, 2; "Dogovor o vzaimopomoshchi

i druzhbe mezhdu Sovetskim Soiuzom i Finliandskoi demokraticheskoi respub-likoi," *Pravda*, December 3, 1939, 1; N. Virta, "Boevye stolknoveniia na Ka-rel'skom peresheike v Teriokakh," *Pravda*, December 5, 1939, 2. Carl Gustaf Emil Mannerheim was the commander in chief of the Finnish military and a decorated officer in the tsarist army during the First World War.

74. See, for example, diary entry from November 30, 1939 in A. T. Mar'ian, *Gody moi, kak soldaty: dnevnik sel'skogo aktivista, 1925–1953 gg.* (Kishinev: Kar-tia Molodoveniaske, 1987), 125.

75. V. Zenzinov, *Vstrecha s Rossiei: kak i chem zhivut v Sovetskom Soiuze—pis'ma v Krasnuiu armiiu, 1939–1940* (New York: n.p., 1944), 481–482, 360–361, 472.

76. Voroshilov "butterflies" were anti-personnel bombs that Red Army troops used against Finnish machinegun nests. See ibid., 424.

77. Ibid., 493, 543.

78. Skuchas anticipated such morale problems in the Red Army, linking them specifically to a post-Terror inability within the ranks to weather ordinary setbacks. "Real problems will begin with the first difficulties. It seems likely that no sooner than difficulties begin—regardless of whether they take the shape of military de-feats, an ammunition shortage or inadequate transportation—you'll see accusations of sabotage, treachery, and so on. Only then will we know the full extent of the harm that was done to the Red Army over the course of this past year." TsA FSB RF, f. 3, op. 5, d. 180, ll. 4–5, quoted in Demidov, "Krasnaia armiia nakanune i v period massovykh repressii po otsenkam innostrannykh razvedok," 151.

79. Diary entry from February 2, 1940 in TsGAIPD SPb, f. 4000, op. 11, d. 85, l. 23.

80. RGVA, f. 9, op. 39s, d. 89, ll. 64, 98.

81. See a report prepared under Voroshilov: "Sovetsko-finliandskaia voina, 1939–1940: 'Ne predstavliali sebe . . . vsekh trudnostei, sviazannykh s etoi voinoi,'" *Voenno-istoricheskii zhurnal* 4 (1993): 7–12; 5 (1994): 45–50; 7 (1994): 35–40. Generally, see Carl Van Dyke, "'Legko otdelalis': kakie uroki izvleklo partiinoe i voennoe rukovodstvo iz finskoi kampanii," *Rodina* 12 (1995): 113–115; Van Dyke, *The Soviet Invasion of Finland, 1939–1940* (London: F. Cass, 1997), chap. 5.

82. On the March 1940 Central Committee plenum, see V. Malyshev, "Proidet desiatok let, i eti vstrechi ne vosstanovish' uzhe v pamiati," *Istochnik* 5 (1997): 110; on the mid-April Central Committee meeting, see RGASPI, f. 17, op. 165, d. 77, ll. 178–212, published in *"Zimniaia voina": rabota nad oshibkami (aprel'—mai 1940 g.)—materialy komissii Glavnogo voennogo soveta Krasnoi Armii po oboboshcheniiu opyta finskoi kampanii* (Moscow: Letnii sad, 2004), 31–42; see also *Zimniaia voina, 1939–1940*, ed. E. N. Kul'kov and O. A. Rzheshevskii, 2 vols. (Moscow: Nauka, 1999), 2: 272–282.

83. *"Zimniaia voina": rabota nad oshibkami*, 35–36; 34.

84. RGVA, f. 4, op. 14, d. 2768, ll. 64–65, published in *"Zimniaia voina": ra-bota nad oshibkami*, 154. This meeting is referred to in Van Dyke, *The Soviet In-vasion of Finland*, 202; *Istoriia Velikoi otechestvennoi voiny Sovetskogo Soiuza*, ed. P. N. Pospelov et al., 6 vols. (Moscow: Voen. izd-vo, 1960), 1:277.

85. RGVA, f. 9, op. 36s, d. 4252, ll. 120–121, 129–130, 133. These sentiments

are expressed differently in the meeting's incomplete stenogram and various drafts of the speech—see ll. 41, 45, 47, 49; and 2, 4–7, 84, 92. For the entire speech and responses from other meeting participants, see *"Zimniaia voina": rabota nad oshibkami,* 329–389.

86. RGVA, f. 9, op. 36s, d. 4252, l. 150; also l. 60. Mekhlis's criticism of study of the *Short Course* within the ranks is ironic, inasmuch as he himself had ordered the obsessive focus—see *Politicheskie zaniatiia v RKKA v 1939 g.* (Moscow: Gosvoenizdat, 1939), esp. 5–7.

87. RGVA, f. 9, op. 36s, d. 4252, l. 131; also ll. 47, 94.

88. RGVA, f. 9, op. 36s, d. 4252, ll. 131–32; also ll. 47–49, 8, 94–95. K. A. Meretskov agreed that internationalist propaganda was no way to fight a war—ll. 166–68.

89. RGVA, f. 9, op. 36s, d. 4252, ll. 121, 116; also ll. 79, 97.

90. RGVA, f. 9, op. 36s, d. 4252, ll. 121, 138–40; also ll. 11, 51, 72, 100–102. Mekhlis apparently borrowed his point about the past experience of the Russian army in Finland from Stalin's comments on the subject to the Red Army command staff on April 17. See the stenographic record published in *I. V. Stalin i Finskaia kampaniia,* 274–275.

91. RGALI, f. 1038, op. 1, d. 1401, ll. 5–6.

92. "Da zdravstvuiut Sovetskaia Bessarabiia i Sovetskaia Bukovina!" *Pravda,* June 29, 1940, 1; "Sovetskaia vlast' v Pribaltiiskikh respublikakh," *Pravda,* July 23, 1940, 1. For an example of how the question of territory loomed large in the popular mind, see diary entries from September 17, 1939, June 27–28, and August 3, 1940 in Mar'ian, *Gody moi, kak soldaty,* 124, 128–129.

93. *Liniia Mannergeima,* dir. V. Beliaev et al. (Leningrad studio "Kinokhronika," 1940); for a review, see L. Nikulin, "Liniia Mannergeima," *Pravda,* April 23, 1940, 4. Marian disliked the film's lack of triumphalism; Vishnevsky reported audiences to be so shocked by the film's brutal realism that "not a single person applauded." See diary entries from July 4 and April 30, 1940 in Mar'ian, *Gody moi, kak soldaty,* 129–130; RGALI, f. 1038, op. 1, d. 2077, l. 46.

94. See, for instance, military planning documents from the spring of 1941—RGASPI, f. 17, op. 125, d. 27, ll. 3–43.

95. See, for instance, "Vospitat' pokolenie, gotovoe k trudu i oborone," *Sovetskaia Belorussia,* February 11, 1941, 1.

96. See *Boi v Finliandii: vospominaniia uchastnikov,* vol. 1 (Moscow: Voennoe izd-vo, 1941). The second volume was never released.

97. Lomagin, "Nastroenie leningradtsev v zerkale politicheskogo kontrolia v preddverii napadeniia Germanii na SSSR," 5–41; HPSSS, no. 1578, schedule A, vol. 36, 21–22, 15; RGVA, f. 9, op. 39s, d. 95, ll. 444, 73, 1–2.

98. RGVA, f. 9, op. 39s, d. 95, ll. 153, 94–95.

CONCLUSION

1. Italics added. RGASPI, f. 89, op. 9, d. 169, l. 4.

2. RGASPI, f. 89, op. 9, d. 169, ll. 4–5.

3. RGASPI, f. 89, op. 8, d. 813, l. 3.

4. Layout reformatted. G. V. Shumeiko, *Iz letopisi Staroi ploshchadi: istorich-eskii ocherk* (Moscow: n.p. 1996), 97–98.

5. Jochen Hellbeck, *Revolution on My Mind: Writing a Diary under Stalin* (Cambridge: Harvard University Press, 2006), 351; Igal Halfin, *From Darkness to Light: Class, Consciousness, and Salvation in Revolutionary Russia* (Pittsburgh: University of Pittsburgh Press, 2000); etc. Such studies have exaggerated the degree to which curious, introspective Soviet citizens were drawn to such a forbidding and inaccessible a subject as party history.

6. See diary entries from January 14, August 3, and November 25, 1937; January 11 and February 22, 1938; August [n.d.] and September 9, 1939 in *Poka stuchit serdtse: Dnevniki i pis'ma Geroia Sovetskogo Soiuza Evgenii Rudnevoi* (Moscow: Moskovskii gos. universitet, 1995), 42, 47–48, 51, 66, 78; David Samoilov, *Pamiatnye zapiski* (Moscow: Mezhdunarodnye otnosheniia, 1995), 157–158; Konstantin Simonov, *Glazami cheloveka moego pokoleniia: razmyshleniia o I. V. Staline* (Moscow: Kniga, 1990), 57–65; Iu. P. Sharapov, *Litsei v Sokol'nikakh: ocherk istorii IFLI* (Moscow: AIRO-XX, 1995), 165–167.

7. Anna Krylova, "Soviet Modernity in Life and Fiction: The 'New Soviet Person' in the 1930s" (Ph.D. diss., Johns Hopkins University, 2000), 207–250; Krylova, "Stalinist Identity from the Viewpoint of Gender: Rearing a Generation of Professionally Violent Women-Fighters in 1930s Stalinist Russia," *Gender and History* 16:3 (2004): 626–653.

8. See, for instance, diary entries from January 11, 1938 and January 26, 1939 in *Poka stuchit serdtse*, 51, 66; diary entry from February 24, 1940 in "Dnevnik Niny Kosterinoi," *Novyi mir* 12 (1962): 87.

9. See, for example, the regular rubric "Boevye epizody," launched in *Pravda* on June 24, 1941; and the memoirs of the editor of *Krasnaia zvezda*, D. I. Ortenberg, *Iiun'-dekabr' sorok pervogo: Rasskaz-khronika* (Moscow: Sovetskii pisatel', 1986), 8, 22, etc. Generally, see Jeffrey Brooks, *"Thank You, Comrade Stalin": Soviet Public Culture from Revolution to Cold War* (Princeton: Princeton University Press, 1999), 175–177.

10. Although situated within the reality of the war, many of these new heroes were as mythologized as Korzh and his compatriots. See N. Petrov and O. Edel'man, "Novoe o sovetskikh geroiakh," *Novyi mir* 6 (1997): 140–151; M. M. Gorinov, "Zoia Kosmodem'ianskaia," *Otechestvennaia istoriia* 1 (2003): 77–92.

11. See, for instance, the famous 1941 Kukryniksy poster, "We are fighting heartily and bayoneting daringly, grandchildren of Suvorov, children of Chapaev!"

12. Memoirists do not discuss these books as reading material during the war, but rather as icons to be hidden from advancing German troops. See the memoirs of G. V. Reshetin, published in *Moskva voennaia, 1941–1945: memuary i arkhivnye dokumenty* (Moscow: Mosgorarkhiv, 1995), 112; and a wartime interview with L. F. Gorbel' at NA IRI RAN, f. 2, raz., III, op. 2, d. 42, l. 5.

13. RGASPI, f. 17, op. 125, d. 221, ll. 28–90, published in *Sovetskaia propaganda v gody Velikoi Otechestvennoi voiny: "kommunikatsiia ubezhdeniia" i "mobilizatsionnye mekhanizmy,"* ed. A. Ia. Livshin and I. B. Orlov (Moscow: Rosspen, 2007), 494–540; d. 254, ll. 218–219.

14. N. Voronov, "Zabota o politicheskom roste molodykh kommunistov,"

Pravda, August 11, 1946, 2; "Marksistsko-Leninskoe obrazovanie kommunistov," *Pravda*, September 7, 1946, 1; V *pomoshch' izuchaiushchim istoriiu VKP(b): konsul'tatsii k I glave Kratkogo kursa istorii VKP(b)* (Moscow: Moskovskii rabochii, 1946).

15. "Ob izdanii Sochinenii I.V. Stalina," *Pravda*, January 20, 1946, 2; P. N. Pospelov, "Klassicheskii trud tvorcheskogo Marksizma-Leninizma: k vos'moi godovshchine vykhoda v svet knigi I. V. Stalina 'Kratkii kurs istorii VKP(b),'" *Pravda*, October 2, 1946, 2. For earlier hints of Stalin's role, see "Vospityvat' molodezh' v dukhe bol'shevistskikh traditsii," *Pravda*, September 11, 1938, 1; V. M. Molotov, "21-aia godovshchina Oktiabr'skoi revoliutsii," *Pravda*, November 9, 1938, 2; *Iosif Vissarionovich Stalin: Kratkaia biografiia* (Moscow: Partizdat, 1939), 78–79.

16. See, for example, the annual 1948–1949 report at RGASPI, f. 17, op. 132, d. 103, ll. 4–8.

17. David Brandenberger, *National Bolshevism: Mass Culture and the Formation of Modern Russian National Identity, 1931–1956* (Cambridge: Harvard University Press, 2002), chaps. 11–13; Amir Weiner, "The Making of a Dominant Myth: The Second World War and the Construction of Political Identities within the Soviet Polity," *Russian Review* 55:4 (1996): 638–660; Brooks, *"Thank You, Comrade Stalin,"* esp. 198–206.

18. RGASPI, f. 558, op. 11, d. 1222, ll. 1–205. Limited updating of the notes in these galleys redirected readers to new postwar editions of the party canon.

19. RGASPI, f. 558, op. 11, d. 1223, ll. 1–140. Aleksandrov's collaborator was P. N. Fedoseev.

20. On the postwar *Short Biography*, see David Brandenberger, "Stalin as Symbol: A Case Study of the Cult of Personality and Its Construction," in *Stalin: A New History*, ed. Sarah Davies and James Harris (New York: Cambridge University Press, 2005), 249–270.

21. RGASPI, f. 558, op. 11, d. 1221.

22. See, for example, his extensive involvement in efforts to release a textbook on political economy—Ethan Pollock, *Stalin and the Science Wars* (Princeton: Princeton University Press, 2006), 168–211. The book was published only after Stalin's death as *Politicheskaia ekonomiia: uchebnik* (Moscow: Gos. izd-vo politicheskoi literatury, 1954).

23. T. Zelenov, "Bibliografiia," *Bol'shevik* 23 (1949): 89–90; generally, N. N. Maslov, "Ideologiia stalinizma: istoriia utverzhdeniia i sushchnost' (1929–1956)," *Novoe v zhizni, nauke, tekhnike: seriia 'Istoriia i politika KPSS'* 3 (1990): 3–64.

24. According to plans for a new edition of the *Short Biography* and a revised Stalin entry in the *Great Soviet Encyclopedia*, authorship of the *Short Course* was reverted to an anonymous Central Committee commission; Stalin was to retain credit only for its section on historical materialism. See RGANI, f. 5, op. 30, d. 7, ll. 49–50; also RGASPI, f. 558, op. 11, dd. 1284–1286.

25. "'O kul'te lichnosti i ego posledstviiakh': Doklad Pervogo sekretaria TsK KPSS tov. Khrushcheva N. S. XX s"ezdu Kommunisticheskoi partii Sovetskogo Soiuza," *Izvestiia TsK KPSS* 3 (1989): 158.

26. *Istoriia Kommunisticheskoi partii Sovetskogo Soiuza*, ed. B. M. Ponomarev

et al. (Moscow: Gospolitizdat, 1959); *Istoriia KPSS*, ed. A. V. Fedorov (Leningrad: Izd-vo Leningradskogo universiteta, 1960); *Istoriia Kommunisticheskoi partii Sovetskogo Soiuza*, ed. P. N. Pospelov (Moscow: Izd-vo polit. lit-ry, 1964); *Istoriia Kommunisticheskoi partii Sovetskogo Soiuza v 6-ti t-kh*, ed. P. N. Pospelov, 6 vols. (Moscow: Izd-vo polit. lit-ry, 1964). On the changes to the historical narrative, see R. Schlesinger, "Soviet Historians Before and After the XX Congress," *Soviet Studies* 8:2 (1956); 157–172; Aleksandr Nekrich, *Forsake Fear: Memoirs of a Historian* (Boston: Unwin Hyman, 1991); L. A. Sidorova, *Ottepel' v istoricheskoi nauke: sovetskaia istoriografiia pervogo poslestalinskogo desiatiletiia* (Moscow: Pamiatniki istoricheskoi mysli, 1997); A. V. Pyzhikov, *Politicheskie preobrazovaniia v SSSR, 50–60-e gody* (Moscow: Kvadrat S—Fantera, 1999), 70–90; Polly Jones, "Myth, Memory, Trauma: The Stalinist Past in Soviet Culture, 1953–68," unpublished manuscript, 2011, chap. 2.

27. Curiously enough, Pospelov played a large role in this process, chairing Khrushchev's commission on Stalin's crimes and assisting in the writing of his Secret Speech. Yaroslavsky had died in 1943, so Pospelov was the sole surviving member of the original brigade.

28. Alexei Yurchak, *Everything Was Forever, Until It Was No More: The Last Soviet Generation* (Princeton: Princeton University Press, 2005), chaps. 2–3; L. A. Openkin, "Mekhanizm tormozheniia v sfere obshchestvennykh nauk: istoki vozniknoveniia, faktory vosproizvodstva," *Istoriia SSSR* 4 (1989): 3–16; I. L. Man'kovskaia and Iu. P. Sharapov, "Kul't lichnosti i istoriko-partiinaia nauka," *Voprosy istorii KPSS* 5 (1988): 57–70; N. N. Maslov, "Politicheskaia istoriia SSSR: predmet, soderzhanie, zadachi," *Novoe v zhizni, nauke, tekhnike: seriia 'Politicheskaia istoriia XX veka'* 11 (1991): 3–62. True change would come only with the launch of M. S. Gorbachev's *glasnost* campaign between 1987 and 1988 and its determination to fill in the "blank spots" in party history.

29. Ronald Grigor Suny, "On Ideology, Subjectivity, and Modernity: Disparate Thoughts about Doing Soviet History," *Russian History/Histoire Russe* 35:1–2 (2008): 251–258, here 253–255.

30. Sheila Fitzpatrick, *Everyday Stalinism—Ordinary Life in Extraordinary Times: Soviet Russia in the 1930s* (New York: Oxford University Press, 1999); *Tear Off the Masks! Identity and Imposture in Twentieth-Century Russia*, ed. Fitzpatrick (Princeton: Princeton University Press, 2005); Golfo Alexopoulos, "Portrait of a Con Artist as a Soviet Man," *Slavic Review* 57:4 (1998): 774–790.

31. Stephen Kotkin, *Magnetic Mountain: Stalinism as a Civilization* (Berkeley: University of California Press, 1995); also David Hoffmann, *Stalinist Values: The Cultural Norms of Soviet Modernity, 1917–1941* (Ithaca: Cornell University Press, 2003). Somewhat different approaches are reflected in Jochen Hellbeck, "Fashioning the Stalinist Soul: The Diary of Stepan Podlubnyi," *Jahrbücher für Geschichte Osteuropas* 44:4 (1996): 233–273; Hellbeck, *Revolution on My Mind*.

32. Ronald Grigor Suny, *The Revenge of the Past: Nationalism, Revolution, and the Collapse of the Soviet Union* (Stanford: Stanford University Press, 1993); Yuri Slezkine, "The USSR as a Communal Apartment, or How a Socialist State Promoted Ethnic Particularism," *Slavic Review* 53:2 (1994): 414; Terry Martin, *The Affirmative Action Empire: Ethnicity and the Soviet State, 1923–1938* (Ithaca: Cor-

nell University Press, 2001); Brandenberger, *National Bolshevism: Mass Culture and the Formation of Modern Russian National Identity, 1931–1956.*

33. On generational cohort, see Anna Krylova, "Identity, Agency, and the 'First Soviet Generation,'" in *Generations in Twentieth Century Europe,* ed. Stephen Lovell (New York: Palgrave Macmillan 2007), 101–120; on the party press, see Brooks, *"Thank You, Comrade Stalin";* on more prosaic issues, see Svetlana Boym, *Common Places: Mythologies of Everyday Life in Russia* (Cambridge: Harvard University Press, 1994); *Stalinism as a Way of Life,* ed. Lewis Siegelbaum and Andrei Sokolov (New Haven: Yale University Press, 2000); etc.

34. On the Great Terror, see Orlando Figes, *The Whisperers: Private Life in Stalin's Russia* (New York: Metropolitan Books, 2007); Hiroaki Kuromiya, *The Voices of the Dead: Stalin's Great Terror in the 1930s* (New Haven: Yale University Press, 2007); on the war, see Weiner, "The Making of a Dominant Myth: The Second World War and the Construction of Political Identities within the Soviet Polity"; Weiner, *Making Sense of War* (Princeton: Princeton University Press, 2000). See also Nina Tumarkin, *The Living and the Dead: The Rise and Fall of the Cult of World War II in Russia* (New York: Basic Books, 1994); Elena Zubkova, *Poslevoennoe sovetskoe obshchestvo: politika i povsednevnost', 1945–1953* (Moscow: Rosspen, 1999).

35. Anna Krylova, "The Tenacious Liberal Subject in Soviet Studies," *Kritika* 1:1 (2000): 119–146.

36. Recent work on ideology appears unaware of the party's failure to popularize its core tenets on the mass level. See Martin Malia, *The Soviet Tragedy: A History of Socialism in Russia* (New York: Free Press, 1994); Andrzej Walicki, *Marxism and the Leap to the Kingdom of Freedom: The Rise and Fall of the Communist Utopia* (Stanford: Stanford University Press, 1995).

Index